FERENCZI DIALOGUES

FIGURES OF THE UNCONSCIOUS 19

Editorial Board

Beatriz Santos (*Université de Paris*),
Philippe Van Haute † (*Radboud University*),
Herman Westerink (*Radboud University*),
Daniela Finzi (*Freud Museum Vienna*),
Jeff Bloechl (*Boston College*)

Advisory Board

Lisa Baraitser (*Birkbeck College, London*),
Rudolf Bernet (*KU Leuven*),
Rachel Blass (*Heythrop College, London*),
Guillaume Sibertin-Blanc (*Université Toulouse II - Le Mirail*),
Richard Boothby (*Loyola University, Maryland*),
Marcus Coelen (*Berlin*),
Jozef Corveleyn (*KU Leuven*),
Monique David-Ménard (*Université de Paris*),
Rodrigo De La Fabián (*Universidad Diego Portales, Santiago de Chile*),
Jens De Vleminck (*Leuven*),
Eran Dorfman (*University of Tel Aviv*),
Tomas Geyskens (*Leuven*),
Patrick Guyomard (*Université de Paris*),
Ari Hirvonen † (*University of Helsinki*),
Laurie Laufer (*Université de Paris*),
Paul Moyaert (*KU Leuven*),
Elissa Marder (*Emory University, Atlanta*),
Paola Marrati (*Johns Hopkins University*),
Claire Nioche (*Université Paris XIII*),
Claudio Oliveira (*Universidade Federal Fluminense*),
Guilherme Massara Rocha (*Universidade Federal de Minas Gerais*),
Elizabeth Rottenberg (*De Paul University, Chicago*),
Vladimir Safatle (*Universidade de Sao Paulo*),
Stella Sandford (*Kingston College*),
Charles Shepherdson (*State University of New York at Albany*),
Celine Surprenant (*Paris*),
Antônio Teixeira (*Universidade Federal de Minas Gerais*),
Patrick Vandermeersch (*University of Groningen*),
Johan Van Der Walt (*University of Luxemburg*),
Veronica Vasterling (*Radboud Universiteit, Nijmegen*),
Wilfried Ver Eecke (*Georgetown University*),
Jamieson Webster (*The New School, New York*)

FERENCZI DIALOGUES

On Trauma and Catastrophe

Raluca Soreanu
Jakob Staberg
Jenny Willner

LEUVEN UNIVERSITY PRESS

Published with the financial support of the Strategic Research Grant,
Department of Psychosocial and Psychoanalytic Studies, University of Essex, UK
and the LMU Mentoring Programme, Fakultät 13,
Ludwig Maximilians University, Munich, Germany.

© 2023 by Leuven University Press / Universitaire Pers Leuven / Presses Universitaires de Louvain. Minderbroedersstraat 4, B-3000 Leuven (Belgium).

All rights reserved. Except in those cases expressly determined by law, no part of this publication may be multiplied, saved in an automated datafile or made public in any way whatsoever without the express prior written consent of the publishers.

ISBN 978 94 6270 352 0
e-ISBN 978 94 6166 486 0
D/2023/1869/6
NUR: 770
https://doi.org/10.11116/9789461664860

Cover design: Daniel Benneworth-Gray
Cover illustration: Hannah Höch: Siebenmeilenstiefel, 1934, © VG Bild-Kunst, Bonn 2022
Lay-out: Friedemann Vervoort

To Philippe Van Haute
(1957–2022)

Contents

Foreword by Adrienne Harris — XI

Reading Ferenczi
A Pirouette Backwards in Seven-League Boots — 1
An Introduction by Jenny Willner, Jakob Staberg and Raluca Soreanu

    Cuts Through the Contemporary Scene — 1
    Ferenczi Dialogues – an Outline — 6
    The Seven Threads of the 'Ferenczi Revival' — 8

PART 1 — 21

Instead of Language: Confusion
Sigmund Freud / Sándor Ferenczi — 23
Jakob Staberg

    Ferenczi in the Psychoanalytic Milieu — 25
    Transference — 39
    Trauma — 49
    The Domain of Dreams — 54
    A Painful Encounter — 62

    'Too much of the father': A Schreberian Pre-History — 73
    RESPONSE *to Jakob Staberg, by Jenny Willner*

    The Tactile Eye and Queer Spectrality — 83
    RESPONSE *to Jakob Staberg, by Raluca Soreanu*

PART 2   89

Catastrophes and Genitality
Ferenczi's *Thalassa* and the Politics of Bioanalysis   91
Jenny Willner

> Freud's Theory of Sexuality Meets Popular Darwinism
> in a Soldiers' Library   93
> The Fish-Orgy:
> Wilhelm Bölsche's Herrings and Ferenczi's *Thalassa*   98
> *Weltanschauung*: Fetishistic Disavowal in Popular Darwinism   102
> Neurotic Evolution: Bioanalysis vs. Biologism   110
> Heroic Organs, Hysteric Organs: The Method of Bioanalysis   113
> The Politics of Bioanalysis   118
>
> Reading Against the Grain: On How Organs Crave Interpretation   131
> RESPONSE *to Jenny Willner, by Jakob Staberg*
>
> What Does an Organ Do?   137
> RESPONSE *to Jenny Willner, by Raluca Soreanu*

PART 3   143

Catastrophe and the Creativity of Fragments
Toward a Phenomenology of the Scene of Trauma   145
Raluca Soreanu

> A Frame: On Ferenczi's Model of Memory   150
> > Repetition   152
> > Scene   153
> > Regression   156
>
> The Dream of Fragments in *The Clinical Diary*   158
> On the Identification with the Aggressor   159
> > Moment 1: Paralysis   164
> > Moment 2: Dematerialisation   166
> > Moment 3: Traumatic Imitation   167

Moment 4: Guilt	168
Moment 5: Getting Beside Oneself	171
Moment 6: Traumatic Progression	173
Moment 7: Autotomy	174
Moment 8: Neo-Formations	175
Moment 9: Orpha	178
Moment 10: Reconstruction	180

There is Hope for Life in Fragments: Thinking with Ferenczi's Images 193
RESPONSE *to Raluca Soreanu, by Jenny Willner*

Toward an Eventful Psychoanalysis 203
RESPONSE *to Raluca Soreanu, by Jakob Staberg*

Bibliography 209

About the Authors 227

Index 229

Foreword

Adrienne Harris

This book delivers such a complex and deep vision of the work and career of Sándor Ferenczi, it is a pleasure to introduce and it was a deep pleasure to read. I found myself thinking of the first conference we in the relational group organized on Sándor Ferenczi. It was Steve Mitchell's idea and he recruited Lewis Aron and myself to organize the meeting. So it was in 1991 that I sat in the large auditorium at Mount Sinai Hospital in New York and listened to a wonderful and distinguished group of scholars describe the work and extraordinary intellectual and clinical arc of Sándor Ferenczi. This arc includes New York, where Ferenczi spent four months in 1926, lecturing at The New School, having been invited to the United States by Alvin Johnson, the president of The New School, who was subsequently to become the founder of the "University in Exile." From Ferenczi's correspondence with Freud during this period, we find out that he lectured, saw patients, and was involved in key aspects of the dissemination of psychoanalysis in the United States. Ferenczi's link to American psychoanalysis was marked by the creation of the Sándor Ferenczi Center at The New School for Social Research in 2008. What Ferenczi brought to the United States in 1926, his influence on developments in clinical theory and practice, is part of a nevertheless interrupted communication across the Atlantic. Interrupted communication is one of the key themes of this volume.

Returning to the scene of the conference at Mount Sinai Hospital in 1991, what I must confess is that at that point I had not read any of Ferenczi's work. As speaker after speaker described the creativity of Ferenczi, his deep commitment and connection to complex early experience, the magical account of clinical process and work, I was overwhelmed. I remember thinking: this is an ancestor, this is an earlier vision/version of Winnicott, and my intellectual and clinical life was transformed.

Reading this book – its particular organization and the depth and breadth of its exploration of Ferenczi, Budapest and Eastern Europe, of early psychoanalysis, the complex engagement of Freud and Ferenczi and his deep creative clinical capacities, his trauma theory – I also have remembered and want to celebrate what the North American and psychoanalytic encounter and revival or Ferenczi's work has meant. I found myself thinking of how much moments and dialogical experiences like this make me particularly sad not to have the company and engagement in these projects with Steve Mitchell (1946–2000) since over 20 years ago and with Lewis Aron (1952–2019) since much more recently, but I venture alone to write this foreword, missing their voices and our discussions.

I want to first notice the particular way in which this book organizes an interdisciplinary set of dialogues. Much more effectively than just a collection of papers by different kinds of scholars, it contains three main parts, each by a scholar representing a different discipline. Each part has two discussants, so that the volume is a series of dialogues, engaged conversations focused on the work of academics and clinicians, all engaged with psychoanalysis in various forms and approaching Ferenczi's work and professional life differently. Jakob Staberg is a psychoanalyst and teaches Aesthetics and Comparative literature at Södertörn University South of Stockholm. Jenny Willner is an assistant professor of Comparative Literature in Munich, teaching literature and psychoanalytic theory, and Raluca Soreanu is a psychoanalyst trained in South America and a professor of psychoanalytic studies at Essex in Great Britain. The interdisciplinarity and the format of dialogue among this threesome has produced a powerful work – in regard to psychoanalytic theory, its history and to the history and importance of Sándor Ferenczi.

The book is introduced with a discussion of the cover, a painting by Hannah Höch in which the authors recognize the theme of regression, the intriguing tension between anger and pleasure, and a focus on splitting as a mechanism. Throughout the book these phenomena are treated, with Ferenczi, as a response to a suffering that is so great that the split is a necessary condition of survival. Right from the beginning of this collection, trauma, catastrophe, life and psyche under threat are center stage. Additionally, throughout this book, the authors keep us aware of and concerned with the surrounding political and social circumstances, in particular, the First World War. Trauma is addressed in the most intimate clinical and personal detail, and set off against the background of the war.

Thinking of and being reacquainted with this history, I want to take notice of Ferenczi's *Thalassa*, a work much considered in this volume and also discussed in one of my own recent publications (Harris, 2020). Intriguingly, Ferenczi worked on *Thalassa* while being stationed during the First World War at a military hospital. Here is how he himself introduces the work:

> In the autumn of 1914 the demands of military service broke in upon the psychoanalytic activities of the author of this work and exiled him to a small garrison town, where he found the duties of chief medical

officer to a squadron of Hussars somewhat of a contrast to the pressure of activity to which he had been accustomed. Thus he came to occupy his leisure hours with the translating of Freud's *Drei Abhandlungen zur Sexualtheorie*; and it was almost inevitable that he should have elaborated in his mind certain ideas suggested by this work and have set down, however sketchily, the results. (Ferenczi [1924] 1989, p. 1)

He goes on to describe composition and work on the project over the next four years and notes its presentation to Freud in 1919, where he is encouraged to prepare the material for publication. War trauma by day and the issues of inheritance and phylogenetics, of the complexly admixed body experiences and energies of sexuality by night. In the progress of this work, Ferenczi struggles with and works over his and Freud's ideas of the death drive. It is interesting that destructiveness survives in *Thalassa* as an aspect of the phylogenetic inheritance of catastrophe.

From the beginning of his writing, Ferenczi's focusses on who is traumatized, who is a victim, who is an aggressor, and who is the witness, a figure who may bear the truth or deny it. His work on the drives keeps a focus on the life drive and the death drive, while introducing new vocabulary: unwelcomeness, mutuality. He was determined to think and bring together elements of psyche and of soma, embodiment and the unconscious. He worked on new formations and meaning for oedipality and a prominent place for regression. His work was crucial for the evolution and importance of the Budapest psychoanalytic community, and he has a deserved place as a psychoanalyst with a deep interest in social and cultural theories.

The chapter by Jakob Staberg, which begins the deep exploration of Ferenczi's life and work, starts at a terrible end point, 1932, a scene involving traumatic rupture of Ferenczi's life and links to Freud, a moment that certainly haunts the book. Ferenczi has come to visit Freud and to read the paper he plans to present at the IPA. Freud is upset, critical and contemptuous. Ferenczi continues to speak of matters and theory Freud has thrown away. In an eerie way, what is reproduced in Ferenczi is the very trauma and scene of attack and contempt he has been trying to theorize.

Staberg uses this disturbing and for Ferenczi tragic ending to his relationship with Freud to examine the authoritarian system in which Freud was determined to move and work. He argues that the problem of authoritarianism forms an uncanny continuity with psychiatry. Ferenczi was himself paying attention to the elements of homophobia and anti-Semitism but his own progressive politics and social conscience put him at risk, even, as we see, from Freud. Ferenczi's modes of practice, his experiments with mutual analysis put him in danger from allies and from opponents.

> [T]hese analyses were born of a reflection on defeat, loss, grief and seclusion, indicative of the Jewish situation during the downfall of the Habsburg monarchy on the threshold of the modernisation of capitalism and the industrial mass murder of the First World War: total war. (Staberg, p. 45)

In her response, Willner has us notice the complexity of the destructive and catastrophic aspects of Freud and Ferenczi's connections, the struggles over authority and interestingly the less obvious implication of the history of Freud's relationship with Fließ, a previous site of conflict. She asks the reader to think of the complexity through a psychoanalytic lens: ironic obedience, traumatic repetition and rebellion. (Willner, p. 74) Raluca Soreanu, in her response, introduces a term she will develop, the notion of the 'tactile eye', a capacity to link seeing and touching. She also alerts us here to another radical aspect of Ferenczi, his consistent attempt to de-oedipalize. (Soreanu, p. 180) In a conception he termed 'amphimixis' he is committed to imagining the force and range of pleasures, not solely genital, available over childhood. Sexuality in this way gains in complexity and depth.

Jenny Willner's chapter takes up Ferenczi on sexuality, on the role of the body and on the *Three Essays*. In a brilliant move she has us notice that Ferenczi is approaching biology in a radically new way. What is crucial is Ferenczi's insistence to link his model of trauma to unconscious wishes. Against this background, Willner argues that Ferenczi uses psychoanalytic ideas to examine and rearticulate biological phenomena, instead of deriving explanations biologistically, from hereditary factors. Many biology driven models are strongly influenced by eugenics and often lead to a racist model of body and mind and the impact of the body on the social. Ferenczi uses psychoanalytic principles to counter Darwinist models that certainly dominated psychiatry. Psychoanalytic bioanalysis in this vision does not reduce the role of mind and unconscious phenomena to biology but rather underwrites the biological discourse.

Raluca Soreanu brings clinical sensibility to her chapter which has a focus on Ferenczi's work on trauma: trauma as a scene and trauma as a catastrophe. Her language captures Ferenczi's intention to expand our understanding of trauma to include not simply events but a 'scene' where fractures, leaks, splits, fragmented psyches can also offer the potential for new growth. Soreanu, in her focus on Ferenczi's language, brings us very close to the intensity of his theorizing, the potential for creativity as an outcome of the frightening collisions of adult and child. In linking carefully and consistently both the asymmetry of relationality and the 'confusion of tongues' – Ferenczi's deeply important and famous phrase – she builds a view of trauma as a confusion between different registers of experience. Above all she sheds a light on the importance Ferenczi ascribed to the presence of a third person in the scene of trauma; the failure to witness and register the trauma and certainly the failure to rescue.

In the dialogical form of each part of the book, one sees the pleasure in this project of revision and reworking of Ferenczi, particularly in the clinical realm. Transference is about ways of relation within the dyad. There is throughout this volume a great appreciation for the hard work of analysis and the power of Ferenczi's subtle but unmistakable revisions of the standard model. The interweave of social and individual aspects can be found on the most intimate scale in clinical moments of stunning force, and in the larger social scale, pulling in the complex role of politics, of ideology and of social force. This book, it its main presentations and in the discussions and intellectual work among all three writers, delivers so much at so many levels.

All three writers stress the difference in Ferenczi's work around organic life and biology. Soreanu emphasizes that his term 'bioanalysis' does not mount up to biological determinism. Rather the opposite, Ferenczi consistently – and these views are beautifully presented throughout this book – wanted psychoanalysis to shape and interpret the natural sciences. It is one of Ferenczi's most dramatic ambitions and this volume brings these ideas freshly to the English-speaking psychoanalytic world.

Reading this book and now writing this foreword has been a great pleasure in this difficult time of emergency and uncertainty. Ferenczi's work, his imagination, and perhaps most importantly his bravery come beautifully alive in this volume. Working with such a rich interdisciplinary text makes these hard times lighter and more hopeful.

November 4, 2022, New York

Reading Ferenczi
A Pirouette Backwards in Seven-League Boots

An Introduction by Jenny Willner, Jakob Staberg and Raluca Soreanu

Cuts Through the Contemporary Scene

The houses seem scattered, as if diced into a landscape as empty and abstract as a map. A blue piece of paper in the upper left corner is perhaps the sea behind the shore, and indefinite black and white shapes take up the foreground, like flames or shades. At the centre there are two female legs, dressed in mid-calf laced boots, leaping over the fragmented landscape. The legs have no torso, there is no head, there are no arms, but a spiral-shaped shell is strapped around the crotch, the shell of a snail or a mollusc. *Siebenmeilenstiefel*[1] is the title of this photomontage, the image on our book cover. It was made in 1934 by Hannah Höch (1889–1978), an active member of the Berlin Dada group. The name *Siebenmeilenstiefel* refers to the mythology of Seven-League Boots in European folklore, boots that allow the bearer to take seven leagues per step in great speed in order to complete a significant, sometimes magical task. In this particular photomontage it is however striking that the giant leap is not directed forwards, but backwards. In Western iconography – and for a Dada monteur acquainted with the visual language of advertising, this must have been obvious – a leap forwards would move from the left to the right. And yet here we see a leap in the opposite direction, towards the past. Moreover, it is a leap with a twist: at a closer look, there is a slight rotation. By performing a pirouette backwards, the legs seem to parallel the spiral of the shell strapped around the crotch. If we were to interpret this shell as any known human accessory, it would be either a loin cloth, a girdle of chastity, or a diaper. But we should perhaps restrain the impulse to interpret and instead stay with this cut-out photographic image of the exoskeleton of a gastropod. It is a calcareous shell that grows per revolution around its coiling axis, providing protection for unsegmented invertebrates known for being slow. Thus the association with a snail brings in a moment of deceleration, a striking contrast to the speed usually associated with Seven-League Boots.

For readers of the Hungarian psychoanalyst Sándor Ferenczi, whose writings are at the heart of this book, Höch's image of a leap backwards brings regressive fantasies into mind: both Ferenczi's interest in regressive states in his patients, and his biological fantasy of a thalassal regressive trend, a longing of all living beings to pre-human, marine forms of life.[2] It is worth underlining that regression in the thought of Ferenczi appears in a catastrophic situation, as a reaction to shock and within a scenario of splitting.[3] When danger is imminent, part of the self unconsciously resorts to the forgotten, evolutionary older coping strategies, as it were. Regression is a flight, one of many means of psychic survival. According to Ferenczi we sometimes take a leap backwards, into the pre-human past, because catastrophe was there, too.

To a far greater extent than Freud, Ferenczi centred his psychoanalytic thought around trauma, focussing on how the traumatic shock leads to radical forms of psychic splitting. Ferenczi thinks of these processes in terms of complex defence mechanisms which we can only understand if we envision the various fragments resulting from splitting as having a psychic 'life' of their own.[4] In his *Clinical Diary*, written during the last year of his life in 1932, he outlines a metapsychology of fragments against the backdrop of both personal and political catastrophes.[5] The form of the diary is itself fragmented: it presents an unfinished theory, containing clinical observations and metapsychological constructions in which Ferenczi draws from his work with severely traumatised patients. His core idea is that, given the enormity of suffering experienced during the traumatic attack, psychic survival would have been impossible without the radical splitting into fragments.

Ferenczi's theory of the subject always contains the story of an encounter with the Other. The consequences of this encounter are catastrophic, which is one of the reasons why our volume bears the title *Ferenczi Dialogues: On Trauma and Catastrophe*. Etymologically, the term 'catastrophe' is derived from the Greek καταστροφή, an overturning, a sudden turn, but also a conclusion: in Greek tragedy, the catastrophe is the change or revolution which produces the final event of a dramatic piece. Although the term 'catastrophe' generally bears the connotation of something disastrous or at least unhappy, it also signifies something that can be viewed in more structural terms: an event producing a subversion of the order or system of things.[6] Ferenczi's biological speculations are closely linked to the idea of primordial catastrophes, going back to Charles Lyell's *Principles of Geology* (1830), which in turn contributed significantly to Darwin's view of the processes involved in evolution. In Lyell, the catastrophe is thought of as an upheaval or convulsion affecting the earth's surface and the living beings upon it. This notion of catastrophe is echoed both in Freud's famous speculation on the primitive organism in 'Beyond the Pleasure Principle' (1921), subjected to traumatic disturbances,[7] and even more so in Ferenczi's catastrophic evolutionary history of human reproductive organs as presented in *Thalassa* (1924).[8]

Throughout this book, we will refer to Ferenczi's last work, his *Clinical Diary*, as a vanishing point even when dealing with his earlier writings. Ferenczi's late theory of psychic fragments tells the story of both partial psychic death and of partial survival, as well as the story of the multiplication of forms of psychic life. His work contributes to pluralising the understanding of catastrophe, as being both destructive and a turning point. What would it mean to systematically think of confusion and disorder as a process with an open outcome? Reading Ferenczi helps us to understand forms of survival beyond restorative illusions. It offers a chance to envision the creative side of survival in terms of what may be called a tragic optimism, in a mode of working through – within the realm of mourning, perhaps melancholia, and also astonishment at the strange forms psychic life may take. Ultimately, Ferenczi's trauma theory is also a theory of the subject that raises new questions of representation. Indeed, the Ferenczian subject bears certain structural similarities to a montage made out of cut-out fragments.

This brings us back to the cover image of our book. There is no history of reception between Sándor Ferenczi and Hannah Höch. However, it makes sense in several ways to think about Dada while reading Ferenczi. While the novels of Thomas Mann remained the most modern art form Freud was willing to engage with, Ferenczi followed the artistic avant-garde of his time with keen interest. In Budapest, he was part of a vibrant intellectual network, which included composers such as Béla Bartók and Zoltán Kodály, and writers such as Sándor Márai.[9] Already in Freud, hysteria appeared as a caricature of art. In Ferenczi, the organism itself is thought of as prepared for art.[10] Without any particular reference to Hannah Höch, Brigid Doherty has convincingly proposed a relationship between two forms of materialisation: on the one hand as a technical procedure in Dada montage, on the other hand as the mechanism of production in hysterical conversion symptoms, as articulated by Sándor Ferenczi in 1919.[11] Indeed, montage-based aesthetic strategies such as Dadaist assemblage and photomontage can be said to respond to problems of representation similar to those addressed by Ferenczi's metapsychology of fragments. While Ferenczi drafts a vision of the self as a mosaic made out of alive and deadened parts, Höch juxtaposes pre-existing materials in wild, often violent ways, producing alienating representations of bodies: she makes 'cuts through the contemporary scene.'[12]

Berlin Dada was formed directly after the world's first full-scale mechanised war that ended with the collapse of several European monarchies. The Berlin Dadaists, among them artists such as Max Ernst, Raoul Hausmann, Richard Huelsenbeck and George Grosz, operated amid everyday social and political conflicts, within a period of significant street fighting, political assassinations, mass strikes, right-wing putsches, and failed revolutionary attempts, creating artistic forms in critical response to nationalism and authoritarianism.[13] It took until the 1990s before Hannah Höch was given a central place within the historiography of the Dada movement. While her images seem to resonate with much later queer theory, they are also responding to medical discourses of her time: both to wartime surgical reconstruction of ripped-off jaws, crushed skulls and blown-away faces and to the genital reassignment surgery performed at the Institute for Sexology in Berlin in the late 1920s.[14] Indeed, Höch consulted Magnus Hirschfeld's vast sexological archive in Berlin, a library dedicated to the deviation of sexual types and drives.[15]

Höch's both attractive and unsettling photomontages have later been elaborated with reference to Julia Kristeva's *The Powers of Horror*: 'because the photograph is intuitively felt to be a mirror of reality, photomontage, with its surprising juxtapositions of disparate photographic images, is inherently more unsettling than paintings or sculptures, that similarly jumble categories.'[16] While alienation, or estrangement in the sense of *Verfremdung*, is an aesthetic key strategy of photomontage in general, Höch's use of alienation is perhaps less to be understood as a method of emotional distancing. Rather, the defamiliarisation in her photomontages 'opens up for the viewer emotional tensions between anger and pleasure'.[17] Speaking in terms of Ferenczian trauma theory, Höch's photomontages represent both shock and survival, destruction and productivity.

The pirouette-like leap backwards in Höch's montage, modelled after the spiral of the shell just like ontogeny was believed to recapitulate phylogeny, is a world away from progressive optimism. Are we to assume that the organ between the leaping legs is comfortably accommodated in this primordial shelter? Any association with something soft, mucous and moist is immediately contrasted by the hard, phallically pointing shell, which has been compared with a 'strapped on phallus'.[18] Apart from this gender trouble, and apart from the troubling associations oscillating between infantility and virility, Höch's image is characterised by the ambiguity of a catastrophic atmosphere intermingled with the sparkling joy of a giant leap. These legs propel towards the past with a deviant, perhaps even somewhat dark kind of pleasure.

We chose *Siebenmeilenstiefel* as a cover image also because we believe that it is fruitful to dwell upon the gesture of moving backwards. In 1918, Ferenczi spoke of shell-shocked soldiers who 'are prevented from going forward through the most violent attacks of shaking, but can carry out the much more difficult task of going backwards without trembling'.[19] In such examples, the historical backdrop of Ferenczi's thinking forces itself upon us. Indeed, the collaboration between Ferenczi and Freud peaked during the years of the First World War, which was already during the Weimar Era interpreted as the first man-made global catastrophe.[20] In the face of this war, Freud and Ferenczi set out together to re-think the role of catastrophes both in the life of the individual and in natural history. At the same time, Ferenczi's interest in war trauma led him to reconsider the trauma theory of hysteria in a way that would ultimately contribute to the break with Freud in 1932, shortly before Ferenczi's death in May 1933.

In the life of Hannah Höch, the year of Ferenczi's death marks the beginning of her inner exile during National Socialism. It is obvious that *Siebenmeilenstiefel* too, made in 1934, bears a historical index. The different gestures and topographies of moving backwards, from Ferenczi's interest in backwards-walking soldiers to Höch's seven-league leap, stand in the tradition of engaging with the past in times of crises. There is a strong correspondence between psychoanalysis and critical theory in this regard. For readers of Walter Benjamin, the figure of a temporal leap is of particular relevance: Benjamin's 'On the Concept of History', written in 1940, shortly before he, fearing Nazi capture, committed suicide in Spain, envisions 'what we call progress' as 'one single catastrophe, which keeps piling wreckage upon wreckage'.[21] Benjamin speaks of a 'tiger's leap into the past':[22] the materialist historiographer 'blast[s] open the continuum of history'[23] and sets out to collect the fragments, to engage with the catastrophes, defeats and crushed emancipatory hopes of bygone times.

Ferenczi Dialogues: On Trauma and Catastrophe situates the legacy of Ferenczi within a broad interdisciplinary landscape – including social sciences, literary theory, psychoanalytic theory, and clinical practice. Our book is the result of a three-year-long dialogue about the philosophical, political and clinical implications of catastrophes in Ferenczi's work, which we try to disentangle from our different disciplinary points of view and against the background of social history. Planned and written during the Covid-19 pandemic, finished during the months in which war in Europe became a dominating subject again, our chapters address Ferenczi's work in terms of thinking in times of crises, considering the present in constellation with scenes from the past: the outbreak of the First World War, the crisis of psychoanalysis as an institution, the disastrous last encounter between Ferenczi and Freud, the rise of fascism and National Socialism, and the impending exile of the founding members of the psychoanalytic movement.

Ferenczi Dialogues – *an Outline*

As we were working on and dreaming up this book, corresponding between different countries and disciplinary contexts, we came to discuss the effect of radical plasticity, the propensity of mind to undergo change, both in terms of clinical imageries and of political counter-narratives. In an attempt to mirror the distances as well as the encounters of our own working process, we decided to divide the book into three main sections, written from each of our different disciplinary angles respectively, and followed by brief responses from the other two authors, hence the title *Ferenczi Dialogues*. The term 'dialogue' is of multiple origin. It can be traced to Spanish, French, Latin and Greek: a discussion, dispute, a literary composition in the form of a conversation, the Ancient Greek meaning to speak alternately, to converse, from Greek $διαλέγεσθαι$ (*dialegesthai*), from *dia* ('through') and *legein* ('speak'). In other words, the prefix *dia-* is not necessarily associated with the number two (*di-*).[24] From the onset, we envisaged a triangular exchange, and this is reflected in three sets of three-way engagements.

In the first part of the book, 'Instead of Language: Confusion. Sigmund Freud / Sándor Ferenczi', Jakob Staberg reflects the psychoanalytic and political milieu of Budapest and Vienna. In particular he explores the complex relation between Ferenczi and Freud departing from a scene of missed encounter: the last meeting between them in 1932, when Ferenczi read aloud his paper in which the notion of an 'identification with the aggressor' was introduced.[25] Staberg develops a new approach to the confusion between Ferenczi and Freud, by showing their theoretical standpoints as coloured by the transference between them. The chapter is theoretically oriented towards Deleuze and Guattari and the approach is guided by a structural psychoanalytic theory. By analysing the different aesthetic atmospheres of their dreams as depicted in analysis, investigating in particular the biological imagery they are containing, Staberg deepens the understanding of their theoretical positions pertaining to the consequences of Ferenczi's reformulation of genital theory. The reading of a concrete scene and its consequences reflects not only Ferenczi's position in the psychoanalytic movement, but also the tensions within its environment, as expressed in the form of authoritarianism, in notions of masculinity and male bonding in light of impending political dangers. In this way, the chapter seeks to articulate the traumatic elements of transference phenomena that dominated the environment of Freud and Ferenczi.

In the second part of the book, 'Catastrophes and Genitality: Ferenczi's *Thalassa* and the Politics of Bioanalysis', Jenny Willner enters an earlier scene, the Hungarian garrison town of Pápa in 1914, where Freud's theory of sexuality met popular Darwinism in a soldiers' library. These were the circumstances under which Ferenczi drafted a first version of his theory of genitality in *Thalassa*, which was to be published in 1924. Willner offers a new frame for reading *Thalassa*, challenging the perception that Ferenczi and Freud sought to provide psychoanalysis with a natural scientific foundation. Instead, her comparative reading shows how their 'bioanalytic' speculations deconstruct precisely what claims such a founding status: Ferenczi reads his sources from nineteenth-century popular biology – Lamarck, Haeckel and Bölsche – against the grain. Combining a poetology of science with psychoanalytic literary theory, Willner's reading foregrounds the diverging ideological implications of the languages of biology. While Freud and Ferenczi's immersion into pre-human history may seem like a retreat from political matters, Ferenczian 'bioanalysis', read against the backdrop of his time, holds the potential of a political intervention against biologism and eugenicist thought. At a time when evolutionary theory begins to inform eugenicist projects, *Thalassa* rewrites the terms of an entire discourse, while using concepts drawn from the psychoanalytic study of hysteria.

In the third part of the book, 'Catastrophe and the Creativity of Fragments: Toward a Phenomenology of the Scene of Trauma', Raluca Soreanu examines Ferenczi's revisions of Freudian theory, which amount to a 'metapsychology of fragmented psyches'. She shows that for Ferenczi the catastrophe is not a single, unitary event, but a 'scene', where several elements hold together and interact. Soreanu provides a phenomenological reading of the creativity of psychic fragments, while discussing ten distinct 'moments' of the scene of trauma. The clinical implication is that we enter the domain of an 'eventful psychoanalysis', where radical change is part of the clinical imagination. Ferenczi's method in arriving at the scene of trauma has a series of political and epistemological implications. He works with analogies from organic life, paying close attention to marine beings, learning from their breathing techniques, their resilience, and their ways of splitting themselves up. The consequence is a clinical imagery of 'wise organs', or, as Ferenczi states: 'when the psychic system fails, the organism begins to think'.[26] Soreanu's reading follows Ferenczi's clinical voice, shares his phenomenological approach and his use of biological analogies, and shows how his reflections on the secret life of organs can be opened up for current theoretical debates in contemporary feminism and new materialism, particularly in works by Donna Haraway and Alexis Pauline Gumbs. Ferenczi too is a thinker who is able to fantasise about life under water, inspired by the resilience of sea critters in times of catastrophe.

One of the most important aims of our project is to give contours to the fundamental *difference* of the Ferenczian project, within psychoanalysis, but also beyond it, in an interdisciplinary conversation. Ferenczi shook the Freudian house, proposing a revised metapsychology. Drawing on different methods, from genealogy, over textual analysis, to clinical reflection, we show that Ferenczi is a contemporary thinker, capable of contributing to questions of otherness, temporality, crisis or creativity. The implications of this journey are profound. By re-reading the relation between Freud and Ferenczi, we show that another psychoanalysis is possible, one that is committed to de-Oedipalising its theoretical imaginary and its key metaphors. By carefully fleshing out insurgent insights in Ferenczi's theory, in relation to the Freudian framework, we explore some possible pathways for a new theory of genitality and a new theory of sexuality. Ultimately, the Ferenczi that we encounter in these pages is a Ferenczi for our times, ridden with questions about how to encounter the Other in an ethical manner.

The Seven Threads of the 'Ferenczi Revival'

The triadic engagement of this book builds on the work of generations of scholars who, to follow the terms used by Adrienne Harris and Stephen Kuchuck, have transformed Ferenczi from 'ghost' to 'ancestor'.[27] This is the result of more than three decades of working-through. As a result of a complex event of forgetfulness, Ferenczi's presence within canonical psychoanalytic literature was almost spectral: the term 'ghost' refers to his unacknowledged influence on theorists such as Melanie Klein, Nicholas Abraham, Mária Torok, Michael Bálint, and Jean Laplanche. The retrospective transformation of Ferenczi into an ancestor, then, is the result of conversations, writings, conferences, seminars, ponderings on archival material, translations and teachings.

In their essay 'Why Psychoanalysis Has No History', Elisabeth Young-Bruehl and Murray Schwartz made an intervention into psychoanalytic historiography, by reminding us about the largely unacknowledged 'trauma history of psychoanalysis'.[28] This refers to two distinct phenomena: firstly, to the migration of Jewish psychoanalysts before and during the Second World War, mostly to England and to the Americas, with deep consequences in terms of dislocation and communal fragmentation. Secondly, the notion of a trauma history refers to intellectual splits, quarrels and fragmentations internal to the field of psychoanalysis. At the intersection of these two forms of forgetfulness, what we are missing is a collective historical consciousness that can organise a set of disparate observations precisely as a trauma history, a reflection on 'a repetitive pattern of splits and consequent distortions'.[29] In particular, the split between Ferenczi and Freud had a crucial role to play in turning Ferenczi into a 'ghost', as many voices have shown.[30] Crucially, turning Ferenczi into an 'ancestor' is not just a matter of setting the historical record straight, but of making sense of an arrest of the psychoanalytic imagination which lasted for nearly five decades, on both matters of theory and technique.

If forgetfulness is of traumatic nature, and has produced profound splits in the psyche, 'revival' cannot be a single act. There will need to be many overlayered revivals, constructions, links, and rearrangements around Ferenczi's voice and his legacy. In 2015, in the introduction of their edited volume *The Legacy of Sándor Ferenczi: From Ghost to Ancestor*, Harris and Kuchuck spoke of 'the inescapable truth that Ferenczi is now canonical.'[31] In the space of our current volume, we imagine ourselves in a field where several acts of revival have been performed over the last three decades in relation to Ferenczi, across national psychoanalytic cultures. Our volume is committed to continuing along these lines, trailing out of Ferenczi's text to contemporary questions at the intersection of literary theory, philosophy, and social theory. The Ferenczi revival thus continues to unfold in a complex temporality. Firstly, it recaptures what Ferenczi was back then, in the initial decades of psychoanalytic craft, in the frame of a past that has not been fully articulated, and which is approached in Staberg's chapter in an archaeological way. Secondly, it situates Ferenczi's voice among the scientific discourses of his time, in Willner's chapter, reassembling his singular voice. Thirdly, it follows orientations to the possible futures, in Soreanu's chapter: where might we travel, and what questions become possible, if we read Ferenczi alongside thinkers like Félix Guattari or Donna Haraway.

The need to revive a forgotten figure more than once also stems from the ethical significance of taking marginal voices seriously. The history of Ferenczi's reception is an example of what Adrienne Harris describes as 'a story about the fate of women or outliers more generally in psychoanalysis, the propensity for eclipse and erasure that "disappeared" a number of figures.'[32] To this question, we add: what structural reconfigurations become possible in psychoanalysis once the 'disappeared' make themselves known again? The revivals that came before us have established some of Ferenczi's contours as a thinker and as a clinician.[33] In what follows, we trace seven crucial 'threads' of the Ferenczi revivals and locate our own enterprise in relation to them. While the story of the revival can be told in different ways, this is our own seven-fold cut into an already vast field of investigation.

The first thread has to do with Ferenczian metapsychological revisions and their particularity. Several scholars have looked at the innovations of Ferenczi's trauma theory,[34] centred on a triadic grammar of psychic positions, where the three presences that make up the scene of trauma are the victim, the aggressor and a third presence, denying the aggression.[35] In 'Confusion of Tongues between Adults and the Child' (1933), Ferenczi develops his probably most famous notion: the identification with the aggressor.[36] This concept belongs to a new way of positioning fantasy and reality. It is crucial to acknowledge that Ferenczi does not revert to Freud's first theory of seduction, privileging the actual event of violation, but rather seeks to reconfigure the relation between seduction theory and the theory of the wish. Our project takes this investigation further by proposing a phenomenological 'stepping in' the scene of trauma, reading it (in the third part of the book) as a complex event that is made up of different moments. We thus encounter the monstrous presences of the scene of trauma from very close.

A second innovation within the revival of Ferenczi's legacy is his contribution to theorising the drives.[37] Ferenczi reconfigures the notion of a life drive, understood as the hypothetically assumed cause of astonishing forms of survival. These forms of life are the subject of Ferenczi's remarkable phenomenological attention. While maintaining the Freudian proposition of a duality of life and death drives, he introduces fascinating 'supplements' to the way in which we imagine their fusion and defusion. Our book engages the matter of the drives from different perspectives, pointing to the destinies of these supplements. One of them is the Orpha fragment of the psyche, a particular combination of life drive and death drive understood by Ferenczi as the result of the traumatic attack.[38] Orpha, a feminine relative of Orpheus, plays a role akin to that of a guardian angel in relation to psychic survival: the name signifies a protective psychic phenomenon, an instance that watches the scene of trauma from the outside, at a time when suffering is unbearable. In the last part of the book, Orpha is given extensive space and it is treated as a new psychic agency, alongside the id, ego and superego.

A third theme explored by the authors of the revival is Ferenczi's new vocabulary on psychoanalytic technique (where ideas such as 'tact' and 'mutuality' are crucial), and his reflections on the importance of countertransference of the analyst to their analysand.[39] In the first part of the book, Staberg builds a genealogical frame so that we can reflect Ferenczi's technical innovations against the background of a series of failed encounters in his short analysis with Freud and in their extra-analytic relationship. In the last part of the book, Soreanu works with the Ferenczian vocabulary in new settings, experimenting with the implications of his metapsychology for understanding the clinical encounter and what psychoanalysis can achieve.

A fourth thread of the Ferenczi revival is the reconfiguration of the relationship between psyche and soma as well as between psychoanalysis, medicine, and biology.[40] This book is traversed by different perspectives on this recomposition. In Staberg's chapter, the analysis of dreams shared by Ferenczi and Freud opens up different mental landscapes oriented around inner organs and body parts. Staberg explores how the dream elements in Ferenczi's analysis are not transcribed in the shape of binary poles but unfold through proximity. In the ramified associations, biological processes of organisms – such as the hermaphroditic binocular worms – bring theoretically useful notions of pollution and infection into play. Willner's chapter, focussing on the conflict of scientific and political debates over evolutionary thought, emphasises how Ferenczi introduces the concept of overdetermination to the natural sciences,[41] thus insisting that there can be no transparent language in which to represent organic life. Which methodological conclusions can we draw from this insight? While Willner's approach foregrounds the necessity to interrogate inherited, ideologically charged scientific concepts, Soreanu stands in closer proximity to what has been termed a post-critical method of reading. She works with the images offered by Ferenczi and demonstrates how these different registers can help us articulate psychic possibilities opened up by trauma and fragmentation: phenomena of radical psychic plasticity.[42] We believe that returning to Ferenczi provides a fresh perspective on the relation between the humanities and the natural sciences in current debates, navigating between the legacy of language-oriented approaches associated with the broad term 'critical theory'[43] on the one hand, and younger paradigms such as 'new materialism' and 'post-criticism'[44] on the other. How can we learn from the latter without falling behind the accomplishments of the former?

A fifth theme that the Ferenczi revivals have brought into focus is Ferenczi's relation to Oedipus and his insistence on the importance of early object relations. It has been argued that Ferenczi's interest in regressive states made it possible for him to articulate new pre-Oedipal preoccupations.[45] In the first part of the book, Jakob Staberg traces a series of different de-Oedipalising interventions, showing how the hysterical symptoms of authority lead Ferenczi to view the Oedipus complex in relation to what Freud's construction according to Ferenczi represses: the existence of trauma. There is a profound link between trauma, authority and masculinity in Ferenczi's work, a constellation which helps us rethink the theory of sexuality beyond heteronormativity.[46]

A sixth thread of the Ferenczi revival places Ferenczi in the context of the Budapest School of Psychoanalysis, a distinctively pluridisciplinary network which brought its own group innovations.[47] What would it mean to take this other metropolis of the crumbling Austro-Hungarian Empire as a vantage point? Jakob Staberg offers a close reading of the difference between Vienna and Budapest, by discerning the 'milieu' where Ferenczi was working and thinking in contrast to Freud's 'milieu'. Both Staberg and Willner's chapters are indebted to a scholarly tradition that emphasises antisemitism as a background for understanding the early years of psychoanalysis.[48] This perspective is of particular relevance in reading Ferenczi. Budapest is the place of departure for the international afterlife of Ferenczi's writings, beginning with the exile of several of his interlocutors only shortly after his death.[49] Up until today, important lines of Ferenczi's reception can be traced along the routes of the Hungarian-Jewish diaspora, and along translations of his work from German and Hungarian into English, Portuguese, French, Italian and Spanish. One of the aims of Willner's chapter is to make Ferenczi's exophonic German language more perceivable to an international readership, his interventions into dominating discourses in the German-language world.

The seventh thread we mention here is one that connects with all aforementioned threads and which we see as opening into many. It has to do with reading Ferenczi as a social theorist, a cultural theorist, and as a critical theorist. Ferenczi's thinking has proven highly compatible with social theory:[50] in his *Clinical Diary*, his metapsychology of fragments is embedded in an analysis of authoritarian structures.[51] Indeed, a subtle line of reception can be traced from Ferenczi via Erich Fromm to Theodor W. Adorno.[52] Ferenczi's insistence that psychoanalysis should always aim for a 'dismantling of the father image'[53] is of particular relevance in the face of the violent return of the phantasm of authoritarian sovereignty today.[54] His strong formulations around the 'confusion of tongues' and the 'identification with the aggressor' also call for further elaborations on modes of representation in the tradition of literary theory.[55] This aesthetic realm is not to be understood in terms of merely exemplifying illustrations of theoretical insights: rather, it provides specific takes on identification, submission, domination, power, ideology, authority, freedom and emancipation. Our book seeks to pluralise the way of relating to a political Ferenczi. Returning to Ferenczi leads to methodically and theoretically relevant encounters between psychoanalysis and different paradigms within contemporary humanities: from critical theory in the tradition of the Frankfurt School, over poststructuralism to new materialism.

Our book project itself is an entanglement that knew a few marked moments. We first met after Raluca Soreanu's talk on 'The Psychic Life of Fragments' at the Ferenczi Conference in Florence in spring 2018, surrounded by the competence and atmosphere of the gathered International Sándor Ferenczi Network.

Our exchange of ideas began at the workshop organised by Jenny Willner in summer 2018 at the Center for Advanced Studies in Munich, dedicated to interdisciplinary approaches. As our entanglements grew and deepened, the initial idea to write a book together was born at a panel organised by Jakob Staberg at the International Society of Psychoanalysis and Philosophy (SIPP/ISPP), organised at Södertörn University, south of Stockholm, in 2019. We received a publication offer from Philippe Van Haute, for the Leuven University Press (LUP) series *Figures of the Unconscious* – he was the first to imagine a book written by the three of us. We are grateful for his invaluable support and encouragement, and for giving us the space and the freedom to experiment with our three sets of triadic constellations. At LUP, we are also indebted to Beatriz Santos, Mirjam Truwant, Annemie Vandezande, Stien Wuyts and Beatrice van Eeghem for guiding us through the production process, and for the fruitful feedback from our two peer-reviewers. Early on we had the important fantasy that we would one day have the words of introduction from Adrienne Harris from the Sándor Ferenczi Center at the New School for Social Research (NYC). We are humbled by the fulfilment of this wish: Harris is a leading voice in the revitalizsed and interdisciplinary conversation on Ferenczi's work. At the end of our writing journey, we received the invaluable editorial assistance of Amber Segal and Johanna Losert as well as a final proof reading by Rebecca Bryan. This was made possible by a Strategic Research Grant from the Department of Psychosocial and Psychoanalytic Studies at the University of Essex and by the financial support from the LMU Mentoring Programme (Ludwig Maximilians University, Munich). We also thank the Hannah Höch estate for giving us the permission to use *Siebenmeilenstiefel* as a cover image.

While our cooperation began several years ago, it was only in the autumn of 2021 that we decided to prioritise this project despite everything. We reflected this explicitly as a means to mentally and intellectually survive another pandemic winter. Our decision meant insisting on research and exchange on our own terms, beyond strategic considerations. It also meant committing ourselves to staying in touch despite institutional pressures that do not always foster experimental working methods. Practically speaking, this book is the result of a dialogue between three talking heads and gesticulating pairs of hands in the scattered windows of digital group meetings between London, Munich, and Stockholm, often late in the evenings, and despite exhaustion, interruptions and disturbances. It is fair to say that the book was written in a state of crisis, for each of us in different combinations of clinical work or parenting, academic teaching and administrative duties, which lead to several postponements due to the logistic and health-related tolls of pandemic working and living conditions.

And yet writing it felt like a glimpse of real utopia. An important aspect was the most generous patience and understanding we performed towards each other each time one of us needed more time, no questions asked, perhaps even needed to regress for a while, in the mood and mode of a Ferenczian reptile. In the end, we felt hesitant towards finishing the book because it would have been quite interesting to just continue this both symptomatic and fruitful mode of writing. We hope that handing in the manuscript will only be the first step towards opening the dialogue even further.

Notes

1. H. Höch, *Siebenmeilenstiefel* [1934], Photomontage, 23.1 x 23.8 cm. Hamburger Kunsthalle.
2. S. Ferenczi, *Thalassa. A Theory of Genitality* [1924], transl. by H. A. Bunker. London, New York: Karnac, 1989.
3. S. Ferenczi, 'On Shock' [1932], in: S. Ferenczi, *Final Contributions to the Problems and Methods of Psycho-Analysis*, ed. by M. Bálint, transl. by E. Mosbacher. London: Karnac, 1994, pp. 253–254.
4. R. Soreanu, 'The Psychic Life of Fragments: Splitting from Ferenczi to Klein', *The American Journal of Psychoanalysis* 78(4), 2018, pp. 421–444.
5. S. Ferenczi, *The Clinical Diary of Sándor Ferenczi* [1932], ed. by J. Dupont, transl. by M. Bálint, N. Z. Jackson. Cambridge, Mass.: Harvard UP, 1995.
6. 'Catastrophe, *n*', *Oxford English Dictionary Online*. Oxford UP, 2022. https://www.oed.com (accessed 14 September 2022).
7. J. Willner, 'Neurotische Evolution. Bioanalyse als Kulturkritik in Jenseits des Lustprinzips', *Psyche. Zeitschrift für Psychoanalyse und ihre Anwendungen* 11(74), 2020, pp. 895–921.
8. J. Willner, 'The Problem of Heredity. Ferenczi's Organology and the Politics of Bioanalysis', *Psychoanalysis and History* 24(2), 2022, pp. 205–218.
9. T. Keve, J. Szekacs-Weisz (eds.), *Ferenczi and His World: Rekindling the Spirit of the Budapest School*. London: Karnac, 2012.
10. B. Doherty, '"We Are All Neurasthenics!" Or, the Trauma of Dada Montage', *Critical Inquiry* 24(1), 1997, pp. 82–132, p. 130 with reference to S. Ferenczi, 'The Phenomena of Hysterical Materialization' [1919], in: S. Ferenczi, *Further Contributions to the Theory and Technique of Psycho-Analysis*, comp. by J. Rickman, transl. by J. I. Suttie. London: Karnac, 1994, pp. 89–104.
11. B. Doherty, '"We Are All Neurasthenics!" Or, the Trauma of Dada Montage', p. 85.
12. M. Lavin, *Cut with the Kitchen Knife: The Weimar Photomontages of Hannah Höch*. New Haven, London: Yale UP, 1993, p. 8.
13. M. Biro, *The Dada Cyborg. Visions of the New Human in Weimar Berlin*. Minneapolis, London: University of Minnesota Press, 2009, p. 27.

14 M. Makela, 'Grotesque Bodies. Weimar-Era Medicine and the Photomontages of Hannah Höch', in: F. S. Connelly (ed.), *Modern Art and the Grotesque*. Cambridge: Cambridge UP, 2003, pp. 193–219. On wartime surgery during the First World War: p. 199; on gender reassignment surgery in the Weimar era: p. 208.
15 Ibid., p. 210. Ferenczi, in turn, was the Budapest representative of Hirschfeld's International, founded in 1905, and advocated for the rights of transvestites, cf.: M. Stanton, *Sándor Ferenczi: Reconsidering Active Intervention*. London: Free Association Books, 1991.
16 M. Makela, 'Grotesque Bodies. Weimar-Era Medicine and the Photomontages of Hannah Höch', p. 195.
17 M. Lavin, *Cut with the Kitchen Knife*, p. 10.
18 Ibid., p. 193.
19 S. Ferenczi, 'Psycho-Analysis of the War-Neuroses' [1918], in: E. Jones (ed.), *Psychoanalysis and the War Neuroses*. London, Vienna, New York: International Psa. Press, 1921, pp. 5–21, p. 15.
20 O. Jahraus, C. Kirchmeyer, 'Der Erste Weltkrieg als Katastrophe', in: N. Werber, S. Kaufmann, L. Koch (eds.), *Erster Weltkrieg. Kulturwissenschaftliches Handbuch*. Stuttgart, Weimar: Metzler, 2014, pp. 495–509, p. 495.
21 W. Benjamin, 'On the Concept of History', in: W. Benjamin, *Selected Writings, Vol. 4, 1938–1940*, ed. by H. Eiland, M. W. Jennings, transl. by E. Jephcott. Cambridge, Mass.: Belknap Press of Harvard UP, 2006, pp. 339–411, p. 392.
22 Ibid., p. 395.
23 Ibid., p. 396.
24 'Dialogue/dialog, *n*', *Oxford English Dictionary Online*, Oxford UP, 2022. https://www.oed.com (accessed 14 September 2022).
25 S. Ferenczi, 'Confusion of Tongues between Adults and the Child' [1933], in: S. Ferenczi, *Final Contributions to the Problems and Methods of Psycho-Analysis*, pp. 156–167.
26 S. Ferenczi, *The Clinical Diary of Sándor Ferenczi*, p. 6.
27 A. Harris, S. Kuchuck (eds.), *The Legacy of Sándor Ferenczi: From Ghost to Ancestor*. London, New York: Routledge, 2015, pp. 5–6.
28 E. Young-Bruehl, M. Schwartz, 'Why Psychoanalysis Has no History', *American Imago* 69(1), 2012, pp. 139–159, p. 140.
29 Ibid., p. 142.
30 M. Bálint, 'The Disagreement Between Freud and Ferenczi and Its Repercussions', in: M. Bálint, *The Basic Fault. Therapeutic Aspects of Regression*. London: Tavistock, 1968, pp. 149–158; A. Haynal, J. E. King, *Controversies in Psychoanalytic Method. From Freud and Ferenczi to Michael Bálint*. New York, London: New York UP, 1990; L. Martín-Cabré, 'Freud-Ferenczi: Controversy Terminable and Interminable', *International Journal of Psychoanalysis* 78(1), 1997, pp. 105–114; É. Brabant, 'Les voies de la passion. Les rapports entre Freud et Ferenczi', *Le Coq-Héron* 3, 2003, pp. 100–113.
31 A. Harris, S. Kuchuck, *The Legacy of Sándor Ferenczi*, p. 2.

[32] A. Harris, '"Language is There to Bewilder Itself and Others": Theoretical and Clinical Contributions of Sabina Spielrein', *Journal of the American Psychoanalytic Association* 63(4), 2015, pp. 727–767, p. 732.

[33] While it would be difficult to paint a full picture of the Ferenczi revival, the mid-1990s were a key moment, with the publication of two edited collections: L. Aron, A. Harris (eds.), *The Legacy of Sándor Ferenczi*. London: The Analytic Press, 1993; P. L. Rudnitzky, A. Bókay, P. Gampieri-Deutsch, *Ferenczi's Turn in Psychoanalysis*. New York, London: New York UP, 1996. A few years later, T. Keve and J. Szekacs-Weisz edited two further volumes: *Ferenczi and His World: Rekindling the Spirit of the Budapest School*. London: Karnac, 2012, and: *Ferenczi for Our Time: Theory and Practice*. London: Karnac, 2012. In 2015, Harris and Kuchuck published the already quoted Routledge anthology *The Legacy of Sándor Ferenczi: From Ghost to Ancestor*. The most recent extensive anthology on Ferenczi was edited by A. Dimitrijević, G. Cassullo and J. Frankel, *Ferenczi's Influence on Contemporary Psychoanalytic Traditions. Lines of Development. Evolution of Theory and Practice over Decades*. London, New York: Routledge, 2018. Considered together, these volumes established a field of exchanges on the contributions of Ferenczi to trauma theory: they are containers of the Ferenczi revival.

[34] For some crucial formulations on psychoanalytic trauma theory in general, see S. Felman, D. Laub, *Testimony. Crises of Witnessing in Literature, Psychoanalysis, and History*. London, New York: Routledge, 1992; C. Caruth (ed.), *Trauma. Explorations in Memory*. Baltimore, London: Johns Hopkins UP, 1995; C. Caruth, *Unclaimed Experience: Trauma, Narrative, History*. Baltimore, London: Johns Hopkins UP, 1996; D. Laub, S. Lee, 'Thanatos and Massive Psychic Trauma: The Impact of the Death Instinct on Knowing, Remembering, and Forgetting', *Journal of the American Psychoanalytic Association* 51(2), 2003, pp. 433–464; W. Bohleber, 'Remembrance, Trauma and Collective Memory: The Battle for Memory in Psychoanalysis', *International Journal of Psychoanalysis* 88(2), 2007, pp. 329–352; R. Luckhurst, *The Trauma Question*. London, New York: Routledge, 2008; W. Bohleber, *Destructiveness, Intersubjectivity, and Trauma: The Identity Crisis of Modern Psychoanalysis*. London: Karnac, 2010; J. Fletcher, *Freud and the Scene of Trauma*. New York: Fordham UP, 2013; D. LaCapra, *Writing History, Writing Trauma*. Baltimore, London: Johns Hopkins UP 2014.

[35] For commentaries on trauma theory in the work of Ferenczi, see M. Schneider, *Le trauma et la filiation paradoxale: de Freud à Ferenczi*. Paris: Ramsay, 1988; J. Frankel, 'Ferenczi's Trauma Theory', *The American Journal of Psychoanalysis* 58(1), 1998, pp. 41–61; C. Bonomi, 'Between Symbol and Antisymbol: The Meaning of Trauma Reconsidered', *International Forum of Psychoanalysis* 12(1), 2003, pp. 17–21; C. Bonomi, 'Trauma and the Symbolic Function of the Mind', *International Forum of Psychoanalysis* 13(1–2), 2004, pp. 45–50; T. Bokanowski, 'Splitting, Fragmenting, and Mental Agony: The Clinical Thinking of Sándor Ferenczi', *International Forum of Psychoanalysis* 13(1–2), 2004, pp. 20–25; F. Borgogno, 'Ferenczi's Clinical and Theoretical Conception of Trauma: A Brief

Introductory Map', *The American Journal of Psychoanalysis* 67, 2007, pp. 141–149; J. Dupont, 'The Concept of Trauma According to Ferenczi and Its Effects on Subsequent Psychoanalytic Research', *International Forum of Psychoanalysis* 7(4), 2010, pp. 235–241; A. Avelar, *Trauma e prática clínica: um percurso entre Freud e Ferenczi* [dissertation]. Universidade Federal do Rio de Janeiro, Instituto de Psicologia, 2013; A. Haynal, 'Trauma – Revisited: Ferenczi and Modern Psychoanalysis', *Psychoanalytic Inquiry* 34(2), 2014, pp. 98–111; A. Bókay, 'The Child as a Traumatic Self-Component in Ferenczi's Later Psychoanalysis', *American Journal of Psychoanalysis* 75(1), 2015, pp. 46–56.

36 J. Frankel, 'Exploring Ferenczi's Concept of Identification with the Aggressor: Its Role in Trauma, Everyday Life, and the Therapeutic Relationship', *Psychoanalytic Dialogues* 12(1), 2002, pp. 101–139; J. Frankel, 'The Persistent Sense of Being Bad: The Moral Dimension of the Identification with the Aggressor', in: A. Harris, S. Kuchuck, *The Legacy of Sándor Ferenczi*, pp. 204–222.

37 J. J. Avello, 'Metapsychology in Ferenczi: Death Instinct or Death Passion?', *International Forum of Psychoanalysis* 7, 1998, pp. 229–234.

38 For commentaries on Ferenczi's 'Orpha' see N. A. Smith, '"Orpha Reviving": Toward an Honorable Recognition of Elizabeth Severn', *International Forum of Psychoanalysis* 7(4), 1998, pp. 241–246; N. A. Smith, 'From Oedipus to Orpha: Revisiting Ferenczi and Severn's Landmark Case', *American Journal of Psychoanalysis* 59(4), 1999, pp. 345–366; H. Gurevich, 'Orpha, Orphic Functions, and the Orphic Analyst: Winnicott's "Regression to Dependence" in the Language of Ferenczi', *American Journal of Psychoanalysis* 76(4), 2016, pp. 322–340; E. Koritar, 'Relaxation in Technique Leading to New Beginnings', *American Journal of Psychoanalysis* 76(4), 2016, pp. 341–353; and G. Hristeva, '"Primordial Chant". Sandor Ferenczi as an Orphic Poet', *The American Journal of Psychoanalysis* 79(4), 2019, pp. 517–539.

39 For commentaries on Ferenczi's technique see: E. Falzeder, 'Sándor Ferenczi Between Orthodoxy and Heterodoxy', *American Imago* 66(4), 2010, pp. 395–404; E. Koritar, 'Ferenczi's Researches in Technique', *The American Journal of Psychoanalysis* 82, 2022, pp. 210–221; particularly on countertransference see A. Haynal, 'Countertransference in the Work of Ferenczi', *The American Journal of Psychoanalysis* 59, 1999, pp. 315–331; I. Hirsch, 'Countertransference and the Person of the Therapist', in: A. Dimitrijević, G. Cassullo, J. Frankel (eds.), *Ferenczi's Influence on Contemporary Psychoanalytic Traditions*, pp. 165–168.

40 G. Hristeva, '"Uterus Loquitur": Trauma and the Human Organism in Ferenczi's "Physiology of Pleasure"', *The American Journal of Psychoanalysis* 73(4), 2013, pp. 339–352. A recent double special issue of the journal *RISS* was dedicated to Ferenczi's take on biology: *RISS. Zeitschrift für Psychoanalyse: Bioanalysen I* 94, 2021, and *Bioanalysen II* 95, 2022.

41 S. Ferenczi, *Thalassa*, p. 34.

[42] Catherine Malabou's notion of plasticity was recently brought into proximity with Ferenczi's theory of genitality: N. Hartmann, A. Wedemeyer, 'Ankündigung eines Austauschs des RISS mit Catherine Malabou anlässlich ihres neuen Buches *Le plaisir effacé. Clitoris et pensée*', *RISS. Zeitschrift für Psychoanalyse: Bioanalysen II* 95, 2021, pp. 113–117.

[43] For a recent autobiographical account of the history of the notion of 'theory' – from Marx and Freud over the French reception of Hegel to Lacan, Foucault, Deleuze, Derrida, Butler, Agamben, the Ljubljana School and more – see: E. L. Santner, *Untying Things Together. Philosophy, Literature, and a Life in Theory*. London, Chicago: University of Chicago Press, 2022.

[44] See R. Felski, *The Limits of Critique*. Chicago: University of Chicago Press, 2015; and R. Felski, 'Postcritical Reading', *American Book Review* 38(5), 2017, pp. 4–5.

[45] H. Stewart, 'Regression Post-Ferenczi', in: T. Keve, J. Szekacs-Weisz (eds.), *Ferenczi and His World: Rekindling the Spirit of the Budapest School*, pp. 129–137; on the influence of Ferenczi's view of regression and of mother–child relations: S. Bar-Haim, *The Maternalists. Psychoanalysis, Motherhood, and the British Welfare State*. Philadelphia: University of Pennsylvania Press, 2021, esp. chapter one.

[46] Ferenczi is of seminal importance in N. Evzonas, 'Countertransference Madness: Supervision, Trans*, and the Sexual', *Psychoanalytic Review* 108(4), 2021, pp. 475–509; see also forthcoming: J. Webster, M. Coelen, 'Two Analysts Ask, "What is Genitality?" Ferenczi's Thalassa and Lacan's Lamella', in: P. Gherovici, M. Steinkohler (eds.), *Psychoanalysis, Gender, and Sexualities. From Feminism to Trans**. London, New York: Routledge, 2023.

[47] For discussions on the Budapest School see J. Mészáros, 'Sándor Ferenczi and the Budapest School of Psychoanalysis', *Psychoanalytic Perspectives* 7(1), 2010, pp. 69–89; F. Erős, 'Some Social and Political Issues Related to Ferenczi and the Hungarian School', in: T. Keve, J. Szekacs-Weisz (eds.), *Ferenczi and His World: Rekindling the Spirit of the Budapest School*, pp. 39–54; A. Rachman (ed.), *The Budapest School of Psychoanalysis. The Origin of a Two-Person Psychology and Emphatic Perspective*. London, New York: Routledge, 2016; H. Bacal, 'The Budapest School's Concept of Supervision: Michael Bálint's Legacy to the Development of Psychoanalytic Specificity Theory', in: A. Rachman (ed.), *The Budapest School of Psychoanalysis*, pp. 140–163; R. Soreanu, 'Supervision for Our Times: Countertransference and the Rich Legacy of the Budapest School', *The American Journal of Psychoanalysis* 79(3), 2019, pp. 329–351.

[48] S. L. Gilman, *Freud, Race, and Gender*. Princeton, NJ: Princeton UP, 1993; D. Boyarin, *Unheroic Conduct. The Rise of Heterosexuality and the Invention of the Jewish Man*. Berkeley: University of California Press, 1997; E. L. Santner, *My Own Private Germany: Daniel Paul Schreber and the Secret History of Modernity*. Princeton, NJ: Princeton UP, 1996; L. Aron, K. Starr, *A Psychotherapy for the People: Toward a Progressive Psychoanalysis*. London, New York: Routledge, 2013.

49 J. Mészáros, *Ferenczi and Beyond. Exile of the Budapest School and Solidarity in the Psychoanalytic Movement during the Nazi Years*. London: Karnac, 2014.
50 For different takes on Ferenczi and social and critical theory: E. Salgó, *Psychoanalytic Reflections on Politics: Fatherlands in Mothers' Hands*. London, New York: Routledge, 2014; S. Gandesha, 'Identifying with the Aggressor. From the Authoritarian to the Neoliberal Personality', *Constellations* 25(1), 2018, pp. 1–18; F. Erős, 'Against Violence: Ferenczi and Liberal Socialism', in: A. Dimitrijević, G. Cassullo, J. Frankel (eds.), *Ferenczi's Influence on Contemporary Psychoanalytic Traditions*, pp. 248–254; R. Soreanu, *Working-Through Collective Wounds: Trauma, Denial, Recognition in the Brazilian Uprising*. London: Palgrave Macmillan, 2018; D. Kupermann, 'Social Trauma and Testimony: A Reading of Maryan S. Maryan's Notebooks Inspired by Sándor Ferenczi', *American Journal of Psychoanalysis* 82(2), 2022, pp. 268–280.
51 F. Erős, 'Freedom and Authority in the Clinical Diary', *American Journal of Psychoanalysis* 74(4), 2014, pp. 367–380.
52 S. Gandesha, 'Adorno, Ferenczi, and the New "Categorical Imperative" after Auschwitz', *International Forum of Psychoanalysis* 28(4), 2019, pp. 222–230.
53 Ferenczi to Freud, 25 October 1912, S. Freud, S. Ferenczi, *The Correspondence of Sigmund Freud and Sándor Ferenczi, Vol. 1: 1908–1914*, p. 417.
54 For a discussion along the lines of Ferenczi's 'Confusion of Tongues': J. Frankel, 'The Narcissistic Dynamics of Submission: The Attraction of the Powerless to Authoritarian Leaders', *The American Journal of Psychoanalysis*, 30 August 2022, online ahead of print: https://link.springer.com/article/10.1057/s11231-022-09369-4.
55 Two different ways of employing Ferenczi's 'Confusion of Tongues' in literary analysis: M. v. Koppenfels, *Schwarzer Peter, der Fall Littell, die Leser und die Täter*. Göttingen: Wallstein, 2012, pp. 19–30, 67–74; B. N. Nagel, 'The Child in the Dark: On Child Abuse in Robert Walser', *New German Critique. An Interdisciplinary Journal of German Studies* 146(8), 2022, pp. 107–132.

PART 1
Instead of Language: Confusion
Sigmund Freud / Sándor Ferenczi

by Jakob Staberg,
with responses from Jenny Willner and Raluca Soreanu

Instead of Language: Confusion
Sigmund Freud / Sándor Ferenczi

Jakob Staberg

En route to the International Psychoanalytic Congress in Wiesbaden, August 1932, the Ferenczis make time for a short visit at the Freud family summer residence in Pötzleinsdorf, Vienna. The matter seems urgent, but the impression made by Sándor Ferenczi is unfavourable from the very start. Although his wife, Gizella, is certainly as charming as ever, there is an icy cold emanating from him according to Freud's later remarks. Making no effort at greeting, Ferenczi rushes in, insisting on reading aloud the paper he is due to give at the upcoming conference. Freud listens but is increasingly 'shocked'.[1] The presentation seems to him 'confused, obscure, artificial'.[2] Abraham Brill, the founder of the American Psychoanalytic Association over which he now presides, is at the time a guest in the household. As he enters the room, the man once venerated as a 'Grand Vizier'[3] has made it halfway through his reading. Freud states that its theme – trauma – should interest Brill and encourages the insistent visitor to summarise what he has read thus far. It deals with the 'repetition' which analysis invites in the patient, not only as recurring themes but also in the form of intensive states during the sessions which spread to nightly anxiety attacks, disturbing nightmares and the like. The patient in particular, Ferenczi argues, develops a heightened sensitivity to desires, tendencies and mood shifts in the analyst, indeed even the latter's dislikes, with which the patient can come to identify. Criticism never crosses the analysand's mind.[4]

For Freud, the attention to these phenomena and the ways in which Ferenczi proposes handling them recall practical and theoretical positions he has long since abandoned. In the middle of all this there are, as he writes to his daughter Anna a few days later, ideas about 'observations of the hostility of patients and the need to accept their criticisms and to acknowledge one's mistakes before them'.[5] Brill, now close by him, leans forward, whispering: 'He is not sincere'.[6] Freud, marked by illness, stares ahead in silence. Both content and behaviour have deeply disturbed him. Two days later, 3 September, he dispatches a telegram to Max Eitingon, the stuttering, wealthy Russian émigré, whom looming Nazism had not yet forced into a second exile in Jerusalem: 'Ferenczi read paper out loud. Harmless, stupid, also inadequate. Impression unpleasant'.[7]

Neither Freud nor Ferenczi knew that this encounter would be their last. But the letters they came to exchange would eventually mean the end of their decades-long contact, saturated as it was theoretically and emotionally with elements that were to form the development of psychoanalysis during its founding years.

Still, at this last meeting things came to a head. While Ferenczi insisted on presenting the discoveries of his theoretical and clinical endeavours, Freud saw his colleague betraying everything he himself had aspired to achieve. The tension between Freud and Ferenczi will, in what follows, be viewed in the light of this last encounter. I will argue that the very form these theoretical conflicts took rests on certain unique contingencies and unconscious desires that characterised the relation between the antagonists. Such circumstances lead us towards a peculiarity specific to the genesis of psychoanalysis as method and theory. With everything it implies by way of a new kind of sensitivity, it is in fact within the framework of the psychoanalytic experience that its praxis is developed. The theoretical findings as well as the complex relations that its milieu contains – with its forces and energies affecting each other – are shaped by, indeed take place in, what we, using a term from its own vocabulary, will call transference. That is, the specific cathexis that arises in and characterises the analytic situation in the shape of the communication of hidden messages, repetitions of earlier, long-forgotten libidinal investments whose traumatic basis is enacted in new forms. It is my contention that the genealogy of psychoanalysis can be seen as a first resistance to the psychiatric power that dominated the medical institutions at the time and in a sense still does. Rather than subordinating the encounter between doctor and patient to the authority exercised by the former by virtue of a scientific legitimacy whose prerequisites are never tested in the encounter, psychoanalysis works with the forces that manifest themselves as symptoms, resistance and idealisation, simulation and imitation; indeed, not least the sexual nature of the symptoms will constitute material for its work. But having said that, it must be recognised that the inner struggles and tensions that we will here come across – the naming of a scapegoat, the fetish of the secret, not least the hysterical acting out of paranoid notions of the name of the father cultivated in the psychoanalytic milieus, as well as the so-called wild analysis of dreams – always run the risk of the return of the phantasmatic power that infests the psychiatric institution.

My aim will thus be to explore the confrontation between Freud and Ferenczi, in particular the theoretical schisms that took place between them regarding the role of authority in psychoanalytic technique, and especially how the transference situation is tainted by trauma, and its manifestations in dream. As major themes I will elaborate on the understanding of trauma, oscillating between external event and fantasy; the presence of the authoritarian paternal function and the possibility of inventing certain answers to the traumatic event whose repetitive capacity presents us with the domain of word-presentations and thing-presentations manifested in dream analysis, no longer subordinated to the authoritarian figure of the father.

We have, hence, begun *in medias res* in order to be able to re-read the oft-told story of psychoanalysis's genesis. However, I will be examining it not from the perspective of a foundation or lost origin, but instead as a scene – *this scene* – observed as if in slow motion or under a microscope. I thereby hope to stir up and muddle a certain trajectory of chronology; I am engaging in a specific *archaeological method* for uncovering tracks of time.[8] Such a method recognises an affinity with the experience of the event in the way it can be gained from the psychoanalytic experience thought of as layered in fragments of time, which is how I interpret the meaning of *deferred action*. To do so is to approach the material with an attentiveness to coincidences – in fact, to everything that relates to particularities, that which sets in motion and results in violence, in approaching the traumatic ground that suddenly manifested itself in Freud's and Ferenczi's last painful encounter.[9]

Ferenczi in the Psychoanalytic Milieu

When Ferenczi had been introduced to the method and theory of psychoanalysis through Freud in 1908, the then young movement had in only a few years expanded from informal Wednesday meetings – where young male Jewish physicians acquired the new ideas in Freud's consulting room on Berggasse in Vienna – to increasingly wider circles, involving established psychiatrists at the large institution of Burghölzli near Zurich as well as practising physicians in Berlin. The following year, Ferenczi, active in Budapest, contributed with an important article that would develop the understanding of the phenomenon of transference by deepening the understanding of the mechanisms of projection and what he would call *introjection*. The article 'Introjection and Transference' expands the understanding of the mental forces that the psychoanalytic situation contains.[10] In the same year, Ferenczi was invited to the USA, together with Freud and Carl Gustav Jung, where Freud, noticeably moved despite his ambivalent attitude towards the country and its culture, was awarded an honorary degree at Clark University, Worcester, Mass. It is during this visit that they – as Jacques

Lacan would put it in a lecture given in Vienna in 1955 – spread the plague to a new continent.[11]

The psychoanalytic circles – whose dominant members in the beginning were men from families who had, in an earlier generation, migrated from provincial, closed environments, *shtetl*, to the cosmopolitan cities of Central Europe – were during these years organised in loosely connected networks. This new science, as they view it, capable of defining and acting on the innermost drives of the human being in a violent and changeable world, never gained a real foothold within the established medical science or at the universities.

Jung, *Sekundärarzt* at Burghölzli, part of the highest social and economic strata of society by marriage, was at this time becoming acquainted with Freud's work and looking forward to a brilliant academic career. In his memoirs, however, he notes that Freud was 'persona non grata' in the academic world. For this reason he was initially somewhat reluctant to recognise a correspondence between his own 'experiments with word association' and the theory elaborated by Freud based on his clinical experience: relating to him was simply not advisable from a career perspective.[12] At the first major international congress in 1910, Ferenczi gave a talk addressing the need to analyse the mechanisms in the organisation of the psychoanalytic environments.[13] The topic of the lecture was more or less provided by Freud, who, aiming for a new, overarching organisation, wanted to place its centre in Zurich and thereby undo the limited conditions of psychoanalysis in the Vienna circle. Freud, so to speak, delegates to Ferenczi the task of handling the tensions that could ensue from this. Freud's ambition brought to the fore a conflict between the representatives from Vienna and the new members from the established Burghölzli in Zurich. But Ferenczi's paper also addressed the psychoanalytic circle's relation to external as well as internal authorities. It is of note how his writing raises the image of psychoanalysis as a secret war machine operating in the institutions dominated by the patriarchal power that surround it. In relation to the established psychiatry, Ferenczi sees them as involved in something to be compared to *guerrilla warfare*. Beyond the current conflict, Ferenczi thus identifies, structurally, the position that psychoanalysis occupies within the medical field. In the following, we will approach this notion of the psychoanalytic movement as a war machine operating in the authoritarian medical world. We will see how it calls forth the existence of a *secret* – on the one hand Ernest Jones's fantasy of a secret committee subordinated to the authority of the father, and, on the other hand, Ferenczi's insights regarding the need to handle the fantasy of the paternal authority, which will also govern his work on transference, theoretically and clinically; his aim can now be formulated as a dissolution of the secret and its phantasmatically operating power.

The multicultural cities of Central Europe were flourishing during the Habsburg monarchy in the years around 1900, an era that has been called *la belle époque*. The circles in which Freud found his patients largely consisted of Jews who had liberated themselves from the ghetto and who, at the heart of the rapidly transforming continent, were engaged in the mapping out of a new future. Not only were they interested in art and embraced free market and political liberalism, they were also inclined to explore themselves. The zeitgeist promised scientific rationality but also dreams of a promised land. Simultaneously, Karl Kraus's linguistic deconstruction, Stefan Zweig's and Arthur Schnitzler's literary projects, as well as Arnold Schönberg's musical formalism, constituted a basis for new visions against a backdrop of a world of old ideas about to perish. Freud's perceived isolation is perhaps rather to be seen as a fantasy, since the reinvention of Hamlet's modern individuality – in *The Interpretation of Dreams* and in the light of the Oedipus myth – corresponds to an emerging aesthetics and new conceptions of the world. Freud, who fully mastered English, French, Italian and Spanish, and had a perfect understanding of Greek and Latin, as well as of Hebrew and Yiddish, can be seen as a product of Viennese culture with its veritable babel of European voices. Large cities like Vienna and Budapest were permeated with German culture; intellectuals in Budapest were in point of fact bilingual. Ferenczi even wrote his diaries in German. In their studies, Lewis Aron and Karen Starr deepen the picture of this era based on the relation between Ferenczi and Freud.[14] Both of them shared an identity characterised by Jewish enlightenment – fruit of a tradition of migration, acculturation and assimilation – while their diverse circumstances illustrate the internal tensions and differences as manifested in the conditions that reigned in Vienna and Budapest, respectively. The Jewish immigrant families that had moved from Eastern to Central Europe, from *shtetls* to cosmopolitan cities, found possibilities within certain specific professions, such as medicine, and especially as private practitioners. In particular, the position of private practitioner allowed for social mobility independent of the institutions that did not allow Jews to be present. But while those in Vienna considered themselves Germans linguistically and culturally, and were politically loyal to Austria, those in Hungary were less integrated, spoke German and Hungarian besides Yiddish. At the same time, while the hope for social change in Budapest lasted longer – up until the collapse of the short Red Commune after the final phase of the First World War – in Vienna the liberal political philosophy that had promised Jewish emancipation and participation in German culture had broken down long before.

The cities of Central Europe were cosmopolitan; writers, thinkers and philosophers gathered in cafés and clubs, around magazines and publishing houses. Unlike Freud, Ferenczi took an active part in this environment. Furthermore, during the 1910s and the 1920s psychoanalysis in Budapest was linked to progressive cultural movements. Thus, the Hungarian political atmosphere remained liberal up until the violent aftermath of the First World War, while Freud, in Vienna, was early on disenchanted by the aggressive right-wing populism and the antisemitism that followed.

Although they were part of the same Jewish enlightenment, Freud's and Ferenczi's conditions in Vienna and Budapest were very different. In Budapest, which around 1900 established itself as a flourishing big city, approximately a fifth of the inhabitants were Jews who took an active part in finance and markets, and played an important role within the cultural field. But in response to that, a new form of antisemitism arose, one that was no longer rooted in religious notions. As a result of the dissolution of the dual monarchy, the basis for the pre-war radical milieus broke down. Ferenczi, however, continued, even after the collapse of the short-lived commune in which he was active in 1919–1920, to work in the city. Freud, for his part, belonged to the most vulnerable group in the upheaval that occurred in connection with Lueger's political takeover in 1897, namely, the liberal Jews of Vienna, who were hit when the previously prevailing opposition between liberals and conservatives was challenged by lower strata in the shape of an aggressive antisemitic agenda. The American historian Carl E. Schorske has noted that beneath the surface of Freud's systematic treatment of the metapsychology of dreams in his *Interpretation of Dreams* can be discerned a deep structure, which, as the author moves from one isolated dream to the next, constitutes a fragmentary but nevertheless autonomous covert plot in the form of a personal history.[15] If Freud, according to Schorske, as a young grammar school pupil still entertained the possibility of politics, he would soon turn into resignation. Although Freud himself was never politically active, he witnessed the takeover by the new right with frustration. In France, the Dreyfus affair was in full swing and, in a letter to Wilhelm Fließ, Freud calls Lueger his *bête noire*, while Zola is ascribed the role of political hero.[16] As a result of the prevailing order, it became increasingly difficult for Jews to maintain an academic career. For Freud, after coming home from his stay at Professor Martin Charcot's clinic of La Salpêtrière, the hope of a career as a researcher seemed increasingly distant, appointments were long in coming, promotion and financial means failed to appear. He withdrew, socially and intellectually, and did not really take part in the surrounding modernism. But Schorske, who has, in his uncovering of layers in dreams – like the one about Irma's injections, the dream about the botanical monograph or the dreams thematically circling around Rome – read into them the tendency to shift the conflict from an external authority to a father complex, also saw Freud's ideas and ambitions as increasingly grandiose: 'Freud's intellectual originality and professional isolation were mutually nourishing'.[17]

Elisabeth Roudinesco – just like André E. Haynal and Véronique D. Haynal, Lewis Aron and Karen Starr, and many others – emphasises antisemitism and the 'Jewish question' as a necessary background to understand the positions taken by Freud and Ferenczi, scientifically, politically and privately.[18] Roudinesco observes the signs of ambivalence that she connects to what she calls the Jewish identity crisis of the late nineteenth century, how they relate to, or rather express, a present dominating discourse. However, neither Freud's nor Ferenczi's projects were ever under the influence of ideas about race – unlike that of Jung, who in his ideas of a specific Jewish and a specific Aryan unconscious later played into the hands of the Nazis.[19] In a letter to Ferenczi on 8 June 1913, Freud insists that there can never be a reason for talking about a specific Aryan or Jewish science. But like so many of his contemporaries, Freud talks without hesitation about differences between Aryans and Jews. Not least in the wake of the break with Jung, these implicit differences come to be understood as the reason for the conflict between them. The Freud–Ferenczi correspondence is full of idioms in Yiddish; for example, Ferenczi writes in a letter that 'all libido is based on "naches" [pleasure]'.[20]

Yiddish has, in Gilles Deleuze and Félix Guattari's analysis of Franz Kafka's work, been considered 'a language that is lacking a grammar and that is filled with vocables that are fleeting, mobilised, emigrating, and turned into nomads'.[21] *Yiddishland* is situated in the heart of what was once the German–Roman realm, the provinces of Galicia, Moravia, Bohemia and Silesia – a territory without definite borders, in which the Jewish population was grouped into communities that migrated from area to area in Poland, Lithuania, Belarus and Romania, many of them finally settling in Hungary and Budapest. Although most professions were closed to them, there were a few possibilities, such as the above-mentioned role of private medical practitioner, and that of the intellectual. As Aron and Starr point out, the correspondence between Freud and Ferenczi expresses a dynamic largely shaped by the two men's reaction to the antisemitic and homophobic culture that surrounded them.[22] Freud and Ferenczi also became prominent within these fields, both of them in touch with, but eventually standing outside of, the established medical science.

At the same time, it is possible to see Yiddishland as language through and through. In his diary, after meeting a Yiddish-speaking theatre group from Lemberg, Kafka expresses enthusiasm for what he calls the 'minor literature' and what it could achieve: 'minor literature is not the literature that is written in a small language, but rather what it, as a minority, achieves in a big language'.[23] The Yiddish words inserted in Freud's and Ferenczi's correspondence can be considered from that perspective, but also, for example, the intricate mixtures of language that are exhibited in the analysis of Sergei Pankejeff, known as the Wolf Man. The language of minority literature is able to express the 'internal tensions' of a language, particularly able to develop 'these tensors or these intensives', according to Deleuze and Guattari's Kafka analysis.[24] The situation of the Jews in the Habsburg Empire, with its migrations, multilingualism and linguistic mixtures, brings forth precisely these kinds of intensities. Kafka's linguistic experiments are an example of this, just like Kraus's exploration of the language of power and the language of modern media. But the linguistic mixture in Freud's analyses, which often form encrypted utterances, can also testify to this. The intensities and the linguistic fragments in *The Interpretation of Dreams*, as well as in the case studies, provide us with examples. Not least those produced in 'From the History of an Infantile Neurosis', whose enigmatic subject, the Wolf Man, constructs an identity from Russian-, English-, German- and French-language fragments, derived from the inner tensions generated by the multitude of languages; as a result, an unconscious populated by multiplicities can be read into the case studies' complex weave of signifiers.[25]

Following and recognising these nomadic movements, inherent for generations among the members of the early circles of the psychoanalytic movement, as well as the institutional conditions – the relation to the established academies, the psychiatric institutions and their establishment, where their activities could be referred to as little war machines involved in guerrilla warfare – brings to the fore the multicultural and linguistic babel of the dual monarchy whose imprint is visible in the case studies of the early psychoanalysis. The fact that the patients were predominantly emigrants from Eastern Europe whose background exhibited, both geographically and socially, an inherent diversity – the case of the Wolf Man is an exemplary – may guide us in our aim to find new ways of thinking of the genealogy of psychoanalysis. The political background – such as the incipient collapse of the empire, the aggressive right-wing populist antisemitism – should also be taken into consideration. The consequence of this can be found in the shape of contingent and accidental traces in the unconscious processes and the symbolic language recorded in the case studies, but most importantly in the way we meet them in the scattered self-analysis that shimmers through *The Interpretation of Dreams* understood as a fragmented biography of a completely new kind. The future development of the movement, oscillating between avant-garde and private practice, resistance to and acceptance of violent authorities, with its inner conflicts and persecutions, indeed, all the paranoia that will characterise the psychoanalytic associations with their exclusions and secret societies, can be traced along the unforeseen lines whose conditions had altered as a result of war, upheavals and deportations. With all this in mind the understanding of the unforeseen creation of its concepts and practices must be rethought starting from a new concept of the genealogy of psychoanalysis. If the question is posed in this way – why psychoanalysis in these places and at these moments in time? – phenomena embarrassing for the medical science emerge as important to note and analyse. Within psychiatry, the hysterised woman was one such embarrassing phenomenon. The hysterical woman's sexualised body was caught in the midst of a dominating psychiatric power – the unsettling simulation so prominent at the institution – and the bourgeois institution of marriage. Within this was the complex role of the family doctor, subordinated to the dominant order of an incipient capitalism in which patriarchy jealously monitors everything that could challenge it. Or for that matter, the very phenomenon of the hysterised male. After all, it has often been asserted that psychoanalysis arose in a context characterised by the crisis of this patriarchal power.

Ferenczi belonged to the intelligentsia that helped to shape Budapest, the capital created by the union of Buda, the district of the aristocratic palaces scattered on the steep verdant hill that rises above the separating river Donau, and Pest, the dense city of the commercial establishments, the craftsmen and the university. This intelligentsia consisted of emigrants from various areas in Eastern and Central Europe, ethnic Germans from Danube Swabia, Jews from western Poland, a country that since Maria Theresa belonged to the dual monarchy, as well as Hungarians from distant provinces such as Transylvania. In this multi-ethnic principality – for decades independent of any central power – the Jewish-Hungarian intellectual elite is born and Budapest becomes a cultural centre. The intelligentsia in Budapest gathered at the Hotel Royal. Among them were radical intellectuals, such as Georg Lukács, who would later break new ground. Ferenczi had studied at the upper secondary school in Miskolc, graduated in medicine in Vienna, and was early on interested in culture, reading Heine and experimenting with hypnosis. After his exam, he practised in Budapest, at the St Rod Hospital and later at St Elisabeth's Charity Hospital, then at a cooperative polyclinic before opening his own practice. For Ferenczi – who alongside his commitments, had from the beginning been concerned with taboo subjects such as spiritism, the meaning of love for science, female homosexuality, ideas of sexually transmitted conditions, even Jung's association experiment – the encounter with Freud's models was to be pivotal. However, for a long time, he continued working in neurology, psychiatry and forensic medicine, continuing to focus on the health of the poor, the criminals and the prostitutes, a focus which leaves its mark on his authorship and clinical studies.

Ferenczi's family had cultivated a great interest in music and literature, an interest that he shared from an early age. His father, né Baruch Frankel in Krakow in 1830 and who participated in the huge migration of Jews from Eastern Europe that took place as a result of a hardening antisemitism, took the name Bernat Ferenczi. The family ran a bookshop in Miskolc that also included a publishing house and a concert agency. The Ferenczis' house thus became a meeting place for artists, musicians and intellectuals, a stimulating environment that was politically and culturally liberal. His mother, Rosa Eibenschütz, ten years younger than her husband, took over the company after the death of the latter when Sándor was merely fifteen years old. She was active and engaged, founding among other things an association for Jewish women, but was later described by Ferenczi as 'strict'.[26] In an analysis of a dream – that we will have occasion to return to – we encounter a day's residue, an evening spent with his mother where a six-year-old grandchild is present and with whom Ferenczi plays, that gives rise to the following interpretation: 'You wanted to show your mother seemingly how a child should be treated, that is, how you yourself should have been treated'.[27] The analysis of the wish-fulfilment of the dream will lead towards the 'primitive, maternal function: to birth'.[28] It is an example of how Ferenczi's own particular experience formed the basis for certain theoretical innovations and the creation of concepts that I will try to shed light on in the following. For now, we note how the enigma of the maternal function is ever present in Ferenczi's work.

Ferenczi and Freud were both surrounded by an antisemitic and homophobic culture, but at an individual level the social conditions of their positions differed. Ferenczi's home was a meeting place for artists, musicians and intellectuals. Freud, on the other hand, distanced himself from the intellectual circles and took little part in what was happening in contemporary art and literature. If Freud's self-analysis revolves around his relationship to his father, Ferenczi's mother is given a far more significant role, a fact that will affect his understanding of the psychoanalytic processes.

The cities and their surroundings – Vienna, Budapest, Zurich and Berlin, dominated by authoritarian forces which the dawning movement occasionally opposes – appear to us as something more than merely historically determined places, or something concerning mere rational interpersonal relations. By paying attention to the accidental and temporary, the recorded oddities and actions revealed by the documents, we approach the sites of these events not only as physical places but also as something mental, something resembling landscapes. We move, so to speak, from the 'cult of an origin', Freud's intrapsychic exploit, his self-analysis as it strikes the historians, to the will to 'acknowledge the power of an environment'.[29] Psychoanalysis is, I argue, in this sense the result of contingence rather than of necessity, of an environment rather than an origin. In particular, I want to acknowledge the ahistorical element that Ferenczi's *Clinical Diary* – still unknown to the circles that would place him in the role of scapegoat, thus delaying its publication for decades – constitutes: a promise that has not yet been fulfilled. We approach the documents, so to speak, in search of the untimely, looking for what is still in genesis, hoping to perceive anew the possibility of this missed encounter between Freud and Ferenczi. Thus, the unforeseen creation of the concept of transference and the inherent power it holds guides the analysis of this patchwork of documents and notes, theoretical discourses and non-discursive practices we have before us. How to access a transference that by definition, necessarily and from the moment of its appearance, withdraws into itself? How to articulate discursively something so fleeting, indeed secretive?[30] How to grasp intellectually something so ephemeral, even mysterious?

At the end of May 1933, Freud writes to Jones a letter that the latter, in his biography, will use as the basis of the image of Ferenczi as a man broken by mental illness, unstable, and whose 'degeneration' explains his theoretical and clinical work as suspect, no longer part or the heritage of psychoanalysis.[31] Freud concludes the letter by adding, 'let us keep his sad end a secret between us'.[32] The secret of the dream, the secret message, the enigma; the secret as 'a way of spreading that is in turn shrouded in secrecy'.[33] The idea of the secret runs like Ariadne's thread through the documents: we come across it in the letters and in the case studies, in the practices and regulations of the psychoanalytic associations.[34] But what forms does secrecy operate by? The question of secrecy, we might say, involves 'the way in which it imposes itself and spreads'.[35] Let us say that it takes the form of a particular series: 'We go from the secret defined as a hysterical childhood content to the secret defined as an eminently virile paranoid form'.[36] First, the secret as the hysterical content that passes between Freud and Fließ; Dora with her little purse that opens and shuts whenever she wants to 'play "secrets"' with her analyst;[37] and then the *insights* about the limits and mechanisms of therapy that can only be imparted to the initiated as if in a *secret tongue*; finally, the paranoid form where it is defined as '*something* that has happened', with constant echoes of a possible patricide.[38] It is when an analysis can no longer be completed that the unconscious as a consequence is finally given the 'difficult task of itself being the infinite form of secrecy'.[39]

It was these and similar phenomena, I believe, that Ferenczi addressed in his paper about the psychoanalytic organisation at the congress in Nuremberg in 1910. Here he considers the advantages and disadvantages of the appeal that the rebellious aura of the movement has had among 'people of artistic gift', attracted by its anti-authoritarian attitude, while also seeing the paranoid overtones created by the movement's cultivation of subservience to an imagined paternal authority. At the very moment that a necessary organisation takes place that also involves correcting at an individual level tendencies that go against the common interest, at that very moment the question of authority returns in the shape of repetitive patterns, structures recognised as 'characteristics of family life'. The organisation is transformed into a 'field in which sublimated homosexuality can live itself out in the form of admiration and hatred'. Now, Ferenczi's vision instead becomes a psychoanalysis, made possible through the educational analysis, where 'the greatest possible personal liberty [is combined] with the advantages of family organisation. It would be a family where the father enjoyed no dogmatic authority'.[40]

At the congress in Nuremberg, Ferenczi proposed that the psychoanalytic movement, which until that point had been centred on the informal Wednesday evening gatherings in Freud's consulting room, should be organised in the form of a psychoanalytic association.[41] More than just outlining the future organisational form of psychoanalysis, Ferenczi identified the necessity of this organisation, as well as the risks it entails. He describes psychoanalysis as a 'young science'. Its practitioners are not just 'innovators and pioneers'; they are, he claims, 'involved in a war'.[42] The fact that psychoanalysis examined hitherto unknown regions and was not yet subordinated to a clear disciplinary order, also contributed to its appeal to new, sensitive spirits being drawn into this 'new scientific field'; but, confronted with the authoritarian forces that surround them – within psychiatry, among the upholders of patriarchal norms and power and not least those forces that emanate from their *own* desire, the charging of paternal authority, as their point of departure – they must 'conduct guerrilla warfare'.[43]

'Secrecy has its origin in the war machine',[44] note Deleuze and Guattari in the seminal work *A Thousand Plateaus*. Secrecy exists as such in a collective milieu but is always a social or sociological phenomenon; it is active in the form of rituals, associations, orders. Now, if the 'wild horde'[45] with which Ferenczi allied himself around 1908 seems like precisely such a secret society, then it was logically also a small war machine whose 'guerrilla war' coincides with what we might call 'the universal project to penetrate all society, to permeate throughout all of society's forms by upending hierarchies and segmentations'.[46] Yet a wild horde of this kind, a herd or a pack like this, is also a possible *ur-horde* with its paranoid contours of potential patricide.[47]

For Ferenczi, 'mutual control' is therefore crucial.[48] Faced with 'the lack of central direction' and the risk of merely gathering around 'the name of Freud' alone, he argues, the specific psychological mechanisms of a group must also be understood – thus, we must be clear about the risks each organisation runs. What Ferenczi's considerations lead to will cut right through the practice of psychoanalysis. Not least, as we noted at the outset, Ferenczi himself became the target of the very forces that such an organised group can mobilise, its paranoia, its need to appoint scapegoats, its idealisation of the paternal authority – everything that was to define the future organisation of the various psychoanalytic associations.

Ferenczi delineates how the organisation is formed according to a desire. Whether scientific, political or social, whatever the organisation, 'childish megalomania, vanity, admiration of empty formalities, blind obedience, or personal egoism' will prevail. This, rather than strenuous work in a joint interest.[49] Ferenczi identifies quite simply 'the characteristics of family life' as they operate in a patriarchy, with its 'flattery of the father figure'. Given this framework, the organisation becomes a field wide open to a sublimated male homosexuality taking the form of admiration and hatred, belittlement and idealisation. Ferenczi thus identifies the dangers to which the psychoanalytic milieu is vulnerable, organised as it is around a phantasmatic father figure with the power to tie individual desires to the machinery of the group.[50] He sees in their disorganised little war cell how

> our intellectual leader is apt in dreams to condense with the father-figure. In our dreams we are inclined in a more or less concealed form to outsore, to overthrow our intellectual father, whom we esteem highly, but whom it is difficult inwardly to tolerate precisely because of his intellectual superiority.[51]

The central complexes being explored by those involved, theoretically and clinically, are impossible to distinguish from the forms that the mutual relations among them take. Namely, the established power structures. This as-of-yet disorganised little group that they constitute is permeated by a patriarchal family structure whose compelling forms are written into the dream life, or in other words, operate in the unconscious. Ferenczi sees the possibility of illuminating the authority of the phantasmal father-figure, and thus neutralising the forces such a figure sets in motion, in the establishment of educational analysis. If only the personal complexes were to be worked through, then the infantile impulses and actions surrounding the insidious notion of the paternal authority might be mastered, thereby finally fulfilling training analysis' promise of another possibility: 'a family where the father enjoyed no dogmatic authority'.[52] The issue of educational analysis would, however, turn out to be much more complicated, while at the same time acquiring a specific role in the future organisation of the association. Initially, it would in fact constitute its secret.

Hanns Sachs remembers in this sense the inner group that formed around Freud; it consisted of himself, Karl Abraham, Eitingon and Jones, as well as the 'disruptive innovators' Otto Rank and Ferenczi.[53] As a sign, they were each given a ring, symbolising that the connection between them rested on the same ground, indeed, emanated from the same centre, namely, the centre that Freud embodied. This inner circle is formed shortly after – and maybe as a reaction to – the break with Jung. Ferenczi was assigned the task of formulating a clarifying critique of the latter's newly published *Wandlungen und Symbole der Libido*. This critique involved issues relating to the meaning of infantile sexuality, the concept of instinct, and other technical matters. In particular, he criticised Jung's view of himself as the authority in the therapeutic setting. For Ferenczi a psychoanalysis must always aim for a 'dismantling of the father image'.[54]

The background of the inner circle is an idea that Ferenczi shares with Rank and Jones during a conversation in Berlin. He envisions a group of analysts, all analysed by Freud, who would represent psychoanalysis and advancing its theory without any personal complexes standing in the way. The idea is embraced by Jones but in him it gives rise to a fantasy that he shares with Freud in a letter about an 'unofficial inner circle in the Verein'.[55] Freud becomes interested, understanding it as a 'secret council' between the foremost.[56] 'This committee', he writes, 'had to be *strictly secret* in his existence and his actions'.[57] Jones seems seduced by the idea of a group of disciples, analysed by Freud and operating, like messengers, in distant countries, just as when they landed in the USA a few years earlier.

> The idea of a united small body, designed, like the Paladins of Charlemagne, to guard the kingdom and policy of their master.[58]

Yet it is Ferenczi that Freud will eventually speak about as his 'Grand Vizier'.[59] By then the machine will have already started to run amok, just as Ferenczi had warned his *guerrilla fighters*.

Organisation is ultimately about technique. Who can, and with what authority, speak about what psychoanalysis is, who is authorised to practise as an analyst. During these years, Freud writes several recommendations on therapeutic technique to doctors. But he is as yet reluctant to publish them as a systematic manual. In fact, he often does not follow his own advice. But there is, nevertheless, the demand on others to publish what they do in their practice, something that the members in turn require of each other – *I can't trust you, I don't know how you work*. At the same time, there is a reluctance to share the methods of one's clinical work. In this situation paranoia seeps through: 'the field was open to espionage'.[60]

Ferenczi shows how the methods of psychoanalysis renegotiate the techniques of contemporary psychiatry – suggestion and hypnosis, the use of medication and not least the authoritarian role of the physician – towards an encounter between the physician and the patient where symptoms are dissolved into meaningful images through the free associations of the talking cure. The mental processes are approached through peculiarities that have so far not been the object of scientific or medical attention: such as slip of the tongue, wit, momentary forgetfulness and dreams. These phenomena had long been well known at the psychiatric institutions but were at the turn of the last century seen as disturbing elements in the treatment of the syndrome of hysteria. The patient's resistance to the authority of the physician and the sexual nature of the symptoms, now become the very core of the psychoanalytic treatment. Ferenczi defines suggestion and hypnosis as an alien will imposed upon the subject, which is why the mental states these techniques generate, used in the therapeutic relation, evoke traces of previous relations and experienced traumas. Based on these phenomena, Ferenczi emphasises the importance of transference in the psychoanalytic process. The 1909 article about transference provides some initial clues that can help us consider the tense relationship between the men: a relationship that will reach a crisis when it comes to the question of the importance of trauma and the role of transference.

Towards the end of his life, Ferenczi will return to these themes in the clinical diary he kept, resignedly formulating his view of Freud's observation of the authority of the psychoanalyst protected by the allegedly *neutral* attitude prescribed by technical writings. When the two, still deeply engaged in the development of the psychoanalytic theory and practice, confront each other at Freud's summer residence in what was to be their last encounter, they are, however, preoccupied with death – the Hungarian aware that his internal organs are affected, Freud long obsessed with the thought of the patriarchal legacy that he will leave to his followers. One of them insists on reporting technical innovations that the other, the elder, can only regard as a violation of everything he has accomplished. In the background, there is a Europe on the threshold of the political events that will redraw its map with unimagined disasters as a result. Ferenczi will not himself experience the mass murders and the deportations, and Freud is not yet inclined to take the threat seriously; not until the outbreak of the war can he be persuaded to seek exile in London. The American writer H.D. – Hilda Doolittle – has described how the Nazi antisemitic slogans, painted on the street outside the clinic, left Freud unperturbed in his relentless work.[61] But around these two antagonists stand other men prepared to reshape psychoanalysis into a uniform practice, no longer a secret cell or war machine operating in the continent marked by authoritarian regimes and institutions.

Freud, who in letters to his confidants, especially Jones and Eitingon, but also directly to Ferenczi, expressed deep scepticism about the direction that the latter's work had taken, was not familiar with the clinical diary that the Hungarian kept during the last year of his life. Here, technical and theoretical findings enforce a revision of central themes in the psychoanalytic theory, not least the understanding of the so-called Oedipus complex. The diary deals with the relationship with Freud and the theoretical positions taken by the former master, which Ferenczi regards with an increasingly critical eye, indeed, considers necessary to reformulate radically. In the clinical approaches tested here, very little remains of Freud's description of the analyst as the *surgeon* of the soul in *Technical Writings*.[62] According to Ferenczi, the acquired capacity for clarity and serene calm – responding to the patient's transference with unmoved neutrality – ought rather to be understood as a way of trying to legitimise the scientific status of practice, and, in the case of Freud, as a defence or protection mobilised when he was suddenly confronted with the 'abyss' opened up for him by the traumatic qualities of transference.[63]

But the diary also deepens the understanding of phenomena that have preoccupied Ferenczi throughout his lifelong practice. Suggestion, seduction and trauma are recurring motifs explored here through the ability, practised in his clinical work, to listen to the child – the child that is dormant in the unconscious of the adult – whose voice is inaccessible to the waking self except in certain dream-like states. The psychoanalytic experience that Ferenczi unearths thus uncovers a *fragmented* individuality. His work will increasingly focus on the ability of the psychoanalytic situation to recall split-off parts of the self, or, as it says in a late diary entry: 'ashes of earlier mental sufferings'.[64] Not until far later, after years of negotiations with Freud's daughter Anna, who finally allows publication, will the diary be published and translated into English, which in the years after the war has become the dominant language of the international psychoanalytic movement. Thereby a documentation of Ferenczi's therapeutic 'experiments' – which, according to Freud's polemic statement in 'Analysis Terminable and Interminable' (1937), did not result in anything – eventually became accessible. Together with the correspondence, *The Clinical Diary* will provide an important source for understanding the conflict areas between the two men and where a driving tension in the praxis of psychoanalysis can be discerned. It is this tension that has been the starting point for the present reflections, and I have sought so far to approach it based on the last encounter between Ferenczi and Freud, contemplated in the light of the long relation that developed between them. I will now seek to deepen the analysis through what psychoanalytic theory calls transference, that is, through what we saw condensed in a moment at their last encounter.

Transference

What is transference? The question haunts psychoanalytic theory. The term transference is implemented in the early work, *Studies on Hysteria* (1895), in which Freud together with Joseph Breuer lays the foundation of psychoanalysis. In *The Interpretation of Dreams* (1900) it still denotes a range of different psychic phenomena. With the first longer case study, 'Fragment of an Analysis of a Case of Hysteria' (1905), however, Freud specifically draws attention to the significance of the phenomenon for the psychoanalytic process, thereby giving the concept a more clearly defined meaning. The transference then refers to the productive ability of neurosis to create a specific form of unconscious figures of thought: new formations of affects and fantasies evoked by the analytic situation where the impressions of past persons are transferred to the analyst. The case study, often referred to as the Dora case, depicts an interrupted psychoanalytic process where a young female patient's decision to end the analysis is provoked precisely by the inability of the analyst to acknowledge and thereby handle the forces developed in the transference. On the basis of this case study, Ferenczi – in his first major contribution to the psychoanalytic literature, the above-mentioned article 'Introjection and Transference' (1909) – treats the phenomenon in a way that highlights the proximity to and the delimitation from the psychiatric techniques and notions of the time. The alleged tendency of the hysteric to simulate, to imitate – 'psychic contagion' so frequently observed at the institution and sometimes referred to as hysterical identification – is here ascribed to phenomena that, understood as symbolic means of representation, must in fact be considered as results of the effect of transference. Michel Foucault has, in his lectures on psychiatric power, analysed hysteria on the basis of this simulation as a phenomenon conditioned by the psychiatric institution and the authority of the doctor – we will have reason to return to Foucault's theories in this regard. The phenomenon of hysteria thus becomes guiding in the analysis of the significance of transference; according to Lacan in his seminar 1964 where he explores the foundations of psychoanalysis: it 'places us […] on the track'.[65] For Ferenczi, the handling of the transference becomes a means of dissolving what he sees as the destructive identification with the sometimes violent authority underpinning the psychiatric power that the institution is dominated by. By so doing he comes to cultivate a sensitivity to the interaction of the psychoanalytic situation, even aspire to a listening where the analyst is able to trust the *dormant child* – as he called it – within the traumatised patient and thus be at her mercy, in order to let her 'split off a sort of fragment of intelligence' giving guidance to the analytic work.[66] In view of these insights, I want to highlight the importance of transference in the metapsychology outlined by Ferenczi. Emphasising the early article from 1909, where the author, based on the Dora case, deepens the understanding of the concept, as well as on the late text 'Confusion of Tongues', I will explore the close relationship between transference and trauma that is expressed. The clusters of motifs that in these texts carry the analysis of transference are further processed in *The Clinical Diary*, as we shall see. In these late, partly fragmented notes, the insights gained into the phenomenon of transference seem to enforce a re-evaluation of the psychoanalytic technique.

'I should like, further', Freud writes regarding the first dream Dora related, 'to draw special attention to the fact that the analysis of this dream has given access to certain details of the pathogenically operative events which had otherwise been inaccessible to the memory, or at all events to reproduction'.[67] In 'Fragment of an Analysis of a Case of Hysteria' transference is identified, for the first time, as the central crux of an analysis, 'by far the hardest part of the whole task'.[68] Freud 'did not succeed in time in mastering' the transference, which leads him to some important insights into clinical processes. Only now at the very end, via the interpretation of a dream, does Freud realise how his own person had become the object of impulses, which have the character of revenge and repugnance, previously directed towards the man whose acts have had a traumatic effect on the young woman in analysis. In the case study, the importance of transference emerges from numerous perspectives, decisive for the relative success of a therapy. It concerns the patient's communication of what is, even to her, *secret* utterances, and also, perhaps in particular, the importance of coping with the patient's negative reactions to the doctor's person that now come to the fore. Through the careful mapping of the development and process of the short analysis, the interpretation of dreams emerges as a key to the domain of transference. The term transference is now used to denote that 'special class of mental structures' that have been brought to life during the analysis in the shape of 'new editions or facsimiles of the impulses and phantasies' which have concerned persons of importance in the past and which are now directed at the doctor.[69] What, in that sense, haunts the analytic situation must not be seen as 'obstacles', but as a 'powerful ally'; thus, the task is understood as seeing through and revealing the phenomena of transference, in particular 'hostile' impulses; raising the awareness of them, Freud believes this means that the transference is 'constantly being destroyed'.[70] In the analysis the dream's message about something untimely can in an instant dispel the veils that make the desire unconscious to its subject. The dream can provide clues to the identification of the phenomenon, thereby giving a direction to our present ambition to uncover the specific discourse in which an inherent tension in the psychoanalytic field is expressed.

In his early analysis of the phenomenon of transference, Ferenczi discusses Freud's case study, in a way that shows how the young female patient's complex of unconscious fantasies is shaped by her relation not only to her parents but to a cluster of important persons – her brother, as well as her governess and a young couple, named Mr and Mrs K, who are close to the family. Ferenczi emphasises that through the catalytic effect of the psychoanalytic situation, her original love objects and the positive and negative affect they are charged with are made present in the transference. The language of the unconscious speaks through small similarities: a gesture, the smoke from a cigar, or through the poetic figures of dreams: 'pars pro toto'.[71] The infantile layers, inaccessible in themselves, now manifest themselves as symptoms – feelings of antipathy, disgust and so on; only when these sexual affects, based on an incestuous fixation and associated with erogenous zones, are recognised in the 'antipathies towards the doctor' that the patient develops can the simulation of hysteria begin to be read as precisely symbolic representations of unconscious wishes. In *The Clinical Diary*, the dividing line between Ferenczi and Freud in their view of the psychoanalytic situation will be articulated, many years later, through the understanding of these phenomena.

The collaboration with Rank, which at the beginning of the 1920s aimed at discursively formulating the psychoanalytic technique, revealed a range of areas of conflict around the therapeutic method that were later addressed in Ferenczi's *Clinical Diary*. Freud, he asserts there, recoiled from 'the problem of countertransference opened up before him like an abyss', and developed, as a protection, the doctrine of psychoanalytic neutrality.[72] By these means he protected himself, according to Ferenczi, against the frightening dimensions of transference, thereby re-establishing a practice subordinated to the authority of the analyst. Insofar as the observed neutrality spares the analyst self-criticism, it places him in a 'situation of almost infantile grandeur', which is why Ferenczi concludes, in an entry on 1 May 1932, that the transference is provoked artificially: 'the doctor's theories (delusions) may not be challenged' other than on condition that the patient is forced to remain in a regressive state of *resistance*.[73] The theoretical models, according to Ferenczi, are not tested in the work done in the analytic situation, which is instead fixed on the preservation of the doctor's authority.

In the scene that unfolds at Freud's summer residence – with Brill's disdainful whisperings, Freud's unease and Ferenczi's insistence on verbalising the dangerous affects and energies of the psychoanalytic situation, transference is manifest. It becomes apparent that the positions taken by the two antagonists are determined by the force field that develops between them. In order to think of this moment as an *event*, in the sense of a composite of active forces, I have here sought to test the possibility to grasp it as embedded in layers of time, layers that a reading of the archived documents can uncover, attentive to what Foucault referred to as the object of genealogy, operating 'on a field of entangled and confused parchments, on documents' that have been scratched over and recopied many times'.[74] Thus the documents, including correspondence and Ferenczi's *Clinical Diary*, can be read as part of a discourse in the Foucauldian sense of the word, discourse that the present reflections seek to draw attention to. This includes peculiarities in the formation of legacy, such as Jones's canonising biography with its pathologisation and defamation of the man who had at one time been his own analyst,[75] that paraphrases Freud's late poisonous judgements in the private letters between them, and can be seen as example of such a hierarchical and patriarchal order that Ferenczi's experiments aimed at dismantling. This was the means by which a truth was established.

The documents referred to also testify to numerous situations where forms of simulation, psychic contagion and hysterical identification are played out: the sharing of dreams followed by so-called wild analysis; peculiar episodes such as Freud's fainting fit in reaction to Jung's preoccupation with the recent discovery of archaic corpses flattened by the pressure of earth segments and embalmed by natural processes found in marshes in the North German lowlands; or, on another occasion, the idea discussed at a conference in Munich of erased paternal names in the hieroglyphic inscriptions of the Egyptian pharaohs.[76] In these examples, the transference is brought into play, if only in the form of *acting-out* which nevertheless shapes the institutional politics that characterise the newly formed association with its paranoid overtones, according to whose logic Ferenczi must be assigned the role of scapegoat. I thus want to insist on the possibility of approaching the documents with a certain astonishment, as if driven by the question: Why these forms of expression? Why these practices? Why like this and not in another way? Why psychoanalysis at this point in time and in these places?

The method that has occurred to me is therefore based on the recognition of the fact that 'the world of speech and desires has known invasions, struggles, plundering, disguises, ploys'.[77] In Lacan's Eleventh Seminar, given in 1964, the year after his *excommunication* from the International Psychoanalytic Association, he refers to a crisis of psychoanalysis that requires the field of psychoanalytic practice to somehow relate to Freud's desire and its connection to the desire of the hysterical women, in a way that identifies certain conceptions of an origin. Lacan's analysis underscores the importance of the analyst's presence in the psychoanalytic encounter, urging analysis to reach the point that designates 'the analyst's desire'.[78] The crisis that Lacan perceives is thereby transformed, in an insistence that psychoanalytic practice must be rethought in relation to its genealogy, which, according to Lacan, is characterised by 'a certain original sin in the analysis', that is to say, the desire of Freud himself, or rather 'the fact that something in Freud was never analysed'.[79] The proximity between Freud's desire and the way in which 'the hysteric constitutes her desire', namely, in relation to language, was the door of perception which he, according to Lacan, entered and so 'discovered the mechanisms of the unconscious'.[80] In my reading of him, Lacan thus insists on a return to an origin, but in order to 'put in question the origin to discover by what privilege Freud's desire was able to find the entrance into the field of experience he designates as the unconscious'.[81] We are here in a search of a theoretical guide. And at the same time, we observe the movements over a continent where crumbling sovereigns give way to other unsuspected forms of authoritarian forces: father figures are dismantled but return phantasmatically in the shape of despots, linking desire to authoritarian control systems. Psychoanalysis is not an isolated laboratory. Nor does the crisis of psychoanalysis necessarily mean that psychoanalysis has come to an end but rather that it, in analogy with Hegel's idea about the end of art, indicates its place in modernity, namely, 'that its position in relation to other fields of experience has changed'.[82] Our analysis of the genealogy of psychoanalysis against the backdrop of the tension between Freud and Ferenczi therefore, ultimately, insists on the necessity of thinking of psychoanalysis and its genealogy politically.

Read alongside a letter to Jones about the Ferenczi incident from the same period, Freud's obituary gives the impression of a strange mixture of respectful mourning and tendentious pathologising that not only can be traced to the previous correspondence but also finds confirmation in Jones's official history of the man who had been his analytic teacher, a characterisation which would be further confirmed many years later in Peter Gay's biography.[83] Both accounts summarise the clinical controversy in terms of how Ferenczi's 'motherly tenderness' for the patient deviated from a correct attitude towards how the fundamental rule should be understood.[84] The so-called psychoanalytic neutrality is at stake, identified as it is with patriarchal power. Freud, in a statement noted by H.D. in her written memories of an analysis during the years 1932–1933, may have disliked being located in the position of the mother in transference – 'I feel so very masculine',[85] as he put it.

Ideas of power and masculinity are set in motion in our material. Running like a common thread in the correspondence between the men is the image of Ferenczi as 'passive and receptive',[86] dreamy, infantile, in relation to the man 'who was too big for me, too much of the father',[87] all of which in this context denotes *feminine* qualities, implicitly of course, as something unwished for, even revolting. In a letter to Jung, Freud writes of Ferenczi: 'I really haven't got enough homosexuality in me to accept him as one [a woman]'.[88] In his *Clinical Diary* Ferenczi will later identify an aversion to female sexuality in Freud, above all when he thinks he can see it in men, as an expression of a certain fear. This theme unfolds along the binary poles of paranoia and hysteria, active and passive, male and female.[89] Eli Zaretsky has shown that the female characteristics which, when found in men, triggered this aversion in Freud are modelled on the image of certain Jewish traits in antisemitic propaganda.[90] Zaretsky emphasises that the circle that formed the core of the so-called Wednesday evenings consisted of Jewish male students and physicians marginalised from the medical establishment in a way that transformed their mutual bonds into a kind of *Männerbund*. Like the male associations of that time they, too, were drawn to a strong and charismatic leader who, in Freud's guise, was given the role of a father figure. As with the *Männerbund* that emerged in that period in the academic world and in the military, the group mobilises passive, dependent and homoerotic feelings among its members, which we saw addressed by Ferenczi in his speech in Nuremberg 1910. Unlike what was the case in the surrounding environments, these feelings can thus here be the object of an analytic interest. The case studies can be read as a series of re-interpretations of masculinity against the background of a so far unfamiliar exploration of mental processes. Indeed, the case studies examine male vulnerability in the age of intensive mechanisation and militarisation. With modern capitalism and militarism, the experience of the male body is transformed, while the family, particularly the bond between father and son, becomes complicated, weakened or marked by conflict. Rather than the picture that Jones and others give of the 'heroic' discoveries Freud made in solitude, these analyses were born of a reflection on defeat, loss, grief and seclusion, indicative of the Jewish situation during the downfall of the Habsburg monarchy on the threshold of the modernisation of capitalism and the industrial mass murder of the First World War: total war.

In his obituary for Ferenczi, Freud asks whether the 'bio-analysis' dreamt of by the *peerless* clinician from Budapest will one day become a reality.[91] He highlights their differences but also foregrounds Ferenczi's exceptional role in the development of psychoanalysis. Even so, the impression remains that Freud – and the inner circle around him – saw something unacceptable in his exploration of psychoanalytic technique; the criticism takes the form of a peculiar pathologisation: in his letter to Jones he writes of 'the regressive intellectual and emotion development' which in Ferenczi's case had its origins in a 'physical decline'.[92] The illness he suffers from, known as 'pernicious anaemia', is merely the organic expression of the morbid;[93] the theoretical models derived from clinical experimentation are accordingly considered in terms of Ferenczi's relation to Freud himself, as the 'mental degeneration'[94] which, with eerie logic, assumes the form of paranoia.

For decades within the psychoanalytic tradition the view of Ferenczi as well as the theoretical models and the technical approach he developed would be perceived wholly in the light of the relation, or better, the transference that was established between him and Freud, in other words: what was acted out and unconsciously communicated between them. But the confrontation, as we understand it, is compelled by a pattern that is as decisive as it is familiar, as archaic as it seems inevitable: the naming of a scapegoat. What do we refer to then when using the word scapegoat if not to that which is forced upon us in a given situation, a crisis? According to René Girard it is thus possible to talk about a stereotypical crisis, in which, both logically and chronologically, one can find the origin of the persecution. Our hypothesis is that the nature of this crisis which provoked the persecution is to be found in the actions that followed the development of notions about paranoia and homosexuality. The semantics of the scapegoat has been studied by Girard, and there are good reasons for invoking it here. By first identifying the destructive forces that are here set in motion – and that remain active – we can perhaps read this image anew. Central to what follows, then, is seeing the *possibilities* which come with locating the theoretical and clinical confrontation in the domain of transference. Girard has examined the 'stereotypes' that give rise to the pattern of scapegoating and persecution. He identifies a 'destabilizing dynamic', a sense of 'confusion of the differences' that brings forth 'patterns' that must be eradicated.[95] 'Eventually, the persecutors become convinced that a small number of individuals, or even a single one, can become extremely dangerous to society as a whole despite their relative weakness.'[96] Those who are victimised are associated with 'extreme characteristics', whether they are 'the symbol of the highest authority' or associated with illness, especially mental illness, that is, someone whose presence seems to dissolve differences, indeed constitute contagion.[97] Freud's 'Grand Vizier' in his alleged 'mental degeneration' fulfils both these criteria.

In the diary that Ferenczi kept during the last year of his life, he tries to analyse the fantasy about himself as 'the proclaimed crown prince' that Freud helped cultivate decades earlier. Ferenczi recalls certain events that unfolded in the years after he joined the movement; how Freud at the time considered him the perfect heir to his ideas and how he, in their relation and in their analytical, theoretical and practical work, would be the son. All this in conflict with the framework conceived by Freud for the psychoanalytic situation. Ferenczi now, late in life, realises that he has been placed in a specific position in an always already established pattern.

> (Fr[eud] seems to have expected something similar of Jung years ago; hence the two hysterical symptoms I observed in him): (1) the fainting spell in Bremen, (2) the incontinence at Riverside Drive, added to the bit of analysis he shared with us: dying as soon as the son took his place, and the regression to childhood, childish embarrassment, when he repressed his American vanity.[98]

Thus, possibly in the very moment of its dissolution, even destruction, Ferenczi appears able to enlighten – even expose – some of the impact that transference made on their relationship, as his analysis focuses on what has been concealed, or repressed, but that can be glimpsed in the opening and closing of transference. Freud, he claims, was constantly seeking to avoid something traumatic by understanding the overdetermined situation in terms of a neurotic complex: in other words, as constant variations of the father theme.

The hysterical symptoms of the authority lead Ferenczi to rethink Freud's construction of the Oedipus complex in relation to what this construction represses, namely, according to Ferenczi, the existence of trauma. The anxiety-provoking thought that the father must die when the son grows up makes Freud unable to let any 'of his sons become independent'. Concealed behind this neurotic fantasy, Ferenczi crystallises the existence of a real trauma, namely, a child who 'really wanted to kill his father'.

> Instead of admitting this, he founded the theory of the parricidal Oedipus, but obviously applied only to others, not to himself. Hence the fear of allowing himself to be analysed, hence perhaps also the idea that in civilized adults primitive instinctual impulses are not in fact real anymore, that the Oedipal disease is a childhood disease, like the measles.[99]

The fact that something remains unanalysed in Freud provokes Ferenczi to insist on the significance of the trauma and thereby a re-evaluation of the Oedipus complex. The castration-oriented aggression that permeates the thought complex and that was acted out in Freud's hysterical symptoms was overdetermined in him, according to Ferenczi, by a wish for a more harmonious father–son relation 'that must be called homosexual'.[100]

The conflicts that I have sought to highlight, concerning technical and theoretical issues, illustrate complexes linked to fantasies revolving around the notion of father-authority that permeated this environment. The power of these fantasies is striking. Jung writes, 'I was alarmed by the intensity of his fantasies', an intensity he perceived to be strong enough to place Freud in a state of impotence: 'they could cause him to faint'.[101] In a letter of 28 November 1912, Ferenczi reminded Freud about this event in the light of another incident, the one mentioned earlier, which took place in Munich. There, Abraham had presented material concerning the Egyptian pharaoh Amenophis IV, known as the founder of a monotheistic religion; the fact that the pharaoh, in that process, is said to have erased the names of his ancestors was interpreted in terms of a patricide. It was practice among new rulers to erase the names of predecessors and fathers 'since they were incarnations of the same god'.[102] Suddenly, during the discussion, Freud falls off his chair in a state of despair. Jung helps him up; in his memoirs he has recorded the event:

> I picked him up, carried him into the next room and laid him on a sofa. As I was carrying him, he half came to, and I shall never forget the look he cast at me. In his weakness he looked at me as if I were his father.[103]

In the arms of the physically more robust Jung, and in a state of weakness, Freud not only sees his father in Jung but embraces, it would seem, a passive, submissive attitude to him, whispering: 'how sweet it would be to die'.[104] The psychological mechanisms of the scene are explored as part of Freud's self-analysis in a late text, 'A Disturbance of Memory on the Acropolis' (1936). In it, Freud recalls a curious event he experienced during his first visit to the Acropolis in 1904. Standing in front of the temple that he has dreamt of visiting since he was a child, he suddenly has a strange feeling of unreality, a kind of vertigo in the shape of a temporary hallucination expressed in the statement: so, *it really exists*. Behind this 'disturbance of memory' are conflicting psychological forces, forces that the author interprets as traces of the child's criticism and disdain of the father who never experienced this, and at the same time a feeling of guilt: as if it were still not permissible to want to surpass him. The observations in this piece of self-analysis lead back to mechanisms he found at work in dreams, whose distortions are motivated by an unconscious wish: 'the forbidden wish to excel his father'.[105]

The fear, the unconscious representation that the father must die, not only creates an unwillingness to let his disciples become independent but also lets the theory circle around a father complex that is, according to Ferenczi, his own. Based on the idea of a real trauma – that Freud actually wanted to kill his father – Ferenczi radically re-evaluates the Oedipus complex that Freud held as the *shibboleth* of psychoanalysis.[106] In *The Clinical Diary*, Ferenczi explores his own position in a milieu wholly oriented around the authority of the father: the impulse to blindly follow the authoritarian leader, the satisfaction of belonging to a small, select circle, and, moreover, the whole crown prince fantasy and what it entails. Furthermore, he writes about the feeling of complacency and comfort that the analytic stance, as practised by Freud, induces: 'the calm, the emotionally detached attitude; the irrefutable assurance that you know better; and the theories, seeking and finding fault with the patients instead of partly in ourselves'. Finally, the realisation that Freud had long since given up faith in the positive therapeutic effect of analysis. That was, in the end, where Ferenczi could no longer follow him. 'Against his will I started to openly devote myself to questions of technique'.[107]

In a letter dated 25 December 1929, Ferenczi summarises the theoretical conflict as an 'overestimation of the imagination' and an 'underestimation of traumatic reality' in Freud's thinking. The insights that *The Clinical Diary* testifies to, according to that line of thought, have consequences for the technique: time and time again Ferenczi returns to the necessity of opposing rigid standards of work. For Ferenczi, a psychoanalysis must always, as we have seen, aim for a 'dismantling of the father image'.[108]

Trauma

It has become clear by now that *trauma* repeatedly becomes the central crux in these theoretical and clinical conflicts. The word, which has a long history within medical science, derives from the Greek word for 'wound', denoting a protective shield torn apart or caused to fracture. This meaning lives on in psychoanalysis where the phenomenon has also come to be defined, in so-called *economic* terms, as a surplus of stimuli impossible for the psychic life to handle. In his early attempts to understand the phenomenon, Freud tends to accept psychiatry's view of trauma as given the difficult task to identify and explain the cause of symptoms, by following traces of a decisive event whose impact on the individual's mental life has become, as it were, a 'foreign body'.[109]

But Freud, who in astonishment notes how, at Professor Charcot's clinic, the insight about the sexual nature of this event remains a secret that medical community nevertheless knowingly shares, in his turn lets this secret be the starting point for both the clinical work with trauma and its systematic determination. If the hysteric suffers from 'reminiscences',[110] they concern precisely reminiscences of a sexual nature, which Ferenczi will, much later, remind him of in that very article he insisted on reading to an increasingly 'shocked' Freud during their last encounter where Freud saw himself confronted with notions of trauma that he had long ago abandoned.

Psychoanalysis, as is well known, was formed as theory and practice during the years 1895–1899 as a result of the treatment of sexual seduction and the discovery of its consequences in the clinical encounter. This period in the history of psychoanalysis can be seen as organised around a turning point in the understanding of not only the consequences of trauma but the very character of seduction as an event, manifested in a famous letter to Fließ on 21 September 1897, in which Freud states: 'I will confide in you at once the great secret, that has been slowly dawning on me in the last few months: I no longer believe in my *neurotica*'. Here the 1964 article 'Fantasy and the Origin of Sexuality' by Jean Laplanche and Jean-Bertrand Pontalis is clarifying. In it they demonstrate how the abandonment of the theory of sexual seduction as an explanation of the origin of neurosis does not eliminate the importance of trauma, instead allowing it to be conceived according to a scheme in which its action is always divided into several temporal series, implying 'the existence of *at least two events*'.[111]

The resulting narrative is, as a consequence, always discontinuous, which is why the mode of presentation in Freud's dream interpretations and case studies would come to make him a kind of involuntary modernist. In the clinical cases,

Freud creates, as Peter Brooks puts it in his article 'Fictions of the Wolf Man: Freud and Narrative Understanding', a narrative that 'perilously destabilizes belief in explanatory histories as exhaustive accounts whose authority derives from the force of closure'.[112] The abandonment of the seduction theory, we might say, makes it possible to think about the event along completely new lines; in the most well-known case study, for instance, the one about the Wolf Man, the decisive event is in fact a child's dream whose presence in Freud's account is given the function of a 'primal text', a condensation, in relation to which the material and strategies of the analysis unfold. This child's dream, retold in the adult's analysis, 'itself is an *event*', indeed the *traumatic* event which will through *a deferred action* determine the patient's neurosis as an answer to '"the primal scene", witnessed two and a half years earlier, and to the "seduction", which occurred several months earlier'.[113]

The traumatic event oscillates in Freud's text between dream and reality, fantasy and external experience. Brooks has explored how the dream, understood as a web of signification, determines the subject as language through and through. 'The psychological subject is present to himself in the text as a linguistic deformation, suggesting the interconnections of anxiety, desire, and language in the problematic identity of' the Wolf Man.[114] The unsatisfactory past of the desire, inaccessible to the individual, 'is persistently repeating its thrust and drive in present symbolic formations'.[115] Hence, we can learn from Freud's mode of presentation something that perhaps the author himself never really intended, namely, 'a radical revision of the conventional notions of narrative causality'.[116] In all its richness of meaning, *Nachträglichkeit* here becomes key, as the chronological order is dissolved in favour of a new understanding of the event. The meaningful elements must now be thought of via 'an analysis that is more nearly structural, a 'mapping of a certain psychic "set" toward neurosis, a network analyzed with extraordinary complexity'.[117] The analysis is inherently interminable, resistance and transference constantly generating new entrances, new exits, new maps. The case study is not oriented around a beginning and an end: its narrative is 'provisional and could always be reopened to take in further circles of meaning and theory'.[118] The mode of aesthetic representation that Freud is forced to invent 'must accord with the complex, twisting, subversive patternings of desire'.[119]

If the entangled network or 'field' of the unconscious is to be regarded as 'structured', it is in the shape of a montage, 'since', in the words of Laplanche and Pontalis, 'it handles, decomposes and recomposes its elements according to certain laws'.[120] The dream analysis makes this clear in an exemplary way. The unconscious creates, according to Freud's models, a determining order, but its elements are made up of a mutually complex and partly self-contradictory network of signifiers. Still, even after 1897, Freud looks for a 'primary reality' – the requirement for a psychological foundation to which the primal scene became the theoretical solution – but is thereby increasingly struck by a vertigo evoked by the elusive character of a truth, when its 'ultimate event, "the scene", disappears over the horizon'.[121]

Ferenczi, who, above all in his clinical work, has observed a corresponding split or fragmentation of psychic life and the attempts at new assemblages that a psychoanalysis can offer the individual, seems for his part to seek a way to take up the seduction theory, albeit in order to see how the event is conveyed linguistically. According to the analysis of Laplanche and Pontalis, Ferenczi fills out Freud's seduction myth with two essential elements, namely, the adult's injection of a language of passion into the child's world and how this language emerges with the experience of annihilation into which pleasure – with its violent character – must be transformed. It was Ferenczi's exploration of this linguistic confusion that may arise between adult and child, therapist and patient, that led him to crystallise his notions of a 'language of passion' that the adult introduces to the infant's language of 'tenderness', a new language marked by 'prohibition, a language of guilt and hatred'.[122] He writes: 'It is hatred that traumatically surprises and frightens the child while being loved by an adult, and that changes him from a spontaneous and innocently playing being to a guilty love-automaton imitating the adult anxiously, self-effacingly'.[123] In this, the fantasy of the primal scene with its violent and compelling nature rather shows the child's introjection of the adult eroticism.[124] For Freud, on the other hand – who in his work constantly witnesses how the foundation he seeks to reconstruct withers and crumbles, threatens to be buried, to sink into the oblivion of the individual – the concept of the primordial fantasy unites his contradictory desires: to find the foundation of the event, but at the same time 'the need to establish the structure of the "fantasy" itself by something other than the event'.[125]

These aspects of trauma which are further explored in Freud's 'Beyond the Pleasure Principle' are developed by Ferenczi, on the basis of his clinical experience. Investigating how parts of the individual appear to be split off, even dead, he is led towards a way of thinking based on fragments. He wants to explore 'a state which – continuing the picture of fragmentation – one would be justified in calling atomization', adding: 'One must possess a great deal of optimism not to lose courage when facing such a state'.[126] Ferenczi thus develops a certain attention, a sensitivity, perhaps, that makes him perceptive to the presence of these fragments or images of states in the analytic work. *The Clinical Diary* testifies to this work and the results are outlined in the 'Confusion of Tongues' article that he insisted on reading to Freud before the upcoming conference that last summer. In the article he takes as his point of departure 'the almost hallucinatory repetitions of traumatic experiences which began to accumulate in [his] daily practice'.[127] This finding enforced a new understanding of what the transference contains; he now realises 'the strain caused by this analytical situation', that the analyst 'imposed on the patient the further burden of reproducing the original trauma'.[128] Only by recognising and admitting how 'apparently willing patients felt hatred and rage' directed at him in his capacity of analyst could he discern their 'repressed or suppressed criticism of [him]', and thus reveal effect of the trauma.[129] The possible recognition of the patient's dislike of the analyst makes a crucial difference. Indeed, if the repetition of the trauma is forced by the analytical encounter, '*the contrast between the present and the unbearable traumatogenic past*' has to crystallise.[130]

As so often in the preceding years, a long silence crept into the two men's correspondence. Only on 27 September 1932 was it broken by Ferenczi, with a letter stating that the meeting had 'deeply shaken' him. Although his speech at the conference was a success, even if he does not say so explicitly, everything was overshadowed by what had taken place at Freud's holiday resort in Pötzleinsdorf. His attempt to take a holiday after the conference, first a stay at Groddeck's clinic in Baden-Baden, possibly on Freud's recommendation, and then a stay at an obscure spot in southern France, turned into a *voyage de lit-à-lit*. The reception he had met with and the presence of a whispering third party had put him in a very dark mood, but far worse was his being urged by the man who had exerted so much influence, indeed power, over him not to publish his speech, the result of many years' work and research. Ferenczi had experienced the pain of being utterly disregarded, yet overcome it, and in consequence dedicated all his energies – having renounced a university career, resigned from the leadership of the Berlin Institute, declined the position of President of the Association – to research that bore no trace of personal ambition.[131]

True enough, the article was nonetheless published in the German-language international psychoanalytic journal under the title 'Sprachvervirrung', but Jones – who by then had been elected President of the Association and who in the 1930s would relocate the Association's centres to the anglophone world – would delay a translation for almost two decades. The term 'censorship' is even used among critical researchers.[132] In his reply to Ferenczi on 2 October, Freud maintains his position that Ferenczi should abandon the theoretical and clinical discoveries in question, which were organised around a conception of a traumatic-hysterical basis for all illnesses, the accessing of which would determine the success or failure of therapy. While he feels reproached by Ferenczi for, among other things having given Brill the role of arbitrator, which he certainly denies, Freud reminds his younger colleague of the objections he still holds concerning shortcomings he believes must be overcome in his work. Opposing publication was merely a concession to the need to 'correct' technical 'faults' in Ferenczi's reasoning. Furthermore, he contends that Ferenczi has increasingly turned away from him, and that a hostility has consequently developed between them – previous rifts haunt him, such as the one with Rank.

Together with Rank, Ferenczi had, as mentioned above, formulated a project about psychoanalytic technique that, in 1924, resulted in a publication in which they sought to change the development of the technique based on a deeper understanding of the significance of the maternal body. Freud increasingly feels that he is unable to convince the Hungarian of the flaws in his theoretical construct concerning the effects of trauma. That same day, Ferenczi recorded in his clinical journal the necessity of reorganising himself, of discovering, so to speak, a new basis for his personality. For him, this enterprise represented a choice between death or becoming someone else, because, as he added with a gesture to Freud, what could be the purpose of living a life on another person's terms? He felt that those around him regarded him as a sick person who must be taken care of: 'Instead of falling into psychical illness, I can only destroy – or be destroyed – in the depths of my organs'.[133] In a letter sent at the beginning of the following year, Freud will remind him of the companionship at one time shared, but insist that its unravelling has its cause in what he calls psychological conditions that he attributes to the friend's shortcomings.

Seven months later, Ferenczi dies. Only those closest to him were aware of his illness, which was not known to Freud's inner circle until just a short while before Ferenczi's death.[134] However, in the correspondence between the 'trio of clowns' surrounding Freud – to borrow Lacan's formulation about the cluster of male colleagues who appear in his dream about Irma's injection (to wit Eitingon, Jones and Brill) – Ferenczi's mental health had been a recurrent concern for several years. Ferenczi is surrounded by a kind of mistrust in which theoretical differences spill over, so to speak, into judgements on his personality, driven in particular by definite notions about masculinity from which Ferenczi's personality is considered to deviate. A few years before, Eitingon had reported on a meeting with Ferenczi in Berlin, declaring that 'I [...] am fairly alarmed'.[135] That same year, 1927, Ferenczi had presented articles and lectures that made the experience of the child the starting point, in a way that in some respects pointed toward many of the models that Melanie Klein, later so influential and once Ferenczi's analysand, would formulate.[136] Klein will never, as is well known, recognise the influence of Ferenczi, the references literally limited to a few footnotes.[137]

In Ferenczi's article, the psychoanalytic approach is focussed on the character of personality, which he understands as a compulsive symptom as the superego develops through identification with a punishing authority.[138] Resigned to what he saw as Ferenczi's tendency towards self-isolation, resulting in turn in the long lacunae in their correspondence, Freud suddenly found himself the object of criticism and insistent demands that he examine himself. 'I don't quite understand him',[139] Freud declared. For his part, Ferenczi, aware of the hostility harboured against him by Jones (a person he considered 'despotic' and 'without scruples', a man who did not hesitate to resort to 'slander'),[140] sought unceasingly both to re-evaluate and to renew the starting points of his work. He strove to find a 'naïve' gaze, 'curious' rather than predetermined by fixed theoretical assumptions, corresponding to the idea of the elasticity of the technique itself, as stated in an article from 1928,[141] and also reflected in the posthumously published *Clinical Diary*.[142] Driven by this ambition, he wrestled with Freud's influence upon him.

The Domain of Dreams

'I ask myself', Freud writes on 10 January 1910, to his friend and colleague, apropos of a dream analysis that the latter has described in a now lost letter, 'if you haven't had a secret reason for disclosing the dream analysis to me'. This purloined letter evokes the presence of a hidden message, of a message whose addressee and sender seem to be constantly interchangeable. This is how the transference operates, manifesting itself in the form of such enigmatic messages, messages caught in the dream's web of signifiers, as a consequence of which an opaque image rises from the meshwork like 'the mushroom out of its mycelium', to use Freud's expression in *The Interpretation of Dreams*.[143]

On 8 September 1914, barely a month before the first phase of his analysis with Freud began, Ferenczi sent him 'a little dream analysis' recorded in the form of a dialogue.[144] It is that dream which initiates Ferenczi's analysis with Freud, the reason it has been given a privileged status. The text was intended for a psychoanalytic journal; the letter's recipient was given the role of a psychoanalyst in a fictional dialogue while the interpretation of the dream was described as part of an 'auto-analysis'. In a meticulous reading Ernst Falzeder has examined the dream and its interpretation, as set out in Ferenczi's article 'The Dream of the Occlusive Pessary' (1915). Falzeder draws attention to the staging of the message, specifically the form of address in the article, the inscribed dialogue between the psychoanalyst and the dreamer as well as the moment of publication and the sending of the letter to Freud, who also – in his role as doctor – is written into the account. According to Falzeder, Ferenczi's staging is a masterpiece of ambivalence, metadiscourse, and hidden messages.[145] Beyond the link to Freud and the theme of auto-analysis, beyond the airless paranoid world of the father complex, however, we are seeking here to extract another layer that hinges on the image of an archaic mother.

Let us therefore follow the notion that this dream, in its network of association, sketches the outlines, or, as it were, registers in distorted form the impressions, of what took place in the meeting between the two men. In a fashion comparable to the classic monograph by Schorske, the aforementioned American historian, it is also possible to trace how, from one dream to another, each entity forms 'a conglomerate which for purpose of investigation, must be broken up once more into fragments'. What we encounter now is not the personal narrative from which the auto-analysis derives, but a *milieu*, a place not merely physical but 'mental, like a landscape'.[146]

During the war, Ferenczi underwent analysis with Freud for three short periods, an analysis that due to different circumstances was never terminated. The first period took place in October 1914, but was suddenly interrupted by Ferenczi's recruitment at the outbreak of the war; the second period was between 14 June and 5 July 1916; and, finally, there was a period of analytic work that lasted for two weeks from 26 September 1916.[147] This unfinished analysis, or the idea of it, will lay the foundation for one of the most important theoretical cruxes formulated during Freud's later phase, and thereby generate insights about the psychoanalytic situation that coming generations of psychoanalysts will have to relate to. How can the bedrock that every analysis – according to Freud – must acknowledge as impenetrable be conceived?

It is therefore important to try to take into consideration the transference that this unfinished analysis, this missed encounter, brought into play. In letters, Ferenczi critically remarks that 'negative feelings and fantasies' were not explored in detail in the analysis. Freud's reply is the above-mentioned influential work 'Analysis Terminable and Interminable' (1937). Ferenczi touched on the subject in texts like 'The Problem of the Termination of Analysis' (1927), but it is in particular in the later text, the one read to Freud in the summer of 1932, that he systematically identifies the importance of addressing negative affects and aggression in the analysis. Phenomena belonging to the field of transference emerge when we try to understand the conflicting, but at the same time intellectually productive, relationship between the two men in its specific expressions and forms. The intrapsychic processes described in the documents – observed through transcribed dreams and their interpretation, hysterical actions, and imaginary complexes extracted through wild analysis – are not considered here to be isolated processes but are linked to forces and energies active in the environments in question.

However, the episode that perhaps most deeply affects the analytic situation between Freud and Ferenczi is the so-called 'Elma affair'. Traces of the event are manifested in the dream interpretation Ferenczi shares with Freud. The event itself takes place in 1911, and the background is an intricate triangular relationship. Since 1900 Ferenczi had courted Gizella Pàlos, who, though still married, lived separated from her husband, Geza Pàlos, with two daughters. They enter into a love relationship, and Gizella, eight years older than Ferenczi, seems to assume something of a maternal function for him. When her daughter, Elma, starts an analysis with Ferenczi on her mother's recommendation, Ferenczi falls in love with the twenty-four-year-old woman, whereupon the analysis is interrupted. In this intricate situation, Ferenczi persuades Freud to let the young woman enter analysis with him, which he agrees to, if reluctantly. The correspondence between them over a number of years testifies to Ferenczi's ambivalent feelings, divided between the older Gizella who could no longer give birth, and her younger, fertile daughter. The idea of the mother, with its roots in infantile sexuality, can be glimpsed in several of the dream analyses that Ferenczi shares. Freud's assumed neutral stance was obscured by his clear position in favour of Ferenczi choosing the older woman; meanwhile, during the ongoing analysis with the younger woman details from it were leaked in the letters between the men. On more than one level, the men are guilty of what would today, in contemporary psychoanalysis, be understood in terms of a break of the frame. The event has huge consequences and leaves deep marks, ultimately causing Ferenczi to regard his analysis as incomplete. Ferenczi will for the rest of his life reproach Freud for his standpoint, as can be seen in the correspondence with Groddeck and in the critical diary from Ferenczi's latter life.

In what follows we will focus on how the dream's meshwork of condensed images and the associations that unfold emerge like mycelial ramifications in relation to a semantic core that its work constantly dissolves, that is the *meaning* of the dream derived from a fantasy of potential patricide. Thus Ferenczi's presentation seems to oscillate between an Oedipal interpretation injected into the text, placed in the analyst's mouth, and a traumatic experience of the archaic mother. The manifest dream that Ferenczi communicates reads:

> I stuff an occlusive pessary into my urethra. I am alarmed as I do so lest it might slip into the bladder from which it could only be removed by shedding blood. I try therefore to hold it steadily in the perineal region from outside and to force it back or to press it outwards along the urethra.[148]

To this are added two interjected details. The first is a fragment of the preceding dream: 'the pessary was stuffed into his rectum', and the second a postscript, 'in the dream I was aware that the elastic thing would spread itself [sic] in the bladder and then it would be impossible to get it out again'.[149]

Thematically, the dream sets in motion an array of interlinked motifs. We can differentiate them into clusters of intricate images involving separate bodily orifices, a surprising interplay between inside and outside, penetration and pregnancy. The dream subject, who otherwise considers himself 'masculine', is effectively taking a feminine contraceptive, which seems 'nonsensical' in the dream work but is linked to a 'wish-fulfilment'.[150] The day residues speak of actual preventative measures taken by his partner, suggesting a preliminary line of interpretation towards his 'in the dream identify[ing] [...] with the woman'.[151] This association is complemented by childhood memories of having inserted objects into his bodily orifices, memories which are displaced by anxiety-causing images of '[t]apeworms and echinococci'.[152] The web of associations around these phenomena also includes eggs and early stages of biological development, all related to how small organisms force their way into bodies so as to grow considerably in size. These series of attributes are concentrated in notions of contagion and spread that interestingly denote fantasies of reproduction, ultimately condensed into images of expansion and enclosures. Infection in the dream work is understood as reproduction.

The images and the complexes of motifs that these images develop are overdetermined by an Oedipal content through the interventions of the psychoanalyst, whose action seems to inject a group of utterances. In the dialogue, the doctor points out: 'you infect yourself as it were with the bladder-shaped instrument, that is, you impregnate yourself'.[153] The dream interpretation's development of sequences derived from the individual elements thus puts into play infantile notions of sexuality, blocks of childhood memories, as well as ramifications of associations in which biological processes of organisms such as the hermaphroditic binocular worms bring into play notions of pollution and infection. Pregnancy becomes analogous to a body hosting parasitic entities, the focal point for contagion. The elements of the dream consistently behave like *self-reproducing* organisms. Against this background, the psychoanalyst's remarks appears like attempts to bring these elements back into a stable – Oedipal – order.

The organising wish impulse of the dream, the possibility to be at once mother and child, is condensed – with reference to the relation with Gizella and her daughter – in the statement: 'if I cannot obtain a child from the older woman, and may not get one from the younger – then I shall make the child myself'.[154] The background is the above-mentioned triangle drama in which Freud played a role for which Ferenczi will later blame him. On 14 July 1911, Ferenczi announced that he had begun analytical work with Elma, daughter of his wife-to-be and soon he confesses to Freud that he has fallen in love with her, for which reason the analysis must be interrupted and that he needs Freud's help. In January of the following year, as mentioned earlier, Freud reluctantly takes over the analytical work with Elma. Ferenczi expresses, in letters at the beginning of that year, his ambivalent relation to the two women, as well as listing his symptoms and expounds on his hypochondria. A few months later, Elma returns to analysis with Ferenczi where, not unexpectedly, things go wrong. A short time before Ferenczi shares the intricate text about his dream with Freud, he had encountered Elma, who was about to get married.

The analysis works with combinations of the deep past and fleeting processes in the present. Another relevant day residue, a meeting with his own mother, has brought their relationship into his thoughts. His own play and interaction with a nephew are contrasted with his own mother's distant manner towards himself. In his interaction with the little boy, he identifies himself with the roles of both child and mother. Underlying this doubled identification lies 'the other, primitive – maternal function; to birth.'[155] The approach to this maternal function is a crucial trace in Ferenczi's development, which leaves its mark not only in his speculative genital theory but in important observations on technical issues based on the concept of transference. The male and female poles of transference allow Ferenczi to rethink the life and death drives Freud had established with 'Beyond the Pleasure Principle'. Ferenczi considers them in *The Clinical Diary* according to two principles, one of which is the female which 'exists as a possibility everywhere',[156] implying a capacity for suffering. In a patriarchal order, subordinated to the paternal principle, whose position, in Freud's view, coincides with the psychoanalytic authority, the female ability establishes itself as a resistance. He writes that 'the feminine principle creates clusters in the strongly masculine principle'.[157] Hence, it becomes linked to the organising life drive called Orpha that he identified in the encounter with his patients, where, based on the image of a fragmented individuality, neglected drives and impulses are mobilised as if by magic. In the article 'Confusion of Tongues', Ferenczi writes about a 'sudden, surprising rise of new faculties after a trauma, like a miracle that occurs upon the wave of a magic wand'.[158] He observes in his clinical experience how the child 'under pressure of such traumatic urgency [...] can develop instantaneously all the emotions of a mature adult and all the potential qualities dormant in him'.[159] The life drive that he identifies as a feminine principle that potentially exists everywhere, and that is thus also accessible to the male analyst, implies 'a slight modification of Freud's assumption of life and death instincts'.[160] 'I would give', Ferenczi writes, 'the same thing other names'. In contrast to 'the egoism and self-assertion of the male' which he conceives as organising the pleasure principle, he seeks in the reality principle a 'conciliation', which is then linked to the female principle.[161]

Furthermore, these principles lead him to think about reproduction as he continues the work he began with *Thalassa*, in which experiments with 'non-sexual fertilization' acquire a central importance. The self-assertion and egoism of the masculine principle are here harboured by the female: 'the pleasure of motherhood is actually a tolerance of parasitic creatures, who develop in a completely egoistic way at the expense of the mother's own body'.[162] The insight that Ferenczi reaches, through an analysis of contemporary biological experiments, as well as experiences gained in the psychoanalytic work, is an insight into 'destructive processes [that] result in productivity'.[163] Applied to the analytic work, it helps him to perceive or listen to a child in the adult analysand who, through trauma, is the victim of an overwhelming aggressiveness, a child present in the form of an abandoned part of the self that is 'dead', a 'ghost'.[164] The analytical work does not aim at removing this ghost, but to tactfully and energetically revive it.

Let us say that the early experiences of the body, or what we may call the archaic mother, form 'the impenetrability of the trauma', that is, 'its resistance to signification', which, according to Lacan, indicates the unconscious as a 'lost cause'.[165] Thus, at the site of the repetition that takes place in the analysis, we find that the transference stumbles on this impermeability. This means that its formations are already put into play and can be perceived in phenomena such as dreams, fallacies or symptoms. In reading Ferenczi's dream analysis, we note a certain syntax that makes it possible to approach the real, that is, sexuality, through the figure of contagion. Lacan asserts that 'what escapes the subject is that the syntax stands in relation to the reserve of the unconscious': the 'core' of the dream is its syntax.[166] We will now look at the peculiarities of Ferenczi's recorded dream analysis explored earlier, in relation to one of the central dream analyses in *The Interpretation of Dreams*.

The dream is Freud's own and depicts a peculiar operation, performed upon a part of the dreamer's own body. The depiction is oriented around the observation of a detail. Part of the dreamer's own body appears in close-up to be clearly divided into two, a visual effect by which a partial object is *given*. Instead of wholeness, with depth, background and perspective, what appears are terrifying fragments. The phenomenon can be compared to peculiarities in other dreams recorded by Freud, like the so-called dream about Irma's injections.[167] The dreamer has been tasked with

> a dissection of my own body, my pelvis and legs, which I saw before me as though in the dissection-room, but without noticing their absence in myself and also without trace of any gruesome feeling.[168]

The image is, so to speak, split off from the affect that should have been attached to it. In the first sequence of the dream, obtrusive images of organs, fragmented body parts, are, as in Ferenczi's dream, observed. 'The pelvis had been eviscerated, and it was visible now in its superior, now in its inferior, aspect, the two being mixed together'. The manifest dream consists of two parts. In the second part the dreamer is suddenly able to recover his legs and take a walk in the city, but is finally too tired to walk. The surroundings change imperceptibly into a mountain landscape, which in turn changes into a swamp, holding a small house and an abyss. The landscape assumes the character of an obstacle, while inserted peculiar details decorate it like inscrutable signs: some people sitting on the ground like '*Indians or gypsies – among them a girl*', a small '*wooden house*' cut off by a '*chasm*', men lying motionless on wooden benches, two sleeping children. Here, as if in contrast to the initial sequence, the dream ends in acute distress: '*It was as though what would make the crossing possible was not the boards but the children. I awoke in mental fright*'.[169]

The dream analyses, Ferenczi's as well as Freud's, bring into play notions of genealogies, gender and reproduction. But they unequivocally open completely different ways of understanding and thinking of these phenomena. In both Freud and Ferenczi, the associations around the elements of dreams form moving fields of signifiers which are condensed into nodes. However, the sensory impressions and affects modelled by Ferenczi evoke a different mental landscape from that found in Freud. We have seen how it involves childhood memories of putting things in the ear and nose, biological phenomena related to reproduction: eggs and larvae spreading and growing in bodies, expansion. These are blended with traces of infantile conceptions of the body relating to specific forms: dispersal, canals that are too dense or too wide, childish theories of pregnancy, and so on.

In both dreams, the fluid networks of signifying elements, alongside references to self-analysis, are linked to different clusters of motifs. In Freud's case they are oriented around a father complex; in Ferenczi's case the associations are woven around representations of gender identity, infantile bodily experiences, pregnancy, complex relations to two women and, ultimately, the emotionally inaccessible mother. For Freud, the emotionally split observation of a part of his own body can be interpreted as self-analysis, in need of self-mastery in order to present the intimate details from which it derives, whereas Ferenczi's dream situates auto-analysis as a potential child within the framework of a fraught relationship with an analyst in the process of turning away from him. In both cases, the dream contains material derived from infantile registers. But Freud retraces the intense images, the shifts, the sudden changes of scene, the landscape with its peculiar details and the 'mental fright' that was unmistakably active in the dream-thoughts, to a specific statement, a *sentence*. The elements – such as a '"wooden house" [that] was also, no doubt, a *coffin*, that is to say, the grave' – are in the dream read like a rebus. They are delineated as *intensities* demanding interpretation; they are transposed in the dream work to a significatory context, a master-signifier. The images of the wooden house, the men lying on the wooden benches and the two sleeping children are carried over by means of a displacement to the image of an archaic sepulchre – an Etruscan tomb visited in Orvieto that consisted of 'a narrow chamber with two stone benches along its walls, on which the skeletons of two grown-up men were lying'[170] – thus, the dream work is completed in a wish-fulfilment:

> The dream seems to have been saying: 'If you must rest in the grave, let it be the Etruscan grave'. And, by making this replacement, it transformed the gloomiest of expectations into one that was highly desirable.[171]

The affect that was split off in the first dream sequence now returns; the fact that he wakes up with fright leads to the constantly recurring father complex; there is something frightening about the children that would 'make the crossing possible', and thus the threatening conceptual figure can be identified as 'the idea that children may perhaps achieve what their father had failed to'.[172]

The infantile layers in Ferenczi's dream analysis form other patterns: the associations to the father set other series in motion, the feeling of his own physical inadequacy in relation to the two women, the regression from object relation to autoeroticism, etc. But the father complex – the Oedipal interpretation of

Ferenczi's feminine attitude, communicated in the dialogue with the analyst – is dissolved, indeed dismantled, in the dream work itself through its presented complex of fragmented images. If the elements in Ferenczi's analysis are contrasted with the forms we encountered in Freud's dream – the almost frozen images whose chains of signifiers move metonymically where the archaic sepulchre is encrypted – these dream elements appear instead as elastic organic-biological forms in which the genital register is manifested *beyond the phallus*. In Ferenczi's analysis the dream elements are not transcribed in the shape of binary poles but unfold through proximity, as interchangeable forms of expansion and repression, inside and outside, where reproduction or procreation appears as contagion.

A Painful Encounter

The meeting on 30 August was, as Judith Dupont puts it, a 'painful' encounter marked by a mutual misunderstanding;[173] we sensed the presence of two men preoccupied with thoughts of death, bodily decay, a lost cause. For Freud, the prospect of death elicited genealogical fantasies, placing his disciples in the role of potential patricides. For Ferenczi, the acquired sensitivity to the neurotic's risk of death, imagined or real, led to a new theory of trauma.

We have identified a certain confusion of tongues manifested between the men, a confusion in which the psychoanalytic discourse finds expression: not as the harmonious development of a prominent man's theories, but as a body determined by conflicts, energies, irreconcilable struggles. If this is the case, psychoanalysis must be treated as the sum of all the forces it allows. Once this is accepted, I believe, it does away with the whole cult of an origin – the perception of Freud's work as rooted in a series of heroic discoveries – in favour of an appreciation of the intrinsic potentialities of a milieu. What matters then is to make amalgams and configurations accessible by means of microscopic analysis where a tactile eye is trained to observe the *grey documents' whirl of contingencies*.

We have sought to outline this milieu in terms of Freud's and Ferenczi's relationship and the tensions within it. Dream analysis and fantasies provided an opportunity to return to the *event* itself in order to dissolve the syntheses by which Ferenczi's intelligence could be regarded as 'exhausted', so as to instead actualise within it that which is singular – that is to say, to reconceptualise the meeting between them as a *missed* opportunity, 'the ever avoided encounter'.[174] The standard biographies rely on observations of transference phenomena – peculiarities played out between the men, symptoms, dreams and acting out – yet these always lead back to a complex which justifies an Oedipal content as the core of psychoanalytic theory even as it activates mechanisms of exclusion. My purpose was to dissolve these syntheses and read the operations of transference in accordance with how Lacan, in his Eleventh Seminar, describes the movement of how something both opens itself up and closes itself off. Instead of a repetition: something remains excluded. The confrontation between Freud and Ferenczi has thus been understood as a missed opportunity, something whose outlines can be traced by means of the phenomenon of transference, which is to say in the details, the accidental: in dreams. By avoiding generalisations – the desire to synthesise the jumble of documents, the wish to restore contingent events to rigid complexes – I sought instead to read this missed opportunity, this opening, as something *untimely*, in Nietzsche's sense, if such a comparison can be sustained. In a word, the attempt was conceived as a possibility followed by a fact: the statements rest upon an unconscious foundation.

My aim has been to explore the possibility of reading the imprint of this always avoided encounter, as I understood the transference established between Freud and Ferenczi. Beyond the link to Freud and the theme of self-analysis, beyond the closed paranoid world of the father complex, I have sought here to deepen the analysis by attempting to uncover other layers revolving around the image of an archaic mother and the enigmatic function of giving birth. In the network of associations of the analysis, a cluster of motifs was grouped around the fragmented story of the love triangle between Ferenczi, his future wife Gizella Pàlos and her daughter Elma, in which Freud also played a role. Here, notions of pregnancy and the mother's body emerged, as well as remnants of unconscious fantasies of birth and reproduction that characterised Ferenczi's text.

Finally, Ferenczi's late notes in *The Clinical Diary* showed how the fundamentals played out in the conflict between him and Freud concerning the question of what truth the psychoanalytic situation is capable of containing or is forced to suppress. Ferenczi's work to overcome psychoanalytic technique, indeed to go beyond all technique in the direction of what he initially calls a mutual analysis, is based on an encrypted trauma. Freud, he argues, sought to defend himself against the experience that the transference confronted him with – the 'abyss' it opened up – by observing the supposed neutrality on which the analyst's all-important 'authority' rested. The conflict can, I think, be traced back to and thus shed light on the genealogy of psychoanalysis, emerging as it does from late nineteenth-century psychiatric practice. Foucault, in his lectures on psychiatric power, to which I alluded earlier, has touched on the origins of psychoanalysis along these lines.[175] In the lectures, he suggests that psychiatric practice gives rise to two discourses – the differentiation of disease types, and their anatomical-pathological correlates – discourses which were never put into play in the encounter and treatment of patients. Rather, these discourses simply guaranteed the truth of psychiatric practice as such, while the regimes and regulations, classifications and treatments of the institution bore no relation to them at all. In short, truth is not at stake between psychiatrist and patient. Foucault identifies from this argument a first retreat of psychiatric power, through the simulation of the inmates – the hysterics – who challenge the authority of psychiatric science, through psychoanalysis, insofar as it takes as its subject the truth the symptom expresses, or rather the game of truth and lie in the symptom as it colours the transference. I believe that it is this question of truth that was at stake in the conflict between Freud and Ferenczi.

Notes

[1] Freud to Ferenczi, 2 October 1932, S. Freud, S. Ferenczi, *The Correspondence of Sigmund Freud and Sándor Ferenczi, Vol. 3: 1920–1933*, ed. by É. Brabant, E. Falzeder, P. Giampieri-Deutsch, transl. by P. T. Hoffer. Cambridge, Mass.: Belknap Press of Harvard UP, 2000, pp. 444–445.

[2] Freud to Anna Freud, 3 September 1932, S. Freud, A. Freud, *Briefwechsel 1904–1938*, ed. by I. Meyer-Palmedo. Frankfurt/M.: Fischer, 2006, p. 527.

[3] Freud to Ferenczi, 13 December 1929, *The Correspondence of Sigmund Freud and Sándor Ferenczi*, Vol. 3, p. 374.

[4] S. Ferenczi, 'Confusion of Tongues between Adults and the Child' [1933], in: S. Ferenczi, *Final Contributions to the Problems and Methods of Psycho-Analysis*, ed. by M. Bálint, transl. by E. Mosbacher. London: Karnac, 1994, pp. 156–167.

[5] Freud to Anna Freud, 3 September 1932, *Briefwechsel*, p. 527.

[6] P. Gay, *Freud: A Life for Our Time*. London: J. M. Dent, 1988, p. 584.

[7] Ibid., p. 583.

[8] G. Deleuze, F. Guattari, *A Thousand Plateaus: Capitalism and Schizophrenia*, transl. by B. Massumi. London: The Athlone Press, 1987, pp. 95–96.

[9] An earlier, shorter version of this line of thought was published in German: J. Staberg, 'Anstatt Sprache: Verwirrung. Eine verfehlte Begegnung zwischen Sigmund Freud und Sándor Ferenczi', *Psyche. Zeitschrift für Psychoanalyse und ihre Anwendungen* 74(5), 2020, pp. 321–343.

[10] S. Ferenczi, 'Introjection and Transference' [1909], in: S. Ferenczi, *First Contributions to Psycho-Analysis*, transl. by E. Jones. London: Karnac, 1994, pp. 35–93.

[11] J. Lacan, 'The Freudian Thing or the Meaning of the Return to Freud in Psychoanalysis', in: J. Lacan, *Écrits: The First Complete Edition in English*, transl. by B. Fink. New York: W.W. Norton, 2006, pp. 401–436, p. 403.

12 C. G. Jung, *Erinnerungen, Träume, Gedanken*. Zurich: Racher, 1962, p. 152; C. G. Jung, A. Jaffé, *Memories, Dreams, Reflections*. London: Fontana, 1993, p. 178.
13 S. Ferenczi, 'On the Organization of the Psycho-Analytical Movement' [1911], in: S. Ferenczi, *Final Contributions to the Problems and Methods of Psycho-Analysis*, pp. 299–307.
14 L. Aron, K. Starr, 'Freud and Ferenczi: Wandering Jews in Palermo', in: A. Harris, S. Kuchuck (eds.), *The Legacy of Sándor Ferenczi: From Ghost to Ancestor*. London, New York: Routledge, 2015, pp. 150–167.
15 C. E. Schorske, *Fin-de-siècle Vienna*. New York: Vintage, 1980.
16 Freud to Fliess, 23 September 1895, S. Freud, *The Complete Letters of Sigmund Freud to Wilhelm Fliess 1887–1904*. Cambridge, Mass.: Belknap Press of Harvard UP, 1985.
17 C. E. Schorske, *Fin-de-siècle Vienna*, p. 185.
18 E. Roudinesco, *Freud in His Time and Ours*, transl. by C. Porter. Cambridge, Mass.: Harvard UP, 2016.
19 C. G. Jung, 'The State of Psychotherapy Today' [1934], in: C. G. Jung, *Collected Works of Carl Jung, Vol. 10: Civilization in Transition*, ed. by G. Adler, transl. by R. F. C. Hull. Princeton, NJ: Princeton UP, 1970, pp. 157–174.
20 Ferenczi to Freud, 15 September 1915, S. Freud, S. Ferenczi, *The Correspondence of Sigmund Freud and Sándor Ferenczi, Vol. 2: 1914–1919*, ed. by É. Brabant, E. Falzeder, P. Giampieri-Deutsch, transl. by P. T. Hoffer. Cambridge, Mass.: Belknap Press of Harvard UP, 1996, p. 80.
21 G. Deleuze, F. Guattari, *Kafka: Toward a Minor Literature*, transl. by D. Polan. Minneapolis: University of Minnesota Press, 1986, p. 25.
22 L. Aron, K. Starr, 'Freud and Ferenczi: Wandering Jews in Palermo'.
23 G. Deleuze, F. Guattari, *Kafka*, p. 16.
24 Ibid., p. 22f.
25 S. Freud, 'From the History of an Infantile Neurosis' [1918], in: S. Freud, *An Infantile Neurosis and Other Works* (1917–1919), SE 17, pp. 1–122; G. Deleuze, F. Guattari, *A Thousand Plateaus*, p. 31ff.
26 S. Ferenczi, 'The Dream of the Occlusive Pessary' [1915], in: S. Ferenczi, *Further Contributions to the Theory and Technique of Psycho-Analysis*, comp. by J. Rickman, transl. by J. I. Suttie. London: Karnac, 1994, pp. 304–311, p. 307.
27 Idem.
28 Idem.
29 G. Deleuze, F. Guattari, *What is Philosophy?*, transl. by H. Tomlinson, G. Burchill. London: Verso, 1994, pp. 95–96; A. E. Haynal, V. D. Haynal, 'Ferenczi's Attitude', transl. by S. K. Wang, in: S. Kuchuck, A. Harris (eds.), *The Legacy of Sándor Ferenczi*, p. 69.
30 J. Lacan, *The Four Fundamental Concepts of Psychoanalysis: The Seminar of Jacques Lacan Book XI*, transl. by A. Sheridan. New York: W. W. Norton, 1998, pp. 136–146.

[31] Jones to Freud, 3 June 1933, in answer to Freud, 29 May 1933, S. Freud, E. Jones, *The Complete Correspondence of Sigmund Freud and Ernest Jones 1908–1939*, ed. by R. A. Paskauskas. Cambridge, Mass.: Belknap Press of Harvard UP, 1993; E. Jones, *Sigmund Freud. Life and Work. Vol. III: The Last Phase 1919–1939*. London: The Hogarth Press, 1957, p. 47: 'Ferenczi more gradually towards the end of his life, developed psychotic manifestations that revealed themselves, among other ways, in a turning away from Freud and his doctrines'.

[32] Freud to Jones, 29 May 1933, *The Complete Correspondence of Sigmund Freud and Ernest Jones*, p. 721.

[33] G. Deleuze, F. Guattari, *A Thousand Plateaus*, p. 287.

[34] Freud to Jung, 6 December 1906, S. Freud, C. G. Jung, *The Freud-Jung Letters: The Correspondence Between Sigmund Freud and C. G. Jung*. Princeton, NJ: Princeton UP, 1994, on 'therapy and its mechanism' as 'intelligible only to the initiate' p. 12.

[35] G. Deleuze, F. Guattari, *A Thousand Plateaus*, p. 287.

[36] Ibid., p. 288.

[37] S. Freud, 'Fragment of an Analysis of a Case of Hysteria' [1905], in: S. Freud, *A Case of Hysteria, Three Essays on Sexuality and Other Works* (1901–1905), *SE* 7, pp. 7–122, p. 78.

[38] G. Deleuze, F. Guattari, *A Thousand Plateaus*, p. 288; on homophobia, homosexuality and paranoia: Letter from Freud to Ferenczi, 6 October 1910, S. Freud, S. Ferenczi, *The Correspondence of Sigmund Freud and Sándor Ferenczi, Vol. 1: 1908–1914*, ed. by É. Brabant, E. Falzeder, P. Giampieri-Deutsch, transl. by P. T. Hoffer. Cambridge, Mass.: Belknap Press of Harvard UP, 1993, pp. 221–223.

[39] G. Deleuze, F. Guattari, *A Thousand Plateaus*, p. 289.

[40] S. Ferenczi, 'On the Organization of the Psycho-Analytical Movement', pp. 302-303.

[41] Ibid.; E. Zaretsky, *Secrets of the Soul: A Social and Cultural History of Psychoanalysis*. New York: Vintage, 2005, p. 57.

[42] S. Ferenczi, 'On the Organization of the Psycho-Analytical Movement', p. 299.

[43] Ibid., p. 301.

[44] G. Deleuze, F. Guattari, *A Thousand Plateaus*, p. 287.

[45] S. Freud, G. Groddeck, *Briefe über das Es*, ed. by M. Honegger. Munich: Kindler, 1974, p. 14, quoted in E. Falzeder, 'Sándor Ferenczi Between Orthodoxy and Heterodoxy', *American Imago* 66(4), 2009, pp. 395–404, p. 397.

[46] S. Ferenczi, 'On the Organization of the Psycho-Analytical Movement'; G. Deleuze, F. Guattari, *A Thousand Plateaus*, p. 288.

[47] C. Bonomi, 'The Penis on the Trail: Re-reading the Origins of Psychoanalysis with Sándor Ferenczi', in: S. Kuchuck, A. Harris (eds.), *The Legacy of Sándor Ferenczi*, pp. 33–51, p. 37.

[48] S. Ferenczi, 'On the Organization of the Psycho-Analytical Movement', p. 303.

[49] Ibid., p. 302; A. E. Haynal, V. D. Haynal, 'Ferenczi's Attitude', p. 65, on authoritarian structures also in the surrounding society.

[50] Ibid., p. 302f.

51. Ibid., p. 303.
52. Idem.
53. H. Sachs, *Freud: Master and Friend*. London: Imago, 1945.
54. Ferenczi to Freud, 25 October 1912, *The Correspondence of Sigmund Freud and Sándor Ferenczi*, Vol. 1, p. 417.
55. Jones to Freud, 30 July 1912, *The Complete Correspondence of Sigmund Freud and Ernest Jones*, p. 146.
56. Freud to Jones, 1 August 1912, *The Complete Correspondence of Sigmund Freud and Ernest Jones*, p. 147.
57. Ibid., p. 148.
58. Jones to Freud, 7 August 1912, *The Complete Correspondence of Sigmund Freud and Ernest Jones*, p. 149.
59. Freud to Ferenczi, 13 December 1929, *The Correspondence of Sigmund Freud and Sándor Ferenczi*, Vol. 3, p. 374.
60. E. Falzeder, 'The Significance of Ferenczi's Clinical Contributions for Working with Psychotic Patients', *International Forum of Psychoanalysis* 13(1–2), 2004, p. 27.
61. H. D. [Hilda Doolittle], *Tribute to Freud*. Boston: Godine, 1974.
62. S. Freud, 'Recommendations to Physicians Practicing Psycho-Analysis' [1912], in: S. Freud, *The Case of Schreber, Papers on Technique and Other Works* (1911–1913), *SE* 12, pp. 111–120.
63. S. Ferenczi, *The Clinical Diary of Sándor Ferenczi*, ed. by J. Dupont, transl. by M. Bálint, N. Z. Jackson. Cambridge, Mass.: Harvard UP, 1995.
64. Ibid., p. 10.
65. J. Lacan, *The Four Fundamental Concepts of Psychoanalysis*, p. 12.
66. S. Ferenczi, *The Clinical Diary of Sándor Ferenczi*, p. 85.
67. S. Freud, 'Fragment of an Analysis of a Case of Hysteria', p. 88.
68. Ibid., p. 116.
69. Idem.
70. Ibid., p. 117.
71. S. Ferenczi, 'Introjection and Transference', p. 43.
72. S. Ferenczi, *The Clinical Diary of Sándor Ferenczi*, p. 93.
73. Ibid., pp. 93–94.
74. M. Foucault, *Essential Works of Foucault, 1954–1984, Vol. 2: Aesthetics, Method and Epistemology*. New York: New Press, 1998, p. 369.
75. E. Jones, *Sigmund Freud. Life and Work. Vol. III: The Last Phase 1919–1939*, p. 134 on Ferenczi's 'mental deterioration' and p. 188 on his 'latent psychotic trends'; 'final delusional state'.
76. C. G. Jung, *Erinnerungen, Träume, Gedanken*; C. G. Jung, A. Jaffé, *Memories, Dreams, Reflections*, p. 187ff.
77. M. Foucault, *Essential Works of Foucault, 1954–1984, Vol. 2: Aesthetics, Method and Epistemology*, p. 369.
78. J. Lacan, *The Four Fundamental Concepts of Psychoanalysis*, p. 10.

[79] Ibid., p. 12.
[80] Idem.
[81] Idem.
[82] S. O. Wallenstein, 'Hegels Shakespeare', *Agora* 37(1), 2019, pp. 25–44, p. 25.
[83] S. Freud, 'Sándor Ferenczi' [1933], in: S. Freud, *New Introductory Lectures on Psycho-Analysis and Other Works* (1932–1936), SE 22, pp. 227–229; É. Roudinesco, *Freud in His Time and Ours*, transl. by C. Porter. Cambridge, Mass.: Harvard UP, 2016, p. 163f.
[84] P. Gay, *Freud*, p. 578; Freud to Ferenczi, 13 December 1931, *The Correspondence of Sigmund Freud and Sándor Ferenczi*, Vol. 3, p. 423.
[85] H. D., *Tribute to Freud*, p. 146.
[86] Freud to Jung, 24 September 1910, *The Freud-Jung Letters*, p. 353.
[87] Ferenczi to Groddeck, 25 December 1921, S. Ferenczi, G. Groddeck, *The Sándor Ferenczi–Georg Groddeck Correspondence*, ed. and transl. by C. Fortune. London: Open Gate Press, 2002, pp. 8–9. Cf. Ferenczi to Freud, 3 October 1910, *The Correspondence of Sigmund Freud and Sándor Ferenczi*, Vol. 1; S. Ferenczi, *The Clinical Diary of Sándor Ferenczi*, pp. 187–188.
[88] Freud to Jung, 24 September 1910, *The Freud-Jung Letters*, p. 353.
[89] L. Aron, K. Starr, 'Freud and Ferenczi: Wandering Jews in Palermo', p. 156.
[90] E. Zaretsky, *Secrets of the Soul*, p. 57.
[91] S. Freud, 'Sándor Ferenczi'.
[92] Freud to Jones, 12 September 1932, *The Complete Correspondence of Sigmund Freud and Ernest Jones*, p. 708 f.
[93] Freud to Eitingon, 20 October 1932, S. Freud, M. Eitingon, *Briefwechsel 1906–1939. Sigmund Freud und Max Eitingon*, ed. by M. Schröter. Tübingen: edition diskord, 2004, p. 834.
[94] Freud to Jones, 29 May 1933, *The Complete Correspondence of Sigmund Freud and Ernest Jones 1908–1939*, p. 721, Jones to Freud, 3 June 1933, p. 721 f.
[95] R. Girard, *Le Bouc émissaire*. Paris: Grasset, 1983, pp. 34–36.
[96] Ibid., p. 27: 'Les persécuteurs finissent toujours par se convaincre qu'un petit nombre d'individus, ou même un seul peut se rendre extrêmement nuisible à la société tout entière, en dépit de sa faiblesse relative.'
[97] Ibid., p. 26: 'le symbole de l'autorité suprême', see further, p. 30f.: 'qualités extrêmes' (p. 31).
[98] S. Ferenczi, *The Clinical Diary of Sándor Ferenczi*, p. 84.
[99] Ibid., p. 185.
[100] Idem.
[101] C. G. Jung, A. Jaffé, *Memories, Dreams, Reflections*, pp. 161, 188.
[102] Ibid., p. 189.
[103] Idem.
[104] E. Jones, *The Life and Work of Sigmund Freud. Vol. I: The Young Freud 1856–1900*. London: The Hogarth Press, 1954, p. 317.

105 E. Jones, *The Life and Work of Sigmund Freud. Vol. II: Years of Maturity 1901–1919*. London: The Hogarth Press, 1954, p. 165.
106 S. Ferenczi, *The Clinical Diary of Sándor Ferenczi*, p. 185.
107 Ibid., p. 186.
108 Ferenczi to Freud, 25 October 1912, *The Correspondence of Sigmund Freud and Sándor Ferenczi*, Vol. 1, p. 417; E. Zaretsky, *Secrets of the Soul*, p. 57. On the case studies as a 're-interpretation of masculinity at the dawn of personal life', emphasising 'male vulnerability in the age of mechanisation'.
109 J. Breuer, S. Freud, 'On the Psychical Mechanism of Hysterical Phenomena: Preliminary Communication' [1893], in: J. Breuer, S. Freud, *Studies on Hysteria* (1893–1895), *SE* 2, pp. 1–18, p. 6.
110 Ibid., p. 7.
111 J. Laplanche, J. B. Pontalis, 'Fantasy and the Origins of Sexuality', *The International Journal of Psychoanalysis* 49(1), 1968, pp. 1–18, p. 4.
112 P. Brook, *Reading for the Plot: Design and Intention in Narrative*. New York: A. A. Knopf, 1984, p. 277.
113 Ibid., p. 274.
114 Ibid., p. 278.
115 Idem.
116 Ibid., p. 280.
117 Ibid., p. 281.
118 Idem.
119 Ibid., p. 282.
120 J. Laplanche, J. B. Pontalis, 'Fantasy and the Origins of Sexuality', p. 9.
121 Idem.
122 Ibid., p. 5.
123 S. Ferenczi, 'Confusion of Tongues between Adults and the Child', p. 167.
124 J. Laplanche, J. B. Pontalis, 'Fantasy and the Origins of Sexuality', p. 5ff.
125 Ibid., p. 9.
126 S. Ferenczi, 'Confusion of Tongues between Adults and the Child', p. 165.
127 Ibid., p. 156.
128 Ibid., p. 159.
129 Ibid., p. 157f.
130 Ibid., p. 160.
131 Ferenczi to Freud, 25 December 1929, *The Correspondence of Sigmund Freud and Sándor Ferenczi*, Vol. 3, pp. 373–374.
132 A. E. Haynal, V. D. Haynal, 'Ferenczi's Attitude', p. 69.
133 S. Ferenczi, *The Clinical Diary of Sándor Ferenczi*, p. 212.
134 Freud to Eitingon, 20 October 1932, *Briefwechsel 1906–1939. Sigmund Freud und Max Eitingon*.
135 Eitingon to Freud, 10 August 1927, *Briefwechsel 1906–1939. Sigmund Freud und Max Eitingon*, p. 542.

[136] S. Ferenczi, 'The Adaptation of the Family to the Child' [1928], in: S. Ferenczi, *Final Contributions to the Problems and Methods of Psycho-Analysis*, pp. 61–76.
[137] R. Soreanu, 'The Psychic Life of Fragments: Splitting from Ferenczi to Klein', *The American Journal of Psychoanalysis* 78(4), 2018, pp. 421–444.
[138] S. Ferenczi, 'The Adaptation of the Family to the Child' [1928], p. 73.
[139] Freud to Eitingon, 3 November 1930, Freud to Eitingon, 26 August 1927, *Briefwechsel 1906–1939. Sigmund Freud und Max Eitingon*, p. 547.
[140] Ferenczi to Freud, 25 December 1929, *The Correspondence of Sigmund Freud and Sándor Ferenczi*, Vol. 3, p. 375.
[141] S. Ferenczi, 'The Elasticity of Psycho-Analytic Technique' [1928], in: S. Ferenczi, *Final Contributions to the Problems and Methods of Psycho-Analysis*, pp. 87–101; cf. F. Borgogno. 'Elasticity of Technique: The Psychoanalytic Project and the Trajectory of Ferenczi's Life', *The American Journal of Psychoanalysis* 61, 2001, pp. 391–407.
[142] Freud to Ferenczi, 17 January 1930, *The Correspondence of Sigmund Freud and Sándor Ferenczi*, Vol. 3, pp. 382–385.
[143] S. Freud, 'The Interpretation of Dreams (II)' [1900], in: S. Freud, *The Interpretation of Dreams (Second Part) and On Dreams* (1900–1901), SE 5, pp. 339–627, p. 525.
[144] Ferenczi to Freud, 8 September 1914, *The Correspondence of Sigmund Freud and Sándor Ferenczi*, Vol. 2, pp. 17–18.
[145] E. Falzeder, 'Dreaming of Freud: Ferenczi, Freud, and Analysis without End', in: E. Falzeder, *Psychoanalytic Filiations*. London, New York: Routledge, 2015.
[146] S. Freud, 'The Interpretation of Dreams (II)', p. 449; see also: C. E. Schorske, *Fin-de-siècle Vienna*, pp. 183, 193; J. Culler, 'Story and Discourse in the Analysis of Narration', in: J. Culler, *The Pursuit of Signs: Semiotics, Literature, Deconstruction*. London: Routledge & Kegan Paul, 1981, pp. 169–187; N. Abraham, M. Torok, *The Wolf Man's Magic Word: A Cryptonymy*, transl. by N. Rand. Minneapolis: University of Minnesota Press, 1986; G. Deleuze, F. Guattari, *What is Philosophy?*, pp. 95–96, from 'the cult of an origin' to the exploration of a 'milieu'; A. E. Haynal, V. D. Haynal, 'Ferenczi's Attitude', p. 69; É. Roudinesco, *Freud in His Time and Ours*, p. 100 about the Jewish environment, and p. 102, about Vienna as a 'Babel of voices'.
[147] J. Dupont, 'Freud's Analysis of Ferenczi as Revealed by Their Correspondence', *The International Journal of Psycho-Analysis* 75(2), 1994, pp. 301–320.
[148] S. Ferenczi, 'The Dream of the Occlusive Pessary', p. 304.
[149] Ibid., p. 304f.
[150] Ibid., p. 305.
[151] Idem.
[152] Idem.
[153] Ibid., p. 305f.
[154] Ibid., p. 307.
[155] Idem.

[156] S. Ferenczi, *The Clinical Diary of Sándor Ferenczi*, p. 41.
[157] Ibid., p. 42.
[158] S. Ferenczi, 'Confusion of Tongues between Adults and the Child', p. 164f.
[159] Ibid., p. 165.
[160] S. Ferenczi, *The Clinical Diary of Sándor Ferenczi*, p. 41.
[161] Ibid., pp. 41–42.
[162] Ibid., p. 42.
[163] Idem.
[164] Ibid., p. 39.
[165] J. Lacan, *The Four Fundamental Concepts of Psychoanalysis*, p. 128f.
[166] Ibid., p. 68.
[167] S. Freud, 'The Interpretation of Dreams (II)', p. 453.
[168] Ibid., p. 452.
[169] Ibid., p. 453.
[170] Ibid., p. 454.
[171] Ibid., p. 454f.
[172] Ibid., p. 455.
[173] S. Ferenczi, *The Clinical Diary of Sándor Ferenczi*, p. xvi.
[174] J. Lacan, *The Four Fundamental Concepts of Psychoanalysis*, p. 128.
[175] M. Foucault, *Psychiatric Power: Lectures at the Collège de France, 1973–1974*, ed. by J. Lagrange, transl. by G. Burchell. Basingstoke: Palgrave, 2006, pp. 133–139, 304, 322f.

'Too much of the father':
A Schreberian Pre-History

RESPONSE

to Jakob Staberg, by Jenny Willner

While preparing this volume – *On Trauma and Catastrophe* – we came to notice that the first chapter of our book does not contain the word 'catastrophe' at all. In Jakob Staberg's reading, the relation between text and disaster is of a different kind: the realm of the catastrophic structures the textual approach from within; it forms the perspective. Staberg's essay is microscopic in its reading, and yet its approach may also be described as hovering over multiple scenes of destruction, taking on a broad angle, searching the ruins and the rubble for what may be of use in drafting a non-phallic concept of psychoanalysis. The ramified reconstruction of the dynamic between Freud and Ferenczi forces us to pay attention in at least two different directions. On the one hand, their last encounter serves as a prism for observing different conflicts of authority within the early psychoanalytic movement. On the other hand, the genealogy of psychoanalysis unfolds against the background of the outside world: an antisemitic, patriarchal, fervently nationalist, homophobic milieu in the wake of fascism.

The transferential dimension of both personal letters and psychoanalytic literature is crucial for Staberg's approach. While both Freud and Ferenczi theorise projective dynamics, they are by no means immune against their force. They become bound up in what Staberg discusses in terms of a secret hysterical content passed on like a hot potato between Ferenczi, Freud and Jung. Many scholars have emphasised how the notion of the 'effeminate', 'hysteric' and 'receptive' male during this time was strongly linked to antisemitic stereotypes.[1] Nobody wants to embody the effeminate hysteric in the long run, and there is a certain smug gratification in the passage from the memoirs of C. G. Jung, quoted by Staberg, where Jung describes carrying a fainted Sigmund Freud in his strong arms: 'I shall never forget the look he cast at me. In his weakness he looked at me as if I were his father'.[2] Staberg's chapter focusses on the stage in which Ferenczi got stuck permanently, as it were, with the role of the deranged hysteric, and was fixated in this function posthumously by his own former analysand Ernest Jones.³ In reconstructing this dynamic, Staberg draws upon both René Girard's notion of scapegoating⁴ and Ferenczi's own insistence to verbalise affects and energies that haunted the psychoanalytic movement: the constant need to handle the fantasy of paternal authority.

Of course, even this story has a pre-history. By only a few years, the constellation between Ferenczi and Freud was preceded by the homoerotically charged relation between Freud and the Berlin-based otolaryngologist Wilhelm Fließ. Of their correspondence (1887–1904) James Strachey once wrote in astonishment to Ernest Jones: 'It's really a complete instance of *folie à deux*, with Freud in the unexpected role of a hysterical partner to a paranoiac.'⁵ Lewis Aron and Karen Starr have argued that the correspondence between Freud and Ferenczi re-enacts the earlier constellation between Fließ and Freud in reversed roles: this time with Ferenczi as the hysteric and Freud as the paranoiac, in split complementarity.⁶ How far back can such chains be tracked? Perhaps we are in need of a theoretical fiction, a mythical primal scene of the chronically impending breakdown of the homosocial.

Staberg's chapter addresses the fact Ferenczi's work seems to be entangled with the processes by which he was excluded from the psychoanalytic community, as if he had become intimately, dangerously associated with the very phenomena he himself brought to the forefront. Deeply unsettling notions at the centre of Ferenczi's later theories – mimetic forms of defence such as 'identification with the aggressor' and 'ironic obedience'⁷ – seem to echo his own fate within the dynamics of the psychoanalytic milieu. The price Ferenczi paid for articulating a set of problems was that he came to embody these problems in the eyes of those who survived him. On the one hand, this was a disastrous dynamic: Ferenczi died in isolation in May 1933, not long after the break with Freud. On the other hand, these dynamics seem inseparable from the late theoretical fragments of his *Clinical Diary* (1932), the very writings our volume seeks to make fruitful within different critical and emancipatory discourses. What does it mean to enter such a grey zone between traumatic repetition and rebellion?

When Ferenczi is pushed into – or perhaps also manoeuvres himself into – the role of the psychotic, the hysteric or the otherwise failing son, we are confronted with an ambivalence which is difficult to bear. How can this traumatically charged material be handled, the suffering be acknowledged without reproducing the pathologising gestures linked to Ferenczi's exclusion from the psychoanalytic movement? And how can we at the same time avoid a romanticising idealisation, becoming part of a new cult centred around the former outsider? By reading theoretical and clinical writings as well as personal letters and diaries against a historical and political background, Staberg finds a nuanced mode of staying with the trouble with several different layers in mind, while breaking with the dynamics of scapegoating.

To further complicate the temporality of Freud's and Ferenczi's last encounter, I will continue on Staberg's path by discussing how the set of problems thematised by his chapter – crises of authority and masculinity, the secret hysterical content passed between Freud and Ferenczi, and the dynamic of scapegoating – resonates with their perhaps earliest conflict. I am thinking of what has been termed their 'primal fight'[8] in the summer of 1910. Ferenczi and Freud had travelled to Palermo together in order to write about Daniel Paul Schreber's *Memoirs of My Nervous Illness* (1903).[9] Schreber (1842–1911) was a former Saxonian judge and a psychiatric patient, whose worst fear was to be transformed into a female body left for sexual misuse and forsaken, left to rot.[10] An extreme tension between authority and masculinity on the one hand and the abject counterpart of these notions on the other can be sensed both in Schreber's memoirs and in the dynamics unfolding in the context of early psychoanalytic engagement with it.[11]

Schreber's *Memoirs* present a detailed account of his psychotic delusions, written in the sophisticated language of a lawyer and a Wilhelmine *Bildungsbürger* of highest education and status. Throughout the book, Schreber insists that he stands in connection with God by means of his severed nerves. We learn that his first symptoms escalated considerably when he became obsessed with the 'idea that it really must be rather pleasant to be a woman succumbing to intercourse'.[12] The pleasure of this thought is brief: soon Schreber comes consider himself the victim of a conspiracy led by his psychiatrist Dr Emil Flechsig and by God himself, who he believes is aiming to transform him, the former judge, into his personal whore, and into a body equipped with inferior Jewish inner organs. The world order is out of joint, but Schreber outsmarts his enemies by gaining insight into what he believes to be the true structure of the universe: a network of divine, nerve-like rays. Freud, in turn, recognises an uncanny structural resemblance between Schreber's psychotic theory of nerves and his own theory of the libido. He concludes his famous 'Psychoanalytic Notes on an Autobiographical Account of a Case of Paranoia' with a gesture of both self-irony and discomfort: 'it remains for the future to decide whether there is more delusion in my theory than I should like to admit, or whether there is more truth in Schreber's delusion than other people are as yet prepared to believe.'[13]

Travelling to Palermo with this highly charged material in 1910, Ferenczi, who would later express his longing for radical openness in his personal relation to Freud, had expected cooperation on equal terms. Instead, he found himself reduced to a secretary taking notes while his master Freud was dictating. In a letter to Groddeck, Ferenczi described the situation as follows:

> [H]e was too big for me, there was too much of the father [*zu viel vom Vater*]. As a result, on our very first working evening together in Palermo, when he wanted to work with me on the famous paranoia text (Schreber), and started to dictate something, I jumped up in a sudden rebellious outburst, exclaiming that this was no working together, dictating to me [*wenn er mir einfach diktiert*].[14]

Freud reacted to Ferenczi's outburst by withdrawing from him. During the rest of the stay in Palermo, he continued his work on the Schreber case alone, and wrote the following crushing assessment in a letter to C. G. Jung:

> My travelling companion is a dear fellow, but dreamy in a disturbing kind of way, and his attitude towards me is infantile. He never stops admiring me, which I don't like, and is probably sharply critical of me in his unconscious when I am taking it easy. He has been passive and receptive, letting everything be done for him like a woman, and I really haven't got enough homosexuality in me to accept him as one.[15]

The correspondences surrounding the Schreber case tend to act out precisely what is brought up through the psychoanalytic engagement with the *Memoirs*.[16] Freud links Schreber's symptoms to the homoerotic realm of the Oedipus complex: he assumes Schreber's father Dr Moritz Schreber to have been particularly fatherly and lovable.[17] Accordingly, Freud detects paternal incarnations everywhere: in Schreber's senior colleagues at court, in his psychiatrist Emil Flechsig, and in his persecutory image of God. When Freud here establishes a relation between repudiated homosexuality and paranoia, no closed door could ever have fended off Ferenczi's influence. This complex forms an early contribution to the theory of what Eve Kosofsky Sedgewick would later term 'homosocial desire',[18] the hidden binding element of heterosexual male bonding. Freud's reading culminates in the insight that Schreber's world has fallen apart, and 'the paranoiac builds it again, not more splendid, it is true, but at least so that he can once more live in it. He builds it up by the work of his delusions. *The delusional formation, which we take to be the pathological product, is in reality an attempt at recovery, a process of reconstruction.*'[19]

It is tempting to speculate what the theoretical reception of Schreber would have looked like had Ferenczi taken up more space. Within the psychoanalytic movement he was notorious for following his patients even into their psychotic delusions, thinking with their symptoms. His willingness to stretch the limits of psychoanalytic practice has been associated with his 'fascination with dangerous intimacy',[20] his interest in 'certain themes which have been seen as anxiety-provoking for Freudian psychoanalysis – thought transference, psychosis, homosexuality, and the seduction theory'.[21] Precisely such transferential fears and desires mark the point where Ferenczi's thought resonates most strongly with the Schreber material.

In discussing the psychoanalytic movement as a war machine, Staberg works with Gilles Deleuze. Indeed, there is a firm link between *Anti-Oedipus* and the Schreber case: Deleuze and Guattari celebrate Schreber as a schizo, a welcome counter-figure to the Freudian neurotic. While Elias Canetti in *Crowds and Power* indirectly but unmistakably compares Schreber to Hitler, rendering the paranoid Saxonian judge a prototype of a totalitarian leader,[22] Deleuze and Guattari read his *Memoirs* as an escape from the seductions of fascism. In Deleuze and Guattari, Schreber is the counter-cultural body: they locate a strong spirit of subversion even in his suffering. There are ongoing changes in Schreber's body, every limb and organ is painfully affected: his genitals, his heart, lungs and skeleton.[23] Occasionally, Schreber's intestines vanish: 'Food and drink taken simply poured into the abdominal cavity and into the thighs',[24] an image which serves as a source for Deleuze and Guattari's vision of a body without organs. Their brief but enthusiastic references to Schreber are written very much in the spirit of their account of Kafka's six-legged protagonist Gregor Samsa. They read both Schreber's *Memoirs* and Kafka's *Metamorphosis* as stories of an anti-Oedipal flight from the seductions of authoritarianism:

> Gregor becomes a cockroach not to flee his father but rather to find an escape where his father didn't know to find one, in order to flee the director, the business, and the bureaucrats, to reach that region where the voice no longer does anything but hum: 'Did you hear him? It was an animal's voice,' said the chief clerk.[25]

The celebratory enthusiasm of Deleuze and Guattari barely takes into account that the insect Gregor Samsa was brutally killed by his father, while Schreber lost his ability to speak and write before he died in an asylum. Is it possible to think theoretically and to write with nuance about deviant identifications and counter-cultural bodies without either reproducing the effects of stigmatisation or disavowing the suffering at stake? Staberg stays with the tensions and contradictions of the Ferenczi material. There is a sense of *Trauerspiel* to his chapter, Staberg is a rather benjaminean Deleuzian. With his approach, we are better equipped to address the dark side of what can nevertheless be most accurately described with the Deleuzian imagery of finding an escape.

In Freud's telling, drafted behind closed doors in Palermo while Ferenczi was longing outside, there is no recognition of the positive attraction femininity held for Daniel Paul Schreber. Deleuze and Guattari's reading makes excessive use of what Freud omits: when God's rays push their way into Schreber's intestines 'like a wedge',[26] it is a frightening experience, which Schreber nevertheless, over the course of several hundred pages, comes to affirm, together with the role of the Wandering Jew. Deleuze and Guattari, who oppose Freud's diagnosis of repressed homosexuality, happily declare: 'Judge Schreber has sunbeams in his ass. *A solar anus*. And rest assured that it works: Judge Schreber feels something, produces something, and is capable of explaining the process theoretically.'[27]

Among all the theological, scientific, literary, juridical and historical references in Schreber's *Memoirs*, the footnotes also contain some of his most intimate confessions: 'I had a female genital organ, although a poorly developed one, and in my body felt quickening the first signs of a human embryo [...]; in other words fertilization had occurred.'[28] Schreber describes the 'greatly increased feeling of voluptuousness'[29] as the result of 'female nerves' entering his body, although his 'whole sense of manliness and manly honor' rises up against it.[30] This is the masculine protest which Freud reflects upon with reference to Adler. A quite different perspective offers itself to us in passages of the *Memoirs* that remain unmentioned by Freud. Schreber's story culminates in the description of a beautiful autumn day with 'heavy morning mist on the Elbe' where the former judge affirms his female body through and through:

> During that time the signs of a transformation into a woman became so marked on my body, that I could no longer ignore the imminent goal at which the whole development was aiming. [...] Soul-voluptuousness had become so strong that I myself received the impression of a female body, first on my arms and hands, later on my legs, bosom, buttocks and other parts of my body.[31]

Along with the horrors and the suffering accounted for in the *Memoirs*, Schreber also describes the joy of producing a glamorous show for his inner eye: to 'make – in day-time or at night – Napoleon or Frederick the Great walk through my room, or the Emperor William I emerge from my wardrobe in full regalia',[32] 'to make the shape of the Matterhorn appear on the horizon',[33] and to lustfully picture himself 'standing in front of a mirror in the adjoining room in female attire [...]. The picturing of female buttocks on my body – *honi soit qui mal y pense* – has become such a habit that I do it almost automatically whenever I bend down.'[34] Despite the inner voices constantly abusing him – 'Fancy a person who was a *Senatspräsident* allowing himself to be f….d'[35] – Schreber proudly declares: 'I have wholeheartedly inscribed the cultivation of femininity on my banner [...]. I would like to meet a man who, faced with the choice of either becoming a demented human being in male habitus or a spirited woman, would not prefer the latter. Such and *only such* is the issue for me.'[36]

These aspects leave no trace in Freud's account.[37] Nevertheless, Freud's androcentric reading does have its advantages: it goes in line with his most famous case studies, which Staberg describes as re-interpretations of masculinity in the age of mechanisation and militarisation. During the course of Staberg's chapter, the difference of the Ferenczian project is fleshed out: the role of the maternal function in his work. Staberg shows how Ferenczi's imagery of the female body stands in contrast to the rather phobic tendency in Freud. The set of queer dreams of reproduction, pregnancy, and maternity discussed by Staberg leads me to the question: how does Ferenczi's dream of playing with a child in front of his mother, to show her what motherhood should be like, relate to Schreber's dream of literally giving birth to new humans of Schreberian spirit? We know that Schreber's adopted daughter Fridoline told an interviewer that her adoptive father was 'more of a mother to me than my mother', so loving and kind.[38]

Ferenczi's theoretical writings can perhaps be read as a lifelong attempt to approach the very problems brought up already in the Schreber material. He keeps challenging Freud while insisting on an intense dialogue. Freud, in turn, repeats the gesture of closing the door, provoking ever more desperate attempts from his counterpart. While Ferenczi reproaches Freud for being 'too much' of a father, it would be hard to describe Ferenczi's own conduct without repeating the coinage 'too much'. Reading his correspondence with Freud is a painful, embarrassing, and fruitful experience, precisely because Freud's distancing is quite understandable too, considering Ferenczi's overt transferential desires, his lengthy unflattering self-diagnoses regarding everything from indigestion to erectile dysfunctions, not to speak of his letter to Freud about a dream in which Freud stands entirely naked before him.[39]

Looking back at the Palermo incident, Ferenczi admits: 'I did, perhaps, have an exaggerated idea of companionship between two men who tell each other the truth unrelentingly, sacrificing all consideration'.[40] Later, a dying man, withdrawing with his *Clinical Diary*, he drafts a theory of the psychic life of fragments which forces us to articulate a sense of escape, of neo-formation, of symptoms and of means of survival without minimising the realm of trauma and catastrophe.

Notes

[1] In psychiatry, there was a consensus according to which Jews were particularly prone to all neurotic diseases, particularly hysteria. S. L. Gilman, *Freud, Race, and Gender*. Princeton, NJ: Princeton UP, 1993, p. 235.
[2] C. G. Jung, A. Jaffé, *Memories, Dreams, Reflections*. London: Fontana, 1993, p. 189; cf. J. Staberg, Part 1, p. 47.
[3] E. Jones, *Sigmund Freud. Life and Work. Vol. III: The Last Phase 1919–1939*, pp. 34, 47, 188.
[4] R. Girard, *Le Bouc émissaire*. Paris: Grasset, 1983.
[5] Strachey to Jones, 24 October 1951, originally quoted in J. M. Masson, *Assault on Truth. Freud's Suppression of the Seduction Theory*. New York: Farrar, Straus and Giroux, 1984, p. 216; further discussed in D. Boyarin, *Unheroic Conduct. The Rise of Heterosexuality and the Invention of the Jewish Man*. Berkeley: University of California Press, 1997, p. 194. On Freud's early self-feminisation and the erotic dimension of the Freud–Fließ correspondence cf. Ibid., pp. 202–203, 220.
[6] L. Aron, K. Starr, 'Freud and Ferenczi: Wandering Jews in Palermo', in: S. Kuchuck, A. Harris (eds.), *The Legacy of Sándor Ferenczi*: From Ghost to Ancestor London, New York: Routledge, 2015, pp. 150–167, pp. 158–159.
[7] S. Ferenczi, *The Clinical Diary of Sándor Ferenczi*, ed. by J. Dupont, transl. by M. Bálint, N. Z. Jackson. Cambridge, Mass., London: Harvard UP, 1995, p. 19.
[8] L. Aron, K. Starr, 'Freud and Ferenczi. Wandering Jews in Palermo', p. 157. The quoted chapter is adapted from chapter 15 in a book by the same authors: L. Aron, K. Starr, *A Psychotherapy for the People: Toward a Progressive Psychoanalysis*. London, New York: Routledge, 2013. For yet another adaptation: L. Aron, K. Starr, 'Freud, Ferenczi, and the Case of Schreber: A Mutual Enactment of Homoerotic Longings, Homophobia, and Internalized Anti-Semitism', in: A. W. Rachmann (ed.), *The Origin of a Two-Person Psychology and Emphatic Perspective*. London, New York: Routledge, 2016, pp. 104–129. The subsequent reading will refer to the first-mentioned version.
[9] D. P. Schreber, *Memoirs of My Nervous Illness* [1903], ed. and transl. by I. Macalpine, R. A. Hunter. New York: New York Review of Books, 2000.

10   Ibid., p. 63.
11   E. L. Santner, *My Own Private Germany: Daniel Paul Schreber and the Secret History of Modernity*. Princeton, NJ: Princeton UP, 1996, p. 42. Cf. M. de Certeau, 'The Institution of Rot', in: D. Allison, P. de Oliveira, M. Roberts, A. Weiss (eds.), *Psychoanalysis and Identity. Toward a Post-Analytic View of the Schreber Case*. Albany: SUNY Press, 1988, pp. 88–100, pp. 91–92.
12   D. P. Schreber, *Memoirs of My Nervous Illness*, p. 46.
13   S. Freud, 'Psychoanalytic Notes on an Autobiographical Account of a Case of Paranoia' [1911], in: S. Freud, *Case History of Schreber, Papers on Technique and Other Works* (1911–1913), *SE* 12, pp. 1–79, p. 79. For a by now classical reading of Freud and Schreber which directs the attention from homophobia to more general issues of influence anxiety: E. L. Santner, *My Own Private Germany*, pp. 20–25.
14   Ferenczi to Groddeck, 25 December 1921, S. Ferenczi, G. Groddeck, *The Sándor Ferenczi–Georg Groddeck Correspondence*, ed. and transl. by C. Fortune. London: Open Gate Press, 2002, pp. 8–9. Cf. M. Giefer (ed.), *Briefwechsel Sándor Ferenczi–Georg Groddeck*. Frankfurt/M.: Stroemfeld, 2006, p. 53.
15   Freud to Jung, 24 September 1910, S. Freud, C. G. Jung, *The Freud-Jung Letters: The Correspondence Between Sigmund Freud and C. G. Jung*. Princeton, NJ: Princeton UP, 1994, p. 353.
16   E. L. Santner, *My Own Private Germany*, p. 19. The above summary is also indebted to the following accounts of the incident: L. Aron, K. Starr, 'Freud and Ferenczi. Wandering Jews in Palermo', p. 154; D. Boyarin, *Unheroic Conduct*; P. Thurschwell, *Literature, Technology, and Magical Thinking*. Cambridge: Cambridge UP, 2001, p. 133.
17   Quite in contrast, later approaches have focussed on Schreber's father as a sadistic perpetrator. W. Niederland, *Der Fall Schreber: Das psychoanalytische Profil einer paranoiden Persönlichkeit*. Frankfurt/M.: Suhrkamp, 1978; M. Schatzmann, *Soul Murder: Persecution in the Family*. New York: Random House, 1973.
18   E. Kosofsky Sedgewick, *Between Men: English Literature and Male Homosocial Desire*. New York: Columbia UP, 1985.
19   S. Freud, 'Psychoanalytic Notes on an Autobiographical Account of a Case of Paranoia', p. 71.
20   P. Thurschwell, *Literature, Technology, and Magical Thinking*, p. 119.
21   Idem.
22   E. Canetti, *Crowds and Power*, transl. by C. Stewart. New York: Continuum, 1984, on Schreber pp. 434–462.
23   D. P. Schreber, *Memoirs of My Nervous Illness*, pp. 142–145, 151.
24   Ibid., p. 144.
25   G. Deleuze, F. Guattari, *Kafka: Toward a Minor Literature*, transl. by D. Polan. Minneapolis: University of Minnesota Press, 1986, p. 13.
26   D. P. Schreber, *Memoirs of My Nervous Illness*, p. 146.

[27] G. Deleuze, F. Guattari, *Anti-Oedipus. Capitalism and Schizophrenia*, transl. by R. Hurley, M. Seem, H. L. Lane. London: Penguin Books, 2009, p. 2.
[28] Schreber, *Memoirs of My Nervous Illness*, pp. 17–18.
[29] Ibid., p. 59.
[30] Ibid., p. 64.
[31] Ibid., p. 163.
[32] Ibid., p. 212, fn.
[33] Ibid., p. 211.
[34] Ibid., p. 211.
[35] Ibid., p. 164.
[36] Ibid., pp. 164–165. In a similar manner, Schreber, whose *Memoirs* circulate the antisemitic imagery of the Bismarck era, in the end affirms his role as a Wandering Jew.
[37] A video installation currently on tour through exhibition halls and musems worldwide celebrates Schreberian femininity explicitly against the Freudian reading and from a contemporary point of view: El Palomar (=Mariokissme and R. Marcos Mota), *Schreber is a Woman,* 4K Video, 2-channel video installation, color, stereo, ca. 30 min, 2020/2021.
[38] R. Dinnage, 'Introduction', in: D. P. Schreber, *Memoirs of My Nervous Illness*, pp. xi–xxiv, p. xiii.
[39] Ferenczi to Freud, 3 October 1910, *The Correspondence of Sigmund Freud and Sándor Ferenczi*, Vol. 1, p. 218; discussed in P. Thurschwell, *Literature, Technology, and Magical Thinking*, p. 119.
[40] Ferenczi to Freud, 3 October 1910, *The Correspondence of Sigmund Freud and Sándor Ferenczi*, Vol. 1, pp. 217–218.

The Tactile Eye
and Queer Spectrality

RESPONSE

to Jakob Staberg, by Raluca Soreanu

I start from the 'tactile eye', which appears and re-appears in Jakob Staberg's writing as part of his genealogical method. What is important here for contemporary psychoanalysis is the capacity to see and touch – while circling or staying with the tactile eye – the possibilities of a milieu, which can unravel in the present and can generate the shape of psychoanalytic futures. As I ponder on the tactile eye, I believe this reading of a missed encounter promises a *queering* of psychoanalytic history and theory. Queer operates at its most political as an *activity* and not as a *noun*. Queer is thus always an intervention, an interruption, a transformational process. This is important because it allows us to invent new ways of thinking about relationality, about the many and beautiful forms in which a relation between two or several things can present itself to us.

How can psychoanalysis *queer itself* by learning to look more closely *at* itself in another temporality – or, with Jakob Staberg, by looking closely at the missed opportunities in the encounter between Ferenczi and Freud? We can here side with Caroline Dinshaw, who writes: 'I [focus] on the possibility of touching across time, collapsing time through affective contact between marginalised people now and then, and I suggested that with such queer historical touches we could form communities across time.'[1] Jakob Staberg unpacks the making of Ferenczi into a 'scapegoat', and this can help us traverse other exclusionary events and inclinations in the field of psychoanalysis. As the description of Ferenczi's and Freud's milieu thickens, I find myself wondering what the touch of this distant time of psychoanalysis can do to its present time. As we enter the different atmospheres of Ferenczi's and Freud's dreams, I find myself wishing to write psychoanalytic theory starting from Ferenczi's dreams.

In my dialogue with Jakob Staberg, I thus wish for a *queer spectrality*, for a moment when the affective force of the past can erupt into the present, speaking of a desire from another time and placing a demand on the present in the form of an ethical imperative. What would it mean to write a theory

RESPONSE to Jakob Staberg, by Raluca Soreanu

of sexuality starting from a landscape that is *beyond the phallus*? Queering our practice meets us here as an ethical imperative.

The 'tactile eye' thus brings another way of knowing, a tentacular exploration. Tentacles are neither fingers nor eyes. In her book *Staying with the Trouble*, feminist thinker Donna Haraway talks about a new tactile mode of knowledge: 'tentacular knowledge'.[2] She reminds us that 'tentacle' comes from the Latin *tentaculum,* which means 'feeler', and *tentare*, meaning 'to feel' and 'to try'. In this book, in our dialogues, Ferenczi emerges as 'tentacular' psychoanalyst and thinker: feeling, trying, experimenting, hesitating, advancing, retracting, revising.

Drawing on Donna Haraway's 'tentacular knowledges', anthropologist Eva Hayward coins the terms 'fingeryeyes'.[3] This starts from an attempt to make sense of an encounter between humans and corals in a bay in California, and it talks about a material-semiotic apparatus, an act of sensuous manifesting between species, between land and sea, between humans and others, perhaps between languages as well. The question that follows from here is a powerful one: 'How, for example, is this […] an arena where species meet not just as different critters, but also as objects and subjects of different sight, sense, sensibility, and sensuality?'[4] There is an investment in *difference*, in what an encounter (or even a missed encounter) can allow us to grasp. The haptic-optic 'fingeryeyes', this tentacular visuality, also carries a synaesthetic quality: senses are amalgamated, superimposed.

The 'tactile eye' brings me to a concept that is central to Ferenczi's theory of genitality, in a landscape that is *beyond the phallus*, and that I consider a de-Oedipalising intervention. Jakob Staberg was particularly attentive to such de-Oedipalising moments in Ferenczi's work. I am referring to Ferenczi's idea of *amphimixis of eroticisms*.[5] In 1924, in his book *Thalassa* (which Jenny Willner will stay with in the second part of this book), Ferenczi brings a striking metapsychological construction that can impact the way we think through different forms of relationality. His focus is not on component instincts, but on the outcome that they can lead to through their *encounter*, while understanding that this will not be a peaceful, harmonious, or conflict-free encounter. It may be a clash. Ferenczi talks about the fusion of different eroticisms, containing different pleasurable and painful experiences, with different object relations and forms of displacement, in a way which transcends any strictly *individual* horizon of reference. He names the fusion of eroticisms 'amphimixis' – a medical term that denotes the mingling of two substances, usually to create a third. In Greek, the prefix 'amphi-' means 'on two sides'. There is no unilinear, irreversible or progressive sexual development of the individual, but rather every act we might wish to analyse will be a mix of infantile, adult, oral, anal and genital components. This mix will be unique, and irreducible to these components. Amphimixis refers to individuals, but also to their *relations*. As I see it, amphimixis is at the heart of a radical revision of sexual theory.

> For what I described in physiological terms as a coordination of urethral and anal innervations may be expressed in the vocabulary of the sexual theory as a synthesis or an integration of anal and urethral erotisms into genital erotism. I may be permitted to emphasize this new conception by giving it a name of its own; let us term such a synthesis of two or more erotisms in a higher unity the *amphimixis* of erotisms or instinct-components.[6]

The consequences of this non-linear conception are profound. In *Thalassa*, we see a democratisation of forms of erotism. Ferenczi creatively de-centres the genital register; he displaces the primacy of the genital over the other component instincts. His language is 'horizontal', as he argues that: 'The genital would then no longer be the unique and incomparable magic wand which conjures erotisms from all the organs of the body; on the contrary genital amphimixis would merely be one particular instance out of the many in which such fusion of erotisms takes place'.[7] Genitality is read in *Thalassa* as a retrogression to the original striving of being immersed in the womb and its gratifications. But beyond the genital amphimixis, the psyche is capable of 'a clever combination of mechanisms of pleasure'.[8]

We enter a relational landscape, of complicated mixtures and transpositions of erotism. As I argue in the third part of the book, in terms of psychic forms that are imaginable with Ferenczi, at times it seems that an 'inter-species' relationship goes on *within* the same self or ego. The Other has already made it to our psychic life, and there are curious 'inter-forms' and fragments that attest to this Other-within. As I show in my chapter, both trauma/confusion and psychic repair take place *between* psychic registers.

A telling example that Ferenczi finds is that of synaesthesias,[9] which he does not cast as displacements or confusions, but he instead regards as a site for the amphimixis of eroticisms: 'synaesthesias […] in which the stimulation of a given sense organ is accompanied by the illusional stimulation of some other (*audition colorée, vision acoustique, audition odorée*, etc.) [coloured hearing, acoustic vision, olfactive hearing] supply evidence for the existence of mixtures of erotic trends'.[10] Jakob Staberg's 'tactile eye' is thus a method that follows the spirit of Ferenczi's text. Tentacular visuality is a mode of making theory where the senses are creatively amalgamated, so that the story told contains the atmospheres of the beginning of the twentieth century, but also letters, disparate notes, theoretical texts, boat journeys, gestures of turning away, sea creatures, silences, half-secrets, noisy quarrels, erotic passions, unfinished analyses, dreams of archaic mothers and inner growths, and father failures. To move across such amalgamations, fingeryeyes are needed. Or, in Laura Marks's words, the critic must 'make the dry words retain a trace of the wetness of encounter.'[11]

At the end of the first part of our book journey, my association is with a very early text by Ferenczi, which is in itself an inter-form: part object of dialogue with the medical establishment of the day, part theoretical intervention, part activist piece taking a stance in the defence of homosexuals. In 1905, in Budapest, the same year that Freud was writing his first version of the *Three Essays*, Sándor Ferenczi presents the text 'Intermediary Sexual States' in front of the Medical Association of Budapest.[12] At this time Ferenczi defines himself as a neurologist, and he has not yet met Freud. We do not have an English translation of this extraordinary text; we have Hungarian and French versions. It is worth noting that in the same year Ferenczi became the Budapest representative of the International Humanitarian Committee for the Defence of Homosexuals, created by the prominent Berlin sexologist Magnus Hirschfeld. He signed petitions calling for legal reforms around the criminalisation of homosexuality and he published the talk we are looking at here. (Freud expressed his sympathy for this Committee, but he did not wish to be associated with the initiatives for legal reform.)

In 1905 Ferenczi speaks to the medical establishment in the hope it would tolerate an intervention, an incision, a political breach, an activist statement in defence of a marginalised and oppressed group. As Ferenczi writes: 'According to Hirschfeld, himself backed up by eminent physicians, individuals do not all progress toward a determined masculine or feminine type. There exist in certain cases certain intermediary forms between the two sexes. In the psycho-physiological organisation of such individuals, the masculine and feminine traits are intermixed.'[13]

The theoretical intervention is also remarkable. To keep to Jakob Staberg's terms, it seems that Ferenczi is speaking from a place beyond the phallus. This place can be discerned already in 1905, before his encounter with Freud. Ferenczi differentiates between *primary sexual traits* (genitals, which he analyses as fundamentally hermaphroditic in nature since the first days of embryonic life); *secondary sexual traits* (gained by bodies in puberty, but occurring in surprising mixes); and, remarkably, *tertiary sexual traits*, or *the psychological character*. This tertiary category involves, on the one hand, the subjective, lived, phantasised experiencing of both primary sexual traits and secondary sexual traits (or, we might say, *'lived' gender*); and sexual attraction, love (or, we might say, with Freud, *object choice*).[14] Although he does place a male and a female character as two types of this tertiary layer, again, remarkably, a study of many cases show us an extreme *variety* of intermediary states, more or less feminine men and more or less masculine women, where the individual's sexual being results from a *modulation* of primary, secondary and tertiary sexual traits. What Ferenczi writes is an anticipation of Patricia Gherovici's succinct formulation on sexual difference: sex needs to be symbolised, while gender needs to be embodied.[15]

Ferenczi also brings in support of his thesis on tertiary sexual traits a letter written by a transvestite, who describes the (voluptuous but also ordinary) experience of wearing women's clothes, also making a case that the transvestite's seduction of their object of love is in effect and if seen from close no different from the seduction of a man by a woman. There is nothing outrageous about it. Ferenczi's 'tactile eye' on this letter is a moment of queer spectrality: a moment when the affective force of the past erupts into the present, speaking of a desire from another time and placing a demand on the present in the form of an ethical imperative. How to write a new theory of sexuality beyond the phallus? How to dismantle all-powerful fathers, including in the work of our dreams?

Notes

[1] C. Dinshaw, L. Edelman, R. A. Ferguson, C. Freccero, E. Freeman, J. Halberstam, A. Jagose, C. Nealon, T. H. Nguyen, 'Theorizing Queer Temporalities: A Roundtable Discussion', *GLQ: A Journal of Lesbian and Gay Studies* 13(2), 2007, pp. 177–195.

[2] D. J. Haraway, *Staying with the Trouble: Making Kin in the Chthulucene*. Durham: Duke UP, 2016, p. 30.

[3] E. Hayward, 'Fingeryeyes: Impressions of Cup Corals', *Cultural Anthropology* 25(4), 2010, pp. 577–599.

[4] Ibid., p. 580.

[5] S. Ferenczi, *Thalassa. A Theory of Genitality* [1924], transl. by H. A. Bunker. London, New York: Karnac, 1989.

[6] Ibid., p. 9.

[7] Ibid., p. 12.

[8] Idem.

[9] Ibid., p. 14.

[10] Idem.

[11] L. Marks, *Touch: Sensuous Theory and Multisensory Media*. Minneapolis: University of Minnesota Press, 2002, p. x.

[12] S. Ferenczi, 'États sexuels intermédiaires' [Intermediary Sexual States] [1905], in: S. Ferenczi, *Les écrits de Budapest* [The Budapest Writings]. Paris: EPEL, 1994, pp. 243–255.
[13] S. Ferenczi, 'États sexuels intermédiaires', p. 244, my translation.
[14] Idem.
[15] P. Gherovici, 'Botched Bodies: Inventing Gender and Constructing Sex', in: V. Tsolas, C. Anzieu-Premmereur (eds.), *A Psychoanalytic Exploration of the Body in Today's World*. London, New York: Routledge, 2017, pp. 159–173.

PART 2
Catastrophes and Genitality
Ferenczi's *Thalassa*
and the Politics of Bioanalysis

by Jenny Willner,
with responses from Raluca Soreanu and Jakob Staberg

Catastrophes and Genitality
Ferenczi's *Thalassa* and the Politics of Bioanalysis

Jenny Willner

In a letter to Freud in the spring of 1915, Ferenczi mentions witnessing young soldiers celebrating the eve of departure to the front: 'Things were very jolly; no trace of the fear of death, everybody sang and danced, everybody volunteered to go'.[1] Such were the scenes in the beginning of the First World War, during the final phase of the 'long 19th century',[2] which came to its end in the horrors of attrition warfare.[3] Since the autumn of 1914, Ferenczi had served as a chief medical officer to a squadron of Hussars, armed cavalry, in the small garrison town of Pápa in Transdanubia. Less than two years later, by then in charge of the section for nervous diseases at the Mária Váleria barrack hospital in Budapest, he was to be confronted with hundreds of victims of shell-shock and with the torturous faradisation treatments supported by several psychiatric colleagues.[4] During the beginning of the war he still had time on his hands, learned how to ride a horse and spent his 'leisure hours'[5] translating Freud's *Three Essays on the Theory of Sexuality* to Hungarian.

Imagine an officer dressed in uniform, surrounded by soldiers, and immersed in the essays in which Freud blended his clinical view on neurosis with metapsychology and blurred the line between sound sexuality and perversion, essays in which hysteria for a short period of time almost came to serve Freud as an anthropological paradigm.[6]

Apart from being his translator, Ferenczi was Freud's friend, follower, for the time being his designated successor, and his patient. During the months in Pápa, via letters and sporadic visits, he attempted to continue his analysis with the founding father himself. Meanwhile he ended up drafting a little book, which was to be published ten years later as *Versuch einer Genitaltheorie*,[7] the attempt of a theory of genitality. In most languages, the book is known as *Thalassa*, named after an assumed regressive trend or gravity, 'die Idee vom "thalassalen Regressionszuge"'.[8] According to Ferenczi's bold hypothesis, all land-living creatures long for earlier, aquatic forms of life. Caught up in complicated detours, they unknowingly strive to restore 'the lost mode of life in a moist milieu'.[9]

Thalassa has been termed 'the silent partner'[10] of Freud's 'Beyond the Pleasure Principle'.[11] It has further been characterised as a masterpiece of ambivalence in relation to Freud, a cumbersome piece of theory where Ferenczi's submission to Freud goes hand in hand with the beginning of a rebellious approach: according to Carlo Bonomi, Ferenczi's theory of genitality is a mockery of Freud's theory of sexuality, exaggerated up until absurdity and deconstructed from within.[12] While Freud's *Three Essays* explain how the sexual development culminates in the primacy of the genital zone, Ferenczi declares his own ambition to 'conform a more definite conception of the meaning [*Sinn*] and biological purpose [*biologischen Zweck*] of the achieving of this primacy'.[13] To put it bluntly, Ferenczi ends up theorising not only genitality, but the genitals themselves. With the morphology of organs as a point of departure, he performs a staggering act of speculation through time and space. The Hungarian title of *Thalassa* is *Katasztrófák*, and indeed Ferenczi considers the act coitus a 'belated abreaction, of not alone an ontogenetic but also a phylogenetic catastrophe.'[14]

In *Thalassa*, a series of catastrophic scenes, situated beyond the realm of empirical approach, form the framework for scrutinising organs in a different light, under the condition of post-catastrophic survival. There are wishes at play in this narrative, but despite Ferenczi's affirmative references to Jean-Baptiste Lamarck, they have little to do with the Lamarckist notion of *besoin*: in *Thalassa*, there is no longing for perfection or domination; rather, the longing is directed backwards and can only be speculatively derived from the somatic reaction formations it has caused. The evolutionary genealogy of the uterus is thus not to be thought of as the result of higher development, but as the melancholic introjection of the lost sea.[15] The penis, in turn, expresses the agony of a fish thrown up on land: it 'enacts [...] the struggles of that primal creature among its ancestors which suffered the great catastrophe of the drying up of the sea.'[16]

Are we to take this seriously? Ferenczi seems to have inserted a disclaimer: 'it is certainly no disgrace if one goes astray in making such flights into the unknown. At the worst, one will have set up a warning post on the road one has traversed which will save others from similarly going wrong.'[17] As Ilse Grubrich-Simitis has pointed out, biological speculation served both Ferenczi and Freud as an experimental field, a site for pursuing a series of unresolved questions in a playful manner, far from the public eye.[18] The issue at stake, according to Grubrich-Simitis, was how to connect the trauma model of Freud's early seduction theory with the theory of the unconscious wish.[19] And indeed, references to Freud's divergent theories of hysteria are crucial for Ferenczi's genital theory.[20]

The following reading discusses Ferenczi's oceanic fantasia against the background of the closing decade of Wilhelmine Germany and the Habsburg monarchy. *Thalassa* holds an eccentric position within the conflict of scientific and political perspectives over evolutionary descent during these years. Far from simply leaning on popular Darwinism and post-Lamarckian theory to fortify the psychoanalytic paradigm, Ferenczi intervenes in these discourses. He precludes the notion of an uncontaminated origin or descent and defamiliarises popular concepts of progression and potency, origins and futures. According to *Thalassa*, organs develop throughout evolutionary time, not on the way towards – or falling short of – completion, but through displacements and responding to traumas that evade capture through observation of the historical record alone. Before exploring Ferenczi's hysteric organology in further detail, we need to take a closer look at his surroundings in the garrison town of Pápa at the beginning of the First World War.

Freud's Theory of Sexuality Meets Popular Darwinism in a Soldiers' Library

Freud's *Three Essays on the Theory of Sexuality* were not the only source of intellectual nourishment at Ferenczi's disposal in Pápa. While translating Freud's theoretical manifesto, he read what the small soldiers' library had to offer. Looking back in his introduction to *Thalassa*, written in 1923, he mentions works of zoology, biology and evolutionary theory: 'the fine Zoology of Hesse and Doflein, and one work each of Lamarck, Darwin, Haeckel, Bölsche, Lloyd Morgan, Godlewsky, H. Hertwig, Piéron and Trömner'.[21] What may appear as an odd field of specialisation for a soldiers' library in fact goes back to the broad political ambition to catapult Hungary into the epoch of enlightenment, among other measures by providing small libraries with popular scientific literature.[22]

Freud and Ferenczi's engagement with nineteenth-century biology has often been read as a futile attempt to provide psychoanalysis with a natural scientific foundation,[23] and indeed Ferenczi's *Thalassa* works with a series of notions from this field. *Thalassa* culminates in a table of two columns and five rows, according to which physiological phenomena in the development of the individual stand in a complex relation to five major catastrophes in the prehistoric past of our species. In this chart, the origin of organic life is enlisted as the primal catastrophe, followed by further disasters such as the 'Recession of the ocean', 'Ice ages' and 'The Coming of Man'. In the second column these catastrophes are echoed at level of the individual: the maturation of germ cells, fertilisation, embryonal development, birth, the development of the primacy of the genital zone and the latency period (fig. 1).

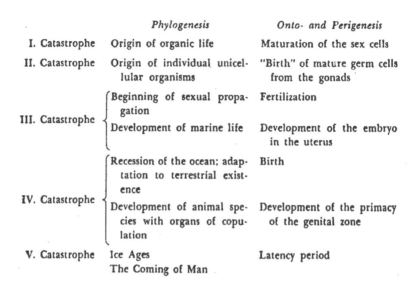

Figure 1: Ferenczi, Thalassa, p. 69.

The headers of the two columns correspond with one of the main sources in the soldiers' library: it was Ernst Haeckel (1834–1919), the highly influential German zoologist and marine biologist, who coined the terms 'phylogenesis', 'ontogenesis' and 'perigenesis'.[24] According to Haeckel's theory of recapitulation, the development of the human embryo recapitulates the evolutionary history of the species: ontogeny (the development of the individual) recapitulates phylogeny (the development of the species). Haeckel himself considered this a basic biogenetic law ('*biogenetisches Grundgesetz*').

Haeckel became famous above all for popularising the work of Charles Darwin in Germany, overcoming the resistances against evolutionary theory by presenting Darwin as the true successor of Goethe. Since the 1860s, Haeckel promoted a version of 'Darwinism' which was not at all – as later in the tradition of August Weismann – seen in opposition to Lamarckism. Haeckel embedded his Darwinism in what he termed a monist world view (*monistische Weltanschauung*): he believed in a seamless continuum of life forms from single-cell beings up until the expressions of human culture and civilisation. Haeckel's psychophysical monism is biologistic in the narrowest sense of this term: all matters of the soul, of society, and of culture are viewed as direct extensions of evolutionary history, which Haeckel conceived of as an inherently progressive process.[25] In a famous speech delivered in Stettin in 1863, he spoke of a 'natural law [...] of progressive development' and a 'continual process of perfection', which, as he argued, also applied to society as a consequence of natural selection's 'war of all against all'.[26] This thought is at the core of his later books: *Generelle Morphologie der Organismen* (1866), *Natürliche Schöpfungsgeschichte* (1868), *Anthropogenie* (1874), and *Die Welträthsel* (1899), to mention but a few.

To highlight another author from Ferenczi's reading list, the popular bestsellers of Wilhelm Bölsche were almost equally formative for the generation that went to war in 1914. Bölsche, a follower of Haeckel, presented a literary account of Haeckelianism, which has been termed 'erotic monism'.[27] Bölsche's *Love-Life in Nature* (1898–1903), a three-volume work of popular scientific prose, is a particularly important intertext for Ferenczi's *Thalassa*. Across hundreds of pages of graphically described pre-human mating acts, Bölsche strives to make the evolutionary history of man both graspable and enjoyable. In his lectures, Freud mentions these volumes as an illustration for how the stages of libido recapitulate pre-human stages of sexuality: 'Among animals one can find, so to speak in petrified form, every species of perversion of the sexual organization.'[28]

Freud's developmental conception of the human psyche has often been said to draw upon a 'strong and literal version'[29] of Haeckel's phylogenetic parallel.[30] Indeed, Haeckel's theory of recapitulation prefigures the much debated parallelisation between infantile psychosexual stages and the early developmental stages of humanity. Haeckelian thought also comes into play when Freud, in 'Beyond the Pleasure Principle', refers to 'embryology, in its capacity as a recapitulation of developmental history'.[31] Such famous references by Freud must however be viewed above all against the background of his intense cooperation with Ferenczi, particularly between around 1913 and 1924, when they worked together on a project they alternatively termed 'metabiology', 'deep biology', the 'Lamarck project', and 'bioanalysis'.[32] While Ferenczi's *Thalassa* can be considered the main opus of bioanalysis, this pursuit can also be traced along fragments and throughout his correspondence with Freud.[33] It has further left its mark wherever either of them speculates over inherited memories from the archaic history of the human species, from Freud's *Totem and Taboo* (1913) to his last major work, *Moses and Monotheism* (1939).[34]

As I will argue, the psychoanalytic use of Haeckel's phylogenetic parallel cannot be sufficiently described merely in terms of influence. While Haeckel's writings form a burdened legacy from the 19th century, bioanalysis must rather be seen as a way of working through this politically charged natural-scientific heritage. Restricting ourselves to the question of Haeckel's *influence* on Freud and Ferenczi would lead to an impasse where only two different conclusions seem possible: to either miss the point by joining Frank Sulloway in declaring

Freud and Ferenczi 'biologists of the mind',[35] or to miss the point by defensively replying that this may be true for the phylogenetic parallel, but that the relevance of psychoanalytic theory lies elsewhere, far from the embarrassing aberrations of biological speculation.

A different approach is possible, but it demands a careful reading. Stephen Gould was one of the first to prominently misread, when he claimed that Ferenczi in *Thalassa* stated 'his desire to import biological conclusions into psychology, particularly Haeckel's version of evolutionary theory'.[36] As a matter of fact, Ferenczi describes a transfer in the opposite direction: 'For I have taken purely psychological concepts, such as repression, symbol formation and the like, and simply transferred them to organic phenomena'.[37] The importance of this idea cannot be overstated: while biologism lies at the core of Haeckel's writings, the tendency to radically reverse biologism is formative for the bioanalytical project.[38] In *Thalassa*, Ferenczi delivers the most elaborate reflection on the method in question: he defines bioanalysis as a speculative science that would 'carry over into the field of the natural sciences in a systematic manner the knowledge gained and the technique used by psychoanalysis'.[39] In other words, Ferenczi does not apply an outdated popular biology to psychoanalysis, but rather subjects the popular biological discourse to a psychoanalytic reading. What can be the outcome of such a wild strategy and why should we engage with it?

While Haeckel's theory of recapitulation was the subject of a widespread obsession in *fin-de-siècle* culture, everything related to the phylogenetic parallel has become somewhat of a source of embarrassment for later psychoanalytic theory. There are good reasons for this discomfort. In 1905, both Haeckel and Bölsche were founding members of the German Society for Racial Hygiene.[40] They remained active in the eugenic movement, which was political from the start, although 'by no means exclusively identified with any one branch of middle-class politics any more than the widely popular theories of race in which it was implicit',[41] and this dimension cannot be isolated from their popular work. Looking back, the contrast between *Thalassa* and its sources from popular biology sheds a light on the fantasies that form both the delusion of biological supremacy and the inextricably entangled fear of degeneration.

Neither Haeckel nor Bölsche can be easily located on a scale between the emancipatory forces and the political dangers of the beginning of the twentieth century. Any involvement with their texts demands from us to face the catastrophic dimension of their popularity. When Ferenczi drafted *Thalassa*, surrounded by war enthusiasm, Haeckel was already deemed outdated within academic biology. Regarding his more far-reaching political influence, the debates about his legacy remain controversial until today.[42] In the early 20th century his work had become a source not only for Social Darwinism in the tradition of economic liberalism, but also, much to his own frustration,[43] for determinist socialism in the evolutionist tradition of Karl Kautsky. Kautsky identified the 'laws of history' with the 'laws of science' and had a formative influence on the Social Democratic movement.[44] Apart from such questions of political reception, Haeckel's writings were embedded in political discourse right from the start: the Franco-German War and the founding of the German Empire had a formative effect not only on the language of bacteriology and immunology but also on the German-language reception of evolutionary theory.[45] In 1914, while Ferenczi used the soldiers' library, this semantic transfer was taking place in both directions: the war itself was rationalised biologistically, with elderly Ernst Haeckel at the forefront.[46]

Bölsche, quite in contrast to Haeckel, considered himself a leftist around 1900. His artistic circles in Friedrichshagen near Berlin were mocked as 'a Bölschewist paradise'.[47] His influence on progressive sexology has been thoroughly documented:[48] both his transgressive style of writing and his affirmative approach towards much of what was deemed perverse runs counter to the repressive Wilhelmine body imagery and to fascist ideals. And yet Bölsche, who lived until 1939, came to consider National Socialism a late confirmation of his own lifelong work.[49]

There is no straight line leading from Haeckel and Bölsche to fascism; reading their work we enter a grey zone. Nevertheless, it can safely be stated that fantasies of racial superiority and inferiority are inextricably entangled with their world view.[50] What is truly remarkable is how the biological speculation in Ferenczi and Freud demarcates itself from this complex – while avoiding any obviously politically charged terms. At a time when evolutionary theory begins to inform eugenicist projects, Ferenczi sets out to rewrite the terms of an entire discourse, while using concepts drawn from the psychoanalytic study of hysteria.

What renders reading *Thalassa* both difficult and fruitful is that the entire material at stake is affectively charged. Pamela Thurschwell has demonstrated how Haeckel's phylogenetic parallel resonated strongly with the transferential fears and desires of his epoch. She also underlines that Freud and Ferenczi's idea of a psychic inheritance of the ancestor's experience tends to insert something ghostly into the social.[51] The role of biology is indeed ghostly, organic life can never be captured and neutrally represented by our categories, it haunts them. And yet, what is at stake here is far more than orgcanic life as the subject matter of biology: what is at stake are notions such as vitality, mastery, and progress in the libidinally charged grey zone between biological discourses and politics. There is a libidinal investment that can be sensed already in Haeckel. It is spelled out overtly in Bölsche's 'erotic monism' and re-interpreted in connection to trauma in Ferenczi's *Thalassa*.

This unfamiliar framing of *Thalassa* allows us to articulate the progressive optimism of Haeckel and Bölsche as part of a catastrophic scenario. In doing so, we foreground our present historical perspective towards the past, a perspective formed by events which neither Freud nor Ferenczi could have known of. This chapter is in other words not to be understood as an attempt to uncover Ferenczi's true original intention. Neither Ferenczi nor Freud could have predicted the extent of genocidal violence that was to be rationalised by evolutionary discourses in the years to come, and there is no evidence to support the claim that Ferenczi would have decided to intervene against eugenicist traditions in general. And yet, to quote Michel Foucault, it is the 'political honour'[52] of psychoanalysis, beginning with Freud's break with the neuropsychiatry of the 1880s, to have formed a counter-model to the idea of hereditary degeneration. Freud and Ferenczi's bioanalysis is not an exception from, but a crucial part of the psychoanalytic pursuit to form a radically different perspective.

What was bioanalysis, what could it have been, and why should it be of any use today? Highlighting the differences rather than the continuities enables us to read Ferenczian bioanalysis as a counter-narrative to biologist discourse in the tradition of Haeckel. Having said this, it is not possible to detect explicit criticism in Ferenczi's reading: he passionately engages with the desires at play in Haeckel's and Bölsche's writings. Ferenczi's *Thalassa* is an elegy, not only for a forever-lost moist milieu, but in the face of the First World War also for the thoroughly scattered world view of progressive optimism and evolutionist enthusiasm. Far from relying on Haeckel as a foundation, Ferenczi's theory of genitality deconstructs precisely that which claims such a founding status. While Ferenczi's method contains a message, his explicit assertions pertaining to the nature of the drive can perhaps be taken with a grain of salt. Sea salt, of course.

The Fish-Orgy: Wilhelm Bölsche's Herrings and Ferenczi's Thalassa

Anyone who wants to understand the enthusiastic reception of Charles Darwin in German-language culture around 1900 should do what Ferenczi did in the soldiers' library: read Wilhelm Bölsche.[53] Published between 1898 and 1903, by 1927 the three volumes of *Love-Life in Nature* had reached 80,000 in copies in Germany alone, and were translated into several languages.[54] These books were equally present in literary salons, in workers' libraries and within the *Lebensreform* movement.[55] It is all the more striking that they have fallen into almost complete oblivion. To compensate for this perhaps symptomatic case of cultural amnesia I will quote extensively from the first volume. These are excerpts from the twenty-page-long 'fish-orgy' (*Fisch-Orgie*), written by Bölsche in the late 1890s, and read by Ferenczi during the early stages of the First World War:

> Do you hear the wind whistle and the waters splash? Norway. The sharp sea air plays with its salty breath and fish smell. […] It is the silvery glare of a many-headed living thing, that presses on, closer and closer. […] The herring draws near, united in millions [*Der Hering naht, zu Millionen vereint*]. […] The island of living fish extends five miles in length as well as breadth. […] Now here, now there, a single body flashes up, as if bluish-white flames played out of the excited, roaring element; as if the island wanted to discharge itself in volcanic convulsions [*in vulkanischen Zuckungen entladen*]. […]
>
> But the colossal mass of fish gets jammed [*staut sich*]. The closeness with which they are pressed and squeezed together suddenly releases the whole restrained voluptuousness of love in a form that like this massed tempest has something almost brutal, in any event something gigantic about it. Thick clouds of male seminal fluid pour through the briny flood [*Durch die Salzflut ergießen sich dichte Wolken männlicher Samenflüssigkeit*]; clouds that are so tremendous that the ocean becomes turbid far and wide, and the whole silver island of voluptuously agitated fish bathes and swims therein [*Wolken so gewaltig, daß der Ozean sich weithin trübt, daß die ganze Silberinsel wollüstig bewegter Fische darin badet, darin schwimmt*].
>
> […] A drama without its equal. / Procreation extended to a joint mass act [*Gesamtakt*], whose quivering and wild outpourings make the ocean swell and froth. Each individual conjointly swimming in the vital force of millions [*Lebenskraft von Millionen*], and giving and taking at the same general source [*allgemeinen Quell*].[56]

The herrings are but the beginning: the fish-orgy is followed by descriptions of copulating dinosaurs, marsupials and mammals, each mating act presented in graphic detail. We are introduced to the mammoth male 'afire with love', his 'glands begin to perspire';[57] another unforgettable protagonist is the crocodile, celebrated by Bölsche as the evolutionary inventor of the penis, which originates in a 'simple guttered plug at the crocodile's anus'; the crocodile is 'a wild fellow in the frenzy of love. It hurls its female roughly on her back and presses belly against belly.'[58]

Together with Paolo Mantegazza's *Fisiologia dell'amore* (1873–1886), Bölsche's books belonged to the first modern affirmative descriptions of sexual acts that were considered acceptable in bourgeois bookshelves.[59] In Freud's 'Fragment of an Analysis of a Case of Hysteria', the over-excitement of the young girl Dora is associated with her habit of reading 'Mantegazza's *Physiology of Love* and books of that sort in their house on the lake'.[60] With 'books of that sort' Freud's contemporaries will most certainly have associated Bölsche: when Dora spent her holiday by the lake with the K. family, the breakthrough of the first volume of *Love-Life in Nature* was already a fact. In 1903, a journal for gynaecology promoted the trilogy as compulsory reading for gynaecologists, to be recommended to adolescents from the age of fourteen.[61]

The popularity of these books – in terms of scientific enlightenment, sexual enlightenment and of crypto-pornography – raises a number of questions pertaining to social psychology. What renders these volumes so important as a document of their time is the way in which Bölsche articulates progressive optimism and evolutionist enthusiasm within the realm of the explicitly sexual. When he speaks of the 'rhythmotropism'[62] of organic life, he has an aesthetic principle in mind, however articulated in a context where the rhythm of copulation seems to be pushing development further, forwards and upwards, towards purification, technological progress, and victory.

This optimism is dialectically linked to a seemingly opposite tendency: in *Love-Life in Nature*, the copulatory scenes invite the reader to regress and chime in with so-called lower forms of life. 'Remember…', the narrator repeatedly murmurs, 'Remember…';[63] '*You* were grotesque creatures without a trace of your form. They crawled on the shore of the sea when this shore was still soft ooze, which to-day forms those adamantine ridges of rock, on which the blue waves break in foam.'[64] As it turns out, Bölsche refers not only to our ancestors at a phylogenetic level, but also to the previous form of life of each and every one of us at the level of ontogenesis:

> And after an interim of the many thousands of years since man first appeared on earth, […] a great, significant mystery manifests itself in the embryo that is just germinating, deep in the mother's womb. The embryo becomes a fish again, before it becomes man. In the dark maternal depths [*dunklen Muttertiefe*], where there is neither land nor sea, the gill-slits appear on the neck of the tiny delicate bud of the future man, the gill-slits by means of which the fish ingeniously separates the vital oxygen from its native element, water. The limbs, too, appear in the rounded form of fins. Once more the picture of the primordial fish

[*Bild des Urfisches*] arises, quivering in the haze; the primordial fish which, in the grey twilight of a passed age gave life to higher beings [*höheren Wesen*], who rose ever higher and higher, until at last man, like a new super-world [*Überwelt*], flamed out of their crown [...] ...

Thus, this wild, grotesque picture is connected also most intimately with you.[65]

Bölsche addresses the inner herring of each and every reader. By quoting him affirmatively in *Thalassa*, Ferenczi, who chose to accompany his suffering patients even into their psychotic hallucinations,[66] readily joins Bölsche in the regressive fantasy. He thinks with Bölsche's images and pushes the phylogenetic fantasy to the extreme. It is important to bear in mind that Bölsche's progressive optimism must have seemed naïve in retrospect, from the point of view of the ongoing war. And yet, Ferenczi's mode of reception in *Thalassa* is almost 'constitutively unsuspicious'[67]: he owns up to the enjoyment at work in Bölsche's volumes, as it were, and acknowledges the enjoyment of this untimely grand narrative. *Thalassa* does not deny the lost perverse pleasures and the reasons to mourn.

As a reader of 19th century biology, Ferenczi conjures the ghosts of our non-human past in specific anatomic detail. He links the appearance of rudimentary gill slits in the human embryo to creatures in the transitional stage between aquatic and terrestrial forms of life, quoting extensively from the twenty-fourth lecture of Ernst Haeckel's *Natürliche Schöpfungsgeschichte*. This is his source when he insists on our intimate relation to the 'peculiar genera of *Dipneusta* and *Protopteri*', the 'American lung fish (*Lepidosiren paradoxa*)' and the 'African mud-eel (*Protopterus annectens*)'.[68] Ferenczi particularly dwells upon the Australian lung fish (*Ceratodus forsteri*), discovered in 1870 and discussed by Haeckel in view of its habit of burying itself under leaves in the drying mud and breathing air during summer time, while living under water in puddles and swamps in the winter, using gills.[69] Haeckel ends the lecture in question by drawing a parallel between the development of the heart muscle in the human embryo and the development of the heart of the fish via the amphibian and the reptile to all warm-blooded mammals.[70]

Departing from Haeckel, Ferenczi takes the speculation even further, along with Bölsche – 'The uterus became the puddle of the salamander'[71] – and arrives at the apodictically stated conclusion that the human embryo is on the one hand entangled with amphibian ancestors, while on the other hand serving as a hidden *tertium comparationis* between sleep and coitus in fully grown human beings.[72] Not only is the act of coitus here understood as the attempt of the male genital organ to re-establish the intrauterine situation. Sleep too recapitulates the life form of both the embryo and our primitive ancestors. Ferenczi's arguments are both dizzying and strictly empirical: in sleep, the body temperature sinks, thereby approaching the state of poikilothermic amphibians. The tendency of the eyes of the human sleeper to rotate outwards and upwards is interpreted by Ferenczi as a return to 'the position of the eyes which obtains in animals without binocular vision (as for example the fishes)', while in the phenomenon of fainting he sees an approximation towards the lower state of blood pressure of a reptile.[73]

These examples may suffice to make us close Ferenczi's book forever, or simply to confirm his well-known foible for transgressive thought, a feature which Ernest Jones associated with 'latent psychotic trends',[74] and which indeed stands in relation to certain obsessions typical for the epoch. What matters most is, however, precisely *how* Ferenczi plays, almost toys around with the imagery of Haeckel and Bölsche.

A positive reason for Ferenczi to read and re-read the books in the soldiers' library is that Haeckel's Lamarckism foregrounds the soma, the living body subjected to sensations both from the outer world and from an unknown past.[75] The idea of a complex, and yet somehow tangible relationship between present bodies to the past is particularly important for Ferenczi's thought.[76] Another reason is of negative nature, related to a growing discomfort with the deeply rooted tendency to think of evolution in terms of intentionality, according to a teleology that remains intimately connected to fantasies of completion and fears of degeneracy. It is far more than a question of taste that Ferenczi consistently drops the language of progress that is so striking in Bölsche: 'rising up',[77] 'ever higher and higher', and '*neue Überwelt*'.[78] In *Thalassa*, evolution is not a triumph, but a tragedy, the untold history of unmourned losses, and a tale of survival that demands a new narrative. Indeed, the 'compulsion to repeat' and the notion of *Nachträglichkeit* introduce a different kind of temporality. These notions bring the old theory of recapitulation out of joint.

Weltanschauung: *Fetishistic Disavowal in Popular Darwinism*

In 'A Difficulty in the Path of Psycho-Analysis' (1917) Freud argued that the 'universal narcissism of men, their self-love' suffered three severe blows (*Kränkungen*, humiliations) from science: the cosmological humiliation associated with the Copernican turn, the biological humiliation associated with Darwin and the psychological humiliation, as it were, through Freud's own discovery of the unconscious.[79] The concept of a blow from biology is of obvious relevance for this context. The relation between human and non-human animals suddenly appears as too close for comfort. In her classic study on *Darwin's Plots*, Gillian Beer provides some poignant examples of how wounded anthropological narcissism manifested itself as disgust in Victorian culture:

> Many Victorian rejections of evolutionary ideas register a physical shudder. In its early readers one of the lurking fears it conjured was miscegeny – the frog in the bed – or what Ruskin called the 'filthy heraldries which record the relation of humanity to the ascidian and the crocodile'.[80]

In striking contrast to the Victorian scenario described by Beer, neither Haeckel nor Bölsche seem to shudder at the thought of our intimate bond with mud-eels or with frogs. The narrator in *Love-Life in Nature* bursts out in euphoria: 'Listen with rapt attention to this cooing and croaking of the frog chorus. From here on there was that too in the world which with you was to become the most wondrous human bond.'[81] How precisely does this celebratory mode relate to the phobic reaction? If the Victorian approach appears as defensive or even reactionary, should then Bölsche's affirmative gesture to embrace the frog, the swamp, and the creatures of the mud as our kin be considered emancipatory, or at least more at ease with man's modest place in nature, as it were?[82] Not necessarily.

The idea of a blow from biology goes far beyond the question of our attitude towards unsightly non-human creatures. It also addresses a more general structure in which organic life, even our own bodies generate surprising, haunting, disorientating effects. What we call biological inheritance and evolutionary development takes place within a scenario which we can never overview. The human subject, then, appears as a creature, not as a creator: as a point within systems, which are not products of human mastery, but rather function 'beyond or above the control of their participants'.[83] While celebrating the human bond with non-human creatures, Haeckel's evolutionary monism distracts the attention from this second aspect of the blow.

Haeckel presented his evolutionary monism as a manifestation of both progressive and epistemological optimism. While this explains the broad appeal of his popular world view, it is equally true that a certain defensiveness lies at the core of his entire edifice. His popularity seems to be built upon a libidinal economy that protects itself from a crisis that ought to have been suffered. Haeckel's and Bölsche's celebratory affirmation of non-human descent presents a particular mode of restorative defence against something that still needs to be spelled out. According to Gillian Beer, the Darwinian blow caused a narrative crisis, one of the greatest shocks resulting from formulations such as the following in *On the Origin of Species*:

> Judging from the past, we may safely infer that not one living species will transmit its unaltered likeness to a distant futurity. And of the other species now living very few will transmit progeny of any kind to a far distant futurity; for the manner in which all organic beings are grouped, shows that the greater number of species of each genus, and all the species of many genera, have left no descendants, but have become utterly extinct.[84]

Ever since Darwin, telling the story of organic life as a triumphant history of progress distracts the attention from a process of dying that exceeds the capacities of imagination. Darwin underlines that the number of living species today is vanishingly small in relation to those genera that have existed but faced extinction.[85] In the distant future, most existing species will not only be dead and gone, but a superlative thereof: 'utterly extinct'. According to the literary theorist Anselm Haverkamp, Darwin 'nearly proclaimed a "Beyond the Pleasure Principle"' – by calling 'extinction' by its name.[86] Quite in contrast, Haeckel's tendency to bypass death is a strategy of domestication. It manifests itself most obviously in Haeckel's later writing, where he extends the concept of the soul to crystals and all inorganic matter in the universe. Here, bios figures as an episode in 'the immeasurable history of Anorgon, of dead nature, as it is falsely called'.[87] By rendering even inorganic matter alive, Haeckel's world view circumvents the concept of death.

An epistemological crisis is part of the scenario as well: Darwin emphasised that the course of evolution can only be inferred through retrospective construction: as a brittle genealogy of the present, faced with the fact that most empirical material has been erased.[88] Only a fraction of all life forms have left fossils behind, and of these fossils, in turn, only a fraction are ever to be found, and if then only in fragmentary form. This constitutive obscurity, highlighted by Darwin through the fractures in his genealogical sketches, turned out to be the most fragile part of his legacy.[89]

In other words the cultural phenomenon of 'evolutionist enthusiasm',[90] most famously represented by Haeckel and Bölsche, only seemingly provides a reason to question the validity of the Darwinian blow as a paradigm.[91] At closer consideration, the popularity of Haeckelian 'Darwinism' confirms rather than confutes the thesis of a narcissist reaction. Celebratory affirmation does not rule out a prior humiliation, particularly not where evolutionist enthusiasm displays a resemblance to mania to a degree that brings the much later notion of an 'inability to mourn'[92] to mind. Haeckel and Bölsche characterised their work as popular scientific *Weltanschauung*. World view in this popular tradition bears the promise of a universal science in touch with intuition, emotion and sensual experience, knowledge attainable and graspable for the subject. It wards off the crisis of modernity insofar as it forms a forceful reaction against the process in which science was increasingly divorced from intuition, rendering 'nature' incomprehensible, less 'natural', as it were. If the literature of popular *Weltanschauung* around 1900 served as a defence against the forces of modernity such as alienation, crisis of language, crisis of power, and the diversification of sciences,[93] then the celebratory 'Darwinism' within this genre offers particularly attractive options for fetishistic disavowal.

From 1924 on, Freud came to use the term 'disavowal' (*Verleugnung*) for a mode of defence in which the subject fails to acknowledge the reality of a traumatic perception, of which castration or the absence of a penis in a girl is seen as a prototype.[94] Freud's understanding of fetishism is linked to this structure: the fetishist simultaneously disavows and acknowledges a traumatic lack.[95] To put it in more general terms, fetishism in the psychoanalytic sense of the term is linked to a loss or a lack that is simultaneously recognised and denied, acknowledged and disavowed. The satisfaction derives from the fact that the fetish represents the lack while keeping it conveniently out of sight. As a fetishistic evolutionary narrative, Bölsche's *Love-Life in Nature* claims to represent 'Darwinism' while simultaneously covering up the disorientating effects of the Darwinian blow.

A devotee of Haeckel's world view, Bölsche argued that the romantic notion of a unity of nature had been scientifically proven by Darwin. There is, however, a striking contrast between Darwin and Haeckel: while Darwin described evolution as a process in which change occurs over unimaginably long periods of time, exceeding the realm of subjective perception, Haeckel offered a manageable format by transforming an essentially disorienting concept into something graphical, clear and vivid, in German *anschaulich*, which implies much more than the term overviewable (*übersichtlich*). Haeckel's notorious chart of embryos in *Anthropogenie* (1874) is an example of this effect: it shows eight creatures in three stages of their embryonal development, their ontogenesis: on the left page a fish, an amphibian, a reptile and a bird; and on the right page four mammals: a pig, a cow, a rabbit and a human (fig. 2).

Jenny Willner

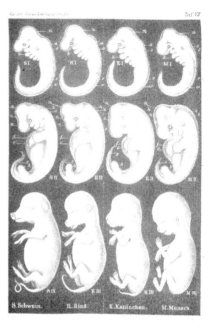

Figure 2: E. Haeckel, 'Vergleichung der Embryonen eines Fisches, eines Amphibiums, eines Reptils und eines Vogels auf drei verschiedenen Entwickelungsstufen' (left); 'Vergleichung der Embryonen von vier verschiedenen Säugetieren (Schwein, Rind, Kaninchen und Mensch) auf drei verschiedenen Entwickelungsstufen' (right), in: E. Haeckel: Anthropogenie oder Entwicklungsgeschichte des Menschen. Gemeinverständliche wissenschaftliche Vorgänge über die Grundzüge der menschlichen Keimes- und Stammes-Geschichte *[1874], Leipzig: Engelmann 1877, charts VI–VII (without pagination); cf. comment Ibid. p. 290.*

In order to observe these eight different creatures separately one would have to read Haeckel's chart vertically, in columns. When moving downwards, each of the columns show the ontogenetic development of one particular creature, under water, in the egg and in utero. Our occidental reading habits, however, make it more likely for us to proceed horisontally, in rows from the left to the right, producing a little flipchart before our inner eye. The lowest row then already implies what is spelled out explicitly by Bölsche: that every pregnant woman literally bears a fish inside her, that we all were all herrings in ontogeny as well.

'[O]ntogenesis [is] a short and rapid recapitulation of phylogenesis'.[96] By means of miniaturisation and acceleration, Haeckel enables his readers to perceive evolution – a process constitutively inaccessible to experience – within the span of an individual life. The womb becomes the site of a metamorphosis, and metamorphosis bypasses death.[97] Most importantly, Haeckel configures the mythically charged circular structure of recapitulation as an element of an upward movement,[98] until, according to Bölsche, 'at last man, like a new super-world',[99] flames out.

According to both Freud and Adorno, popular *Weltanschauung* is characterised by the boundless narcissism of a subject that claims to grasp the entire universe, as if the modern diversification of sciences had never taken place.[100] The catchword of Haeckelian evolutionary monism is 'All-Einheit', and Haeckel indeed framed his scientific world view as a substitute for religion. The libidinal appeal of this concept is related to what Freud calls the oceanic feeling. In 'Civilization and its Discontents' (1930) he links both religion and the transgressive fantasy of coalescence to infantile megalomania.[101] What may appear modest, the distinct feeling of closeness to nature and matter, reverts into omnipotence when the subject claims to grasp the entire universe. This leads us to the malign side of Bölsche, a dimension which has no counterpart in Ferenczi.

If we read Bölsche's *Love-Life in Nature* as a fetishistic evolutionary narrative in this sense, both scientific complexity and vulnerability are the wounding aspects at stake, and the fetish is linked to potency both in terms of efficacy or capability and of virility. The idea of an intimate connectedness with non-human animals promises participation in what is conceived of as uncontaminated natural potency. In *Love-Life in Nature*, the narrator envisions an invigorating repetition of life as a herring by means of 'primordial memory'[102] and suggests that our connection to pre-human ancestors can be reactivated for further empowerment and growth, against the looming threat of degeneration. The insistence on intimate participation with the entire copulating ancestral line altogether leaves the impression of an attempt to conjure a sense of physical force despite the fears of degeneration, alienation and nervousness that were typical for the epoch. Bölsche's celebration of procreation exposes the libidinous undertones of entire discourses: evolution, heredity, growth and, by extension, the realm of cultural progress.

> The social ideal! How it comes down to the gruesomely bright reality of our time, heaving, sweating, bleeding [*dampft, blutet, wogt*]! This, too, is in a last analysis but a question of love. […] It is latent [*angelegt*] in the fish that sexual love sifts out of the ocean, until like a silvery isle they rise in a mass from the waters, a community of birth-giving sexual creatures [*Gemeinschaft zeugender Geschlechtswesen*] for whom the narrow, shallow fjord is one large bridal bed.[103]

There is a notion of power (*Kraft*) at play here, for which it is essential to conceive of oneself as part of the animalistic herd. Bölsche derives his notion of 'the social' directly from biology. A fundamental aspect of Haeckelian monism manifests itself when Bölsche's image of the swarm passes smoothly via the herd into the image of a human crowd. Bölsche swims with the current of late nineteenth-century mass psychology, which derives human group behaviour directly from the herd instinct of animals. A common denominator between Bölsche and Gustave Le Bon lies in the biologist tradition formed precisely by Ernst Haeckel,[104] combined with the nineteenth-century notion of the unconscious seen as a mere prolongment of the spinal cord.

Having said this, Le Bon's conservatism goes along with a phobic attitude towards the crowds: they appear as threatening, closely associated with the looming danger of revolution and of a bio-social degradation of the nation.[105] Quite in contrast, Bölsche affirms the forces of the herd. The point is that this does not make his vision emancipatory. Bölsche's *Love-Life in Nature* sets off deep in the ocean, but the vision is directed upwards, towards the sky. In the fish-orgy, the euphoric affirmation of everything that threatens the borders of the subject merges seamlessly with the fantasy of being part of a larger, forceful unity:

> To-day you see it only as through a break in the clouds [*Riss in den Wolken*]. The new conception of the universe [*Weltanschauung*] is still in the making. It condenses, consolidates, and casts off rings, like a star in process of formation. Who can tell what bodies will some day circle around it and what will be its sun [*wer ihre Sonne werden wird*]?[106]

Who (*wer*) will become the sun of the crowd? In *Love-Life in Nature*, Bölsche still has the development of humanity as a whole in mind. Three decades later he will speak of Germans only.[107] Already in *Love-Life in Nature* the literary figuration of the swarm and herd structurally resembles the authoritarian crowd, waiting for a strong leader. In 1934, Bölsche fills the break in the clouds, the space left over in *Love-Life in Nature*, with Adolf Hitler, who appears unnamed as the greatest in a line-up of German geniuses:

> More powerfully than anywhere else, these persons go straight up through our German history. Where the great person sinks, the people appear to sink; where he suddenly appears between us, it is always as if the mists were torn again. What a personality, radiating through times, was Goethe, or Freiherr von Stein, Friedrich the Great, and Luther! I need

not to mention the name of which we are all thinking at the moment, and before which even the fiercest opponent must admit this miracle of personality.[108]

The escalatory line drawn here, from a libidinally charged description of a shoal of herrings to the crowd awaiting Hitler, is in itself catastrophic, perhaps even hysteric. Were the readers who enjoyed the fish-orgy already preparing themselves for participation in the Nazi crowds?

It is worthwhile dwelling at the fact that Bölsche blurs several categories of our social-psychological sensorium. *Love-Life in Nature* stages the overcoming of inhibition, a pathos directed against the repressive side of civilisation in general and of Wilhelmine society in particular. While it can easily be acknowledged that the Wilhelmine society was utterly repressive, the case of Bölsche demonstrates the limited usefulness of what Foucault called the repressive hypothesis as a theoretical tool. *Love-Life in Nature* defies the categories offered by thinkers such as Wilhelm Reich or Klaus Theweleit in his study of *Male Fantasies*, which revolves around the opposition between a militaristic, proto-fascist imagery of the body as opposed to everything feminine that floods its borders.[109] The appreciation of floods, swamps, and the dynamic capacities of matter is not in and of itself counterhegemonic.[110] Bölsche positions himself on the side of the critters – but that does by far not make him immune to the seduction of fascism.

A defender of liberated, orgiastic sexuality, a rebel against the inhibiting effects of civilisation, Bölsche insists that our connection with the animalistic swarms and herds can be grasped intuitively. He challenges the anthropocentric account – however in a way that is incompatible with any Deleuzian notion of becoming small. Bölsche's fish is bound for glory. Awaiting a future of healthy, strong men, the liberated humans in Bölsche's third volume follow the ideals of *Lebensreform*: they eat raw vegetables and exercise naked in the sun (*nackte Gymnastik*) to overcome the weakness of the cultured and prevent degeneration.[111] In the same spirit, Bölsche proposes that science should intervene into the processes of human procreation for the health of future strong generations – 'zum Heil immer gesünderer, kräftigerer, glücklicherer Generationen.'[112]

While eugenic thought as represented in the work of both Haeckel and Bölsche is typical for a much broader tendency at the time, it is striking that *Thalassa*, despite entering Bölsche's marine world, moves against the current. Ferenczi remains consistent with his statement from 1909, according to which psychoanalysis is never to be used as a prolongment of natural selection:

> Psycho-analysis wishes to individualise, while Nature disdains this; analysis aims at making capable for life and action persons who have been ruined by the summary repression-procedure of that Nature who does not concern herself with the weakly individual being.[113]

In an epoch marked by the fear of degeneration, psychoanalysis entertains a sympathetic relation to neurotics and hysterics. Bioanalysis takes this tendency even further: as an eccentric experimental field of psychoanalytic theory, bioanalysis inserts the dynamics of neurosis and hysteria into the evolutionary narrative.

Neurotic Evolution: Bioanalysis vs. Biologism

At this point it should have become obvious that bioanalysis can hardly be charged for being biologistic. While the derogatory term 'biologism' refers to the application of biological standards and terms to psychology and society, *Thalassa*, methodically speaking, does the opposite. Ferenczi does not apply biology to psychoanalysis; rather, he applies psychoanalytic terms to biology. If *Thalassa* is grandiose, it is because Ferenczi, as opposed to elevating the laws of biology to a world principle, actually claims the interpretational sovereignty of psychoanalysis over natural sciences. In *Thalassa*, psychoanalytic notions are the models, 'Vorbilder', at stake:

> I believe that as prototypes [*Vorbilder*] of bioanalytic mechanisms the structure of the neuroses and psychoses, with which we are best acquainted, will always serve.[114]

Ferenczi's drastic reframing of organic phenomena by means of psychoanalytic notions forms a link between *Thalassa* and Freud's speculation on the primitive cell in 'Beyond the Pleasure Principle'. In Freud, we find a similar defamiliarisation of popular evolutionary narratives:[115]

> The processes involved in the formation of a neurotic phobia, which is nothing else than an attempt at flight from the satisfaction of an instinct, present us with a model [*Vorbild*] of the manner of origin of this supposititious 'instinct towards perfection'[.][116]

In 'Beyond the Pleasure Principle', Freud pictures 'a living organism in its most simplified possible form'[117] as a creature that would, to quote Bartleby, 'prefer not to'.[118] This stands in contrast to the ideologically charged notion of an instinct toward completion. In Freud, a disturbance from the outside sets in motion a dynamic which is 'bound to give a deceptive appearance of being forces tending towards change and progress'.[119] The burdensome life-path of Freud's primitive organism consists of 'ever more complicated *détours*',[120] and if we read closely, these detours result *from the effort to avoid any kind of effort*. Similarly, Ferenczi forces his readers to envision creatures that would have *preferred not to conquer land*. But how are we, then, supposed to account for the indisputable fact that land-living creatures exist?

As if by all means challenging the familiar idea of an innate progressive striving, Ferenczi draws upon the psychoanalytic notion of neurosis as a flight 'from the pleasure that has become disagreeable'.[121] According to *Thalassa*, the regressive tendency manifests itself as a reaction formation:[122] 'we should thus have in the hysterical and pathoneurotic type of reaction a prototype of the energy displacements that take place in the accomplishing of every adaptation and development.'[123] Ferenczi takes the bioanalytical experiment further than Freud ever did, and he, indeed, does not share Freud's reserved approach towards the oceanic.[124] Having said this, *Thalassa* – despite its title – is less oceanic than it may seem. Neither does Ferenczi partake in Haeckel's vision of science as a substitute for religion, nor does his epistemology render any original purity accessible: while the psychosomatic theories of Georg Groddeck, Felix Deutsch and Franz Alexander followed the goal of ridding the affected organ of its entanglement with the psyche and of purifying the organs from their psychic cathexis, Ferenczi's organology does not allow for any such ideal.[125]

While Haeckel's morphology presupposes that truth becomes evident in the form and the structure of organs and tissues, Ferenczi pursues what he calls utraquism: a method of analogy which stands in striking contrast to the transparent and holistic theory laid out in Haeckel's *General Morphology of Organisms*. In the foreword of *Thalassa,* Ferenczi defines the utraquistic method as a free use of analogies 'drawn from a field as remote as possible', to 'grasp for analogies in alien scientific fields.'[126] In his later work, where he articulates psychoanalytic observations in dialogue with vignettes on animal behaviour, he does not provide a biological substratum of the theory, but rather engages in producing meaning by means of an oscillation between both parts in an analogy.[127]

Ferenczi thoroughly demarcates his thought from the concept of the human mind as an unbroken extension of the biological. Later, in 'Freud's Influence on Medicine' (1933), he reflects this explicitly, emphasising that the psychoanalytic method avoids both a Cartesian dualism of body and soul and the methodological error of materialist-monism, which Ferenczi refers to as an overhasty unification of the psychic and the physical.[128] According to Ferenczi, such a 'unification is not possible at present, nor in the near future, and perhaps cannot be ever achieved completely. On no account should we confuse Freud's dualism with the naïve separation of a living organism into a body and a mind.'[129]

Ferenczi describes what may be termed a methodological or perhaps even strategic dualism as opposed to any ontological claim. Despite the view of the human as a psychosomatic being, Ferenczi stresses that there is no neutral, transparent language that can represent the organic. The consequence is the primacy of language within the methodological approach, acknowledging a gap, a remainder within any form of scientific representation. Ferenczi's bulkiest gift to biology is the psychoanalytic notion of overdetermination:

> It seems that we must familiarize ourselves with the idea of the overdetermination of one and the same process, as psychoanalysis teaches us in the case of psychical processes, as well as in its explanation of physiological processes.[130]

These lines break with the dream of a transparent language of what is today called the hard sciences. *Thalassa* applies the notion of overdetermination to organs, tissues and their elements. Quite differently from Haeckel's paradigm of morphology, Ferenczian organs do not come clear, but demand interpretation. Ferenczi's pattern of interpretation and construction – and this goes for psychoanalytic methods in general – runs counter to the paradigm of *Anschaulichkeit*: it is profoundly theoretical and counterintuitive. Ferenczi explains that 'the same force which impels to regression operates, when it is prevented therefrom by a censorship, in a progressive sense – in the sense, that is, of adaptation and constructiveness.'[131]

In bioanalysis, the hypothesis of an originary neurosis replaces the notion of an innate progressive striving. A relevant question remains: why bother to replace one biological fantasy – the idea of a tendency towards progression and completion – by another more complicated one?

What the bioanalytical narrative achieves, is, firstly, a deconstruction of progress and of evolutionary monism. Secondly, it destabilises the relation between pathology and normalcy. By bringing the structure of neurosis and hysteria into the centre of the evolutionary narrative, Ferenczi breaks with a basic feature of his explicitly praised pre-texts. Furthermore, he brings into the centre precisely that which was understood as a threat to development per se: neurosis and hysteria. In Ferenczi's narrative, these features neither lead to a lineage towards extinction, nor do they demand eugenically motivated biopolitical intervention. The very features that were commonly perceived as a threat against the health of future generations are reframed by Ferenczi as the organising structures of organic life itself: life as post-catastrophic survival.

In order to appreciate this intervention it is crucial to acknowledge the preoccupation with alienation, degeneracy and neurasthenia in the early twentieth century, and how antisemitism became established within medical discourse. In psychiatry, there was consensus that Jews were particularly prone to all neurotic diseases. Sander Gilman has demonstrated how psychiatric discourse linked the clinical image of the (male) hysteric with Judaism.[132] This was partly attributed to the diasporic living conditions, and partly to a supposed hereditary susceptibility to all pathogenic effects of modernity.[133]

On a lighter note, which is nevertheless crucial for the narrative strategy at play, Ferenczi's complicated fantasy of neurotic evolution brings comic relief. In a letter to Freud, Ferenczi wrote that the idea for *Thalassa* had come to him 'at first as a bad joke', continuing: 'but I forced myself to take it seriously, though I am ready for the whole thing to turn out to be nonsense'.[134] Nonsense or not: a certain gain lies in estranging the common perception and conceptualisation of organic life. This *defamiliarising* effect brings tension into Haeckel's famous exclamation that we – since Darwin – *are all one family* with the animal kingdom.[135]

To summarise before proceeding further, Ferenczi's genital theory fundamentally disturbs several forms of fetishistic disavowal at play in both Haeckel and Bölsche, the very aspects that were decisive for their immense popularity. The contrast is connected to a series of different epistemological underpinnings. While carefully avoiding the notion of a vitalist striving for perfection, Ferenczi interprets the development of reproductive organs as the result of a reaction formation against a striving in the opposite direction: here, development occurs as the neurotic reaction to a regressive trend which, in turn, was traumatically induced. This is where the theory of hysteria comes into the picture – applied above all to the male genital organ, the grand hysteric.

Heroic Organs, Hysteric Organs: The Method of Bioanalysis

In *Thalassa*, Ferenczi expresses his seemingly unrestricted admiration for Bölsche: 'It is only in the imaginative and spirited writings of Bölsche, so well-known as a populariser and so underrated even now as an original thinker, that there recurs again and again, albeit expressed only in poetic images, a point of view similar to the one here set forth'.[136] While Haeckel, according to Ferenczi, only ascribed the developmental stages of the embryo 'value as a historical document',

Ferenczi declares himself a follower of Bölsche insofar as he believes in the historiographic value of the sexual organs themselves. They '*represent a kind of recapitulation* – the recapitulation, namely, of the environmental situations which have been experienced during the development of the species.'[137]

Ferenczi illustrates this thesis by referring to the second volume of *Love-Life in Nature*, where Bölsche tells the legend of Melusina, a woman who surpassed every other human female in beauty, except for when she was regularly transformed into a snake from the waist down. According to Bölsche's interpretation, 'she had to feel the old fish-tail of a connection with a lower world in herself', a feeling that is too close for comfort for the civilised subject: a 'dull Melusinian fear still dogs us all.'[138] Bölsche, staging the triumphant overcoming of any fearfulness, then proceeds to proclaim that the 'male member' indeed is 'Melusine's fish-tail'.[139] Ferenczi agreeingly quotes Bölsche's euphoric exclamation: 'It is a Melusinian member. With it, man turns off at the fish from which he came in purple days'.[140] It is, however, telling, that Ferenczi refrains from quoting the next sentence in Bölsche, which is exemplary for evolutionary monism as a paradigm:

> But there is more to it. In it [the first penis in evolutionary history] lies the entire upward road of evolution to man, the crown of all. [...] Every step forward once gleamed here like a doubtful little flame ... will the wind suddenly blow it out or fan it to a bright flame ...? All humanity's geniuses once slumbered here, ready for resurrection. Behind this member the dice were shaken for your existence and mine and that of all of us...[141]

For Bölsche, the non-human origin of the penis contains a prefiguration of subsequent development, of man, and of further growth and glory. Quite differently, the organ according to *Thalassa* is ridden by inherited ancestral coping mechanisms that defy the categories of pathology and normalcy and have nothing to do with vitalism. Ferenczi conceives of organs in general and of the penis in particular according to a pattern presented by Freud in 'Fragment of an Analysis of a Case of Hysteria' (1905), which is why we need to return to the young girl Dora, who presumably read both Mantegazza and Bölsche by the lake.

In his case study of Dora, Freud famously stated that '[t]he subject of erection solves some of the most interesting hysterical symptoms.'[142] He was, of course, referring to women's reactions when confronted with 'the outlines of men's genitals as seen through their clothing'.[143] Ferenczi seems to have read this sentence against the grain: while Freud argues that the erection provides an opportunity to analyse hysteric reactions in women, Ferenczi treats the erection itself as a hysterical phenomenon, the example *par excellence* of hysteria understood as psychosomatic conversion. In *Thalassa*, the physiology of erection, coitus and ejaculation appear as symptoms of a hysteric fit. This is on the one hand to be understood in the sense of a traumatically induced conversion disorder: the organ is a living remnant of multiple primordial catastrophes; the erection is a displaced expression of anguish. On the other hand, Ferenczi analyses the erect penis along the lines of the theory of the wish, following the same pattern in which Freud argued that a symptom 'signifies the representation – the realisation – of a phantasy with a sexual content'.[144]

While the sexual content at stake in case of an erect penis may seem all too obvious, for Ferenczi, the organs are not what they seem. His point lies in distracting our attention from any habitual notion of goal-orientated utility and reconsidering the expressive value of organs against the background of a hypothetically assumed regressive longing. Within this particular setup, he develops an organology for which Dora's nervous cough in Freud's case study appears to have served as a model.

Dora's *tussis nervosa* is one of Freud's most prominent examples of overdetermination.[145] As a symptom, her nervous cough corresponds with at least six different meanings, and Freud underlines that 'it is not necessary for the various meanings of a symptom to be compatible with one another'.[146] Dora's cough is thus an imitation of her father's illness, of her relation to Mr K., of the regret at his absence, of her wish to make him a better wife, of sexual intercourse with her impotent father, of identification with her father's lover Mrs K. and last not least of her homosexual desire towards this woman.[147] Freud assures that 'this series is by no means complete'[148] – the symptom resembles an old wineskin (*alter Schlauch*) into which new wine is poured.[149]

In *Thalassa*, the penis is this 'alter Schlauch'.[150] Ferenczi may have spared us the image of a coughing penis.[151] Nevertheless, at a closer look, it becomes obvious how the overdetermination of Dora's nervous cough is uncannily echoed in the diversity of determinations ascribed to the erect penis in *Thalassa*. In coitus, the penis acts out a compromise between the anal desire to retain and the urethral desire to desire to give out,[152] while the frictional movements express the wish for 'a kind of self-castration',[153] the wish to 'tear away the itching part of the body'.[154] The penis is a 'symbol of the more primitive boring implement, the tooth',[155] while also playing 'the rôle of executive manager [*Prokurist*]' who 'provides for the discharge of sexual tension [*Lustabfuhrgeschäft*] on behalf of the entire organism'.[156] It is a 'miniature of the total ego',[157] while it, last but not least, signifies 'the fish, set down on land':[158] it 'enacts […] the struggles of that primal creature among its ancestors which suffered the great catastrophe of the drying up of the sea.'[159]

In *Thalassa*, the penis is not identical with itself, it has no coherent goal or meaning and it derives its eroticism from elsewhere. The penis is acting out, it literally makes a scene, appearing to be immediately present and alive in erection and coitus as a current event, while signifying what is absent. The primordial catastrophes that structure Ferenczi's narrative appear less as past causes in terms of linear causality, but are rather hypothetically reconstructed departing from the observed seizures of genitality. The result is a radical reconfiguration: in Ferenczi's own words, the penis is 'no longer […] the unique and incomparable magic wand which conjures erotisms from all the organs of the body; on the contrary, genital amphimixis would merely be one particular instance out of the many in which such fusion of erotisms takes place.'[160]

It is remarkable here how Ferenczi appropriates August Weismann's term 'amphimixis' against the intention of the originator: while Weismann related the term exclusively to the fusion of hereditary substance in the germ cells, Ferenczi defines amphimixis as a transferential relationship between organs, whereby the soma of the susceptible individual enters the scene. This corresponds more closely with the Lamarckian approach, which takes environmental influences into account. Indeed Weismann's deterministic theory of heritage, which considers only natural selection and genetics, effectively displaced Lamarckism from academic biology in the 1890s.

Ferenczi's organology stands in contradiction both with Weismann's biodeterminist doctrines of heredity and with central features of Lamarck, which were decisive for his reception in Haeckel and Bölsche. By re-interpreting the erection along the lines of a hysteric symptom, Ferenczi subverts not only Weismann's notion of amphimixis but also the organology of Lamarck. While Ferenczi's preoccupation with a catastrophic past may very well resonate with Lamarckism, the similarity ends where the organs in Lamarck emerge strengthened from each crisis: what does not kill them makes them stronger. Kyla Schuller has convincingly argued that the erection serves Lamarck as a paradigm for development in general: according to Lamarck, organs develop because fluids flow into the activated body part when stimulated and used. This curbs development, strengthening and growth.[161] Ferenczi's Lamarckism turns Lamarck on his head by using hysteria as a paradigm for re-interpreting organs in general and the penis in particular.

Ferenczi at times explicitly spoke of his 'Lamarck project'.[162] Freud, too, insisted on his Lamarckism, like on his interest in telepathy, his smoking habit and his Judaism.[163] Focussing on the contrast between Lamarck and the

Freudo-Ferenczian approach to his concepts challenges the common perception of phylogenetic speculation in psychoanalysis. Freud's stubborn sympathy for Lamarck has been explained by the politically progressive potential of the concept of inheritance of acquired characteristics.[164] Indeed, within several socially progressive movements, Lamarckism was linked to the hope of biological upgrading of disadvantaged minorities. Neo-Lamarckist eugenics in particular was often coupled with public health reforms and efforts for improving environmental conditions. The advantages of assimilation were thought of in this sense: as a means to reverse supposed hereditary effects of oppression and ghettoisation of earlier generations.

In *Thalassa*, however, such a logic of biopolitical optimisation plays no role. In bioanalysis, the strategy is of a different kind: it declares precisely that which the antisemitic norm delegates to Jewish bodies to be the structural law of organic life in general. This may not enable any course of practical political action. Nevertheless, by refusing to think of organs in terms of their goal-oriented utility, Ferenczi partakes in denaturalising our habitual notions of organs. This is worth dwelling upon. Considering the political dangers connected to the notion of heredity at the time, the organology of *Thalassa* bears the potential of an intervention.

While the importance of environmental factors and the notion of a transgenerational transfer of acquired characteristics do form a common denominator with Lamarck, Ferenczi breaks with the Lamarckist notion of heredity by declaring: 'What we call heredity is perhaps, therefore, only the displacing upon posterity of the bulk of traumatically unpleasurable experiences in question.'[165] While Lamarck emphasises the inheritance of positive features, gains and capacities, Ferenczi's wording prefigures the reconceptualisation of tradition in Freud's *Moses and Monotheism*, where a series of repressed, violent and unverifiable events are conceived of as more influential than what was willingly recorded, written down and consciously passed on to future generations. Heredity, in bioanalysis, is not a transmission of achievements and abilities, but a transgenerational transfer of something burdensome and unknown, across generations of latency. Ferenczi's notion of heredity as the displacement of a 'bulk of traumatically unpleasurable experiences'[166] is further echoed in the theory of transgenerational trauma transmission as developed by Abraham and Torok, according to which 'the dead do not return, but their lives' unfinished business is unconsciously handed down to their descendants.'[167]

Some of the thought experiments in *Thalassa* are continued in Ferenczi's later metapsychological concepts. The theoretical notion of a 'traumatic progression'[168] in individuals, so termed by Ferenczi in 'Confusion of Tongues'

(1932), is playfully anticipated in *Thalassa*, where Ferenczi conceives of organic development as a trauma-induced flight. While *Thalassa,* strictly speaking, presents an interpretation of the male erection as a hysteric fit, we find a structurally similar figure of thought when Ferenczi reflects masculinity as a post-traumatic phenomenon in his *Clinical Diary* of 1932.[169] There, neither the framework of evolutionary history nor the comical qualities of *Thalassa* remain. But when read along with this late diary, it appears almost as if *Thalassa* was written already under the impression of astonishment that life survived, despite the catastrophes, and that death did not occur in the fastest possible way. *The Clinical Diary,* with its sharpened attention towards the consequences of shock, is a book of mourning.

The Politics of Bioanalysis

How does sexuality relate to war? In *Thalassa,* Ferenczi envisions the sexual act as the discharge of accumulated unpleasurable tensions.[170] In a later text, 'A Lecture for Judges and Barristers' (1926), this thought does not refer to coitus, but to the 'paroxysms of revolutions and wars': they are 'like hysterical discharges of pent-up primitive instincts'.[171] And yet, despite recurrent passing remarks on 'the entire genital warfare',[172] *Thalassa* neither mentions the ongoing war, nor any social context of human sexuality. In 1932, shortly before his death, Ferenczi closed his essay 'Confusion of Tongues' with a critical return to *Thalassa*, as if to prevent biologist conclusions that may be drawn from his earlier work:

> [W]e shall have to revise certain chapters of the theory of sexuality and genitality. […] How much of the sadomasochism in the sexuality of our time is due to civilization (i.e. originates only from introjected feelings of guilt) and how much develops autochthonously and spontaneously as a proper phase of organization, must be left for further research. […] The 'Theory of Genitality' that tries to found the 'struggle of the sexes' on phylogenesis will have to make clear this difference between the infantile-erotic gratifications and the hate-impregnated love of adult mating.[173]

It is true that *Thalassa* appears to leave behind any ambition to link psychoanalytic theory to the institution of the family, let alone to symbolic order, language, society at large, and the effect of its norms. It is nevertheless worth acknowledging that Ferenczi, when highlighting that sexuality cannot be explained by biology only, distances himself from a stance that was never his own in the first place. Considering his earlier eminently political readings of libidinal attachments, especially regarding questions of authoritarianism and patriarchal violence, it seems unlikely that he should have omitted society from *Thalassa* out of naivety. Bioanalysis is a political pursuit insofar as it intervenes with politically influential notions of popular biology.

There is no ideologically neutral discourse on nature, biology, and heredity. Ferenczi's genital theory subverts its politically influential sources by means of a new organology informed by different paradigms of hysteria. On the one hand, this is an example for how phylogenetic speculation served Freud and Ferenczi as an experimental field for pursuing a series of unanswered questions: how to connect the trauma model of Freud's early seduction theory with the theory of unconscious wish.[174] On the other hand, apart from inner-psychoanalytic debates, the hysteric organology sets Ferenczi apart from the biopolitical fantasies that were formative for the generation that went to war in 1914. These tendencies were prevalent all over the political spectrum at the time, and across the division between adepts of Weismann and of Lamarck.

The grey zone between biology and politics forms the background against which Ferenczi's bioanalytic idea emerges in all its eccentricity. Freud's theory of sexuality meets popular Darwinism in a soldiers' library. Imagining what Ferenczi's writing desk may have looked like during the months in Pápa, it appears as if the contradictions of his time were condensed in this scene of reading and writing, in this constellation of books.

Around the outbreak of the First World War, Haeckel supported Germany for eugenic reasons: while Ferenczi was translating Freud's *Three Essays*, Haeckel claimed to explain the Great War 'according to the laws of natural development'.[175] While Ferenczi was drafting *Thalassa*, Haeckel drew a clear line from 'unicellular protists'[176] to the necessity of a German victory in the interest of the human species.[177] While Ferenczi reflected the macabre scenes of joyous departure to the front, Bölsche had already published his essay collection *Stirb und Werde* – with a proud phoenix on the front cover, rising from the flames and ashes in a ray of light.[178]

There is a libidinal investment that can be sensed already in Haeckel. It is spelled out overtly in Bölsche's 'erotic monism'. And it is re-interpreted, and connected to trauma, in Ferenczi's *Thalassa*. This does not make it less sexual. Rather, it locates sexuality within the context of post-traumatic survival and reconfigures the role of sexuality within a discourse formation where its presence cannot be denied.

Notes

1. Ferenczi to Freud, 1915, S. Freud, S. Ferenczi, *The Correspondence of Sigmund Freud and Sándor Ferenczi, Vol. 2: 1914–1919*, ed. by É. Brabant, E. Falzeder, P. Giampieri-Deutsch, transl. by P. T. Hoffer. Cambridge, Mass.: Belknap Press of Harvard UP, 1996, p. 60.
2. The period termed by historians as the 'long 19th century' stretches from the beginning of the industrial revolution in Britain in the 1770s until the outbreak of the First World War. E. Hobsbawm, *The Age of Empire 1875–1914*. New York: Vintage, 1987, p. 8.
3. E. Hobsbawm, *The Age of Empire 1875–1914*, p. 326: 'In 1914 the peoples of Europe, for however brief a moment, went lightheartedly to slaughter and to be slaughtered. After the First World War they never did so again.'
4. On the formative effect of Ferenczi's wartime experience for his later theory of trauma A. Harris, 'Ferenczi's Work on War Neuroses', in: A. Harris, S. Kuchuck (eds.), *The Legacy of Sándor Ferenczi. From Ghost to Ancestor*. London, New York: Routledge, 2015, pp. 127–133; see also F. Erős, 'Violence, Trauma, and Hypocrisy', in: A. Borgos, J. Gyimesi, F. Erős (eds.), *Psychology and Politics: Intersections of Sciences and Ideology in the History of Psy-Sciences*. Budapest, New York: Central European UP, 2019, pp. 81–94, pp. 85–87.
5. S. Ferenczi, 'Introduction', in: S. Ferenczi, *Thalassa. A Theory of Genitality* [1924], transl. by H. A. Bunker. London, New York: Karnac, 1989, pp. 1–4, p. 1.
6. P. v. Haute, H. Westerink, 'Hysterie, Sexualität und Psychiatrie. Eine Relektüre der ersten Ausgabe der *Drei Abhandlungen zur Sexualtheorie*', in: P. v. Haute, C. Huber, H. Westerink (eds.), *Sigmund Freud: Drei Abhandlungen zur Sexualtheorie (1905)*. Göttingen: V&R unipress, 2015, pp. 9–56, p. 27.
7. S. Ferenczi, 'Versuch einer Genitaltheorie' [1924], in: S. Ferenczi, *Schriften zur Psychoanalyse II*, ed. by M. Bálint. Gießen: Psychosozial-Verlag, 2004, pp. 317–400.
8. Ibid., p. 363; 'the idea of a "thalassal regressive trend"': S. Ferenczi, *Thalassa*, p. 52.
9. S. Ferenczi, *Thalassa*, p. 54.
10. T. Dufresne, *The Late Sigmund Freud: Or, the Last Word on Psychoanalysis, Society, and all the Riddles of Life*. Cambridge, New York: Cambridge UP, 2017, p. 11.
11. For an extensive reading of 'Beyond the Pleasure Principle', departing from Freud's collaboration with Ferenczi: J. Willner, 'Neurotische Evolution. Bioanalyse als Kulturkritik in Jenseits des Lustprinzips', *Psyche. Zeitschrift für Psychoanalyse und ihre Anwendungen* 11(74), 2020, pp. 895–921.
12. C. Bonomi, *The Cut and the Building of Psychoanalysis, Vol. 2: Sigmund Freud and Sándor Ferenczi*. London, New York: Routledge, 2018, p. 65.
13. S. Ferenczi, *Thalassa*, p. 15; S. Ferenczi, 'Versuch einer Genitaltheorie', p. 330.
14. S. Ferenczi, *Thalassa*, p. 51.

15 S. Ferenczi, *Thalassa*, p. 56: 'the amniotic fluid represents a sea "introjected", as it were, into the womb of the mother – a sea in which, as the embryologist R. Hertwig says, "the delicate and easily injured embryo swims and executes movements like a fish in water"'.
16 Ibid., pp. 49–50.
17 Ibid., p. 44.
18 I. Grubrich-Simitis, 'Trauma oder Trieb – Trieb und Trauma. Lektionen aus Sigmund Freuds phylogenetischer Phantasie von 1915', *Psyche. Zeitschrift für Psychoanalyse und ihre Anwendungen* 41, 1987, pp. 992–1023, p. 995.
19 I. Grubrich-Simitis, 'Trauma oder Trieb – Trieb und Trauma: Wiederbetrachtet', *Psyche. Zeitschrift für Psychoanalyse und ihre Anwendungen* 61, 2007, pp. 637–656, p. 647.
20 A much shorter version of the main line of thought was published in: J. Willner, 'The Problem of Heredity: Ferenczi's Organology and the Politics of Bioanalysis', *Psychoanalysis and History* 24(2), 2022, pp. 205–219, transl. by N. E. Levis from J. Willner, 'Das Problem mit dem Erbe. Ferenczis Organologie und die Politik der Bioanalyse', *RISS. Zeitschrift für Psychoanalyse: Bioanalysen I* 94, 2021, pp. 81–97.
21 S. Ferenczi, 'Introduction', p. 1.
22 P. Berz, 'Die Einzeller und die Lust. Bölsche, Freud, Ferenczi', in: C. Kirchhoff, G. Scharbert (eds.), *Freuds Referenzen*. Berlin: Kadmos, 2012, pp. 15–33, p. 20, with reference to Verena Hofer.
23 F. J. Sulloway, *Freud, Biologist of the Mind. Beyond the Psychoanalytic Legend*. Cambridge, Mass., London: Harvard UP, 1992.
24 The terms onto- and phylogenesis were introduced in E. Haeckel, *Generelle Morphologie der Organismen. Allgemeine Grundzüge der organischen Formen-Wissenschaft, mechanisch begründet durch die von C. Darwin reformirte Descendenz-Theorie*. Berlin: Georg Reimer, 1866. Haeckel's later theory of perigenesis, articulated in 1875, held that acquired characters become hereditary through particular molecular movements, cf. B. Kleeberg, *Theophysis. Ernst Haeckels Philosophie des Naturganzen*. Cologne, Weimar, Vienna: Böhlau, 2005, p. 166, fn 571.
25 For a profound account of Haeckel's monism: B. Kleeberg, *Theophysis*; S. J. Gould, *Ontogeny and Phylogeny*. Cambridge, Mass., London: Belknap Press, 1977 remains a standard reference on the history of the phylogenetic parallel in relation to evolutionary concepts.
26 E. Haeckel, 'Ueber die Entwicklungstheorie Darwins' [Jungfernrede, Stettiner Rede], in: C. A. Dohrn, Dr. Behm, *Amtlicher Bericht über die acht und dreißigste Versammlung deutscher Naturforscher und Ärzte in Stettin im September 1863*. Stettin: Hesselands Buchdruck, 1864, pp. 17–30, p. 24.
27 A. Kelly, *The Descent of Darwin: The Popularization of Darwin in Germany, 1860–1914*. Chapel Hill: UNC Press, 1981, p. 38.

28 S. Freud, 'Some Thoughts on Development and Regression – Aetiology' [1917], in: S. Freud, *Introductory Lectures on Psycho-Analysis (Part III)* (1916–1917), *SE* 16, pp. 339–357, p. 354.
29 For a young example: G. Marcaggi, F. Guénolé, 'Freudarwin: Evolutionary Thinking as a Root of Psychoanalysis', *Frontiers in Psychology* 9, 2018, pp. 1–9, p. 5.
30 Freud's years in *Gymnasium* (1865–1873) coincided with Haeckel's breakthrough as a populariser of the theory of evolution. It was only after he began studying under Ernst Wilhelm Brücke that physicalism came to have a decisive influence on his thinking. Until then, he was most likely not averse to Haeckel's interpretation of Darwin along the lines of natural philosophy (Cf. L. Ritvo, *Darwin's Influence on Freud: A Tale of Two Sciences*. New Haven: Yale UP, 1990, p. 10).
31 S. Freud, 'Beyond the Pleasure Principle' [1920], in: S. Freud, *Beyond the Pleasure Principle, Group Psychology and Other Works* (1920–1922), *SE* 18, pp. 7–64, p. 26.
32 A particularly important letter: Ferenczi to Freud, 15 September 1915, *The Correspondence of Sigmund Freud and Sándor Ferenczi*, Vol. 2, pp. 84–85.
33 For a reconstruction of this unfinished project, see I. Grubrich-Simitis, 'Metapsychologie und Metabiologie. Zu Sigmund Freuds Entwurf einer "Übersicht der Übertragungsneurosen"', in: S. Freud, *Übersicht der Übertragungsneurosen* [1915], ed. by Ilse Grubrich-Simitis. Frankfurt/M.: Fischer, 1985, pp. 83–119; U. May, 'Der dritte Schritt in der Trieblehre. Zur Entstehungsgeschichte von Jenseits des Lustprinzip', *Luzifer-Amor. Zeitschrift zur Geschichte der Psychoanalyse* 26(51), 2013, pp. 92–169; J. Willner, 'Neurotische Evolution'.
34 P. T. Hoffer, 'Freud's 'Phylogenetic Fantasy' and His Construction of the Historical Moses', in: L. J. Brown (ed.), *On Freud's 'Moses and Monotheism'*. London, New York: Routledge, 2022, pp. 35–51.
35 F. J. Sulloway, *Freud, Biologist of the Mind. Beyond the Psychoanalytic Legend*.
36 S. J. Gould, *Ontogeny and Phylogeny*. Cambridge, Mass., London: Belknap Press, 1977, p. 163. This misreading within an otherwise invaluable source has persisted in several subsequent interpretations.
37 S. Ferenczi, *Thalassa*, p. 102.
38 In my reading, this appears to be decisive for Freud and Ferenczi's common pursuit, quite in contrast to the Jungian understanding. On Freud and Jung cf.: P. T. Hoffer, 'The Concept of Phylogenetic Inheritance in Freud and Jung', *Journal of the American Psychoanalytic Association*, 40(2), 1992.
39 Ibid., p. 82.
40 B. Kleeberg, *Theophysis*, p. 201, fn 684.
41 E. Hobsbawm, *The Age of Empire 1875–1914*, p. 253.
42 D. Gasman polemically drew a straight line from Haeckel to Hitler: D. Gasman, *Haeckel's Monism and the Birth of Fascist Ideology*. New York: Lang, 1998. For a more solid and nuanced account: K. Bayertz, 'Darwinismus als Politik. Zur

Genese des Sozialdarwinismus in Deutschland 1860–1900', in: E. Aescht, G. Aubrecht, E. Krausse (eds.), *Welträtsel und Lebenswunder. Ernst Haeckel – Werk, Wirkung und Folgen*. Linz: Oberösterreichisches Landesmuseum, 1998, pp. 229–289. For a comprehensive attempt to rehabilitate Haeckel as a humanist thinker: R. J. Richards, *The Tragic Sense of Life: Ernst Haeckel and The Struggle over Evolutionary Thought*. Chicago: University of Chicago Press, 2008.

[43] D. Pick, *Faces of Degeneration: A European Disorder 1848–1918*. Cambridge: Cambridge UP, 1993, p. 28.

[44] On Haeckel and Kautsky: W. Michler, *Darwinismus und Literatur. Naturwissenschaftliche und literarische Intelligenz in Österreich 1859–1914*. Vienna, Cologne, Weimar: Böhlau, 1999, p. 165f.; R. Weikart, *Socialist Darwinism: Evolution in German Socialist Thought from Marx to Bernstein*. San Francisco: International Scholars Publication, 1999, pp. 157–188.

[45] C. Gradmann, 'Unsichtbare Feinde. Bakteriologie und politische Sprache im deutschen Kaiserreich', in: P. Sarasin, S. Berger, M. Hänseler, M. Spörri (eds.), *Bakteriologie und Moderne. Studien zur Biopolitik des Unsichtbaren 1879–1920*. Frankfurt/M.: Suhrkamp, 2007, pp. 327–353, p. 332.

[46] E. Haeckel, *Ewigkeit. Weltkriegsgedanken über Leben und Tod, Religion und Entwicklungslehre*. Berlin: Georg Reimer, 1915, p. 10.

[47] P. Sarasin, 'Zäsuren biologischen Typs: Der Kampf ums Überleben bei Wilhelm Bölsche, H. G. Wells und Steven Spielberg', in: H. Schramm, L. Schwarte, J. Lazardzig (eds.), *Spuren der Avantgarde*. Berlin: De Gruyter, 2011, pp. 443–459, p. 447.

[48] S. Azzouni, 'Populärwissenschaft als fachwissenschaftliche Autorität: Wilhelm Bölsches "Das Liebesleben in der Natur" und die Anfänge der Sexualwissenschaft', *Jahrbuch Literatur und Medizin* 3, 2009, pp. 13–38.

[49] G.-H. Susen, E. Wack, 'Einleitung', in: G.-H. Susen, E. Wack (eds.), *'Was wir im Verstande ausjäten, kommt im Traume wieder'. Wilhelm Bölsche 1861–1939*. Würzburg: Königshausen & Neumann, 2012, pp. 7–16, p. 12.

[50] There is a history of leftist eugenics, linked to the idea of promoting welfare. What Daniel Pick has clarified regarding theories of degeneration, is applicable to any nuanced account of the history of eugenics too: 'The aim is […] to reconstruct some of the political and cultural contradictions at issue in nineteenth-century scenarios of degeneration, and moreover to refuse the comforting mythology which (often by reading backwards from the 1930s and the War) allies them exclusively with the intellectual world of the far Right'. D. Pick, *Faces of Degeneration*, p. 30.

[51] P. Thurschwell, 'Ferenczi's Dangerous Proximities: Telepathy, Psychosis, and the Real Event', *differences: A Journal of Feminist Cultural Studies* 11, 1999, pp. 150–178, p. 158.

[52] M. Foucault, *Histoire de la sexualité I. La volonté de savoir*. Paris: Gallimard, 1976, pp. 197–198: 'l'honneur politique de la psychanalyse', cf. p. 157.

[53] For a more extensive reading of the trilogy: J. Willner, 'Vom Fisch an aufwärts giebt es keinen Rückfall. Bedrohlicher Optimismus in Wilhelm Bölsches *Das Liebesleben in der Natur*', in: C. Ortlieb, P. Ramponi, J. Willner, *Das Tier als Medium und Obsession. Zur Politik des Wissens von Mensch und Tier um 1900*. Berlin: Neofelis, 2015, pp. 265–302.

[54] A. Berentsen, *Vom Urnebel zum Zukunftsstaat – Zum Problem der Popularisierung der Naturwissenschaften in der deutschen Literatur (1880–1910)*. Berlin: Oberhofer, 1986, pp. 175–176.

[55] M. Hagner, P. Sarasin, 'Wilhelm Bölsche und der "Geist". Populärer Darwinismus in Deutschland 1887–1934', *Nach Feierabend. Zürcher Jahrbuch für Wissensgeschichte* 4, 2008, pp. 47–68, p. 52. On Bölsche's popularity cf. A. Kelly, *The Descent of Darwin*.

[56] W. Bölsche, *Love-Life in Nature. The Story of the Evolution of Love*, Vol. I, transl. by C. Brown. New York: Albert & Charles Boni, 1926, pp. 15–18.

[57] Ibid., p. 87.

[58] W. Bölsche, *Love-Life in Nature*, Vol. II, p. 185.

[59] S. Azzouni, 'Populärwissenschaft als fachwissenschaftliche Autorität', pp. 21–22.

[60] S. Freud, 'Fragment of an Analysis of a Case of Hysteria' [1905], in: S. Freud, *A Case of Hysteria, Three Essays on Sexuality and Other Works* (1901–1905), *SE* 7, pp. 7–122, p. 26.

[61] F. Freudenberg, 'Liebesleben in der Natur', *Der Frauenarzt* 18(2), 1903, pp. 65–68, quoted in S. Azzouni, 'Populärwissenschaft als fachwissenschaftliche Autorität', p. 28.

[62] W. Bölsche, *Love-Life in Nature*, Vol. II, pp. 364–366.

[63] W. Bölsche, *Love-Life in Nature*, Vol. I, pp. 7, 8.

[64] Ibid., p. 7, emphasis in the original.

[65] Ibid., p. 20.

[66] S. Ferenczi, *The Clinical Diary of Sándor Ferenczi* [1932], ed. by J. Dupont, transl. by M. Bálint, N. Z. Jackson. Cambridge, Mass., London: Harvard UP, 1995, pp. 31–34 [entry from 14 February 1932].

[67] To borrow a term from E. L. Santner, *Untying Things Together: Philosophy, Literature, and a Life in Theory*. London, Chicago: University of Chicago Press, 2022, p. xiii.

[68] S. Ferenczi, *Thalassa*, p. 55; without mentioning the title, he is quoting from E. Haeckel, *Natürliche Schöpfungsgeschichte*. Berlin: Reimer, 1872, pp. 616ff.

[69] S. Ferenczi, *Thalassa*, p. 55; cf. E. Haeckel, *Natürliche Schöpfungsgeschichte*, p. 616.

[70] E. Haeckel, *Natürliche Schöpfungsgeschichte*, p. 619; no equivalent in *Thalassa*.

[71] S. Ferenczi, *Thalassa*, p. 47, cf. W. Bölsche, *Love-Life in Nature*, Vol. II, p. 182.

[72] S. Ferenczi, *Thalassa*, pp. 73–74.

[73] Ibid., p. 76.

[74] E. Jones, *Sigmund Freud. Life and Work. Vol. III: The Last Phase 1919–1939*. London: The Hogarth Press, 1957, p. 188.

[75] On Haeckelian temporality cf. S. Ferguson, 'The Face of Time between Haeckel and Bergson; Or, Toward an Ethics of Impure Vision', *Qui Parle* 19(1), 2010, pp. 107–151.
[76] R. Soreanu, 'Ferenczi's Times: The Tangent, the Segment, and the Meandering Line', *American Imago* 73(1), 2016, pp. 51–69, p. 54: 'Only through analogy, not through chronology, could one grasp originary time. It could not even be elucidated as regression from present to past. Instead, originary time appeared as a tangent of the lived present. This tangent-out might be imagined as a line of highly accelerated travel touching two temporal periods in which two series of elements stand in similar relations to one another. Analogical thinking meant sustaining contact with *both* series of elements, as a tangent touches on two circles.'
[77] W. Bölsche, *Love-Life in Nature*, Vol. I, p. 5.
[78] Ibid., p. 20.
[79] S. Freud, 'A Difficulty in the Path of Psycho-Analysis' [1917], in: S. Freud, *An Infantile Neurosis and Other Works* (1917–1919), SE 17, pp. 137–144, p. 139.
[80] G. Beer, *Darwin's Plots. Evolutionary Narrative in Darwin, George Eliot and Nineteenth Century Fiction*. Cambridge, New York: Cambridge UP, 2009, p. 7.
[81] W. Bölsche, *Love-Life in Nature*, Vol. I, p. 450.
[82] W. Bölsche, *Love-Life in Nature*, Vol. II, p. 178: 'The little toads with the little white necks in the puddle over there are already veritable past masters of the art of holding fast with the legs for sexual purposes. Or with the arms, to put it better. For their short forelegs work exactly like arms.'
[83] Elisabeth Grosz sees a structural resemblance here regarding the passivity of the subject in relation to economic and linguistic rules. E. Grosz, 'Darwinian Matters: Life, Force, Change', in: E. Grosz, *The Nick of Time. Politics, Evolution, and the Untimely*. Durham: Duke UP, 2004, pp. 17–39, p. 39.
[84] C. Darwin, *On the Origin of Species: A Facsimile of the First Edition* [1859]. Cambridge, Mass.: Harvard UP, 1964, p. 489.
[85] Cf. G. Beer, 'Darwin and the Uses of Extinction', *Victorian Studies* [Special Issue: Darwin and the Evolution of Victorian Studies] 51(2), 2009, pp. 321–331.
[86] A. Haverkamp, 'Undone by Death. Umrisse einer Poetik nach Darwin', in: C. Blumenberg, A. Heimes, E. Weitzman, S. Witt (eds.), *Suspensionen. Über das Untote*. Paderborn: Wilhelm Fink, 2015, pp. 35–51, p. 37.
[87] E. Haeckel, *Gott-Natur (Theophysis). Studien über die monistische Religion*. Leipzig: Alfred Kröner, 1914, p. 46.
[88] G. Beer, *Darwin's Plots*, p. 79f.
[89] J. Voss, 'Das erste Bild der Evolution. Wie Charles Darwin die Unordnung der Naturgeschichte zeichnete und was daraus wurde', in: K. Bayertz, M. Gerhard, W. Jaeschke (eds.), *Weltanschauung, Philosophie und Naturwissenschaft im 19. Jahrhundert. Bd. 2: Der Darwinismus-Streit*. Hamburg: Felix Meiner, 2007, pp. 47–82, p. 78.
[90] W. Michler, *Darwinismus und Literatur. Naturwissenschaftliche und literarische Intelligenz in Österreich 1859–1914*, p. 100.

[91] Ibid., p. 102.
[92] A. Mitscherlich, M. Mitscherlich, *The Inability to Mourn: Principles of Collective Behaviour*, transl. by B. R. Platzeck. New York: Grove Press, 1975.
[93] H. Thomé, 'Weltanschauungsliteratur. Vorüberlegungen zu Funktion und Texttyp', in: L. Danneberg, F. Vollhart (eds.), *Wissen in Literatur im 19. Jahrhundert*. Tübingen: Max Niemeyer, 2002, pp. 338–380; J. Willner, 'Weltanschauung', in: T. Erthel, R. Stockhammer (eds.), *Welt-Komposita. Ein Lexikon*. Munich: Fink, 2019, pp. 15–25.
[94] J. Laplanche, J.-B. Pontalis, *The Language of Psychoanalysis*. London, New York: Routledge, 2018, p. 118.
[95] S. Freud, 'Fetishism' [1927], in: S. Freud, *The Future of an Illusion, Civilization and its Discontents and Other Works* (1927–1931), SE 21, pp. 152–157, p. 156: 'In very subtle instances both the disavowal and the affirmation of the castration have found their way into the construction of the fetish itself.'
[96] E. Haeckel, *Generelle Morphologie der Organismen. Allgemeine Grundzüge der organischen Formen-Wissenschaft, mechanisch begründet durch die von C. Darwin reformirte Descendenz-Theorie*. Berlin: Georg Reimer, 1866, p. 300, transl. JW.
[97] G. Beer, *Darwin's Plots*, p. 104.
[98] Ibid., p. 104.
[99] W. Bölsche, *Love-Life in Nature*, Vol. I, p. 20.
[100] T. W. Adorno, *Philosophische Terminologie. Zur Einleitung*. Frankfurt/M.: Suhrkamp, 1973, p. 92; cf. S. Freud, 'The Question of a *Weltanschauung*' [1933], in: S. Freud, *New Introductory Lectures on Psycho-Analysis and Other Works* (1932–1936), SE 22, pp. 158–182, p. 158: 'In my opinion, then, a Weltanschauung is an intellectual construction which solves all the problems of our existence uniformly on the basis of one overriding hypothesis'; p. 160: 'but we cannot nevertheless overlook the fact that it would be illegitimate and highly inexpedient to allow these demands to be transferred to the sphere of knowledge. For this would be to lay open the paths which lead to psychosis'.
[101] Cf. S. Freud, 'Civilization and its Discontents' [1930], in: S. Freud, *The Future of an Illusion, Civilization and its Discontents and Other Works* (1927–1931), SE 21, pp. 21–145, p. 72.
[102] W. Bölsche, *Love-Life in Nature*, Vol. I, p. 9.
[103] Ibid., p. 36.
[104] On Le Bon's Haeckelianism: D. Gasman, 'The Monism of Georges Vacher de Lapouge and Gustave Le Bon', in: D. Gasman, *Haeckel's Monism and the Birth of Fascist Ideology*.
[105] D. Pick, *Faces of Degeneration*, p. 90.
[106] W. Bölsche, *Love-Life in Nature*, Vol. I, p. 40.
[107] Cf. M. Hagner, P. Sarasin, 'Wilhelm Bölsche und der "Geist"', p. 61.
[108] W. Bölsche, *Was muß der neue deutsche Mensch von Naturwissenschaft und Religion fordern?*. Berlin: Buchholz & Weißwange, 1934, quoted in M. Hagner, P. Sarasin, 'Wilhelm Bölsche und der "Geist"', p. 61, transl. JW.

[109] Theweleit's approach in *Male Fantasies. Women, Floods, Bodies, History* is essentially Reichian. According to Wilhelm Reich, the societal development leading from the earliest clan-based society to the capitalist state exhibited two interacting processes: the development of production was accompanied by the development from natural sexual freedom via monogamous marriage to the 'continuous confinement, repression, distortion of genital sexuality'. In Reich's view, this is the root of all neuroses. W. Reich, 'The Imposition of Sexual Morality', in: W. Reich, *Sex-Pol*, ed. by L. Baxandall. New York: Vintage Books, 1972, p. 226.

[110] K. Schuller, *The Biopolitics of Feeling. Race, Sex, and Science in the Nineteenth Century*. Durham, London: Duke UP, 2018, p. 26.

[111] W. Bölsche, *Das Liebesleben in der Natur. Eine Entwicklungsgeschichte der Liebe*, Vol. III. Leipzig: Diederichs, 1903, p. 143.

[112] Ibid., pp. 332–333.

[113] S. Ferenczi, 'Introjection and Transference' [1909], in: S. Ferenczi, *First Contributions to Psycho-Analysis*, transl. by E. Jones. London: Karnac, 1994, pp. 35–93, p. 56.

[114] S. Ferenczi, *Thalassa*, p. 87.

[115] On Freud's bioanalysis in 'Beyond the Pleasure Principle', cf. J. Willner, 'Neurotische Evolution', esp. pp. 896–904.

[116] S. Freud, 'Beyond the Pleasure Principle', p. 42.

[117] Ibid., p. 26.

[118] H. Melville, *Bartleby, the Scrivener* [1856], in: H. Melville, *Billy Budd, Bartleby, and Other Stories*. New York: Penguin, 2016, pp. 17–54, p. 25.

[119] S. Freud, 'Beyond the Pleasure Principle', p. 38.

[120] Ibid., p. 39.

[121] S. Ferenczi, 'Introjection and Transference', p. 45.

[122] Cf. Freud in 'Beyond the Pleasure Principle': 'The backward path that leads to complete satisfaction is as a rule obstructed by the resistances which maintain the repressions. So there is no alternative but to advance in the direction in which growth is still free – though with no prospect of bringing the process to a conclusion or of being able to reach the goal. The processes involved in the formation of a neurotic phobia, which is nothing else than an attempt at flight from the satisfaction of an instinct, present us with a model of the manner of origin of this supposititious "instinct towards perfection"' (S. Freud, 'Beyond the Pleasure Principle', p. 42).

[123] S. Ferenczi, *Thalassa*, p. 91.

[124] M. Wegener, 'Seinem großen Ozeanischen Freund das Landthier S. Fr.', *RISS. Zeitschrift für Psychoanalyse: Bioanalysen II* 95, 2021, pp. 27–41.

[125] E. Wilson, *Gut Feminism*. Durham, London: Duke UP, 2015, pp. 57–59. Cf. p. 59: 'Under Ferenczi, biology is strange matter, proficient at the kinds of actions (regressions, perversions, strangulations, condensations, displacements) usually attributed to nonbiological systems'.

[126] S. Ferenczi, *Thalassa*, p. 3.

[127] R. Soreanu, 'Sándor Ferenczi's Epistemologies and their Politics: On Utraquism and the Analogical Method', in: F. Erős, A. Borgos, J. Gyimesi (eds.), *Psychology and Politics*, pp. 95–106.
[128] S. Ferenczi, 'Freud's Influence on Medicine' [1933], in: S. Ferenczi, *Final Contributions to the Problems and Methods of Psycho-Analysis*, ed. by M. Bálint, transl. by E. Mosbacher. London: Karnac, 1994, pp. 143–155, p. 146.
[129] S. Ferenczi, 'Freud's Influence on Medicine', p. 147.
[130] S. Ferenczi, *Thalassa*, p. 34.
[131] Ibid., p. 89.
[132] S. L. Gilman, *Freud, Race, and Gender*. Princeton, NJ: Princeton UP, 1993, p. 235.
[133] J. Willner, 'The Problem of Heredity. Ferenczi's Organology and the Politics of Bioanalysis'; for an account of Freud's distancing from the antisemitic milieu of Charcot's hereditary theory cf. E. Roith, 'Hysteria, Heredity and Anti-Semitism. Freud's Quiet Rebellion', *Psychoanalysis and History* 10(2), 2008, pp. 149–168.
[134] Ferenczi to Freud, 13 January 1915, *The Correspondence of Sigmund Freud and Sándor Ferenczi*, Vol. 2, pp. 44–45.
[135] E. Haeckel, 'Ueber die Entwicklungstheorie Darwins', pp. 22–23.
[136] S. Ferenczi, *Thalassa*, p. 46.
[137] Ibid., p. 46.
[138] W. Bölsche, *Love-Life in Nature*, Vol. II, p. 168.
[139] Idem.
[140] Ibid., p. 169; cf. in a different, less exact translation from the German original, S. Ferenczi, *Thalassa*, p. 46.
[141] W. Bölsche, *Love-Life in Nature*, Vol. II, p. 169. The translation (from 1926) omits details typical for the German context around 1900: mentions of Goethe were omitted, references to 'Kraft' were replaced by chromosomes. The German original: 'Aber es liegt mehr darin. Es steckt auch der ganze Weg empor zur Menschenkrone darin. […] Und auf das Mannesglied, hinter dem die Aeonen-Perspektive der ewigen Generationen sich ins uferlose Blau der zeitlichen Weltenfolge verliert. Goethes Augen etwa. Und das Mannesglied eines gesunden Menschen, auf dem die Kraft weiter wandert, in Goethes Namen zu siegen, an Goethes Werk weiterzubauen und eines Tages selbst Goethe zu überbieten, so daß die Augen noch von abermals höheren Sternen strahlen' (W. Bölsche, *Das Liebesleben in der Natur. Eine Entwicklungsgeschichte der Liebe*, Vol. II. Florence, Leipzig: Diederichs, 1900, p. 265).
[142] S. Freud, 'Fragment of an Analysis of a Case of Hysteria', p. 32.
[143] Ibid., p. 32, fn.
[144] Ibid., p. 47.
[145] Ibid., p. 31, fn; cf. p. 60: 'But in the world of reality, which I am trying to depict here, a complication of motives, an accumulation and conjunction of mental activities – in a word, overdetermination – is the rule'.
[146] Ibid., p. 53.

[147] Ibid., pp. 46–47, p. 83.
[148] Ibid., p. 83.
[149] Ibid., p. 54.
[150] The phallic connotation of 'Schlauch' is lost in Strachey's translation to 'bottle': The German term 'Schlauch' refers to a wineskin, but also signifies a hose or a tube.
[151] He however thematises erectile disturbances in terms of 'genital stuttering', S. Ferenczi, *Thalassa*, p. 9.
[152] Ibid., p. 17.
[153] Ibid., p. 29.
[154] Ibid., p. 30.
[155] Ibid., p. 22.
[156] Ibid., p. 16.
[157] Idem. Ferenczi's original term 'Lustabfuhr*geschäft*' (business of lust disposal) plays with the peculiar assonance between '*Geschäfts*verkehr' (business connections) and '*Geschlechts*verkehr' (sexual intercourse).
[158] Ibid., p. 47.
[159] Ibid., p. 49f.
[160] Ibid., p. 12.
[161] K. Schuller, *The Biopolitics of Feeling. Race, Sex, and Science in the Nineteenth Century*, pp. 47–51.
[162] Ferenczi to Freud, 15 September 1915, *The Correspondence of Sigmund Freud and Sándor Ferenczi*, Vol. 2, pp. 84–85.
[163] On telepathy, smoking and Judaism cf. S. Frosh, 'Psychoanalysis and Ghostly Transmission', *American Imago* 69(2), 2012, pp. 241–264, pp. 254–255.
[164] E. Slavet, *Racial Fever. Freud and the Jewish Question*. New York: Fordham UP, 2009.
[165] S. Ferenczi, *Thalassa*, p. 66.
[166] S. Ferenczi, *Thalassa*, p. 66.
[167] N. T. Rand, 'Secrets and Posterity: The Theory of the Transgenerational Phantom. Editor's Note', in: N. Abraham, M. Torok, *The Shell and the Kernel. Renewals of Psychoanalysis*, Vol. 1, ed. and transl. by N. T. Rand. Chicago, London: The University of Chicago Press, 1994, pp. 165–169, p. 167.
[168] S. Ferenczi, 'Confusion of Tongues between Adults and the Child' [1933], in: S. Ferenczi, *Final Contributions to the Problems and Methods of Psycho-Analysis*, p. 165.
[169] S. Ferenczi, *The Clinical Diary of Sándor Ferenczi*, p. 188.
[170] S. Ferenczi, *Thalassa*, p. 29.
[171] S. Ferenczi, 'A Lecture for Judges and Barristers' [1913], in: S. Ferenczi, *Further Contributions to the Theory and Technique of Psycho-Analysis*, comp. by J. Rickman, transl. by J. I. Suttie. London: Karnac, 1994, pp. 424–434, p. 433.
[172] S. Ferenczi, *Thalassa*, p. 17, cf. pp. 26, 58.

[173] S. Ferenczi, 'Confusion of Tongues between Adults and the Child', p. 166.
[174] I. Grubrich-Simitis, 'Trauma oder Trieb – Trieb und Trauma. Lektionen aus Sigmund Freuds phylogenetischer Phantasie von 1915', pp. 992–1023, and 'Trauma oder Trieb – Trieb und Trauma: Wiederbetrachtet', pp. 637–656, p. 647.
[175] E. Haeckel, *Ewigkeit. Weltkriegsgedanken über Leben und Tod, Religion und Entwicklungslehre*, p. 10.
[176] Ibid., p. 27.
[177] Ibid., pp. 35–37.
[178] W. Bölsche, *Stirb und Werde! Naturwissenschaftliche und kulturelle Plaudereien*. Jena: Diederichs, 1913.

Reading Against the Grain:
On How Organs Crave Interpretation

RESPONSE

to Jenny Willner, by Jakob Staberg

In the work of Jenny Willner, the relationship between biology and psychoanalysis is, in a sense, put out of joint. She presents us with a new reading of old themes, of what we thought familiar. Freud's and Ferenczi's engagement with nineteenth-century biology has often been read as an attempt to provide psychoanalysis with a natural scientific foundation. However, as Willner's chapter shows, Ferenczi's genital theory 'deconstructs precisely that which claims such a founding status':[1] he reads his sources 'against the grain'.[2] The same can be said about Willner's own approach: she reads her sources against the grain.

What does it mean to read against the grain? In Willner, let us say we encounter *a new archivist*; extracted through an approach of the archivist's thoroughness and keen eye, her reading pertains to a certain cheerful positivism. More important, it opens up a whole series of fields possible to explore. Her approach invites further writing, further speculations, but at the core we encounter an archivist who looks at her material with a certain astonishment – an effect we, her readers, must marvel at. Thus the map is redrawn, new territories become available. Let us reflect on where this method can lead us. I sense a broader intellectual landscape enabled here involving literary critique, political history, as well as psychoanalytic theory with implications for its clinical practice. What is at stake, it seems to me, is a new way of thinking about forces.

The way Willner analyses Ferenczi's work on hysteria, on thinking masculinity, reflects, in my mind, a certain experience of the body in terms of forces. It brings to mind Gilles Deleuze's reassessment of the concept of genealogy: 'What defines a body is this relation between dominant and dominated forces. Every relationship of forces constitutes a body – whether it is chemical, biological, social or political'.[3] With Willner's careful readings, Ferenczi's position can be understood as a potential expanding of such a view. The body's capability for transformation and survival as a response to overwhelming experience in Ferenczi's writing gives us an example:

RESPONSE to Jenny Willner, by Jakob Staberg

'Concussion', reaction to an 'unbearable' external or internal stimulus in an autoplastic manner (modifying the self) instead of an all-plastic manner (modifying the stimulus). A neoformation of the self is impossible without the previous destruction, either partial or total, or dissolution of the former self. A new ego cannot be formed directly from the previous ego, but from fragments, more or less elementary products of its disintegration. (Splitting, atomization.)[4]

Let us dwell for a moment on this articulating of forces, this new way of thinking organs that Willner brings to the fore in Ferenczi's writing. We can see it played out in Ferenczi's intricate relationship and confrontation with Freud. 'While Freud's *Three Essays* explain how the sexual development culminates in the primacy of the genital zone, Ferenczi declares his own ambition to "conform a more definite conception of the meaning [*Sinn*] and biological purpose [*biologischen Zweck*] of the achieving of this primacy." [...] Ferenczi ends up theorising not only genitality, but the genitals themselves',[5] Willner writes. An extraordinary observation on her part. This allows us to see how Ferenczi connects to a certain art of interpretation, where, by activating such Freudian notions as overdetermination and deferred action, the body, organs and organisms themselves are approached, whereby the transformations that intersect them now can begin to be articulated. Again to resonate with Deleuze: 'Consciousness is essentially reactive; this is why we do not know what a body can do, or what activity is capable of'.[6] In my mind, Willner acknowledges in an intricate way how Ferenczi's preoccupation with organs, hysteric fits of the body, lead to a specific art of interpretation. 'Ferenczi stresses that there is no neutral, transparent language that can represent the organic [...] Ferenczian organs do not come clear, but demand interpretation'.[7] Ferenczi's challenge to the biologist imaginary of his time, with its glorification of the dominant forces it contained, involves a radical reassessment in which what were thought of as so-called active forces are revealed as reactive, indeed, in which evolution itself, what is considered as development, must suddenly be understood as effects of catastrophes that have created trauma. Understanding bodies, psychic life, microscopic processes in this way involves the recognition of changes, mutations, indeed, the play of chance and coincidences; what appear to be stable entities, products of a given evolution, can in this reading be thought of as neurotic responses to chaotic, unknowable events imbued with the hidden Darwinian insight, that of *complete extinction* as an ever-forming principle: the death drive is at hand.

When it comes to the place of biology in Ferenczi's project, as stated earlier, Jenny Willner turns the relationship around. Contrary to previous notions, she shows that his 'bio-analysis' does not seek a basis or find justification in biopolitics rooted in the natural sciences; in fact, he directs the tools of psychoanalysis against contemporary discourses on biological processes themselves. As Willner points out, Ferenczi 'defines bioanalysis as a speculative science that would "carry over into the field of the natural sciences in a systematic manner the knowledge gained and the technique used by psychoanalysis"'.[8] Willner's analytical strategy makes it possible to see how Ferenczi's speculative manoeuvres are precisely effective deconstructions of a world of imagination according to which developmental optimism and the idealisation of progress understood as biological necessity could nurture an aggressive nationalism as well as affirm the interpretative primacy of natural science. Ferenczi's series of catastrophes, the notice of shock, convulsion and ubiquitous trauma, replace the notion of 'Wonders of Nature', which was seminal both for Haeckel's reception of Darwin and for Bölsche's narrative. For psychoanalysis itself, Willner's analysis becomes effective in that through these observations it dismantles the supposed notion within the psychoanalytic milieu that Ferenczi's critique of Freud could be undermined by reducing his thought to the product of a certain biologism. Willner's reading shows how Ferenczi's psychoanalytic work contains speculative models in which Freud's world of thought is at once challenged and taken to its extreme rather as a re-evaluation of all values.

The possibilities I would like to sketch given by Willner's work concern not only Ferenczi's re-evaluation of the contemporary popular science idealisation of violence and progress but his relationship to Freud and in particular the restructuring of the death drive he outlines towards the end of his life. If 'Beyond the Pleasure Principle', with its introduction of the death drive, constitutes an alien body in metapsychology that subsequent psychoanalytic theory has sought either to incorporate or displace, it is important for us to see how it operates, so to speak, in the thinking to which Ferenczi's work invites us. Willner's reminder of how the death drive, as it were, haunts Ferenczi's theoretical and clinical models right up to the crucial articles of the last few years and *The Clinical Diary* he kept can make us sense the outlines of a potential discourse within psychoanalytic metapsychology, a thinking yet to be realised. In other words, the question concerns how the impact of this alien body can be read in Ferenczi's work, perhaps in particular in the later texts, and, so my suggestion, as something *untimely* in Nietzsche's sense of the word. By following the reformulations and displacements of the death drive and its effects that *The Clinical Diary* in particular makes possible, I would argue in an attempt to follow Willner's line of thought that we can begin to discern new layers in Ferenczi's intellectual and clinical legacy. Willner's incisive analyses, which have drawn our attention to Ferenczi's thinking about bodies, organs and active forces, invite new readings of how the death drive works as an alien body in Ferenczi's corpus, being the object of certain yet unimagined transformations. Against this background, I would like to set Ferenczi's analyses in relation to lines of thought that at once reach towards our time, with its challenges and possible catastrophes, while at the same time seeming to emanate from the question Deleuze saw formulated in Spinoza's philosophy: a question that concerns precisely the nature of the forces whose interactions shape bodies and produce meaning, an observation that rests on the fact that we do not yet know what a body is capable of. 'Spinoza suggested a new direction for the sciences and philosophy. He said that we do not even know what a body can do, we talk about consciousness and spirit and chatter on about it all, but we do not know what a body is capable of, what forces belong to it or what they are preparing for'.[9] In this sense, Willner's reassessment of Ferenczi's relation to biology opens up certain trajectory lines in which questions of body, organs and thought can be raised.

To conclude, let's look at some details in Ferenczi's *Clinical Diary*. On 21 and 23 February 1932, he makes some interesting remarks that might shed light on what I have tried to highlight in Willner's work and the openings into Ferenczi's world of thought she offers. The context is the analytical task of working with traumatised patients in whom parts of the self have been split off, as it were, and the analytical approach being, in Ferenczi's words, to 'remove this split'. The reasoning concerns the exploration of how 'a destructive process results in productivity'.[10] In this way, a mental landscape is uncovered, a landscape Raluca Soreanu in her chapter of this book will explore in a way that amounts to a rethinking of the so-called metapsychology. The aim of psychoanalytic work is described by Ferenczi as a method 'to revive tactfully yet energetically the "ghost"'.[11] In other words, the psychoanalytic process strives 'slowly to persuade the dead or split-off fragment that it is not dead after all'.[12] The project revolves in this way around issues of death and survival; it explores psychic life in the form of encrypted fragments, ghosts, haunting dead parts but also the capacity for life within this processes. The note made on 23 February develops this notion, and deals subsequently with processes of awakening and 'transformation' which are explored in greater depth.[13] As so often in Ferenczi's *Clinical Diary*, we notice how the analysis follows 'a conscious lead by the patient'.[14] Here he states how, temporarily, certain 'principles' embodied in nature crystallise, which he designates on the basis of differences why they may be analysed qualitatively.

What is at stake here, and subsequently can be related to the death drive, is that something in 'the female organism' is contrasted with 'the egoism and self-assertion of the male'.[15] This leads the analysis to a re-evaluating of forces, but also a modification of the death drive itself.

Ferenczi interprets the forces at stake as an expression of a 'maternal willingness to suffer and capacity for suffering'.[16] Ferenczi's way of interpretation grasps organs qualitatively as forces: 'whenever a force or substance has been "subjected" to the changing, modifying, destructive influence of another force […] one must also reckon equally with the influence of the feminine principle, which we must assume to exist as a potential everywhere'.[17] What Ferenczi's argument amounts to is a way of thinking the models Freud elaborated in 'Beyond the Pleasure Principle' in a new way: 'All this would represent only a slight modification of Freud's assumption of life and death instincts. I would give the same thing other names'.[18] Rather than a supposedly male aggressiveness associated with the death instinct, Ferenczi instead presents a haunting insight that connects the death drive with the perception of an archaic mother. 'Egoism is the impulse to rid oneself of a quantity of unpleasure-producing tension at all costs'.[19] Against this ability stands the feminine principle that can seem frightening and overwhelming to the individual. 'Death=feminine, mother'.[20] How to understand this? I think that against the background of the death drive, the forces Ferenczi explores and associates with a feminine principle function as a capacity for life, bordering on death and at the same time acknowledging life beyond the individual: 'conciliatory drives and impulses are mobilized from everywhere and summoned as if by magic: just as in human society the feminine principle clusters in the strongly masculine principle'.[21] The prime example Ferenczi gives is the maternal function, understood as 'a toleration of parasitic beings, which develop a completely egoistic manner at the expense of the mother's own body'.[22] Perhaps it is in light of this capacity that his conception of masculinity as a hysterical fit should be understood: 'that masculinity only takes its place for traumatic reasons (primal scene), as a hysteric symptom'.[23] Willner's reading against the grain leads us to an understanding of Ferenczi's re-evaluation of the Oedipus theory – in contrast to an assumption of him turning to biology in search of a scientific foundation – as derived from an interpretation of organs as charged with meaning.

Notes

1. J. Willner, Part 2, p. 98.
2. J. Willner, Part 2, p. 7, 114.
3. G. Deleuze, *Nietzsche and Philosophy*, transl. by H. Tomlinson. London: Athlone Press, 1983, p. 40.
4. S. Ferenczi, *The Clinical Diary of Sándor Ferenczi*, 1988, p. 181.
5. J. Willner, Part 2, p. 95; S. Ferenczi, *Thalassa. A Theory of Genitality* [1924], transl. by H. A. Bunker. London, New York: Karnac, 1989, p. 15; *Versuch einer Genitaltheorie* [1924], in: S. Ferenczi, *Schriften zur Psychoanalyse II*, ed. by M. Bálint. Gießen: Psychosozial-Verlag, 2004, pp. 317–400, p. 330.
6. G. Deleuze, *Nietzsche and Philosophy*, p. 41.
7. J. Willner, Part 2, p. 112.
8. J. Willner, Part 2, p. 96; S. Ferenczi, *Thalassa*, p. 82.
9. G. Deleuze, *Nietzsche and Philosophy*, p. 39.
10. S. Ferenczi, *The Clinical Diary of Sándor Ferenczi*, p. 42.
11. Ibid., p. 39.
12. Ibid., p. 39f.
13. Ibid., p. 41.
14. Idem.
15. Idem.
16. Idem.
17. Idem.
18. Idem.
19. Ibid., p. 42.
20. Ibid., p. 183.
21. Ibid., p. 42.
22. Idem.
23. Ibid., p. 188.

What Does an Organ Do?

RESPONSE

to Jenny Willner, by Raluca Soreanu

I start from the 'coughing penis', a surprising and inspiring figuration that appears in Jenny Willner's writing. This curious figuration guides us through an important move in Ferenczi's text: the use of hysteria as a paradigm for interpreting organs. I believe we could not have made it as far as the 'coughing penis' without Willner's method. Its orientation is to the ways in which the Ferenczian text can be *used* in the psychoanalytic world, and perhaps beyond it, in cultural, social and political thinking and practice, and not to uncovering its hidden 'truths'. Her reading means that we take into account experiences of identification (of Ferenczi with Freud, of ourselves with Freud and Ferenczi, to name the first ones that come to mind), empathy and failures of empathy (Freud's failure of empathy with Ferenczi as analyst, which Jakob Staberg approached in the first part of this book), immersion in texts and in the world of discourse (Ferenczi's immersion in the biological readings of the time, while he was a chief medical officer in Transdanubia in the First World War, but also his capacity to read them against their grain). Addressing the issue of the *uses* of a text, Rita Felski[1] talks about post-critique, its being geared to the messiness of examples and it paying close attention to the multiple ways in which texts and persons connect. It is a post-critical exercise of imagination to wonder what the books on Ferenczi's desk were, during the First World War, while he was translating Freud's *Three Essays in the Theory of Sexuality*[2] to Hungarian, and while he was writing paragraphs of his *Thalassa*. Willner offers us a double experience of 'against the grain': she looks at how Ferenczi was reading biological texts against their evolutionist grain and she offers a reading against the grain of Ferenczi's speculative organology in *Thalassa*.[3] This double gesture does not turn the text against itself; instead, it turns it toward the future, it reveals its possibilities, it makes it ever more usable by psychoanalysts and social theorists of our time.

The 'coughing penis' is thus a useful post-critical fantasy, emerging from reading Freud's Dora case alongside Ferenczi's speculative organology in *Thalassa*. For me, it is also a useful *clinical* fantasy: while in the psychoanalytic consulting room with my patients, the question 'what does an organ *do*?' is more useful than the questions 'what *is* an organ?' or 'what is an organ *for*?'.

RESPONSE to Jenny Willner, by Raluca Soreanu

I believe that Ferenczi himself stays very close to this question, 'what does an organ do?', and his understanding of hysteria is a radically reconfigured one, in the sense that it has a complex way of discussing the creativities of the hysterical symptom. In his own writings on hysteria, Ferenczi is less interested in coughs and paralyses, and more fascinated by the mobilisation of the 'inside' of bodies in a phenomenon that he calls 'hysterical materialisation'.[4] Discussing the globus hystericus (a lump in the throat), he 'descends' into the digestive tract, and becomes interested in the material transformations that take place in the patients' throats: 'The patients themselves speak of a lump stuck in their throats, and we have every reason to believe that the corresponding contractions of the circular and longitudinal musculature of the oesophagus produce not only the paraesthesia of a foreign body, but that a kind of foreign body, a lump, really is brought about'.[5] The accent here is on the productive and materialising force of hysteria: the lump in the throat is not merely a hallucination, but it is part of a new 'grammar' of organs, a stirring up of the tissues of the throat, or of the contents of the stomach, or of the intestinal matter, which implies a capacity for condensation, displacement, repetition, or identification. This showcasing of the creativities of the hysterical symptom has important implications for how we can imagine the relationship between the psyche and the soma. In short, there is a 'horizontalising' gesture here, where the soma is just as capable of complex acts as the psyche. Willner follows Ferenczi in *Thalassa*, and guides us through his conception of the psychosoma.

Psychoanalytic theory is thus re-embodied, even if the bodies are those of fish, squid, jellyfish, octopi and amphibians, humans or raccoons. In dialogue with Jenny Willner and Donna Haraway, I share an interest in 'neural extravaganzas, fibrous entities, flagellated beings, myofibril braids, matted and felted microbial and fungal tangles, probing creepers, swelling roots, reaching and climbing tendrilled ones'.[6] The 'coughing penis' is a figuration in the spirit of Ferenczi's theory, maintaining a curiosity about what organs *do*, and not fixated into what they are *for*, or, in Willner's terms, alert to the fact that 'organs are not what they seem'.[7] Or, sometimes, '[t]he penis literally makes a scene'.[8]

In dialogue with Jenny Willner, I picture an enlarging of our imaginary around the forms of the life drive. This imaginary of the life drive comes from taking seriously the instances of *radical plasticity* of organs, psychic fragments, blood vessels or nerve fibres. In certain circumstances, they are able to create new shapes or new configurations. I believe that one of the most important contributions of Ferenczi's work is that of pluralising our imaginary of the fusion of and defusion of the life drive and the death drive. Ferenczi preserves the dualism of the drives. This comes through in his 1929 text 'The Unwelcome

Child and His Death-Instinct', where he talks about the 'unwelcome child' and the 'dropped child' and their proximity to the death drive.[9] But as he makes clear in *The Clinical Diary*, our interest in the death drive should not obscure an equally attentive eye to the manifestations of the life drive.[10] In *Thalassa*, the immersion in the sphere of the life drive takes the form of an investigation of a variety of 'protective' formations that the psychosoma can create. He looks at various ad hoc protective bladders, vesicles or pustulae filled with fluid, usually developed under the strain of the traumatic attack. In the third section of the book, I discuss the psychic agency Orpha as a complicated result of the fusion of life drive and death drive, and also as another kind of protective psychic phenomenon, a 'guardian angel' that watches over the trauma scene from the outside, at a time when the suffering is unbearable. The value of this 'life drive imaginary' can only come through as something-other to a naïve vitalism, a generic optimistic image of the prevalence of life over death. Willner's reading thus renders Ferenczi's life drive imaginary usable precisely by specifying the ways in which it is not a form of vitalism, but it is articulated as an ingenious counter-narrative to the vitalisms of his time. Unlike Wilhelm Bölsche's fish-orgy,[11] Ferenczi's fish are not 'bound for glory'.[12]

In Ferenczi's narrative, smaller or larger catastrophes interrupt progress and linear development. Jenny Willner captures this interruption brilliantly, in terms of its internal poetics, its historical context and its political implications. To the many images of radical plasticity in *Thalassa* she assembles for us, I would like to add two closely interlinked ones: the cooperation of organs and the layering of organs.

In *Thalassa*, Ferenczi talks about an internal qualitative differentiation in the sphere of the libido, which can lead to an 'organ libido' and even an 'organ individuality'.[13] As he writes: 'According to the "theory of genitality", the cooperation of organs and of their component parts does not consist simply of the automatic adding together of useful workmen to give a sum total of performance. Each organ possesses a certain "individuality"; in each and every organ there is repeated that conflict between ego- and libidinal interests which, too, we have encountered hitherto only in the analysis of *psychic individualities*'.[14] Ferenczi differentiates between the 'altruistic' functioning of organs and autoerotic or self-gratifying processes in the tissues. Organs are thus capable of cooperation, but this is not a guaranteed outcome; it takes struggle and a complicated negotiation between opposing forces.

Ferenczi constructs a whole new series of terms, which are both clinically and politically interesting: cooperation, conciliation, endurance of suffering, selflessness, appeasement, adaptation to renunciation, self-denial, compromise. In one entry of *The Clinical Diary,* Ferenczi even experiments with a modification to the sphere of the dualism death drive/life drive. He renames them the 'drive of self-assertion' and the 'drive of conciliation'.[15] The 'selflessness' he evokes, including the 'selflessness' of organs, emerges in relation to the scene of trauma. The 'drive for conciliation' appears as a basis of the reality principle. To survive, as any sort of individuality, means to practice a kind of politics of self-limitation. In the same spirit, Jenny Willner argues against Ferenczi's being a monistic thinker: what we find in his texts is not a fantasy of coalescence of everything into 'one', but of cooperation. This is important because of the structural parallels between the coalescing swarm/herd and the authoritarian crowd waiting for the leader, which Willner captures so well.

The second instance of radical plasticity I evoke here is that of a layering of organs: it appears that in the moment of trauma '[n]ewly created organs in respect to their functions are only superposed upon the old without destroying them; even when the new functions make use of the material medium of the old, the latter organisation or function, although apparently given up, remains 'potential', 'biologically unconscious', and may again become active under certain circumstances'.[16] This layering or superposition of organs means that any idea of evolution is questioned. The layered organs contain many times within themselves, many references to other moments, including to other catastrophes. It is a curious concentricity of catastrophes, where forward movement or progress will almost certainly involve a level of denial of this multiplicity of temporal references.

Jenny Willner qualifies *Thalassa* as a book of 'creatures that would have *preferred not to conquer land*'.[17] This is a political image of self-limitation, of abstaining. These creatures are not bound for glory. They have their own insurgent breathing techniques, their improbable forms of resilience, their modes of memory, their ways of splitting themselves into fragments, but also of cooperating with one another. Even the penis is not what it seems; it is perhaps a 'coughing penis', one that stutters and cannot advance in a linear fashion, cannot conquer new foreign territories, and is instead interrupted by previous catastrophes.

The perspective in *Thalassa* turns away from a modernist narrative of progress: we do not meet the gaze of the settler, encompassing the land from controlling heights, but the unsettled and uncertain view of the sea creatures and their observer. They both seem to be located in the sea, amid moving waters, ridden with doubts and the constant threat of dissolution. With Jenny Willner, we understand that in *Thalassa*, 'evolution is not a triumph, but a tragedy, the untold history of unmourned losses, a tale of survival that demands a new narrative'.[18]

Notes

1. See R. Felski, *The Limits of Critique*. Chicago: University of Chicago Press, 2015; and R. Felski, 'Postcritical Reading', *American Book Review* 38(5), 2017, pp. 4–5.
2. S. Freud, 'Fragment of an Analysis of a Case of Hysteria' [1905], in: S. Freud, *A Case of Hysteria, Three Essays on Sexuality and Other Works* (1901–1905), *SE* 7, pp. 7–122.
3. S. Ferenczi, *Thalassa. A Theory of Genitality* [1924], transl. by H. A. Bunker. London, New York: Karnac, 1989.
4. S. Ferenczi, 'The Phenomena of Hysterical Materialization' [1919], in: S. Ferenczi, *Further Contributions to the Theory and Technique of Psycho-Analysis*, comp. by J. Rickman, transl. by J. I. Suttie. London: Karnac, 1994, pp. 89–104.
5. Ibid., p. 92.
6. D. J. Haraway, *Staying with the Trouble: Making Kin in the Chthulucene*. Durham: Duke UP, 2016, p. 32.
7. J. Willner, Part 2, p. 115.
8. J. Willner, Part 2, p. 116.
9. S. Ferenczi, 'The Unwelcome Child and His Death Instinct' [1929], in: S. Ferenczi, *Final Contributions to the Problems and Methods of Psycho-Analysis*, ed. by M. Bálint, transl. by E. Mosbacher. London: Karnac, 1994, pp. 102–107.
10. S. Ferenczi, *The Clinical Diary of Sándor Ferenczi* [1932], ed. by J. Dupont, transl. by M. Bálint, N. Z. Jackson. Cambridge, Mass., London: Harvard UP, 1995.
11. W. Bölsche, *Love-Life in Nature. The Story of the Evolution of Love*, Vol. I, transl. by C. Brown. New York: Albert & Charles Boni, 1926.
12. J. Willner, Part 2, p. 109.
13. S. Ferenczi, *Thalassa*, p. 82.
14. Ibid., p. 82.
15. S. Ferenczi, *The Clinical Diary of Sándor Ferenczi*, p. 41.
16. S. Ferenczi, *Thalassa*, p. 93, fn.
17. J. Willner, Part 2, p. 111.
18. J. Willner, Part 2, p. 102.

PART 3
Catastrophe and the Creativity of Fragments
Toward a Phenomenology of the Scene of Trauma

by Raluca Soreanu,
with responses from Jenny Willner and Jakob Staberg

Catastrophe and the Creativity of Fragments
Toward a Phenomenology of the Scene of Trauma

Raluca Soreanu

What does it mean to have survived a psychic catastrophe? What happens to the psyche at this time of catastrophe? With Sándor Ferenczi, we can imagine a catastrophe that is not a single, unitary event, but a *scene*, where several elements hold together in relation and interact, sometimes in a violent manner, where certain structures and psychic positions are formed, and others are destroyed. What kind of scene are we following here? How might we make sense of the different moves or psychic events that happen in this scene?

Catastrophe, event and trauma are at the core of Ferenczi's vocabulary. They are not identical or interchangeable terms, but together they constitute a way of talking about psychic processes that implies a series of important revisions to Freudian metapsychology. In what follows, with Ferenczi, we step into the domain of an *eventful psychoanalysis*. The images that predominate here are those of fractures, splits, atomisations, pulverisations, leakages, detritus, but also new formations, protective membranes, expansions, contagions, and inner growths.

We also step into the domain of a *metapsychology of fragmented psyches*, which is closely connected to the notion of the event. Ultimately, the events we are looking at are events of psychic fragmentation. Ferenczi's great interest in psychic splitting amounts to filling a phenomenological gap in psychoanalysis, by giving precise descriptions of what is being split in the psyche and of the 'life' of the fragments that result from the splitting.[1]

To the series catastrophe–event–trauma, we can add a fourth term: 'the shock of what is'. We can start with the voice of Cornelius Castoriadis: for him, 'the shock of what is' (*Anstoß*) is not a case of the environment causing a determinate outcome in the subject or in the living being. Instead the kind of shock he has in mind 'sets in motion the formative (imaging/imagining, presenting and relating) capacities of the living being'.[2] It is thus a sort of creative and consequential collision with the environment. This is already suggested in Fichte's original development of this idea. Literally, *Anstoß* is a 'stimulus' or a 'push'. For Castoriadis, just as for Ferenczi, the challenge is not to explain how the living being (or the subject) is determined by the environment, but to explain how the living being's self-determination is *affected* by the environment. In other words, taking seriously 'the shock of what is' means that we take seriously the fact that we have a relationship with the world that lies beyond our representations. It is however an encounter that sets in motion the process of representation that affects representations, without determining them. Ultimately, this shock marks the capacity of the self for being affected.

Set against the backdrop of this capacity of the self of being affected, the psychic catastrophe that I will capture in the following pages describes an *asymmetric encounter*, one between large and small, between powerful and vulnerable, between rigid and plastic. Indeed, we will see that Ferenczi's paradigm of relationality is an asymmetric one.

Asymmetry is written into Ferenczi's formulation on the 'confusion of tongues'. Trauma occurs in the form of a 'confusion of tongues' between the children and the adults. Children speak the 'language of tenderness' which is an experimental, playful and expansive register, through which more and more of the outside world is taken inside. Adults speak the 'language of passion', the register of adult sexuality, which has known repression and guilt. The meeting of the two languages causes children shock, a sense of intrusion, and an unbearable intensity. There is always some violence in the meeting of the two registers, as they do not just intersect, or cross one another: instead, there is a clash, and the language of passion intrudes into the language of tenderness.

In describing the psychic effects of the encounter of the two registers – of tenderness and of passion – Ferenczi acts as a phenomenologist. In what follows, I explore the phenomenology of this fragmentation. For now, let us succinctly note that Ferenczi shows how the fragile ego of the child is pulverised, atomised, de-materialised, only to afterwards take the shape, through a process of imitation, of the closest form that she encountered at the moment of the attack: the shape of the aggressor. I argue that this is the tragic side of the identification with the aggressor: it is perhaps not best seen as a mere introjection of the aggressor into a still existing ego, but literally replicating the shape of the aggressor, at a time when the psyche has become no more than a cloud of disparate particles, in search of a form. As Ferenczi tells us in a short note 'On Shock', in the hour of the attack, the self is 'unfest, unsolid' and it loses its form only to adopt an imposed form easily and without resistance, 'like a sack of flour'.[3]

The confusion of tongues is thus an *asymmetric encounter between two psychic registers*.

For Ferenczi, any traumatic event occurs in two moments and it includes three presences. A first moment is when the language of passion intrudes into the language of tenderness (and this can take the form of an actual sexual assault or of a psychic transmission). The second moment is that of denial (*Verleugnung*), when a third adult called upon to recognise the intrusion fails to do so. It is only through the action of denial that an intrusive event becomes a trauma, bringing a near-death of the self, producing a gap in memory, and destroying the capacity of the subject to trust their own senses.

The 'confusion of tongues' is more than a narrow proposition for understanding sexual abuse and early trauma. It is a theory of the subject. The scene of the trauma that we will be disentangling over the next pages is also a scene of becoming-subject. For Ferenczi, no one can be 'outside' of the confusion of tongues. Existing purely in the register of tenderness is more of a clinical-theoretical fiction, which we need in order to better understand the encounter with the Other. Neither of the two registers can exist on its own; they are bound up together. In my interpretation, the register of passion is structurally prefigured in the register of tenderness. There is a structural *impossibility* of *not* having an encounter with the Other. There are resonances here between Sándor Ferenczi and Jean Laplanche in terms of the importance given to the Other for the formation of subjectivity. For Laplanche, the subject is defined by the fact that she has an originary relationship with the enigma of the Other or with the enigmatic messages pertaining to adult sexuality. The originary mechanisms are not 'in person' but 'in otherness', and there is a constant reference to implantation (by the other) and to intromission (of something coming from the other).[4] What brings the two theorists together is a kind of 'clinical anthropology' that grounds their theories, which establishes 'the child' and 'the adult' as different, not as developmental ages or as individual psyches, but precisely as *psychic positions*. We are thus confronted with a universally asymmetrical situation.

Ferenczi's confusion of tongues leaps out of the consulting room: it is relevant for making sense of social scenes of submission, misrecognition and denial. The social world also has its own 'tongues'. Whenever a demand of recognition is not being addressed in its own 'tongue', this causes a traumatic wound. Or it causes the re-actualisation of a traumatic mark caused by a similar crossing between 'tongues'. Through this shock of registers, the capacity for collective symbolisation is interrupted. The capacity for social polysemy is affected. The social imaginary cannot create new contents and new connections; and it cannot mourn for its losses. Denial, as it functions at the level of groups and societies, is not a refusal to acknowledge some real traumatic fact, but it is equivalent to the very negation of the possibility of plurality of meanings.[5]

Donna Haraway writes: 'It matters what stories we tell to tell other stories with; it matters what concepts we think to think other concepts with'.[6] Ferenczi has important concepts to think our concepts and our impasses with: catastrophe, trauma, event. They constitute a vocabulary for making sense of the eventfulness of our time: the Covid-19 pandemic, extreme weather events, the climate crisis. Ferenczi's psychoanalytic thinking is eventful.

The dialogues of this book are starting from Ferenczi's stories and trying to tell other stories with them, be they stories about epistemology, about metapsychology, or stories about the clinical encounter. In his writing, Jakob Staberg (the first part of this book) reminded me of the atmosphere of a 'tactile eye' present in Ferenczi's stories. This tactile mode of knowledge is assembled by post-humanist and feminist thinker Donna Haraway in her book *Staying with the Trouble*, where she talks about 'tentacular knowledge'.[7] She reminds us that 'tentacle' comes from the Latin *tentaculum,* which means 'feeler' and *tentare*, meaning 'to feel' and 'to try'. In the story of ten qualitatively different psychic events of Ferenczi's scene of trauma that I tell below, we encounter him as 'tentacular' psychoanalyst and thinker: feeling, trying, experimenting, hesitating, advancing, retracting, revising.

With Jenny Willner (the second part of this book), we come close to some of the odd critters that populate Ferenczi's sea in *Thalassa*,[8] to their destinies and to the extraordinary importance they play in our attempt to make sense of psychic process and its extreme plasticity. Ferenczi establishes an analogy between sleep, dreams, sex life and the life of fantasy, to look at a continuous regressive trend manifest in psychic life, which strives for the re-establishment of the intrauterine situation. But he also stays with the fish-becoming-amphibian, which is a reminder of the creative edge of catastrophe, of what the receding of the oceans can enable, in terms of creative adaptations and the formation of new organs, and ultimately of new forms of existence. The spirit of this immersion in the sea is close to Haraway's 'sf', which stands for more than one thing. As she writes:

> The tentacular ones tangle me in sf. Their many appendages make string figures; they entwine me in the poiesis – the making – of speculative fabulation, science fiction, science fact, speculative feminism, *soin de ficelle,* so far. The tentacular ones make attachments and detachments; they make cuts and knots; they make a difference; they weave paths and consequences but not determinisms; they are both open and knotted in some ways and not others. sf is storytelling and fact telling; it is the patterning of possible worlds and possible times, material-semiotic worlds,

gone, here, and yet to come. I work with string figures as a theoretical trope, a way to think-with a host of companions in sympoietic threading, felting, tangling, tracking, and sorting. I work with and in sf as material-semiotic composting, as theory in the mud, as muddle.

Theory, including psychoanalytic theory, is thus re-embodied. It is equally the case if the bodies are those of fish, squid, jellyfish, octopi and amphibians, or 'fingery beings' like humans or raccoons.[9] Both Haraway and Ferenczi, and the three of us, tangled in the dialogue of this book, share an interest in 'neural extravaganzas, fibrous entities, flagellated beings, myofibril braids, matted and felted microbial and fungal tangles, probing creepers, swelling roots, reaching and climbing tendrilled ones'.[10]

What is important in Ferenczi's writing is that this keen interest in fish and amphibians does not amount to biologism, or biological determinism. His 'bioanalysis' in *Thalassa* is an attempt to show the existence of a *psychic* sub-stratum manifest in all organic and inorganic matter. I believe his gesture of turning to sea critters is in resonance with contemporary feminist thinkers, who show us how to pay close attention to marine beings, and to learn from their breathing techniques, their resilience, their modes of memory, their ways of splitting themselves into fragments and also of relating to one another. This is the case in Alexis Pauline Gumbs's writings, *Undrowned: Black Feminist Lessons from Marine Mammals* and *Dub: Finding Ceremony*.[11] As Gumbs tells us, her project is 'an artefact and tool for breath retaining and interspecies ancestral listening'.[12] And a few striking questions follow, all relating to interspecies imaginaries: 'what if you could breathe like whales who sing underwater and recycle air to sing again before coming up for air? What if you could breathe like coral from a multitude of simultaneous openings connected to one source built upon the bones of all your dead? What if you could breathe like cyanobacteria who made the sky into oxygen millions of years ago and sent their contemporaries to a world of sulphur deep under the ocean and ground?' All these questions invoke a radical plasticity, the ability to become-whale, and then become-coral, and then become-cyanobacteria. For Ferenczi, it is the scene of trauma that contains the possibility of such radical and surprising plasticity, as we will see in the following pages, across ten different moments of the scene.

In *Thalassa*, Ferenczi invites us to his own psychoanalytic interspecies story of listening:

> Let me ask you to picture the surface of the earth as still entirely enveloped in water. All plant and animal life still pursues its existence

in an environment of sea-water. Geologic and atmospheric conditions are such that portions of the ocean bed become raised above the surface of the water. The animals and plants thus set upon dry land must either succumb or else adapt themselves to a land and air existence; above all, they must become habituated to obtaining from the air, instead of from the water, the gases necessary to their existence – oxygen and carbon dioxide.[13]

Ferenczi's starting from the sea, in his myth of *Thalassa*, constitutes a fresh direction to think with. In our times, voices of the 'blue humanities' start from the sea as a political act, placing cultural history in an oceanic rather than terrestrial context. Human civilisation and development have been situated mostly in pastoral fields, enclosed gardens or cities. What happens if we start from the sailor and swimmer, from the movement across oceans, and from estrangements at sea, rather than progressive settlements on land? One of the things that happen is that the perspective changes: it is no longer the gaze of the settler, encompassing the land from controlling heights, but it is the unsettled and uncertain view amid moving waters, ridden with doubts and the constant threat of dissolution. As Steve Mentz argues in *Shipwreck Modernity: Ecologies of Globalization, 1550–1719*,[14] from an oceanic perspective, even the story of modernity is ultimately a story of shipwrecks; it is a catastrophe-ridden epic where expansion happens in relation to sea crossings, and to the many disasters waiting to happen. In our times traversed by migrant crises, and with boats capsizing while vulnerable humans are trying to get across borders and walls, it appears ever more important to start from the sea.

A Frame: On Ferenczi's Model of Memory

In an intriguing note of 1932, Ferenczi argues: '[m]emory is […] a collection of *scars of shocks* in the ego'.[15] A curious third element appears here: it is not just *wounds* (unmourned forms of suffering) and *scars* (mourned forms of suffering), but also a *scar*-tissue, which I read as the structural effect in the psyche of an accumulation of acts of mourning. Ferenczi speaks of 'the development of memory from the mental scar-tissue created by bad experiences'.[16] To have memory is to possess the capacity to be affected, and this most of the time includes being overwhelmed, broken, split.

It is not surprising that we find a note on 'wounds' at the core of Ferenczi's definition of psychoanalytic process. Psychoanalysis is work on wounds. Psychoanalysis is a form of endurance across wounds:

> Psycho-analysis […] is a proceeding that seeks to cure neurotic conflict not by a fresh displacement or temporary repression, but radically. It endeavours not to tie up psychic wounds but to lay them bare, to render them conscious. Of course, not without 're-educating' the patient, and accustoming him to endure the painful ideas instead of fleeing from them to disease.[17]

I argued that 'memory-wounds' are not to be read as 'wounds of memory' or 'wounds to memory'.[18] Instead, memory-wounds are those kinds of wounds out of which memory is made. They are 'wounds-toward-memory'. They are the wounds that through particular transformations can come to form someone's memory. Or the 'scar-tissue' that Ferenczi talks about.[19]

Ferenczi's constructions around 'wounds', 'scars' and 'scar-tissues' point to an important quality of the traumatic shock: one of the results of the trauma is precisely the precipitation of representation, of images, of capacities of relating, of specific faculties and even hyper-faculties, and not the interruption of symbolisation. That is to say that the relationship between traumatic shocks, on the one hand, and creativity and memory, on the other hand, is not a simple or obvious one and it calls for further elucidation.

For Ferenczi, this precipitation of the imaginative process happens through the operation of the 'unresting Eros':

> I have no hesitation in regarding even memory-traces as scars, so to speak, of traumatic impressions, i.e. as products of the destructive instinct, which, however, the unresting Eros nevertheless understands how to employ for its own ends, i.e. for the preservation of life. Out of these it shapes a new psychical system, which enables the ego to orientate itself more correctly in its environment, and to form sounder judgements. In fact it is only the destructive instinct that 'wills evil', while it is Eros that 'creates good' out of it.[20]

In Ferenczi's theory, memory operates both through the ego and through the id, constituting two different regimes or tracks of memory, defined in their difference by their object-relatedness.[21] In the *regime of id memories*, we find 'bodily sensations', referring to primal life and death trends (*Züge*). When these are elaborated retrospectively by the ego, they are lived as emotions. In the *regime of ego memories*, we encounter 'projected sensations', referring to the environment and to external occurrences. These tend to produce effects of objectivity, and they are experienced as verifiable consciously. The crux of the matter is how these regimes of memory interact, and whether the emotionality of the bodily sensations and the objectivity effects of the projected sensations come to be connected.

This image of a system of memory functioning across different registers has important consequences in terms of our understanding of repetition, the scene of trauma, and regression. This triad – *repetition/scene/regression* – is at the core of Ferenczi's metapsychology of fragmented psyches and his revisions to Freudian metapsychology. It is also our frame for the discussion of the ten moments of the scene of trauma.

Repetition

In 1920, Freud discovered a new form of repetition, which is not in service of the pleasure principle. When he solidified this important discovery, because of its strong anchoring in the primacy of the death drive, he closed the path to exploring other kinds of repetition. Our imaginary on repetition became partly 'frozen' after the uncovering of its 'daemonic' aspect. In a succinct formulation, in 'Beyond the Pleasure Principle', Freud theorises two types of repetition.[22] The first one is in service of the pleasure principle and it proceeds by linking. It happens in the transference, in the psychoanalytic setting, and it leads to recollection. The second type of repetition is in service of the death drive, and it is an attempt to restore a previous state of things, an attempt to return to the inanimate by way of a total extinction of tension in psychic life. This second kind of 'daemonic' repetition represents the core discovery of the text 'Beyond the Pleasure Principle'.

With Ferenczi, we can imagine a kind of repetition that does not serve directly the pleasure principle, nor does it bear its first and most important connection to the death drive. It is primarily a *reparative repetition* aiming at eliminating residues of unworked-through traumas and at restoring some elements of a pre-traumatic state of the ego (or of the proto-ego). This repetition takes the form of an *eventful reliving* of the trauma. The 'eventfulness' of this sort of reliving is manifested primarily in traumatic dreams and in the consulting room.

Ferenczi gave a whole different meaning to the series repetition/remembering/reliving. Freud contrasted remembering with repeating and distinguished sharply between insight (memory or recollection) and experience (repetition or regression). Ferenczi saw repetition, and particularly regression or experiential reliving, as one of the tracks of remembering. Importantly, reliving is the way of gaining access to the child in the adult, or what Ferenczi speaks of in terms of 'child analysis in the analysis of adults'.[23]

Scene

The Freudian *Nachträglichkeit*, translated by Laplanche as 'afterwardsness',[24] refers to a temporal logic that governs the psychic world, and where we have a system of 'scenes', a kind of psychic scenography emerging through the *interaction* effects between different moments in time.[25] In short, the traumatic consequences of the first scene are only released in the form of a (hysterical) symptom as a result of the retrospective action of the second scene, which has the power to reactivate or revitalise the memory traces of the first scene. As Freud explains when he discusses the case of Katharina, the memory of the first scene persists, in a defensively isolated state, in a kind of limbo, or 'in storage'. It is somewhat like a foreign body, constituted by way of the intensity of the excitation experienced at the time. The second scene reactivates it by way of connections and homologies. There is thus no exclusive power of the initial mnemonic trace. The power emanates precisely from the interaction between the different moments. The effect of afterwardsness depends on the articulation of the various scenes, and crucially includes processes of defence and repression.

John Fletcher takes us through some very interesting tensions that pass through the Freudian system of notions around the *Nachträglichkeit*.[26] Crucially, in my reading, he points to Freud's insistence on the centrality of the first scene (which he will then trace back to an originary seduction scene). He refers to the other scenes as 'auxiliaries'. This statement on auxiliaries is counterintuitively accompanied by the assertion that there is a kind of infantile sexual indifference or apathy in relation to the first scene of abuse. The first scene only gains its status through the occurrence of the subsequent ones. Thus, memory comes to be lived as a contemporary event. In simpler terms, without the second moment, there would have been no trauma in the first moment. This thesis on infantile sexual indifference or apathy is very difficult to defend. It installs a certain sense of *equality* among mnemic traces that is also implausible. The idea of a very fragile ego, still unable to handle certain types of stimulation and easily broken by overstimulation, escapes any kind of systematic articulation.

Here, the Ferenczian metapsychology of fragmented psyches can lead to useful questionings. The young fragile ego is neither apathetic nor indifferent; on the contrary, it is very sensitive to the moments when adults cease to address it in what Ferenczi referred to as 'the language of tenderness' and start to address it in the incomprehensible and overburdening (at the time) 'language of passion', which is specific to a register of sexuality that is unliveable by the child but with the cost of the fragmentation of the ego. While Freud would say that there was no trauma as such in the first moment, with Ferenczi we come to understand how the selection between the mnemic traces is done, so that not all memories have the potential of the subsequent contribution to the complicated palimpsest of different scenes and temporalities that can constitute a 'trauma'. In brief, the stimulation of the child via the language of passion results in the 'pool' of scenes that the psyche can then weave, via composing different temporalities, into a trauma.

In what follows, I would like to discuss the quality of the relation between the different scenes/elements that come to constitute a trauma. Fletcher suggests that in the construction of his idea of 'screen memories',[27] Freud is primarily guided by a metonymical logic. This means that 'the displacement from experience to screen takes place [...] between two adjacent elements within a simultaneous ensemble'.[28] Fletcher goes on to argue that Freud oscillates between this metonymic interpretation of memory (where there is a substitution of insignificant for significant parts within a large whole) and a metaphoric interpretation (where the elements are put in a relation of similitude or analogy). It is crucial to note that in his *Nouveaux fondements pour la psychanalyse*, Jean Laplanche proposed a use of the couple metaphor/metonymy that is crucial in making sense of the functioning of the life drive and the death drive, respectively.[29]

According to Laplanche, the life drive and the death drive are two aspects of the sexual drive. The life sexual drive corresponds to a total and totalising object. It is linked (which in a Freudian sense, in Laplanche's account, means that it is maintained more or less coherent and it is not split in pieces) by a relation to an object in view of or in process of an act of totalisation.[30] This means that the life drive is more inclined to metaphorical, than to metonymical displacements. This is the case because precisely the kinds of structures that present a certain totality, a certain internal articulation, are susceptible to become the matter of analogies. This gesture toward some sort of totality makes an operation of analogy thinkable. The death drive seems to correspond more to metonymical operations, because it is always achieving a partial object: an object that is unstable, formless and in fragments. By this reasoning, it is of crucial importance if we can qualify a relation between different elements as metaphorical or metonymical.

This brings us to Ferenczi, to his conception of the symbol, and to his ideas on analogical thinking. Association – linking across levels of sensoriality and signification – brings an alteration of material structures, and a re-organisation of the very fleshiness of the body. '[T]he symbol – a thing of flesh and blood', Ferenczi writes.[31]

The implications of this conception of the symbol are profound. I would like to ponder here idea of the non-arbitrary that emerges from Ferenczi's work and from his philosophical ideas on mimetism and analogy. Even language imitates the body and body parts in a complicated manner. This means that associations have a *necessary* aspect to them, and thus they also need to be very *precise*. Marion Oliner has recently drawn to our attention that although there is a growing body of work in psychoanalytic theory on the irrepresentable, the non-represented or non-represented mental states, we are still confronted with an unsettling clinical-empirical puzzle in the fact that there is often a very striking *accuracy* in the enactments and actualisations of the traumatic events, even when the memory of them remains inaccessible to consciousness.[32] This is to say that the psycho-soma is able to re-stage the traumatic events with a great level of precision. This precision and minuteness of detail leads us to believe that the crux of the matter is not that these marks were not presented in any way to the psyche, or that they belong to the realm of the irrepresentable. Oliner uses 'non-represented' in inverted commas,[33] to draw our attention to the overuse of this term to cover situations where what is actually missing is the associations between different modes of representation (or, we would say, between different modes of presentation in the psyche). The crux of the matter, rather, is another Ferenczian theme: that of *splitting* of the psyche during a moment of excessive stimulation, when the psyche cannot convert the amount of free energy invading it into linked energy. In short, we can say that the reason association is at times very difficult and painful across different sensorial modalities is because we are dealing with modes of presentation belonging to different split-off parts of the psyche, rather than because the traumatic event has not presented itself to the psyche in any way that produces a mark.

Returning to Freud, this brings a significant challenge to the thesis of the infantile sexual indifference. All the details that appear in the reliving of the traumatic scene have to have made a sensorial inscription, which was retained in some way. The choice of elements in the trauma scene and their relations are non-arbitrary. Also, non-traumatic memories compose details that needed to have had a personal significance at the time of their selection. Freud got disturbingly far from being able to account why one *particular* scene (and not another one!) out of the countless moments of a child's life becomes the scene of trauma, and why some sensory elements and not others are tied into a non-traumatic memory.

The Ferenczian reading of *Nachträglichkeit* would entail, firstly, a psychoanalytically plausible version of a type of 'time-travel', where, via what Ferenczi calls memory of the id, or sensorial memory, we become able to 'touch' another time. Here, I use 'touch' as a metaphor for multi-sensorial access, not just the strictly tactile one – it may be acoustic, olfactive, kinetic etc. Secondly, a Ferenczian *Nachträglichkeit* also involves in the structure of the traumatic scene a third presence, which 'locks-in' the trauma, via denial (or misrecognition of the nature or of the magnitude of the child's experience, whose world was broken by the intrusion of the language of passion of the adult). When, in a clinical setting, different sensorial modalities become linked with one another, and the memory of the id becomes connected in stronger ways to the memory of the ego, what we achieve is *effects of authenticity*. Originally, the trauma brought the splitting of sensorial modalities and of parts of the more or less developed ego, producing *effects of inauthenticity*. It is crucial to mark that the memory of the id is capable of some form of inscription. This means that both in the 'locking-in' of the trauma, and in its subsequent unpacking and working-through, the memory of the id has a leading role. The reliving of a different moment in time and the recuperation of the split-off parts of the ego unfold *in the spirit of the marks inscribed via the memory of the id*. In other words, healing occurs guided by and in the spirit of the memory of the id.

Regression

In the second part of this book, Jenny Willner took us through the ontogenetic-phylogenetic parallels that structure Ferenczi's *Thalassa*. This surprising tracing of the overlaying of catastrophes across different registers of memory brings an important insight: there is a kind of regression that is not best seen as a return to a more 'primitive' developmental stage, but as accessing a more ancient way of putting elements in relations. In *The Clinical Diary*,[34] Ferenczi argues: 'under certain conditions, it can happen that the (organic, perhaps also the inorganic) substance recovers its psychic quality, not utilized since primordial times'; and '[i]n moments of great need, when the psychic system proves to be incapable of an adequate response, or when these specific organs or functions (nervous and psychic) have been violently destroyed, then the primordial psychic powers are aroused, and it will be these forces that will seek to overcome disruption. In such moments, when the psychic system fails, the organism begins to think.'[35] What is surprising here is that the Freudian logic of hysterical conversion is turned on its head. For Freud, conversion is a scene where organs, limbs and nerves are transformed according to a psychic logic, which challenges strict anatomical laws. For Ferenczi, in contrast, there exists a 'language of organs', where various elements (tissue, limbs, cells, nerves) are arranged in meaningful relations. Anatomy is already impelled by psychic 'motives'.

In her book *Gut Feminism*, Elizabeth Wilson discusses the different perspectives on the relationship between the psyche and the soma in Freud's work and Ferenczi's work, and some of the implications of this difference.[36] In the Rat Man case history, Freud argues that there is 'leap from a mental process to a somatic innervation' that is characteristic of conversion hysteria, but he also claims that this leap 'can never be fully comprehensible to us'.[37] In other words, there is a dissociation of somatic symptoms from anatomical constraint.[38] We are thus met with image of a leap or a gap between the mental or the somatic, or a spatial divide between a psychic event and a bodily one. Conversion hysteria enigmatically bridges this gap, but we cannot account for *how* this bridging takes place. Furthermore, I believe that the Freudian text here puts psyche and soma in a hierarchical arrangement: the psyche *prevails* over anatomical laws and makes an inscription into the body, rearranging tissue, limbs, cells and nerves.

With Ferenczi, there is no leap, or gap, or enigmatic, mysterious space between the psyche and the soma. Ferenczi brings a different solution, an escape from a 'flat biology',[39] where the biological stratum is also capable of different kinds of regressions, 'perversions, strangulations, condensations, displacements, which we usually attribute to the psychic stratum, or to nonbiological systems'.[40] Ferenczi's work is thus surprisingly contemporary, in line with critiques of a reductionist, deterministic, flat and mechanistic understanding of matter.

In what follows, as we enter the scene of trauma, we encounter images of radical plasticity. The hysterical body is not a body possessed by fantasy, or by hallucinations, or by the psyche. It is a body that has gained 'semifluid' qualities, and where the tissue, limbs, cells and nerves speak the language of organs. Ferenczi's 'hysterical materialisations'[41] involve a material transformation that does not cease to have meaning, or to arrange elements in meaningful relations.[42]

In a fascinating entry of *The Clinical Diary*, Ferenczi writes:

> if the psychically dormant substance is rigid, while the nervous and mental systems possess fluid adaptability, then the hysterically reacting body could be described as semifluid, that is to say, as a substance whose previous rigidity and uniformity have been partially redissolved again into a psychic state, capable of adapting. Such 'semisubstances' would then have the extraordinarily or wonderfully pleasing quality of being both body and mind simultaneously, that is, of expressing wishes, sensations of pleasure-unpleasure, or even complicated thoughts, through changes in their structure or function (the language or organs).[43]

Regression is a way of manifesting this radical plasticity of the psycho-soma, where tissue, limbs, cells and nerves become capable of perversions, strangulations, condensations and displacements.

The Dream of Fragments in The Clinical Diary

We will enter the scene of trauma through a dream of psychic fragments, which Ferenczi analyses in his *Clinical Diary*. The dreamer is the protagonist of *The Clinical Diary*, Elizabeth Severn, whose appears in the text as patient 'R.N.'. One of the most important Ferenczian revisions to Freud's ideas on dreams is the great importance given the *traumatolytic function* of the dream. This means that the dream is the place of return for unmastered traumatic sensory impressions which struggle for a (better) solution. The dreams that Ferenczi writes about are often accounts of complicated scenes of psychic fragmentation. They are also tied up with the reparative repetition that I discussed above: through dreams, the impressions inscribed in the register of memory of the id can gain form.

Let us step into the dream:

> R.N.: frequently recurring form of dream: two, three, or even several persons represent, according to the completed dream-analysis, an equal number of component parts of her personality. The dream analysed today, for instance, was dramatized as follows: the dreamer herself receives a written message from the beloved person who is closest to her, which reads: 'Here I am. I am here.' The dreamer attempts to tell this to a third person, a man, but she can contact him only indirectly, by a long-distance telephone call, and in fact the whole conversation with this man sounds very indistinct, as if coming from an immense distance. The difficulty increases to the point of a nightmarish and helpless struggle because of the fact that the text of the message cannot be read directly; the dreamer sees it only in mirror-writing, as light shines through the postcard; she is sitting in a kind of tent, and can see the writing only as mirror-writing.[44]

After we entered the atmosphere and landscapes of Ferenczi's dreams with Jakob Staberg in the first part of the book, we approach Elizabeth Severn's dream, which Ferenczi qualifies as nightmare.[45] One of the key images here is that of an agonising breakdown of communication. As Ferenczi writes in his interpretation of the dream, 'this personality, shattered and made defenseless by suffering and poison, is attempting, over and over again but always unsuccessfully, to reassemble its various parts into a unit, that is, to understand the event taking place in and around her'.[46] Integration is impossible and the psychic life of fragments is marked by confusion and distortion. The dream even records the impossibility of direct representation, by the reference to 'mirror writing', which is a painful and inversed inscription, in need of a transposition before the message can be understood. The radical splitting of various parts of the psyche is symbolised as the long-distance telephone call and the 'immense distance'. The 'I' of the dream, perhaps standing for the conscious ego, is unable to deliver the written messages. The fragments are linked to one another in a precarious way (if at all), and the connection can collapse at any point. Holding in mind the atmosphere of this dream of fragments, we enter the scene of trauma. The psychic process of identification with the aggressor is at its core.

On the Identification with the Aggressor

Psychic splitting is a crucial psychoanalytic theme. Despite its importance, there is a 'phenomenological gap' in psychoanalysis around the problem of splitting. I understand this phenomenological gap as a deficit of precise descriptions about what is being split in the psyche; about the process of splitting; and about the psychic life of the fragments that result from the splitting. Not all these fragments map on to the three Freudian agencies of the psyche: id, ego and superego. There are kinds of splitting that make demands from us and that point to a need for metapsychological revisions.

I argue that Ferenczi gets closer to addressing the phenomenological gap that I mentioned above, and that he proposes a true metapsychology of fragmented psyches. In his work, we find a series of original formulations on processes of splitting (centred on the idea of identification with the aggressor) and new kinds of psychic fragments (such as the Orpha fragment of the psyche, functioning between the life drive and the death drive; or the teratoma, a parasitic deadened 'double' of the self, living inside the psyche), which I discuss in the following pages.

When looking at psychic splitting, it is useful to have in mind a field of questions that can guide the inquiry. A central question is: what is the 'stuff' that the psyche is splitting? Is it the ego? Is it the self on the whole (including the ego, but also other agencies)? Is it a part of the ego where a particular introjection happened? Or is it even a part of the ego that an other has successfully projected something onto?

An important interlocutor when we discuss psychic splitting is Melanie Klein, with her work on the complicated notion of 'projective identification'.[47] As Spillius argues, for Klein 'projective identification' is an unconscious phantasy, an intrapersonal and not an interpersonal concept.[48] In a number of 1958 notes that Spillius finds in the Melanie Klein Archive, Klein distinguishes between projection and projective identification as two steps in the same process. The first step, 'projection', means that something that is very unpleasant or something that one feels one does not deserve is attributed to somebody else. The second step, 'projective identification', means that something – either good or bad – is split off from the self and deposited into the object. As Klein notes, these two steps 'need not be simultaneously experienced, though they very often are'.[49]

There is an important tension built into the construction of 'projective identification' emerging from the very polarity of good object/bad object. The good/bad polarity functions as a proxy for a processual elucidation of psychic splitting, but it does not manage to do the phenomenological work that is needed for understanding what happens to the psyche at the time of splitting. Even if Klein anchors the good/bad polarity psychoanalytically, tying 'good' in the same chain with 'satisfaction' and 'bad' in the same chain with 'frustration', the two function as fundamentally *moral* notions. There is thus no processual elucidation, no *quality* that can be added in describing the object, the internal phantasy of the object, or the effect the object has on the subject, which can disturb the circular and morally coded relationship that the pair good/bad presupposes. I believe this moral duality and the circularity it inscribes (from good to bad and back again) gives a certain circularity to Klein's work, and to her conception of splitting in particular, where we move from projection to introjection and back again. There is thus a level of 'mundane' splitting assumed to be going on all the time in the psyche, which does not dictate major metapsychological revisions.

Psychic life is from the onset based on *qualities*, and not on sheer polarities. We might be frustrated or satisfied, both by the object and in phantasy, but the question of remarkable significance is: in which particular way does frustration/satisfaction occur? What is the eroticisation of the body that accompanies both frustration and satisfaction?

What we might miss if we remain faithful to the 'mundane' splitting that I discussed above is a more 'eventful' kind of splitting, resulting in de-libidinised stable fragments of the psyche. There are very limited grounds in Melanie Klein's work to consider the tremendous difficulty of the libidinal operation of projecting the bad or unwanted contents of the psyche. While this tremendous libidinal endeavour is attributed to very primitive states, we are left with the open question of whether, for such a successful and constant projection, an actually less primitive state of the ego is required, capable of channelling the libido in such way that the unwanted contents can be discarded.

Yet another difficulty with the Kleinian conception of splitting rests in the fact that splitting functions in a silent or explicit duality with integration/cohesion. The psychoanalytic process itself is seen as aiming at achieving a better integration of the psyche. Working from the Ferenczian metapsychology of fragmented psyches, I argue that integration is not the polar opposite of splitting, nor is it the ultimate goal of analysis. Sometimes splitting is so profound and it results in such stable psychic fragments that the psychoanalytic process is more accurately described as one of re-libidinisation of 'deadened' parts of the psyche, rather than one of integration.

While it is important to avoid radicalising the distinction between splitting *by* the ego, and splitting *of* the ego (to do so would mean to misrecognise a point that Klein rightly directs us to, which is that any splitting *by* the ego brings into action a certain amount of splitting *of* the ego) – the question that remains unanswered in Klein's work relates precisely to the psychic 'life' of the fragments that are the result of the splitting.

In what follows, I argue that Ferenczi's formulation on the 'identification with the aggressor' is one of the most phenomenologically thick accounts of psychic splitting that we possess in psychoanalysis to this day. The identification with the aggressor stands at the very core of Ferenczi's conception of trauma, as many contemporary authors have shown.[50] What we can remark in the case of the identification with the aggressor is that the scheme discussed in Klein's work – organised around the polarity between good/bad objects – loses its applicability. For Ferenczi, splitting is *qualified*, not driven by polarities. It is not useful to ask whether the introjection is of a good object or a bad object – we could argue that the identification that Ferenczi talks about is a tragic one: it contains a primary element of *imitation* of form; and an *introjection of guilt feelings*. This introjection of the guilt feelings, however 'dark' in itself, allows the child to continue living, after having gone through an overwhelming and potentially deadly experience. In a note in his *Clinical Diary*, in an entry of 10 May 1932, the kind of splitting that Ferenczi describes appears to us as qualified:[51] it is not between good and bad, but instead it is between reason and emotion. The two faculties become separated from one another, and gain quasi-autonomous functioning. Both become hyper-faculties – enhanced but also split.

There are moments of *The Clinical Diary* when Ferenczi maps out the psychic fragments of his patient, Elizabeth Severn.[52] How did he arrive here, and what are the implications of such a psychic topography? Ferenczi differentiates in his work between two kinds of responses of the ego to a powerful stimulus from the outside. One response is 'alloplasticity' or 'alloplastic adaptation', where the psyche acts by 'the alteration of the environment in such a way as to make self-destruction and self-reconstruction unnecessary, and to enable the ego to maintain its existing equilibrium, i.e. its organization, unchanged'.[53] The other response is autoplasticity, where the psyche acts by its own modification, by fragmentation, or by its partial self-destruction. One of the questions that animates Ferenczi regards the different *modes of autoplasticity* that are possible in the psyche. It does not suffice to say that 'splitting' operates in the psyche, but it is necessary to elucidate what kind of splitting we are talking about and what kind of psychic fragments the splitting process has generated.

If we consider a psychic world of autoplastic reactions, this produces a considerable topographic surprise: the effect of predominantly autoplastic actions is that the ego almost disappears or is suspended, so that the psyche appears to be made up only of id and superego. As Ferenczi notes:

> One part of [the traumatised subjects'] personalities, possibly the nucleus, got stuck in its development at a level where it was unable to use the alloplastic way of reaction but could only react in an autoplastic way by a kind of mimicry. Thus we arrive at the assumption of a mind which consists only of the id and super-ego, and which therefore lacks the ability to maintain itself with stability in face of unpleasure – in the same way as the immature find it unbearable to be left alone, without maternal care and without a considerable amount of tenderness.[54]

In *The Clinical Diary*, we meet the same idea of an effect of inexistence of the ego produced by autoplastic acts. The ego becomes completely flexible, it loses its solidity, or the level of resistance that is needed for its being a separate psychic agency. In other words, the ego itself is entirely 'repressed'. In the entry of 29 May 1932, Ferenczi writes:

> Fear dissolves the rigidity of the ego (resistance) so completely that the material of the ego becomes as though capable of being moulded *photochemically* – is in fact always moulded – by external stimuli. Instead of my asserting *myself*, the external world (an alien will) asserts itself at my expense; it forces itself upon me and *represses* the ego. (Is this the primal form of 'repression'?)[55]

This 'photochemic moulding' of the ego is at the heart of having a memory. We return here to the idea of memory as a collection of scars of shocks suffered by the ego. A certain amount of autoplastic reactivity is unavoidable. Memory-wounds, as I showed above, are 'wounds-toward-memory'. To be wounded is to be in possession of the capacity of being affected. This being said, in another entry of his *Clinical Diary*, Ferenczi put activity before passivity, by referring to an alloplastic act that he thought preceded any autoplastic reaction. In other words, there seems to be always a version of the ego or of the proto-ego that offers some resistance to being moulded or un-done:

> This observation indicates that hatred and rage play a part in the processes that precede repression; if that is so, then no analysis is complete as long as this emotion has not been worked through as well. It is possible that, at each overwhelming shock, an initial attempt at aggressive, alloplastic defense is made, and only faced with the full realization of one's own utter weakness and helplessness does one submit entirely to the aggressor or even identify with him.[56]

Some of Ferenczi's most important and original ideas on trauma are built around a series of biological analogies. What is remarkable is how Ferenczi records vignettes on animal behaviour, how he humbly learns from them, and how he construes the psychoanalytic observations in dialogue with them, in the spirit of a clinical empiricism. A very particular way of filling the phenomenological gap around the problem of splitting in psychoanalysis emerges from here. Meaning springs from his own utraquistic[57] oscillation between the example in biology (or sometimes chemistry or physics) and his thesis in trauma theory. We can argue that his metapsychology is the fruit of these forms of utraquistic elucidation. This type of minute observation of animals and cells is close in spirit to that of philosophers and social theorists such as Donna Haraway, Gregory Bateson or Félix Guattari, in the sense of acknowledging the plurality of semiotic codes that traverse the living being.[58] I am thus not insisting on the fact that Ferenczi's theory of trauma has a biological substratum, but on the fact that Ferenczi is able to take insights from biology according to his own utraquistic method.

Over the next pages, I describe several 'moments' of the identification with the aggressor, and I reflect on the psychic fragments that result from these moments. I will discuss the following psychic processes: the moment of the attack and traumatic paralysis, dematerialisation, the process of traumatic imitation, the introjection of the guilt of the aggressor, getting beside oneself, traumatic progression or precocious maturity, self-caring and the emergence of the Orpha fragment of the psyche, autotomy, the emergence new organs (neo-formations), psychic reconstruction. The ten moments are not there to suggest a temporal sequence. They do not follow one after the other. Several of these processes can take place at the same time, or can become entangled with other processes in complicated ways, following the particular 'composition' of life drive and death drive. The ten moments aim to *qualify* the catastrophe, to capture its many facets. They also work toward a Ferenczian vocabulary on the psychic life of fragments.

Moment 1: Paralysis

Paralysis is the result of the asymmetric encounter with the Other. The clash between the register of tenderness and the register of passion is experienced by the subject as an overwhelming psychic attack. The result is a motionless psychic state, perhaps one that mimics death.

In a previous section, I offered a reconstruction of Ferenczi's take on the problem of infantile sexual indifference, which is implicit in Freudian theory. I showed how children are in no sense 'indifferent' to overwhelming and sexualised psychic transmissions received from adults. There is a clash of registers here which leads to a state of traumatic confusion. While Ferenczi insists that the adaptive potential 'response' of very young children to sexual or other passionate attacks is much greater than one would imagine, it is worth stressing that what is at stake is not necessarily an act of sexual abuse. Indeed, what is at stake is a *psychic transmission*. In 'On Shock', Ferenczi clarifies this point: 'Shock can be purely physical, purely moral, or both physical and moral. Physical shock is always moral also; moral shock may create a trauma without any physical accompaniment'.[59] As Jay Frankel has shown, the place of the aggressor is here occupied in most cases by a narcissistically compromised caregiver.[60] The 'attack' therefore consists of parts of the caregiver's mind *intruding* into the child; *appropriating* aspects of the child's mind and using it for the caregiver's own purposes;[61] or *inverting the parent–child relationship*, so that it responds primarily to the caregiver's needs and not to those of the child.[62]

The first response to the attack is a state of traumatic paralysis, which is incompatible with any sort of psychic spontaneity or activity of psychic defence. The paralysis is not a fleeting state or a moment of adaptation. Instead, it is capable of changing the structural organisation of the psyche, and it generates a 'frozen fragment' of the psyche, which is silent, deadened and fully de-libidinised. As Ferenczi describes:

> This process gives us an opportunity of observing something of the mechanism of the genesis of a trauma. First, there is the entire paralysis of all spontaneity, including all thinking activity and, on the physical side, this may even be accompanied by a condition resembling shock or coma. Then there comes the formation of a new – displaced – situation of equilibrium. If we succeed in making contact with the patient even in these phases, we shall find that, when a child feels himself abandoned, he loses, as it were, all desire for life or, as we should have to say with Freud, he turns his aggressive impulses against himself. Sometimes this process

goes so far that the patient begins to have the sensations of sinking and dying. He will turn deadly pale, or fall into a condition like fainting, or there may be a general increase in muscular tension, which may be carried to the point of opisthotonus.[63]

The absolute paralysis of motility in the moment of the attack includes the inhibition of perception and, with it, the inhibition of thinking.[64] The traumatic impressions that occur at the time of the attack cannot be recorded via the system of memory of the ego, because this would involve the presence of thinking, even if we are talking about processes of repression. These impressions are thus taken up by the psyche without any sort of resistance. Ferenczi hesitates between suggesting that 'no memory traces of such impressions remain, even in the unconscious, and thus the causes of the trauma cannot be recalled from memory traces' and describing the elements of the new system of memory of the id.[65] I have shown that the precision of the traumatic re-enactments leads us to believe that some marks, in the first instance incompatible with thoughts, are presented to the psyche.

The fact that the traumatised subject survives the moments of traumatic paralysis, psychically and physically, is a highly improbable event, in terms of the state of the drives. In other words, it is a time that is so radically dominated by the operation of the death drive and so prone to un-linking, that 'the event of survival' requires an explanation.

Alongside the 'frozen fragment' of the psyche that moves outside time, there are other psychic forces at play. Ferenczi speaks of a psychic dimension always latent in the soma, and, interestingly enough, in all material substance. This manifests as a series of ontogenetic and phylogenetic inclinations (or 'motives'). Ferenczi discusses this primal substrate in the first pages of his *Clinical Diary*, pointing to a process when different organs or body parts produce effects of thinking, and are able to perform surprisingly minute calculations that have as a result the preservation of life. In his words, 'when the psychic system fails, the organism begins to think'.[66]

In the hour of the traumatic attack, the event of survival means maintaining a beating heart or getting air into the lungs, against all odds. All available psychic energy is concentrated on one task, an apparently simple one, but without which preserving life would be impossible. The lungs, at this time, become 'thinking lungs'. Let us remember one of the questions posed by Alexis Pauline Gumbs: 'what if you could breathe like whales who sing underwater and recycle air to sing again before coming up for air?'[67] The radical plasticity invoked here traverses both interspecies imaginaries and the 'wild' imaginaries of the trauma scene. The transformations in this scene often carry something *beside* the human, and thus appeal to ancestral forms of listening that are analogous to interspecies listening.

Moment 2: Dematerialisation

The psychic process of dematerialisation is one of the markers of Ferenczi's vocabulary on psychic splitting. This appears in series of terms, which also includes pulverisation (*Pulverisierung*) and atomisation (*Atomisierung*). It is one of the catastrophic events of the trauma scene.

Unlike Anna Freud's idea of the 'identification with the aggressor',[68] Ferenczi's one does not wish to capture a kind of ego defence, where an aggressor is taken as object of identification by a (quite mature) ego. Instead, what Ferenczi means by his 'identification with the aggressor' refers to a much more complicated and more primary process. Here, the notions of dematerialisation and traumatic imitation are crucial. Ferenczi does not use 'psychic dematerialisation' or 'pulverisation' as a metaphor through which we would gain a better understanding of some other kind of psychic process. Instead, he has in mind particular moments in the traumatic scene, when the ego is literally pulverised into bits, and when it loses whatever stable shape it had before.

In his short piece 'On Shock', Ferenczi writes:

> Shock – annihilation of self-regard – of the ability to put up a resistance, and to act and think in defence of one's own self; perhaps even the *organs* which secure self-preservation give up their function or reduce it to a minimum. (The word *Erschütterung* is derived from *schütten*, i.e. to become 'unfest, unsolid', to lose one's own form and to adopt easily and without resistance, an imposed form – 'like a sack of flour'). Shock always comes upon one *unprepared*. It must needs be preceded by a feeling of *security*, in which, because of the subsequent events, one feels *deceived*; one trusted in the *external world too much* before; after, too little or not at all. One had to have overestimated one's own powers and to have lived under the delusion that *such things* could not happen, not *to me*.[69]

The process of pulverisation assumes the existence of a kind of 'proto-ego'. There is always some form that can be shattered through traumatic shock or the confusion of tongues, even for an ego that is not very developed. Pulverisation is accompanied by both positive and negative hallucinations. Through the positive hallucinations, the subject reverts to the previous state of tenderness that preceded the trauma, in the form of the clash between the register of tenderness and the register of passion. Through the negative hallucinations, the subject creates a psychic position grounded in asserting 'this is not happening to me'. We can see that this position produces a fundamental alteration of the reality principle: the subject has in their repertoire the denial of overwhelming and unpleasant feelings, often through a combination of negative and positive hallucinations.

In 1930, in a fragment titled 'Each Adaptation is Preceded by an Inhibited Attempt at Splitting', Ferenczi prefigures an important theme, to which we turn in the following pages: that of the reconstruction of the psyche out of the fragments that resulted from the traumatic attack.[70] What he notes is that even fragments that are apparently shapeless, that bear no articulation with the ego, and that appear to us as mere 'psychic energies' (marking a sort of reversibility of the formation of the ego from instinctual forces, a re-falling into the realm of the drives) can serve as a ground for a psychic reconstruction:

> In the extreme case when all the reserve forces have been mobilized but have proved impotent in the face of the overpowering attack, it comes to an extreme fragmentation which could be called dematerialization. Observation of patients, who fly from their own sufferings and have become hypersensitive to all kinds of extraneous suffering, also coming from a great distance, still leave the question open whether even these extreme, quasi-pulverized, elements which have been reduced to mere psychic energies do not also contain tendencies for reconstruction of the ego.[71]

Moment 3: Traumatic Imitation

Respecting a psychic rule where any form is better than no form, a part of the psyche, pulverised by the power of the traumatic attack, borrows the shape of that which is closer: the shape of the aggressor. This is a phenomenon of traumatic imitation which brings into being one of the deadliest fragments of the psyche: a fragment that performs a direct mimicry of the manner or the psychic ways of the aggressor. From a kind of 'cloud of particles', the psyche stabilises into the form of the aggressor. This insight is important for understanding how intergenerational transmission of trauma takes place: it will undoubtedly involve phenomena of traumatic imitation, by which a traumatic residue will *intrude* in the psyche, causing first a dematerialisation, and afterwards a re-materialisation that observes the form of the aggressor.

This kind of radical plasticity becomes thinkable if we turn to Ferenczi's conception of language, and to his idea of mimesis between words and things. Language is both physical and psychic. There is an inscription of materiality at the core of every word. This inscription results from the operation of analogy, through which symbols are made. The primary analogies take us back to the body and to the act of the child of establishing correspondences between body parts and the external reality. Just as symbols express the body, words imitate things. As Ferenczi writes: 'In its origin, language is imitation, in other words, vocal reproduction of sounds and noises produced by things, or that are produced through them'.[72] And, later in his *Clinical Diary*, he adds: 'To speak is to imitate. The gesture and speech (voice) imitate objects of the world around. "Ma-ma" is magic of imitation'.[73]

There is thus a direct connection between traumatic impressions and the reconstruction of the scene of trauma. Ultimately, Ferenczi sees speech as a form of permanent imitation, which the victim develops so as to tell the story of the trauma: 'a part of the ego remains undestroyed, indeed, it seeks to profit from this demolition (scars). The traumatic *mimicry impressions* are utilised as memory-traces, useful to the ego: "dog" = bowwow, bowwow. When I am frightened of a dog, I become a dog'.[74]

Yet another important theme is that of traumatic hyper-sensitivity and the development of traumatic hyper-faculties. These hyper-faculties come into being, at least to some extent, through processes of imitation. In one of the next sections, we will discuss the psychic life of the Orpha fragment of the psyche, characterised by hyper-faculties, intuitions and sensitivities, and even by a new form of radical mutuality, a new relationality resulting from a particular form of fusion between life drive and death drive.

Moment 4: Guilt

There is one distinctive psychic fragment that comes into being through the incorporation of the guilt feelings of the aggressor. Here, we would have to distinguish traumatic guilt from neurotic guilt. Traumatic guilt is a catastrophic kind of guilt, it is sudden, and it propels the subject into a state of traumatic confusion. Ferenczi gives an important phenomenological insight about how this fragment of the psyche comes into being:

> These children feel physically and morally helpless, their personalities are not sufficiently consolidated in order to be able to protest, even if only in thought, for the overpowering force and authority of the adult makes them dumb and can rob them of their senses. *The same anxiety,*

> *however, if it reaches a certain maximum, compels them to subordinate themselves like automata to the will of the aggressor, to divine each one of his desires and to gratify these; completely oblivious of themselves they identify themselves with the aggressor.* […]
>
> The most important change, produced in the mind of the child by the anxiety-fear-ridden identification with the adult partner, is *the introjection of the guilt feelings of the adult* which makes hitherto harmless play appear as a punishable offence.[75]

What Ferenczi describes here is how the aggressor ceases to be a part of external reality (extrapsychic) and instead becomes intrapsychic. What he calls 'identification with the aggressor' or 'introjection of the aggressor' actually presents itself as an 'incorporation of the aggressor'. The psyche of the victim 'swallows' the aggressor whole, as if in a single psychic act. This 'swallowing up' is centred on the guilt feelings, which represent one of the least 'metabolisable' psychic facts of the scene. If we refer to the phenomenon of traumatic imitation discussed above, we can say that non-neurotic guilt functions as the necessary core of the imitation. We are dealing with a new psychic organisation, structured around guilt.

The suddenness of this incorporation creates a trance-like state, which is dominated by 'positive or negative hallucinations'.[76] As reality has become too terrifying, the hallucinations serve a precise function. The positive hallucinations restore the situation of tenderness, or the situation before the intrusion of the language of passion into the language of tenderness. In other words, the child recreates in fantasy the pre-traumatic state, which has been lost. The negative hallucinations manifest themselves as an overwhelming feeling of 'being bad', because the 'wrongness' of the traumatic scene has been incorporated and curved inwards. All aggression is now masochistically directed toward the inside. Frankel has recently discussed the facets of this traumatic feeling of 'badness' in the contemporary clinic.[77] This 'badness' results from the child taking upon himself the badness which resides in his objects. We could say that this 'badness' is a negative hallucination of a very particular sort, which takes a part of the self as the object. The ego punishes the subject through a kind of 'strike', through hyper-sensitivity and lack of energy. As Ferenczi put it, '[c]ertain observations suggest that an oppressive sense of guilt can occur even when one has not transgressed against oneself at all'.[78]

The result of this catastrophic incorporation is that the child enters a state of traumatic confusion, where the 'confidence in the testimony of his own senses is broken'.[79] In other words, the child now confuses inner and outer reality, and is dominated by an omnipotence of thoughts, where it becomes impossible to distinguish what is imagined from what is real. This is the result of 'knowing terrible things'.[80]

There are important political implications deriving from the existence of such a psychic position. Bragin argues that victims of torture experience the fear that some hidden and terrible badness resides in them.[81] They start to believe that their own childhood fantasies of harm are congruent, read, and enacted by the perpetrator, who can somehow respond to their own pre-existing internal choreography of destructiveness. Thus, they start to feel that they resemble their torturer in their familiarity with the 'terrible things'. These 'terrible things' and the hallucinations that surround them bind the victim and the perpetrator together, because there emerges a sense of sharedness in something that others are ignorant of. The originary traumatic confusion thus creates an omnipotent belief in one's own badness that allows further forms of abuse and exploitation to take place. This form of 'being bad' is incompatible with feelings of self-esteem, social worth or social entitlement.

The psychic fragment that results from the incorporation of the guilt feelings of the aggressor is directly implicated in social compliance and submission. Any demand of 'blind' compliance, which does not entail a deliberative process, will appeal to the 'mechanical, obedient automaton' that the subject was reduced to in the scene of the trauma.[82]

I would like to stress the consequences of the phenomenon of hyper-attunement with the feelings and intentions of the aggressor and its role in maintaining structures of domination. At the time of the attack, the child develops thoughts and feelings that they sense the aggressor needs from them, which increase the chances of surviving the terrifying situation. On the one hand, this means developing hyper-sensitivities and hyper-intuitions. On the other hand, it means failing to perceive certain aspects of reality, which would counter the traumatic 'script' that was implanted in the child or that would threaten the hyper-attuned traumatic adaptation. We could thus say that while certain aspects of reality are hyper-perceived, other are dissociated from. Any political system of domination will demand from its subjects similar kinds of traumatic 'selectiveness' that result in perfect mental and behavioural compliance. The atrocities and murders of the regime are to be erased from memory, while the political rituals that maintain and celebrate the regime are to be diligently observed.

A new important series of terms emerges in *The Clinical Diary:* guilt, implantation of an alien will, alien transmission, alien transplant. Guilt is the object of the enigmatic and violent transmission that comes from the Other.

The presence of guilt, alongside repression, is what qualitatively differentiates the register of passion from the register of tenderness.

Moment 5: Getting Beside Oneself

In contrast with the Kleinian 'projection' of the unwanted aspects of the self, we encounter in Ferenczi's work a curious libidinal and topical act that can be read more as a temporary re-location or ex-corporation of the ego, rather than a mere projection. In his text 'On the Analytic Construction of Mental Mechanism', Ferenczi will call this ex-corporation of the ego 'getting beside oneself'.[83] This psychic act requires tremendous psychic energy. Although this fragment is associated to a temporary state in the scene of the trauma, I believe it should not be treated fleetingly. It generates a kind of psychic 'trail' that the psyche can later repeat or reconstitute in situations of abuse or strain:

> Another process requiring topical representation is characterized in the phrase 'to get beside oneself'. The ego leaves the body, partly or wholly, usually through the head, and observes from outside, usually from above, the subsequent fate of the body, especially its suffering. (Images somewhat like this: bursting out through the head and observing the dead, impotently frustrated body, from the ceiling of the room; less frequently: carrying one's own head under one's arm with a connecting thread like the umbilical cord between the expelled ego components and the body.)[84]

Many clinicians working with traumatised patients have noted the peculiar moment of exiting the body, of observing oneself from the ceiling, as if the self were an other. This 'othering of the self' produces an important dissociation, a sense of exteriority from their own experience. This psychic position of exteriority to the self is available to the subject in subsequent situations that mimic the scene of the trauma. The psychic fragment 'observing from the ceiling' marks what I call a 'pre-Orpha function'. It develops after the moment of traumatic paralysis, which we described above, and which was experienced as a near-death, as a cessation of all thought and feeling; and before the coagulation of the Orpha fragment of the psyche, which, as we will see in what follows, comes in the shape of a 'guardian angel' – a true, stable and fully shaped dissociation, capable of watching over the abused child, abandoned by all external helpers and subjected to the overwhelming force of the aggressor.

The psychic imagery that accompanies the formation of this psychic position is very striking. The subject does not only 'find' themself looking from the outside to their own suffering, but often has a sense of a physical journey to the new ex-corporated state. The movement can be that of leaving the body through the head. Another possible movement can be an image of 'losing one's head' and carrying it under one's arm. What is crucial here is the representation of the dissociation of faculties. Seeing and thinking (standing for objective perception) are relocated elsewhere, while the rest of the body is left in agony on the ground.

In *The Clinical Diary*, Ferenczi makes a series of interesting observations on this distinctive topical catastrophe of the scene of trauma. He clarifies the alterations to the sense of time that the act of 'getting beside oneself' comes with. He points to a non-human or trans-human imagery that accompany the ex-corporation. The subject no longer feels reduced to spatial and temporal constraints, and acquires a sense of a radical plasticity: they can be condensed, enlarged, or even change states of aggregation.

> If I am to believe what my patients repot about similar states, this 'being gone' is not necessarily a state of 'non-being', but rather one of 'not-being-here'. As for the 'where', one hears things like: they are far away in the universe; they are flying at a colossal speed among the stars; they feel so thin that they pass without hindrance through the densest substances; where they are, there is no time; past, present and future are simultaneous for them; in a word, they feel they have overcome time and space. Seen from this gigantically wide perspective, the significance of one's own suffering vanishes, indeed there develops a gratifying insight into the necessity for the individual to endure suffering, when opposed and combatant natural forces meet in one's own parson.[85]

What we can discern here is a state of traumatic omnipotence, based on a particular kind of violent temporal relations. The particular kind of timelessness described is one where a part of the subject feels triumphant over time or feels like they have overcome time or 'killed' time altogether.

There is also a particular kind of alienation that derives from different parts of the psyche being in their own times. We are referring to a violent internal plurality of the times of the subject, where the different psychic fragments 'living' inside a different time create an overall effect of a-synchrony. The times of some fragments seem to attack, displace or negate the times of other fragments. Here, the time resulting from 'being beside oneself' attacks the sense of unfolding of the more conscious and well-adapted parts of the ego.

Moment 6: Traumatic Progression

When subjected to an overwhelming psychic transmission or to an attack, the child can go through an instantaneous maturation, and develop the emotions of an adult. This premature coming of age is often accompanied by being able to perform roles more easily associated with motherhood or fatherhood than with childhood. The playful, spontaneous, gradual appropriation of the world stops, while the traumatised child migrates to a place of 'carer' for the narcissistically compromised adults around him, for other children, or even for parts of the self, as we will see further. Another facet of this precocity refers to sexual roles. It is worth noting that it is a *fragment* of the psyche that goes through what Ferenczi 'traumatic progression' or 'precocious maturity', and not the entire personality.[86] There is a traumatic bifurcation that happens, which produces a markedly paternal/maternal fragment, and other fragments that are still 'childfull', in their needing the presence of the register of tenderness, of gentle care and gradual learning, in order to mature.

Traumatic progression extends to the sphere of the intellect: the traumatised child will be capable of surprisingly wise utterings, sometimes to the delight of the adults around him, who will gratify and encourage faculties that are in fact results of traumatic dissociation. As Ferenczi poetically puts it: 'It is natural to compare this with the precocious maturity of the fruit that was injured by a bird or insect'.[87] Ultimately, Ferenczi regards the intellect as born out of suffering.

The splitting that leads to the birth of intellect is recorded in the unconscious in the form of dreams where a 'wise baby' enters the scene, speaking in the voice and with the contents of an adult conversation. Babies in the cradle or very young children are present in these dreams, and they are able to talk or write fluently, they find solutions to complicated puzzles, they offer intelligent advice and guidance to adults, or they offer scientific explanations. Ferenczi records this type of dream in his short 1923 piece, 'The Dream of the "Clever Baby"'.[88] The 'wise baby' became an important psychoanalytic construction for Ferenczi, through which he was able to better discern the effects of the particular arrangement of the trauma scene on his patients. This dream plays an important role in understanding precocious maturity, a traumatic kind of maturity, or a sudden split between faculties, between reason and emotion, where the intellect comes to function autonomously and disconnected from both emotion and the body.

Moment 7: Autotomy

Let us recall that there are two kinds of responses of the ego to the trauma, according to Ferenczi. The first one, corresponding to a highly developed sense of reality, he terms 'alloplastic adaptation', which means that the ego is able to alter the environment, the world outside, in such way that self-destruction and self-reconstruction are not necessary, and in such way that the ego maintains its equilibrium.[89] The second one he names 'autoplastic adaptation',[90] which means that ego does not have or loses its capacity to mould the external world, and proceeds to operations on itself.

Perhaps the most tragic form of autoplastic adaptation is autotomia, where the ego cuts off, dis-attaches and leaves behind a part of itself. It is here that Ferenczi relies on the image of the animal shedding a body part that has been wounded. Let us think of lizards cutting off their tail. In 'Psycho-Analytical Observations on Tic', Ferenczi writes:

> Here I will touch on the analogy of the third kind of tic, i.e. the motor discharge ('turning against one's own person', Freud), with a method of reaction that occurs in certain lower animals, which possess the capacity for 'Autotomia'. If a part of their body is painfully stimulated they let the part concerned 'fall' in the true sense of the word by severing it from the rest of their body by the help of certain specialized muscular actions; others (like certain worms) even fall into several small pieces (they 'burst asunder', as it were, from fury). Even the biting off of a painful limb is said to occur.[91]

In one of the entries of *The Clinical Diary*, Ferenczi brings another vignette on animal behaviour, where the adaptation to the anticipation of unbearable pain and complete submission is suicide:

> As an analogy I refer to a reliable account of an Indian friend, a hunter. He saw how a falcon attacked a little bird; as it approached, the little bird started to tremble and, after a few seconds of trembling, flew straight into the falcon's open beak and was swallowed up. The anticipation of certain death appears to be such torment that by comparison actual death is a relief.[92]

Ferenczi derives crucial metapsychological reflections from these images. In the first one, on autotomia, we see 'an archaic prototype of the components of the masochistic instinct'.[93] In the second one, we see the limits of passivity, and a certain primacy given to activity, in that an active death is preferred to the anticipation of complete surrender to the aggressor. In a fragment on 'Trauma and Anxiety', Ferenczi strengthens the same idea: '*[s]elf-destruction* as *releasing some anxiety* is preferred to silent toleration'.[94] It appears that the easiest to break apart is the conscious system, responsible for the integration of mental images into a unit. Ultimately, splitting is an act that is more readily available to the psyche than we are used to consider. Autotomy refers to a kind of splitting where a part of the psyche becomes permanently unavailable to any form of linking.

Moment 8: Neo-Formations

Ferenczi is aware of the importance for clinical thinking of the point of contact between autoplastic and alloplastic adaptations. He observes how self-fragmentation and splitting are at times bound up with the creation of new organs and new capacities – or, as he calls them, 'neoformations'.[95] In his 1926 essay on 'The Problem of Acceptance of Unpleasant Ideas', he discusses how certain kinds of self-destruction lead to an enlarged recognition of the surrounding world and lead closer to the formation of objective judgement.[96] Here Ferenczi cites Sabina Spielrein's (1912) paper on destruction as a 'cause of being',[97] which is in itself notable, given the lack of acknowledgement of her ideas at the time, and given the fact that her ideas, as Adrienne Harris (2015) comments, seem to have been absorbed rather than referenced, turning her into a ghost rather than into an ancestor.[98] Resonating with Spielrein, Ferenczi argues that a partial destruction of the ego is tolerated, but with the purpose of constructing a stronger and more resilient ego from what remains. We here encounter a biological analogy:

> This is similar to the phenomena noted in the ingenious attempts of Jacques Loeb to stimulate unfertilized eggs to development by the action of chemicals, i.e. without fertilization: the chemicals disorganize the outer layers of the egg, but out of the detritus a protective bladder (sheath) is formed, which puts a stop to further injury. In the same way the Eros liberated by instinctual defusion converts destruction into growth, into a further development of the parts that have been protected.[99]

As he notes four years later, in 1930, in a short writing on 'Trauma and Striving for Health', fragmentation as a result of trauma does not appear at all to be a sort of mechanical consequence of shock, but instead it is already a form of defence, an adaptation. Here, he makes another analogy with lower animals, which, subjected to extreme stimulation, break up and continue their existence in fragments. He goes on to imagine the logic of a defence by splitting.[100] Fragmentation might prove useful to the subject because it creates a bigger surface open to the external world, such increasing the possibility of discharging the many and unbearable affects of the scene of trauma. Fragmentation is also advantageous because it can dissolve the sense of unified perception. It is often the case that the suffering experienced in the scene of trauma is so great that the subject could not survive it. Splitting into pieces means that 'single fragments suffer for themselves; the unbearable unification of all pain qualities and quantities does not take place'.[101] The integration of all pain would be the equivalent of psychic death.

Another important note is that the 'new organs' produced at the time of the trauma emerge in a sudden manner. They are psychic events. It is a kind of 'teleplastic' transformation,[102] producing ad hoc organs, which become responsible for some of the organism's functions. Teleplasty is another term that that is key to Ferenczi's eventful psychoanalysis. In *The Clinical Diary*, he shows that in some cases the hallucination of breathing can maintain life, even where there is total somatic suffocation.[103] It is as if the subject generates ex-corporated lungs, which are the teleplastic double of the physical lungs. For the purposes of defence and survival, the subject can also generate 'receptacles, gripping tools, tools of aggression',[104] which will still fight for life, although the organism can find itself in a lifeless state or in deep coma. To further concretise this intriguing idea of teleplasty, Ferenczi evokes the case of R.N., Elizabeth Severn, who imagined an infinitely expandable bladder formed at the back of her head, where all her pain can accumulate.[105] This pain-collecting bladder has a function in surviving the intensity of suffering in the scene of trauma. Ferenczi pays close attention in his clinical work to such odd organs, swelling up and disintegrating, in relation to some detail of the scene. Among these odd organs, the protective bladder has a special place, allowing some partial and hallucinatory integration, in a psychic time where the danger of complete disintegration looms.

The connections that Ferenczi makes between destruction, creativity and the creation of new organs should not however seduce us into a celebration of fragments, a sort of enthusiasm for a post-catastrophic subjectivity. Such triumphalism of fragments is not in the spirit of Ferenczi's work. Ferenczi remains lucid on the dark implications of splitting, which pass through a particular kind of narcissism, where the deadened fragments of the ego are denied. The ego becomes a kind of mosaic of dead and still-alive parts, but the deadened and de-libidinised ones are 'forgotten'. Some of the fragments 'assume, as it were, the form and function of a whole person'.[106] Here, Ferenczi construes another analogy with the animal world. As he writes in 'Child Analysis in the Analysis of Adults':

> I have been told little tales like the one about the wicked animal which tries to destroy a jelly-fish by means of its teeth and claws, but cannot get at it because the jelly-fish with its subtleness eludes each jab and bite and then returns to its round shape. This story may be interpreted in two ways: on the one hand it expresses the passive resistance with which the patient meets the attacks of his environment, and on the other it represents the splitting of the self into a suffering, brutally destroyed part and a part which, as it were, knows everything but feels nothing.[107]

The attention to the jellyfish brings a reminder of both creative and destructive dimensions of catastrophe. The jellyfish, critter of the sea, is radically plastic during the attack. It re-becomes round, avoiding death. But at the same time, it momentarily dies, it is frozen in a passive state that mimics death. Paradoxically, the jellyfish survives because it had the ability to get closest to death.

In the analytic situation, the traces of this sort of splitting resurfaces when the patient feels hurt and disappointed, and as a result 'he starts playing by himself like a lonely child'.[108] In some instances, some parts of the body – hands, fingers, feet, genitals, head, nose, or eye – become 'representatives' of the entire person.[109] The tragic pain of the scene of trauma is re-enacted, using these body parts. This re-enactment, in the analytic situation, is equivalent to striving for a better solution to the one found at the time of the trauma. This gives us an insight into the precision and non-arbitrary nature of the symptom: very particular parts of the body are selected for the symptom, and they are tied with exact details of the trauma scene.

Ferenczi's biological analogies allow him to extend his trauma theory and to observe that new faculties emerge at the time of the trauma. This opens new paths in psychoanalytic theory in terms of how we think about repair, and how the 'new organs' created in traumatic times can be part of this repair. In the 30 July 1932 entry of his *Clinical Diary*, Ferenczi concludes: 'A neoformation of the self is impossible without the previous destruction, either partial or total, or dissolution of the former self. A new ego cannot be formed directly from the previous ego, but from *fragments*, more or less elementary products of its disintegration. (Splitting, atomization)'.[110]

Moment 9: Orpha

The splitting processes that I described above are forms of *narcissistic splitting*. Under the strength of the traumatic attack, the psyche is forced to devise new ways to care for itself, and at times the only way to do so is by fragmenting itself into parts that care and parts to be cared for. We are thus speaking about a tragic narcissism of fragments, where the self does not take itself for an object, but the self treats one of its parts as an 'other' and takes *it* as an object. A narcissism of fragments comes with very particular forms of denial. It also comes with what Ferenczi calls 'autosymbolism',[111] which can perhaps be understood as an effort to find an expression for a psychic state of being in fragments, by focussing a great part of the libido on body parts or organs, which become a corporeal enactment of the psychic splits.

One of the most fascinating results of the narcissistic splitting is Orpha. Orpha is more than a mere mechanism of defence: I argue that we can treat it as a new psychic agency, a fourth agency alongside the id, ego and superego. In *The Clinical Diary*, we come across an entire Orphic vocabulary, which allows us to imagine the psychic life of Orpha. Among the terms of this new vocabulary, I note: 'guardian angel';[112] 'ancient substitute (to thinking)';[113] 'substitute mother';[114] 'dissociation of fragments and organs'; 'explosion'; 'destruction of psychic associations'; 'anarchy of organs (where reciprocal cooperation is compromised)'.[115]

Orpha is the result of traumatic self-caring. It defends the psyche from sensations of unbearable intensity of the scene of trauma. This curious psychic agency is named 'Orpha' because it is a feminine Orpheus. Orpha is the form that the organising life instincts take at the time of the trauma, precisely when the enormity of suffering has resulted in a renunciation of any expectation of external help. As Ferenczi notes, '[t]he absent external help [...] is replaced by the creation of a more ancient substitute'.[116] Orpha is a sort of 'guardian angel', a healing agent, and a principle of salvation: by surprising minute calculations around what it would mean to continue living (often in a basic sense of continuing breathing or maintaining a beating heart), Orpha acts in the direction of self-preservation. Orpha also 'produces wish-fulfilling hallucinations, consolation phantasies; it anaesthetises the consciousness and sensitivity against sensations as they become unbearable'.[117] What is remarkable here is that with Orpha any dichotomy between reason and passion collapses. Orpha is created by the intrusion of the language of passion in the realm of the language of tenderness. Orpha is wise, but it is a fragment, it is split-off from other faculties. Orpha is formed when death is very near, but it acts as an organising life instinct.

As I see it, Orpha brings an account of the emergence of hyper-faculties and of over-performance. A strange product of the traumatic shock, Orpha manifests itself, Ferenczi writes, as 'an unperturbed intelligence which is not restricted by any chronological or spatial resistances in its relation to the environment'.[118] The construction of Orpha is based to a large extent on the analysis of Elizabeth Severn (marked in *The Clinical Diary* as patient 'R.N.'). Ferenczi records a series of trans-human images that R.N. shares with him in the analysis. She experiences sensations of exploding into the universe, accompanied by images of shinning constellations. She is populated by hallucinatory phrases, such as 'I am the universal egg'. This enigmatic image points to a fantasy that she is the centre of the world and has incorporated the entire universe within herself.[119]

Orpha is a metapsychologically plausible account of a particular kind of clairvoyance. On the couch, Orpha appears as a fragment of the psyche that sometimes instructs, directs or guides the analyst with great precision as to what to do, how to speak, how to be silent, in order to allow the reliving of the traumatic sequence of events.

We could argue that Ferenczi offers a metapsychological account of clairvoyance and even messianic dispositions. An Orphic time is one when individuals become aware of their hyper-faculties, and are able to use them for the benefit of others, not only for narrow self-interest. 'For the visionary adult', Ferenczi writes, 'the infantile amnesia disappears, and, due to the lifting of the barriers of repression, he is able to establish communication with the visionary child, and the capacities of the latter stay with the adult'.[120]

The many children populating Ferenczi's work, with Orpha as a central figure, align themselves as the messengers of a kind of sensorial messianism. After the scene of trauma, some of the psychic fragments resulting from traumatic splitting gain semi-autonomous lives, they become curious 'sites' for hyper-faculties. Like Orpheus's head after his death, they are both dead – since they have become separated from the body – and alive – since they can function as an oracle and open a window onto the future.

Let us start with Ovid's myth of Orpheus. Orpheus is the son of Muse Calliope, 'of the beautiful voice', and of a mortal father, Oiagros, a Thracian king 'who hunts all alone'.[121] Orpheus is a poet who, with his gift of the lyre, descends on his own into the Underworld, into 'Persephone's sad realm', to bind Eurydice in love. As Kerényi tells us, Orpheus's name is related to *orphne* – a sombre garment that Orpheus wore when he made sacrifice to Hecate on behalf of the Argonauts; it thus stands for darkness and gloom. Indeed, Orpheus lives between the luminous beauty of the lyre and this sombre garment. We also know that Apollo was Orpheus's divine father and that he offered him his lyre, while it was the Muses who taught him how to play it.[122] The music of Orpheus's lyre was unlike that of any mortal: when he played trees would be drawn to him, wild animals were tamed, while the inhabitants of the Underworld became uncharacteristically moved by feelings of compassion for others. Orpheus went along with the Argonauts in their journey to obtain the Golden Fleece and the magical sound of his lyre drowned the Sirens' song. After Eurydice's untimely death, he descends in the Underworld to save her, but because he fails to keep to the condition of not looking at her during the journey, Eurydice returns to the dead, while Orpheus's lyre fails him, and he is unable to enter the Underworld yet again to bring her back. When Orpheus dies, his body becomes dismembered, but, as ancient writers tell us, his head is enshrined and survives as an oracle, separated from the body.

I believe that when Ferenczi feminises Orpheus and speaks of the disembodied Orpha, he does not adopt each and every aspect of the myth, as presented above. Our focus is precisely on the death of Orpheus and on his dismemberment. Orpheus's head is a tragic fragment, both dead and alive. It is alive in the sense of being able to contribute in a striking, improbable, clairvoyant way to the collective life, by way of a hyper-faculty.

What emerges from here is a novel and non-Oedipal clinical and theoretical imaginary. A kind of Orphic register. Nancy Smith marks the difference between the Oedipal register and the Orphic register: '[the myth of Oedipus] throbs with conflict, murderous aggression, incest, and guilt',[123] while '[t]he Orpheus and Eurydice myth, in contrast to the Oedipus myth, aches with fragmentation, separation, suffering due to acts of violation, as well as an attempt at reclamation motivated by love'.[124] In this Orphic atmosphere, improbable survival meets deadly omnipotence.

Moment 10: Reconstruction

If the psyche presents itself as a kind of mosaic of parts, some of which are alive and some of which are deadened (de-libidinised), then what does it mean to say that some form of post-catastrophic reconstruction is possible and what does such a reconstruction rest upon? In his *Clinical Diary* Ferenczi makes an intriguing note: 'in a manner which to us appears mystical, the ego fragments remain linked to one another, however distorted and hidden this may be'.[125] To achieve a fresh start in thinking about psychic healing we are to think about this note as a metapsychological assumption, rather than a metaphorical statement. This is confirmed by the fact that the 'link' preserved between the split parts of the psyche also makes its apparition in dreams and dream-like images and states. Patients sometimes bring us dreams of a cut-off body part that is still connected by one thread to the body. In such dream imagery, what is represented is not only the severed organ/head, but also the *thread* that connects to it to the body. In one of the sections above, we analysed a dream of fragments of patient R.N., as it was recorded in *The Clinical Diary*. This dream contained an imagery of threads and their collapse, such as that of an interrupted long-distance telephone call.

If we take this proposition seriously, what emerges as a question is: where and how can this thread be found and in which way can it be used for psychic healing? In the consulting room, this question brings us to the crucial importance of *regression* for the healing of trauma. The clinician will know that as a result of a traumatic shock, one part of the personality can 'die' (or, in other words, the libido can fully withdraw from a part of the personality), while the part that survives the trauma can wake up from the shock with a 'gap in memory' (or, to be more precise, with a gap in conscious memory, or the system of memory of the ego). The 'thread' that we are discussing passes through the system of memory of the id, which has an entirely different inscription mechanism from the system of memory of the ego. This does not mean that nothing was ever presented or preserved in the unconscious, but that to be able to access it, a re-enactment by way of regression is needed. Ferenczi noted that often in the second part of the analytic cure, what the patient experiences is a 'collapse of the intellectual superstructure', accompanied by a 'breaking through of the fundamental situation, which after all is always primitive and strongly affective in character'.[126]

This kind of regression will make possible a 'new beginning' – a term that Michael Bálint will later put at the centre of his propositions on 'benign regression' and 'the basic fault'.[127] What is repeated in this state of regression is the original conflict between the ego and the environment and the painful intrapsychic solutions found for this conflict, in search of fresh and better solution.

***

To make sense of the scene of trauma what is needed is a kind of knowledge that can feel, try, experiment, hesitate, advance, retract and revise. To get closer to the Ferenczian catastrophe – which is not a single or unitary event, but precisely a scene, where several elements hold together and interact and where both creation and destruction take place – what is called for is a 'tentacular knowledge' (Haraway) or the presence of a 'tactile eye' (Staberg). Indeed, we have felt, touched, and theorised our way into and through ten different moments of the scene of trauma, alert to the detail of various forms of psychic splitting and fragmentation. Our interest in neural extravaganzas and the radical plasticity of psyche and soma led us to approach the catastrophe through ten distinct stories about fragments.

Keeping to the spirit of a tentacular knowledge, Ferenczi's writings point to an awareness about the erotics of objectivism and offer important insights on horizontalising the encounter between knower and known. As he writes: 'The last and logically irrefutable word of the pure intellectuality of the ego on the relationship to other objects is a solipsism, which cannot equate the reality of other living beings and the whole outside world of personal experience, and speaks of them as more or less living phantoms or projections'.[128] We have thus left the realm of phantoms, projections and other forms of non-materiality, and encountered fish, squid, jellyfish, octopi and amphibians, as well as 'fingery beings', including aggressors and attackers. The alternative to the kind of solipsism interested in living phantoms and projections is what he calls 'conviction'. Conviction, as opposed to mere belief, cannot be derived solely through logical insight; instead, it needs to be lived as an affective experience, and even felt in one's body.[129]

The implications of this change of orientation away from phantoms and projections are profound. It is possible, with Ferenczi, to think through the catastrophe as *both destructive and creative.* Understanding this tension between radical destruction and radical creativity appeals to our psychoanalytic tentacular knowledges. A curious formation appears in Ferenczi's work precisely at this difficult crossing: it is the *teratoma* – the fruit of one of his medical analogies, where he compares the growth of a complicated (cancerous) tumour with a psychic phenomenon. In his 1929 paper 'The Principle of Relaxation and Neocatharsis', Ferenczi notes:

> For it is no mere poetic licence to compare the mind of the neurotic to a double malformation, something like the so-called teratoma which harbours in a hidden part of its body fragments of a twin-being which has never developed. No reasonable person would refuse to surrender such a teratoma to the surgeon's knife, if the existence of the whole individual were threatened.[130]

Georg Groddeck had used a similar term in a literary context,[131] when he spoke of 'horror stories': teratomae were a particular type of monsters, either constructed from parts of different bodies, like Frankenstein, or the result of fantasy and the transformations of the body that fantasy brings.[132] Medically, the teratoma is a tumour, made up of various types of tissue, which may or may not be cancerous. The implications of Ferenczian teratomae are, however, much deeper. Ferenczi argues that in some cases of neurosis, the greater part of the personality becomes a teratoma, while the task of adaptation to reality falls upon the (smaller) fragment of the personality that was spared. I believe the work of the psychoanalytic process is to deal with this very disproportion, where the deadened 'twin-being' occupies most of the psychic space. This is perhaps the Ferenczian uncanny: a meeting with the twin-inside. The act of the (Ferenczian) narcissist is that of denying the very existence of the teratoma.

As early as 1908, in a text on 'Psycho-Analysis and Education', Ferenczi was already noting the existence in the unconscious of a parasitic double of the conscious self, 'whose natural egotism and tendency for unscrupulous wish-fulfilment represents the dark phantom, the negative of all the good and beautiful on which the higher consciousness prides itself'.[133] This type of split psychic functioning creates 'introspective blindness', which is preserved through moralising education. Through the 'prohibiting and deterring commands of moralising education',[134] the person settles into a state akin to that of hypnosis, with diminished mental energies flowing in the conscious part of the ego and with considerably impaired capacity for action. What is remarkable here is that, in contrast with the writings of Melanie Klein, projection is much less readily available to the psyche. It is often the case that internal 'badness' (especially that resulting from various facets of the identification with the aggressor) is retained in the psyche, and while it is retained it also generates structural modifications of the psyche which require important metapsychological revisions.[135] This is why Ferenczi feels the need to name this psychic place, which he refers to as an internal 'parasite' at an earlier point in his works. Two decades later, this parasitic psychic place will become the 'teratoma'.

I believe that the 'teratoma' is involved in the development of a particular aspect of the superego. In 'Fantasies on a Biological Model of Super-Ego Formation', Ferenczi returns to a scene of devouring and swallowing whole that he attributes to the identification with the aggressor.[136] We discussed above this sort of incorporation of an unmetabolised whole. It is important to stress that the 'scene of devouring' is quite fluid and it circulates freely in the psyche: from the act of having swallowed the aggressor whole, the psyche easily produces fantasies of having swallowed somebody else, and of having swallowed itself. The twin-being of the teratoma is also created through a fantasy of having swallowed oneself. What develops from here is a kind of 'mad superego' that is not an introjection of a person or of an aspect of a person, but of a *scene*. What is incessantly replayed in this scene is the encounter between an 'over-great (fat) aggressor' and 'a much smaller, weaker person, oppressed and dominated by the aggressor'.[137] This is the fundamental asymmetry that we marked above in the discussion of the identification with the aggressor.

After taking this journey with the teratoma, we return to tentacular knowledge. This 'dark' creation, this monstrous agglomeration of psychic fragments of different sorts can only be apprehended by a tactile eye. To put it in Goodfield's terms, 'if you really want to understand about a tumor, you've got to be a tumor.'[138]

The teratoma is an instance of radical psychic plasticity. This means that sometimes parts of the organism can appear dead, but they retain the capacity to build a new psychic formation or fragment, out of their own detritus. This is an important implicit conversation that Ferenczi has with Freud, on the place of the death drive, marking that 'organisms are not so eager to die'.[139] Indeed, this is not, in my reading, an abandonment of the death drive as clinical-theoretical construct. It is instead a curiosity about the many forms that the life drive can and does take. In *Thalassa*, an image that Ferenczi ponders over is that of a 'protective' bladder, membrane, vesicle, pustule or 'place of abode' filled with fluid.[140] Such protective creations are directly implicated in psychic survival at the time of catastrophe, and they count as a manifestation of the life drive. Another facet of this complex analogy is the 'supposition that the amniotic fluid represents a sea "introjected", as it were, into the womb of the mother – a sea in which, as the embryologist R. Hertwig says, "the delicate and easily injured embryo swims and executes movements like a fish in water"'.[141]

The keen interest in radical plasticity takes one other shape. Within the story of trauma, Ferenczi gives space to something I would call 'inter-forms'. Ferenczi is alert to creations that are not of pure essence, and to becomings. With him, we learn to pay close attention to marine beings and to learn from their breathing techniques, their resilience, their modes of memory, their ways of splitting themselves into fragments, and also of becoming deeply entangled with one another. What does it mean, in psychoanalytic terms, that we are able to observe the ability to become-amphibian, become-whale, and then become-coral, and then become-cyanobacteria? Ferenczi is interested in the paradoxical (and creative) breathing that takes place in the scene of trauma, when it remains surprising that any sort of breathing is still going on. This is the kind of breathing that creates new lungs, or adds a new unexpected layer to existing lungs. Drawing on Ernst Haeckel, Ferenczi notes the breathing techniques of the American lung fish (*Lepidosiren paradoxa*) of the Amazon area and the African mud-eel (*Protopterus annectens*). During the dry season, these creatures bury themselves in the drying mud in a nest of leaves and then breathe air by means of lungs, just like amphibians. During the rainy season, they live in the water and breathe water through gills, just like fish. In terms of psychic forms, we can say that at times something that looks like an 'interspecies' relationship goes on *within* the same self or ego. The Other has already made it to our psychic life, and there are curious 'inter-forms' and fragments that attest to this Other-within.

As our journey is coming to an end, it is a good time to wonder what becomes of the time *after* the catastrophe. Is there such a thing as a 'post-traumatic time'? In his writing 'The Two Extremes: Credulity and Scepticism', Ferenczi speaks of 'psychognosis' or 'gnosis', which he sees as 'the hope that it is possible, through an adequate profound relaxation, to gain access to a direct path to a past experience, which can be accepted without any other interpretation as being true'.[142] Here, the pre-traumatic time and the post-traumatic time touch, creating an opening for understanding a particular kind of utopia. What we arrive at through 'psychognosis' is not direct access to the experience 'of how things truly were' at the time of the catastrophe, but an *effect of authenticity* and an *effect of veridicity*. The post-traumatic state is, paradoxically, fuller in possibilities for enrichment and more radically relational than the pre-traumatic state. In other words, the catastrophe has curiously brought about both forms of radical destruction and forms of radical creativity. Utopia is the multiplication and expansion of such psychic effects of authenticity and veridicity.

Notes

1. R. Soreanu, *Working-Through Collective Wounds: Trauma, Denial, Recognition in the Brazilian Uprising*. London: Palgrave Macmillan, 2018.
2. C. Castoriadis, 'Done and to Be Done', in: D. A. Curtis (ed.), *The Castoriadis Reader*. Oxford: Blackwell, 1989, pp. 361–417.
3. S. Ferenczi, 'On Shock' [1932], in: S. Ferenczi, *Final Contributions to the Problems and Methods of Psycho-Analysis*, ed. by M. Bálint, transl. by E. Mosbacher. London: Karnac, 1994, pp. 253–254.
4. J. Laplanche, *Essays on Otherness*. London, New York: Routledge, 1999, p. 257.
5. R. Soreanu, *Working-Through Collective Wounds*.
6. D. J. Haraway, *Staying with the Trouble: Making Kin in the Chthulucene*. Durham: Duke UP, 2016, p. 10.
7. Ibid., p. 30.
8. S. Ferenczi, *Thalassa. A Theory of Genitality* [1924], transl. by H. A. Bunker. Albany: The Psychoanalytic Quarterly, 1938.
9. D. J. Haraway, *Staying with the Trouble*, p. 32.
10. Idem.
11. A. P. Gumbs, *Undrowned: Black Feminist Lessons from Marine Mammals*. Chico: AK Press, 2020; A. P. Gumbs, *Dub: Finding Ceremony*. Durham: Duke UP, 2020.
12. A. P. Gumbs, *Dub*, p. xiii.
13. S. Ferenczi, *Thalassa*, p. 99.

[14] S. Mentz, *Shipwreck Modernity: Ecologies of Globalization, 1550–1719*. Minneapolis: University of Minnesota Press, 2015.
[15] S. Ferenczi, *The Clinical Diary of Sándor Ferenczi* [1932], ed. by J. Dupont, transl. by M. Bálint, N. Z. Jackson. Cambridge, Mass.: Harvard UP, 1995, p. 111.
[16] S. Ferenczi, 'The Birth of Intellect' [1931], in: S. Ferenczi, *Final Contributions to the Problems and Methods of Psycho-Analysis*, pp. 244–246, p. 244.
[17] S. Ferenczi, 'The Analytic Conception of the Psycho-Neuroses' [1908], in: S. Ferenczi, *Further Contributions to the Theory and Technique of Psycho-Analysis*, comp. by J. Rickman, transl. by J. I. Suttie. London: Karnac, 1994, pp. 15–30, p. 29.
[18] R. Soreanu, *Working-Through Collective Wounds*.
[19] S. Ferenczi, 'The Birth of Intellect', p. 244.
[20] S. Ferenczi, 'The Problem of Acceptance of Unpleasant Ideas: Advances in Knowledge of the Sense of Reality' [1926], in: S. Ferenczi, *Further Contributions to the Theory and Technique of Psycho-Analysis*, pp. 366–379.
[21] M. Stanton, *Sándor Ferenczi: Reconsidering Active Intervention*. London: Free Association Books, 1991, p. 84.
[22] S. Freud, 'Beyond the Pleasure Principle' [1920], in: S. Freud, *Beyond the Pleasure Principle, Group Psychology and Other Works* (1920–1922), *SE* 18, pp. 7–64.
[23] S. Ferenczi, 'Child-Analysis in the Analysis of Adults' [1931], in: S. Ferenczi, *Final Contributions to the Problems and Methods of Psycho-Analysis*, pp. 126–142.
[24] J. Laplanche, *Notes sur l'après-coup*, 1998. Paper presented at the Conference on psychoanalytical intracultural and intercultural dialogue. International Psychoanalytical Association, Paris, 27–29 July.
[25] See L. Baraitser, *Enduring Time*. London: Bloomsbury, 2017; D. Birksted-Breen, 'Time and the Après-Coup', *International Journal of Psychoanalysis* 84, 2003, pp. 1501–1515; G. Dahl, 'The Two Time Vectors of *Nachträglichkeit* in the Development of Ego Organization: Significance of the Concept for the Symbolization of Nameless Traumas and Anxieties', *International Journal of Psychoanalysis* 91, 2010, pp. 727–744; H. Faimberg, 'A Plea for a Broader Concept of *Nachträglichkeit*', *The Psychoanalytic Quarterly* 76, 2007, pp. 1221–1240; J. Fletcher, *Freud and the Scene of Trauma*. New York: Fordham UP, 2013.
[26] J. Fletcher, *Freud and the Scene of Trauma*.
[27] Ibid.
[28] Ibid., p. 116.
[29] J. Laplanche, *Nouveaux fondements pour la psychanalyse*. Paris: PUF, 1987.
[30] Ibid., p. 144.
[31] S. Ferenczi, 'The Symbolism of the Bridge' [1921], in: S. Ferenczi, *Further Contributions to the Theory and Technique of Psycho-Analysis*, pp. 352–356, p. 352.
[32] See M. Oliner, '"Non-Represented" Mental States', in: H. B. Levine, G. S. Reed, D. Scarfone (eds.), *Unrepresented States and the Construction of Meaning: Clinical and Theoretical Contributions*. London: Karnac, 2013, pp. 152–171; A. Green, *On Private Madness*. London: Karnac, 1996; R. Roussillon, *Primitive Agony and Symbolization*. London: Karnac, 2011.

33 M. Oliner, '"Non-Represented" Mental States'.
34 S. Ferenczi, *The Clinical Diary of Sándor Ferenczi*, pp. 5–6.
35 The fuller excerpt reads as follows: 'Inorganic and organic matter exist in a highly organized energy association, so solidly organized that it is not affected even by strong disruptive stimuli, that is, it no longer registers any impulse to change it. Substances are so self-assured in their strength and solidity that ordinary outside events pass them by without eliciting any intervention or interest. But just as very powerful external forces are capable of exploding even very firmly consolidated substances, and can also cause atoms to explode, whereupon the need or desire for equilibrium naturally arises again, so it appears that in human beings, under certain conditions, it can happen that the (organic, perhaps also the inorganic) substance recovers its psychic quality, not utilized since primordial times. In other words the capacity to be impelled by motives, that is, the psyche, continues to exist potentially in substances as well. Though under normal conditions it remains inactive, under certain abnormal conditions it can be resurrected. Man is an organism equipped with specific organs for the performance of essential psychic functions (nervous, intellectual activities). In moments of great need, when the psychic system proves to be incapable of an adequate response, or when these specific organs or functions (nervous and psychic) have been violently destroyed, then the primordial psychic powers are aroused, and it will be these forces that will seek to overcome disruption. In such moments, when the psychic system fails, the organism begins to think.' See S. Ferenczi, *The Clinical Diary of Sándor Ferenczi*, pp. 5–6.
36 E. Wilson, *Gut Feminism*. Durham: Duke UP, 2015.
37 S. Freud, 'Notes upon a Case of Obsessional Neurosis' [1909], in: S. Freud, *The Cases of 'Little Hans' and the 'Rat Man'* (1909), *SE* 10, pp. 151–249, p. 157.
38 E. Wilson, *Gut Feminism*.
39 Ibid., p. 59.
40 Idem.
41 See S. Ferenczi, 'The Phenomena of Hysterical Materialization' [1919], in: S. Ferenczi, *Further Contributions to the Theory and Technique of Psycho-Analysis*, pp. 89–104: 'The patients themselves speak of a lump stuck in their throats, and we have every reason to believe that the corresponding contractions of the circular and longitudinal musculature of the oesophagus produce not only the paraesthesia of a foreign body, but that a kind of foreign body, a lump, really is brought about.'
42 S. Ferenczi, 'The Phenomena of Hysterical Materialization'.
43 S. Ferenczi, *The Clinical Diary of Sándor Ferenczi*, p. 7.
44 Ibid., p. 157.
45 Ibid., p. 158.
46 Idem.
47 M. Klein, 'Notes on some Schizoid Mechanisms' [1946], in: M. Klein, *The Writings of Melanie Klein*, Vol. 3. London: The Hogarth Press, 1975, pp. 1–24.

48 E. Spillius, *Encounters with Melanie Klein: Selected Papers of Elizabeth Spillius*. London, New York: Routledge, 2007, p. 109.
49 M. Klein cited in E. Spillius, *Encounters with Melanie Klein*, p. 122.
50 See J. Frankel, 'Ferenczi's Trauma Theory', *American Journal of Psycho-Analysis* 58(1), 1998, pp. 41–61. J. Frankel, 'Exploring Ferenczi's Concept of Identification with the Aggressor: Its Role in Trauma, Everyday Life, and the Therapeutic Relationship', *Psycho-Analytic Dialogues* 12(1), 2002, pp. 101–139; J. Frankel, 'The Persistent Sense of Being Bad: The Moral Dimension of the Identification with the Aggressor', in: A. Harris, S. Kuchuck (eds.), *The Legacy of Sándor Ferenczi: From Ghost to Ancestor*. London, New York: Routledge, 2015, pp. 204–222; K. Lénárd, T. Tényi, 'Ferenczi's Concept on Trauma, connected with the Katonadolog – "Soldiers can take it" Concept', *International Forum of Psycho-Analysis* 12(1), 2003, pp. 22–29.
51 S. Ferenczi, *The Clinical Diary of Sándor Ferenczi*, p. 103.
52 Ferenczi writes, in the 12 January 1932 entry of his *Clinical Diary*: 'She managed, however, as if by a miracle, to get this being back on its feet, shattered as it was to its very atoms, and thus procured a sort of artificial psyche for this body forcibly brought back to life. From now on the "individuum", superficially regarded, consists of the following parts: (a) uppermost, a capable, active human being with a precisely – perhaps a little too precisely – regulated mechanism; (b) behind this, a being that does not wish to have anything more to do with life; (c) behind this murdered ego, the ashes of earlier mental sufferings, which are rekindled every night by the fire of suffering; (d) this suffering itself as a separate mass of affect, without content and unconscious, the remains of the actual person' (S. Ferenczi, *The Clinical Diary of Sándor Ferenczi*, p. 10).
53 S. Ferenczi, 'Autoplastic and Alloplastic Adaptation' [1930], in: S. Ferenczi, *Final Contributions to the Problems and Methods of Psycho-Analysis*, p. 221.
54 S. Ferenczi, 'Confusion of Tongues between Adults and the Child' [1933], in: S. Ferenczi, *Final Contributions to the Problems and Methods of Psycho-Analysis*, pp. 156–167, p. 163.
55 S. Ferenczi, *The Clinical Diary of Sándor Ferenczi*, p. 111.
56 Ibid., p. 176.
57 Derived from the Latin *utraque*, meaning 'one and the other', *utraquism* [*Utraquismus, Utraquistische Arbeitsweise*] is the work of establishing relationships of analogy between distinct elements that belong to distinct fields of knowledge and strata of reality with the aim of discovering or going deeper into the *meaning* of certain processes (See S. Ferenczi, *Thalassa*). For Ferenczi, utraquism is a method. It is an epistemologically consistent disposition. Ferenczi borrowed this term from a sixteenth-century Protestant group, the Utraquists. What distinguished the Utraquists among the Protestants was their belief that it is not only the clergy that should have the privilege of taking both the bread and the wine during communion, but this symbolic reuniting of the flesh and blood of Christ should be extended to laity. As Martin Stanton notes, Ferenczi's interest in

this term is quite a curious event in itself, given the fact that he was an agnostic Jew. I believe that Ferenczi's attraction to the Utraquists rests in his own strand of materialism, which is succinctly and poetically formulated in a 1921 essay: '[T]he symbol – a thing of flesh and blood'. See S. Ferenczi, 'The Symbolism of the Bridge' [1921], in: S. Ferenczi, *Further Contributions to the Theory and Technique of Psycho-Analysis*, pp. 352–356. See also M. Stanton, *Sándor Ferenczi*.

58 See D. J. Haraway, *Crystals, Fabrics, and Fields: Metaphors of Organicism in Twentieth-Century Developmental Biology*. New Haven, London: Yale UP, 1976; G. Bateson, *Mind and Nature: A Necessary Unity*. New York: Dutton, 1979; F. Guattari, *The Machinic Unconscious: Essays in Schizoanalysis*, transl. by T. Adkins. Los Angeles: Semiotext(e), 2011.

59 S. Ferenczi, 'On Shock', p. 254.

60 J. Frankel, 'The Persistent Sense of Being Bad: The Moral Dimension of the Identification with the Aggressor'.

61 See Ibid.; H. Faimberg, *The Telescoping of Generations: Listening to the Narcissistic Links between Generations*. London, New York: Routledge, 2005.

62 J. Frankel, 'The Persistent Sense of Being Bad: The Moral Dimension of the Identification with the Aggressor'.

63 S. Ferenczi, 'Child-Analysis in the Analysis of Adults', pp. 137–138.

64 S. Ferenczi, 'On the Revision of the Interpretation of Dreams' [1931], in: S. Ferenczi, *Final Contributions to the Problems and Methods of Psycho-Analysis*, pp. 238–243, p. 240.

65 Idem.

66 S. Ferenczi, *The Clinical Diary of Sándor Ferenczi*, p. 6.

67 A. P. Gumbs, *Dub*, p. xiii.

68 A. Freud, *The Ego and the Mechanisms of Defence*. London: The Hogarth Press, 1936.

69 S. Ferenczi, 'On Shock', pp. 253–254.

70 S. Ferenczi, 'Each Adaptation is Preceded by an Inhibited Attempt at Splitting' [1930], in: S. Ferenczi, *Final Contributions to the Problems and Methods of Psycho-Analysis*, p. 220.

71 Idem.

72 S. Ferenczi, 'Stages in the Development of the Sense of Reality' [1913], in: S. Ferenczi, *First Contributions to Psycho-Analysis*, transl. by E. Jones. London: Karnac, 1994, pp. 213–239, p. 228.

73 S. Ferenczi, *The Clinical Diary of Sándor Ferenczi*, p. 151.

74 Ibid., pp. 112–113.

75 S. Ferenczi, 'Confusion of Tongues between Adults and the Child', p. 162.

76 Idem.

77 J. Frankel, 'The Persistent Sense of Being Bad: The Moral Dimension of the Identification with the Aggressor'.

78 S. Ferenczi, *The Clinical Diary of Sándor Ferenczi*, p. 188.

79 S. Ferenczi, 'Confusion of Tongues between Adults and the Child', p. 162.

80. See M. Bragin, 'Knowing Terrible Things: Engaging Survivors of Extreme Violence in Treatment', *Clinical Social Work Journal* 35(4), 2007, pp. 229–236; J. Benjamin, *Beyond Doer and Done to: Recognition Theory, Intersubjectivity and the Third*. London, New York: Routledge, 2018.
81. M. Bragin, 'Knowing Terrible Things: Engaging Survivors of Extreme Violence in Treatment'.
82. S. Ferenczi, 'Confusion of Tongues between Adults and the Child' [1933], p. 163.
83. S. Ferenczi, 'On the Analytic Construction of Mental Mechanism' [1930], in: S. Ferenczi, *Final Contributions to the Problems and Methods of Psycho-Analysis*, p. 222.
84. Ibid.
85. S. Ferenczi, *The Clinical Diary of Sándor Ferenczi*, p. 32.
86. S. Ferenczi, 'Confusion of Tongues between Adults and the Child', p. 165.
87. Idem.
88. S. Ferenczi, 'The Dream of the "Clever Baby"' [1923], in: S. Ferenczi, *Further Contributions to the Theory and Technique of Psycho-Analysis*, pp. 349–350.
89. S. Ferenczi, 'Autoplastic and Alloplastic Adaptation', p. 221.
90. Ibid.
91. S. Ferenczi, 'Psycho-Analytical Observations on Tic' [1920], in: S. Ferenczi, *Further Contributions to the Theory and Technique of Psycho-Analysis*, pp. 142–174, p. 160.
92. S. Ferenczi, *The Clinical Diary of Sándor Ferenczi*, p. 179.
93. S. Ferenczi, 'Psycho-Analytical Observations on Tic', p. 161.
94. S. Ferenczi, 'Trauma and Anxiety' [1931], in: S. Ferenczi, *Final Contributions to the Problems and Methods of Psycho-Analysis*, pp. 249–250, p. 249.
95. S. Ferenczi, 'The Problem of Acceptance of Unpleasant Ideas: Advances in Knowledge of the Sense of Reality'.
96. Ibid.
97. S. Spielrein, 'Destruction as the Cause of Coming into Being' [1912], *Journal of Analytical Psychology* 39(2), 1994, pp. 155–186.
98. A. Harris, S. Kuchuck (eds.), *The Legacy of Sándor Ferenczi: From Ghost to Ancestor*. London, New York: Routledge, 2015.
99. S. Ferenczi, 'The Problem of Acceptance of Unpleasant Ideas: Advances in Knowledge of the Sense of Reality', p. 377.
100. S. Ferenczi, 'Trauma and Striving for Health' [1930], in: S. Ferenczi, *Final Contributions to the Problems and Methods of Psycho-Analysis*, pp. 230–231.
101. Ibid.
102. S. Ferenczi, *The Clinical Diary of Sándor Ferenczi*, p. 117.
103. Idem.
104. Idem.
105. Ibid., p. 121.

[106] S. Ferenczi, 'On the Analytic Construction of Mental Mechanism', p. 222.
[107] S. Ferenczi, 'Child-Analysis in the Analysis of Adults', p. 135.
[108] Ibid.
[109] Ibid.
[110] S. Ferenczi, *The Clinical Diary of Sándor Ferenczi*, p. 181.
[111] S. Ferenczi, 'Autoplastic and Alloplastic Adaptation', p. 221.
[112] S. Ferenczi, *The Clinical Diary of Sándor Ferenczi*, pp. 8–10, pp. 102–106.
[113] Ibid., pp. 102–106.
[114] Ibid., pp. 63–66.
[115] Ibid., pp. 68–70.
[116] Ibid., p. 105.
[117] Ibid., p. 8.
[118] S. Ferenczi, 'The Birth of Intellect', pp. 245–246.
[119] S. Ferenczi, 'Child-Analysis in the Analysis of Adults', p. 29.
[120] S. Ferenczi, 'The Birth of Intellect', pp. 244–245.
[121] K. Kerényi, *The Heroes of the Greeks*. London: Thames and Hudson, 1959, p. 280.
[122] R. Graves, *The Greek Myths, Complete Edition*. New York: Penguin Books, 1992.
[123] N. A. Smith, 'From Oedipus to Orpha: Revisiting Ferenczi and Severn's Landmark Case', *American Journal of Psychoanalysis* 59(4), 1999, pp. 345–366, p. 345.
[124] Ibid.
[125] S. Ferenczi, *The Clinical Diary of Sándor Ferenczi*, p. 176.
[126] S. Ferenczi, 'Child-Analysis in the Analysis of Adults', p. 140.
[127] M. Bálint, *The Basic Fault. Therapeutic Aspects of Regression*. London: Tavistock, 1968.
[128] S. Ferenczi, 'The Symbolism of the Bridge', p. 229.
[129] S. Ferenczi, 'Transitory Symptom-Constructions during the Analysis' [1912], in: S. Ferenczi, *First Contributions to Psycho-Analysis*, pp. 193–194.
[130] S. Ferenczi, 'The Principle of Relaxation and Neocatharsis' [1929], in: S. Ferenczi, *Final Contributions to the Problems and Methods of Psycho-Analysis*, p. 123.
[131] G. Groddeck, *The Book of the It*, transl. by V. M. E. Collins. New York: Funk & Wagnalls Company, 1923.
[132] M. Stanton, *Sándor Ferenczi*, p. 174.
[133] S. Ferenczi, 'Psycho-Analysis and Education' [1908], in: S. Ferenczi, *Final Contributions to the Problems and Methods of Psycho-Analysis*, pp. 280–290, p. 287.
[134] Ibid.
[135] See M. Klein, 'The Early Development of Conscience in the Child' [1933], in: M. Klein, *The Writings of Melanie Klein*, Vol. 1. London: The Hogarth Press, 1975, pp. 248–257; M. Klein, 'Notes on some Schizoid Mechanisms' [1946], in: M. Klein, *The Writings of Melanie Klein*, Vol. 3, pp. 1–24; M. Klein, 'On Identification' [1955], in: M. Klein, *The Writings of Melanie Klein*, Vol. 3, pp. 141–175.

[136] S. Ferenczi, 'Fantasies on a Biological Model of Super-Ego Formation' [1930], in: *Final contributions to the Pproblems and Methods of Psychoanalysis*, pp. 227–230, p. 228.
[137] Ibid.
[138] J. Goodfield, *An Imagined World: A Story of Scientific Discovery*. New York: Harper & Row, 1981, p. 213.
[139] S. Ferenczi, *Thalassa*, p. 90.
[140] Ibid., p. 64.
[141] Ibid., p. 56.
[142] S. Ferenczi, 'The Two Extremes: Credulity and Scepticism' [1932], in: S. Ferenczi, *Final Contributions to the Problems and Methods of Psycho-Analysis*, p. 263.

There is Hope for Life in Fragments: Thinking with Ferenczi's Images

RESPONSE

to Raluca Soreanu, by Jenny Willner

Over the last years, Raluca Soreanu has been spelling out a metapsychology inherent to the clinical and theoretical fragments from Sándor Ferenczi's *Clinical Diary* of 1932.[1] In Ferenczi's notes, especially on his patient R.N. (Elizabeth Severn), there is a striking sense of urgency that stands out even within the vast archive of psychoanalytic writing on trauma. The imagery connected to this case is chilling:

> From now on the 'individuum', superficially regarded, consists of the following parts: (a) uppermost, a capable, active human being with a precisely – perhaps a little too precisely – regulated mechanism; (b) behind this, a being that does not wish to have anything more to do with life; (c) behind this murdered ego, the ashes of earlier mental sufferings, which are rekindled every night by the fire of suffering; (d) this suffering itself as a separate mass of affect, without content and unconscious, the remains of the actual person.[2]

Soreanu invites us to think of these images not in terms of metaphors, but as metapsychological assumptions. Ferenczi, she holds, maps out psychic layers and fragments. Departing from her reading of *The Clinical Diary* as a collection of fragments about fragments, Soreanu continues Ferenczi's project by arranging and systematising images collected from the dreams, hallucinations and fantasies of patients – both Ferenczi's and her own. What does it mean to work with the imagery in this way? Soreanu's approach is centred around a hypothesis she shares with Ferenczi, according to which we can learn something crucial from the severely traumatised: that splitting is more readily available to the psyche than we are used to think.

Soreanu's chapter is the most clinical part of our volume. There is no clinical vignette, and yet it can be felt that the material is drawn from the consulting room, that these reflections derive from the question of how to approach the most extreme forms of traumatisation. Why, then, should a literary scholar and a mere admirer of the art of psychotherapy write a response about such matters? The possibility of an interdisciplinary dialogue opens up due to the intricate questions of representation brought up in this material. One of Soreanu's leading thoughts is that trauma is to be understood less as an interruption of symbolisation but rather as the precipitation of images and ways of relating. Catastrophes set strange processes of representation in motion and Soreanu, following Ferenczi, is a careful collector of the images produced. Even the ghastliest fragments are safe in her hands.

As the title of her chapter shows, 'Catastrophe and the Creativity of Fragments', the notion of creativity plays a crucial role for her actualisation of Ferenczi's theory of splitting: Soreanu discusses what she terms the 'creativity' of different modes of survival and attempts at self-healing. This is an extension of Ferenczi's vocabulary: while he explicitly reflects how 'a destructive process results in productivity',[3] the word 'creativity' does not occur in his textual universe.[4] Since 'creativity' is a cultural-politically loaded term,[5] the implications of this terminological extension are worth reflecting.

The social expectation of creativity is deeply imbedded in our culture, as expressed in inspirational phrases such as 'take crisis as a chance' or in euphemisms such as 'flexibility' when referring to the individual adapting to exploitative employment conditions. Faith in the creative potential of the individual, it has been said, belongs to 'the secular religion of the entrepreneurial self'.[6] The demand to be creative is what 'pushes modernity's optimization imperative to the limit'.[7] From a sociological point of view,[8] the demand for creativity can be seen as the epitome of the pressure which the neoliberal system exerts on the individual, exploiting its flexibility and ability to adapt. At the same time, the term still carries the association of artistic expression and artistic freedom as a vehicle to defy oppressive norms. It has however been argued, that precisely this positive notion of creativity, in the tradition of the repressive hypothesis and the hippie movement, has turned out to be more than compatible with commodification.[9]

How precisely does Soreanu's acknowledgement of the creativity of traumatic fragments relate to the imperative to take crisis as a chance for creative solutions? While it is obvious that Soreanu's use of the term is different, I believe it is important to try to articulate why this is the case. Soreanu does something with the way we usually understand 'creativity'. Her use of the term stands crosswise to what has been called the *creativity dispositif* in the above-described sense.[10] This is partly because the notion of creativity at play in Soreanu's chapter is not structured around efficiency. In the context of our book, creativity appears as an inseparable aspect of traumatic splitting under catastrophic circumstances. Soreanu follows Ferenczi in focussing on the dark implications of all processes involved:

> The connections that Ferenczi makes between destruction, creativity and the creation of new organs should not [...] seduce us into a celebration of fragments, a sort of enthusiasm for a post-catastrophic subjectivity. Such triumphalism of fragments is not in the spirit of Ferenczi's work. Ferenczi remains lucid on the dark implications of splitting, which pass through a particular kind of narcissism, where the deadened fragments of the ego are denied. The ego becomes a kind of mosaic of dead and still-alive parts, but the deadened and de-libidinised ones are 'forgotten'. Some of the fragments 'assume, as it were, the form and function of a whole person'.[11]

To reverse the perspective, we should perhaps take precisely these abysmal dimensions into account when dealing with notions of creativity outside the psychoanalytic discourse. A crucial difference between Soreanu's notion of creativity and the popular *creativity dispositif* can be articulated departing from the question of whether there is something to be mourned. The neoliberal idealisation of creativity promotes a kind of mania which can be seen as the reverse side of melancholia, dismissing the catastrophe in fetishistic disavowal and false reassurance.

The reassurance offered in Soreanu's Ferenczian metapsychology of splitting is of an different kind. Soreanu's writing leads us deep into a frightening world. Indeed, any involvement with Ferenczi's 'Confusion of Tongues' is utterly destabilising. With his understanding of mimetic modes of defence we enter a grey zone where suffocated anger may hide underneath complete subordination and adaption, where abused children may develop thoughts and feelings they sense the aggressor needs from them, where perpetrators may speak through their victims. This concept is not only difficult to grasp intellectually. Even the beginning of an insight generates a painful disturbance. It is an ethical challenge to endure the impact of this material. Practically speaking, such an approach is probably the precondition for any kind of free-floating phenomenological attention towards the most disturbing sides of victimhood: phenomena of submission, self-abandonment, and mimetic forms of defence, repetition compulsion and suffocated impulses of rebellion. In cases where even the most annihilating self-reproach is easier to bear for the subject than the knowledge of one's complete helplessness during an attack, there is no space left unaffected

RESPONSE to Raluca Soreanu, by Jenny Willner

by the catastrophe, no victimhood uncontaminated by the wrongness of the violation, no steady ground under our feet. Introjection of the aggressor means that the attack ceases to be part of external reality and becomes an intrapsychic reality within the victim. In metapsychological terms, Soreanu speaks of a psychic organisation structured entirely around introjected guilt, where 'the "wrongness" of the traumatic scene has been incorporated and curved inwards'.[12]

Soreanu ends up drafting ten moments that capture different facets of catastrophic splitting: paralysis, dematerialisation, traumatic imitation, guilt, getting beside oneself, traumatic progression, autotomy, neo-formations, Orpha, and reconstruction. Along these ten moments, we are presented with a series of traumatic re-enactments and of recurring bodily symptoms. We are confronted with children who subordinate themselves to their aggressors like automata and with images of frozen, deadened, silent psychic fragments. According to Ferenczi, such fragments testify to a situation where falling into traumatic paralysis may have been the only way to survive a violently induced shock.

Whatever caused these reactions is not part of the discourse: Soreanu's chapter does not take up what kind of attacks may have taken place. Instead, her approach is strictly oriented towards peculiar aftereffects in the psyche: the sense of leaving one's own body, observing it from outside, locating seeing and thinking elsewhere 'while the rest of the body is left in agony on the ground'.[13] It is noteworthy that the omission of references to the external cause of the trauma at stake does not reduce the urgency and the triggering effect of the examples. Soreanu argues that fantasies about new organs may testify to a state in which the victim barely maintained a beating heart, or to a situation in which death was prevented only by means of a hallucination of breathing, under the condition of somatic suffocation.[14] From such constellations, Ferenczi drew the speculative conclusion that there must be an instance in the unconscious which produces minute calculations on what it would mean to continue living when death is near: Orpha, a feminine version of Orpheus, the man who descended into the underworld.[15]

Although Orpheus' *katabasis*, his journey to Hades, belongs to Greek mythology, I have caught myself associating Soreanu's ten moments of psychic catastrophe with another underworld: the rings of the *Inferno* in Dante Alighieri's *Divina Commedia*. Dante depicts hell in nine concentric circles of torment, added to the zone of the devil in the middle. His literary alter ego descends into these depths guided by Virgil, who embodies a principle of anaesthesia that has been associated both with Freud's notion of the dream as the guardian of sleep and with the aesthetic distance of art.[16] Soreanu's style of writing indeed displays a calmness which stands in stark contrast to the catastrophic scenes evoked. We are guided through the ten moments in a way that enables us to take in more than we could normally bear.

This calm approach is everything but cold. A discrete tenderness of tone distinguishes Soreanu's scholarly style from scientific dispassion. Her writing embodies an approach which according to her conclusions from clinical work is crucial for any kind of healing, an approach in line with Ferenczi's critique of Freud's distance and withdrawal. Soreanu's voice in writing generates the impression of sympathy, even while she mobilises the imagery out of which nightmares are made: cut-off body parts still connected to the body by one thread, victims of torture who feel that they resemble their torturer in their intimate familiarity with 'terrible things'.[17]

Ferenczi's willingness to follow his patients even into their psychotic hallucinations, thinking with their images, has sometimes been considered a psychotic trait in himself: a tendency to take dreamed-up imagery at face value. Quite differently, Soreanu underlines the epistemological implications of his use of analogies: Ferenczi draws upon different registers of imagery and switches between them. Soreanu describes this as a methodological consequence of an unsettling clinical-empirical puzzle: the fact that there can be a striking precision in the enactments and actualisations of the traumatic event in the consulting room even while the memory at stake remains inaccessible to consciousness.[18] The lack of associative links between the different registers allows for the assumption that splitting must have occurred. Accordingly, it is precisely where associations fail that the clinician assumes this specific mode of attention, led by the hypothesis that what is enacted belongs to different parts of the split psyche, different modes of representation.

Soreanu puts Ferenczi's vocabulary to work: a vocabulary dominated by fractures, splits, atomisations, pulverisations, protective membranes, expansions, contagions and new organs. Her approach focusses on the arrangement of the material rather than on the interpretative act. This alludes to the assumption that dreams may tell strange stories of psychic splitting, of specific means of survival and of fragments which cannot be consciously felt or known. While according to Ferenczi there is no shock without a splitting,[19] this very fragmentation is already to be understood as more than a causal result of the blow: it is a form of defence. Each one of the ten moments presents us with yet another form of survival, a new form of life. Soreanu's insistence on the creativity of fragments picks up a feature that can be sensed throughout Ferenczi's writing: astonishment at the fact that survival was possible at all.

Something breaks into pieces and continues life in fragments. Because the unification of all pain would be unbearable, each of the fragments stubbornly suffers for itself. There is a strange comfort in this view: a sense of recalcitrance of fragments that continue living. Clinical work, then, consists of linking the different sensorial modalities to one another. The integration of the fragments is not the ultimate goal of this linking: '[s]ometimes splitting is so profound and it results in such stable psychic fragments that the psychoanalytic process is more accurately described as one of re-libidinisation of "deadened" parts of the psyche, rather than one of integration'.[20] Soreanu speaks of a mosaic of dead and alive fragments. We may also imagine a photomontage, like the one on the cover image of our book,[21] or even a cyborg consisting of machine-like and organic parts. It may be monstrous, but it is recognised in its different eccentric components. This recognition means everything. While reading Soreanu, it is as if even the most terrifying fragments were somehow both interpellated and contained by her Ferenczian voice.

What can we learn from severe traumatisation? To return to the initial reflection of this response, Soreanu's notion of creativity can be used to shift the common understanding of the term. Outside the consulting room, it is perhaps precisely the fetishistic ideal of a flexible, adapted, managerial and creative individual, displaying hyper-faculties under pressure that needs to be viewed with Ferenczian eyes. Recently, Ferenczi's notion of an identification with the aggressor has been used to analyse how authoritarianism works under neoliberal conditions: according to Samir Gandesha, the neoliberal subject, facing privatisation and upward redistribution of wealth due to the destruction of social security networks, willingly takes on the responsibility for displaying successful entrepreneurial activity, introjecting guilt in the face of failure.[22] This line of thought can perhaps be taken even further: when Ferenczi describes the surface of 'a capable, active human being with a precisely – perhaps a little too precisely – regulated mechanism',[23] we may assume that pain and protest have been annihilated, that a catastrophe has occurred. The *creativity dispositif* is part of a catastrophic scenario in which the individual, cast under the spell of the neoliberal demand to be creative, at a closer look indeed displays a psychic organisation structured entirely around debt and introjected guilt. The wrongness has been curved inwards.

Soreanu's understanding of the 'tension between radical destruction and radical creativity'[24] operates in close proximity to the 'creativity complex'.[25] This is partly because psychoanalysis in general relates in a secondary manner to prevalent discourses, observing, re-arranging, interpreting or deconstructing different notions at work. There is no strictly demarcated line between the dominant discourse and the psychoanalytical; even the most emancipatory coinages of the latter may be re-appropriated by precisely those tendencies psychoanalytic thinking set out to deconstruct in the first place. Therefore, it demands a persistent effort to articulate the relation between different notions at work.

This leads me to my last point, namely that Soreanu's and my own approach to the relation between psychoanalytic theory and organic life are in a way complementary. While expanding the Ferenczian vocabulary towards a theory of the creativity of fragments, Soreanu draws upon imagery derived from new materialist writing, above all Donna Haraway.[26] The accomplishment of this paradigm lies in a non-determinist approach to organic matter, according to which biology does not constitute a foundation, but rather directs our attention towards the somatic as a realm that goes beyond our representations, as a site of indeterminacy, surprising and unpredictable effects.[27] While Soreanu convincingly makes new materialism fruitful for an actualisation of Ferenczi's metapsychology, my own approach has more to do with how old and new epistemologies can be situated within a larger social arena, including the history of science and ideology.[28] Quite in contrast to the paradigm of post-criticism, I remain rather fond of interrogating concepts, for instance in order to articulate how Ferenczi's use of the phylogenetic parallel differs from the eugenicist world view of Haeckel and Bölsche – and how Soreanu's use of the term creativity differs from the neoliberal *creativity dispositif*.[29] As Kyla Schuller has emphasised, the new materialist 'recognition of the dynamic capacities of matter is not in and of itself counterhegemonic; rather, its political implications depend on *how* plasticity is deployed within scientific discourse'.[30] Hence, a critical interrogation of concepts such as plasticity, vitalism, and material agency remains useful for understanding the concepts we inherit and what we risk re-animating.[31]

To put it differently, the critters and marine animals populating Ferenczi's writings attract Soreanu's and my own respective scholarly attention from quite different directions. Coming from philology, always preoccupied with the archive, with words and discourses as such, I doubt that we have ever left the 'realm of phantoms, projections' and truly 'encountered fish, squid, jellyfish, octopi and amphibians'.[32] My point of departure is rather that Ferenczi's work, his replacement of biologism by bioanalysis, can help us handle the unavoidable gap that remains. In his methodological writings, he describes what I termed a 'strategic dualism'[33] as opposed to any ontological claim. Ferenczi states that a unification of the physical and the psychic 'is not possible at present, nor in the near future, and perhaps cannot be ever achieved completely.'[34] By returning to Ferenczi we are reminded that there is no neutral, transparent discourse on organic life.

RESPONSE to Raluca Soreanu, by Jenny Willner

Having said this, in Soreanu's work, the benefit of *thinking with* the images of organisms and organs – as opposed to suspiciously interrogating them – becomes obvious. This too belongs to the legacy of Ferenczi. To a precise observer like Soreanu, our fantasies of the organic display a structure, tell fragmented fairy tales of metapsychological relevance. Her – and Ferenczi's – references to marine life have nothing to do with the oceanic ambition of using regression in order to tap energy from some supposedly uncontaminated vital force. Rather, we must assume that in times of crisis, new forms of representation occur, both through theoretical fictions and through re-arrangements of the imagery of the infantile and the world of non-human animals. As Soreanu has pointed out,[35] we need to remain speculative on precisely how the different registers of representation relate to each other. We re-articulate our relation to the past, take a leap backwards – to the past of the child and of the species – because there are reasons to believe that catastrophe was there, too. In order to represent processes of the living psyche and soma, the pressures of the present, we must assume that something happened, and that it continues to produce effects as we go along.

Right now, I imagine a squid, pulling its tentacles together, squirting thick, dark ink to confuse any follower before propelling deeper into the sea by taking in water through its gills and forcing it through a muscular syphon, diving into depths inaccessible to us, escaping our frames of representation entirely, blissfully unaware of what it brought to the *Ferenczi Dialogues*.

Notes

[1] R. Soreanu, 'The Psychic Life of Fragments: Splitting from Ferenczi to Klein', *The American Journal of Psychoanalysis* 78(4), 2018, pp. 421–444.

[2] S. Ferenczi, *The Clinical Diary of Sándor Ferenczi* [1932], ed. by J. Dupont, transl. by M. Bálint, N. Z. Jackson. Cambridge, Mass.: Harvard UP, 1995, p. 10.

[3] S. Ferenczi, *The Clinical Diary of Sándor Ferenczi*, p. 42.

[4] At some other occasion, it would be intriguing to investigate how this notion relates to Winnicott's use of the term, as discussed in R. Roussillon, 'Creativity: A New Paradigm for Freudian Psychoanalysis', in: G. Saragnano, C. Seulin (eds.), *Playing and Reality Revisited*. London: Karnac, 2015, pp. 89–110.

[5] J. N. Howe, 'Kreativität', in: C. Benthien, E. Matala de Mazza, Uwe Wirth (eds.), *Handbuch Literatur und Ökonomie*. Boston: DeGruyter, 2019, pp. 182–184.

[6] U. Bröckling, *The Entrepreneurial Self. Fabricating a New Type of Subject*, transl. by S. Black. Los Angeles, London: Sage, 2016, p. 101.

[7] A. Reckwitz, *The Invention of Creativity. Modern Society and the Culture of the New*, transl. by S. Black. Malden, Mass.: Polity, 2017, p. iix.

8   L. Boltanski, È. Chiapello, *Der neue Geist des Kapitalismus*, transl. by M. Tillmann. Konstanz: UVK, 2003; D. Bell, *The Cultural Contradictions of Capitalism*. New York: Basic Books, 1976.
9   I am referring, here, to the idea of a structural compatibility between the cultural critique of the late 1960s and neoliberal modes of self-modelling. It has been argued that the field of art since then has become a blueprint for managerial creativity, even far beyond the realm of the creative industries. Cf. L. Boltanski, È. Chiapello, *Der neue Geist des Kapitalismus*; A. Reckwitz, *The Invention of Creativity*, originally published in German in 2012.
10 A. Reckwitz, *The Invention of Creativity*, p. vii. Reckwitz uses the term *dispositif* in the sense of Michel Foucault.
11 R. Soreanu, Part 3, p. 176-177.
12 R. Soreanu, Part 3, p. 169.
13 R. Soreanu, Part 3, p. 172.
14 R. Soreanu, Part 3, p. 176; cf. S. Ferenczi, *The Clinical Diary of Sándor Ferenczi*, p. 117.
15 R. Soreanu, Part 3, p. 179-180, cf. S. Ferenczi, *The Clinical Diary of Sándor Ferenczi*, p. 8.
16 My source here is admittedly the protagonist of a novel, a fictive reader of Dante: '[I]n a dream the no-longer-endurable led to awakening, just as in literature it is freed by the translation into words. Anesthesia, he [Heilmann] went on, was likewise part of extremely participatory art that took a stance, for without the help of anesthetic we would be overwhelmed either by feeling compassion with other people's torments or by suffering our own misfortune'. P. Weiss, *The Aesthetics of Resistance* [1975], Vol. 1, transl. by J. Neugroschel. Durham, London: Duke UP, 2005, p. 71.
17 R. Soreanu, Part 3, p. 170, with reference to M. Bragin, 'Knowing Terrible Things: Engaging Survivors of Extreme Violence in Treatment', *Clinical Social Work Journal* 35(4), 2007, pp. 229–236; cf. S. Ferenczi, *The Clinical Diary of Sándor Ferenczi*, p. 162.
18 R. Soreanu, Part 3, p. 155: 'what is actually missing is the associations between different modes of representation'.
19 S. Ferenczi, 'On Shock' [1932], in: S. Ferenczi, *Final Contributions to the Problems and Methods of Psycho-Analysis*, ed. by M. Bálint, transl. by E. Mosbacher. London: Karnac, 1994, pp. 253–254.
20 R. Soreanu, Part 3, p. 161.
21 H. Höch, *Siebenmeilenstiefel* [1934], Photomontage, 23.1 x 23.8 cm. Hamburger Kunsthalle.
22 S. Gandesha, 'Identifying with the Aggressor. From the Authoritarian to the Neoliberal Personality', *Constellations* 25(1), 2018, pp. 1–18, pp. 9–10.
23 S. Ferenczi, *The Clinical Diary of Sándor Ferenczi*, p. 10 [entry from 12 January 1932].
24 R. Soreanu, Part 3, p. 182.

25 T. Beyes, J. Metelmann (eds.), *The Creativity Complex. A Companion to Contemporary Culture*. Bielefeld: transcript, 2018.
26 D. J. Haraway, *Staying with the Trouble: Making Kin in the Chthulucene*. Durham: Duke UP, 2016.
27 See also E. Grosz, *The Nick of Time. Politics, Evolution, and the Untimely*. Durham: Duke UP, 2004.
28 P. Ramponi, J. Willner, 'Nachdarwinistische Obsessionen. Eine Vorgeschichte der Human-Animal-Studies', in: C. Ortlieb, P. Ramponi, J. Willner (eds.), *Das Tier als Medium und Obsession. Zur Politik des Wissens um Mensch und Tier um 1900*. Berlin: Neofelis, 2015, pp. 9–46.
29 While trying to understand what it means that Soreanu's response to my own chapter brings my method into proximity with post-criticism (p. 137), I was delighted by Eric L. Santner's use of the term 'post-critical': he undermines the common post-critical gesture of a break with 'critical theory' and instead celebrates the libidinally charged, transferential nature of any serious engagement with theory. For Santner, being post-critical implies being 'constitutively *unsuspicious*, willingly *enchantable*' in relation to the text, given, however, that precisely this transferential trust forms the precondition for any proper criticism. '[T]hose who assume from the start the critical posture, perhaps especially one fortified by psychoanalytical theory, to avoid being duped are the ones who are really duped'. E. L. Santner, *Untying Things Together: Philosophy, Literature, and a Life in Theory*. London, Chicago: University of Chicago Press, 2022, p. xiii, xiv.
30 K. Schuller, *The Biopolitics of Feeling. Race, Sex, and Science in the Nineteenth Century*. Durham, London: Duke UP, 2018, p. 26; cf. A. Willey, 'A World of Materialisms: Postcolonial Feminist Science Studies and the New Natural', *Science, Technology, and Human Values* 41(6), 2016, pp. 991–1014.
31 K. Schuller, *The Biopolitics of Feeling*, pp. 26–27. Schuller's study investigates the structuring role of ideas of vital matter and plasticity in the deployment of biopower over the last two centuries.
32 R. Soreanu, Part 3, p. 182.
33 J. Willner, Part 2, p. 112, regarding S. Ferenczi, 'Freud's Influence on Medicine', in: S. Ferenczi, *Final Contributions to the Problems and Methods of Psycho-Analysis*, ed. by M. Bálint, transl. by E. Mosbacher. London: Karnac, 1994, pp. 143–155, pp. 146–147.
34 S. Ferenczi, 'Freud's Influence on Medicine', p. 147.
35 R. Soreanu, 'Sándor Ferenczi's Epistemologies and their Politics: On Utraquism and the Analogical Method', in: F. Erős, A. Borgos, J. Gyimesi (eds.), *Psychology and Politics: Intersections of Science and Ideology in the History of Psy-Sciences*. Budapest, New York: Central European UP, 2019, pp. 95–106.

Toward an Eventful Psychoanalysis

RESPONSE

to Raluca Soreanu, by Jakob Staberg

Raluca Soreanu's analysis of Ferenczi's exploration of psychic fragments conjures up a new map of the mental landscape that goes beyond Freud's model of the self, the id and the superego. She argues that the forms of splitting Ferenczi discovered in his clinical practice point to the need for a revision of metapsychology. To this end, Soreanu engages in a mapping of the 'new' types of psychic fragments Ferenczi uncovers, where in particular the Orpha fragment, understood as a female Orpheus oscillating between the urges of life and death, plays a crucial role in turning attention to the forces or forms that help an individual to survive. 'Ferenczi was much more curious about how subjects survive, in fragments, through the action of intrapsychic forces, rather than how they are held together by the environment'.[1] This leads to certain questions I would like to ponder from the perspective of Soreanu's world of thought. How to think the nature of these fragments? How to think the substratum that makes up this psychic life and what paths does such an investigation and analysis open?

These questions invite a plurality of images and landscapes; Soreanu's work especially creates ways of thinking catastrophes and transformations, shipwrecks, losses, transitions between oceans and land, sudden opening of biological possibilities. This way of thinking and reading Ferenczi's work takes us on multiple paths and engages new understandings that resonate with our catastrophes, the challenges we are facing. Ferenczi's concepts of catastrophes, trauma and event constitute with Soreanu 'a vocabulary for making sense of the eventfulness of our time'.[2] Psychoanalytic thinking becomes eventful, in this sense, as it evolves around the question: 'What does it mean to have survived a psychic catastrophe?'[3] Thus imagining the catastrophe, not as a singular, unitary event, but as a *scene* where qualitative forces are held together, the whole world of fragments become intense, vibrating with particular elements of becoming. In my view, this way of thinking eventfulness opens up intellectual and emotional operations that are interlaced with aesthetics, thus Soreanu's work enables me to connect psychoanalysis to literature and poetry in new ways. With Edouard Glissant we can think of this operation as a certain *poetics of relation*. If this eventful psychoanalysis is thus re-embodied we enter not only a psychic sphere of fragments. Soreanu finds an interlocutor in Donna Haraway with whom she can articulate Ferenczi's interest in 'neural extravaganzas, fibrous entities, flagellated beings, myofibril braids, matted and felted microbial and fungal tangles, probing creepers, swelling roots, reaching and climbing tendrilled ones'.[4] In particular, we enter a certain aquatic register where 'the bodies are those of fish, squid, jellyfish, octopi and amphibians'.[5]

The link between trauma and catastrophes to aquatic life, remembering or experiencing as an unconscious impact voyages over an abyss, resonates with the writing of Glissant. In an important essay, he has explored the lived experience that traverses generations of the survivors of colonialism and slavery, an experience of unimaginable losses that cries for poetry and creates nomadic uprooted subjects. 'For the Africans who lived through the experience of deportation to the Americas, confronting the unknown with neither preparation nor challenge was no doubt petrifying'.[6] What, in his word, 'partakes the abyss is linked to the unknown'; the boat that dissolves is a 'womb, a womb abyss', the depth of the sea, and paralleling this mass of water there is the creation of metamorphosis of the abyss that 'thus projects a reverse image of all that had been left behind, not to be regained for generations except […] in the blue savannas of memory or imagination'.[7]

This referring to aesthetics always resonates with lived experience, and in a way it can shape our understanding of the psychoanalytical situation, something I find particularly developed in Soreanu's images drawn from her clinical work, where she depicts analytical processes with depth and calm clarity. Together with a careful reading and remarkable analysis of Ferenczi's text, her own findings give insight into what has hitherto constituted a, in her words, *phenomenological gap* in the understanding of psychic fragments. Her research leads to a new understanding of the field she has marked out, constituted as it were between Ferenczi and Melanie Klein. 'The images that predominate here are those of fractures, splits, atomisations, pulverisations, leakages, detritus, but also new formations, protective membranes, expansions, contagions, and inner growths'.[8] We find ourselves brought to strange environments and mental states, landscapes of cut-off parts, of fragments. With the help of Soreanu, we can experience forms of psychic life that go beyond ego, even beyond consciousness, perhaps emanating from the organs themselves. Her critique of Klein's positioning becomes crucial for articulating this particular field, in a further approach. Let us now dwell on this.

Soreanu's analysis is prompted by certain questions: what does it mean to think the psychic life of a fragment? how to understand its forces? its substratum? What, in this sense, are organs, and most of all, what do they do? What are they capable of? We move from the neat binary coupling of good and bad of the world of partial objects to something that at first seems strange and perhaps uncanny. Soreanu forces us through her intrinsic reading of Ferenczi to think further the concept Freud developed in his writing on unconscious processes. In this sense, Soreanu's work partakes in a renewed interest in Ferenczi that we have seen in the last decades; her findings insist quite simply on a certain rethinking of the psychoanalytic tradition. This is close at hand to a certain genealogical method, but her structural analysis of metapsychology is always rooted in a strong insight extracted from the clinical work of Ferenczi, as well as her own practice. Not least *The Clinical Diary* shows how closely Ferenczi's understanding of metapsychology is related to his work with patients, always following leads from them. We experience it in the whole process of mutual analysis, in his way of scrutinising himself, constantly exploring the possibilities and failures of the psychoanalytical situation. It is also here that his disappointment with Freud becomes apparent.

In his late work Ferenczi reports the results of his explorations through the psychoanalytic situation and transference in particular, of what he calls autoplastic reaction patterns. That shock or horror, phenomena which bear traces of a split in personality, can produce a regression to a state of the event that is, he argues, at the same time strange and familiar. But in his work, Ferenczi sees, confronting death and anxiety, other mechanisms at work: 'I mean the sudden, surprising rise of new faculties after a trauma, like a miracle'.[9] As in the writings of Glissant, trauma and its effects exist virtually like an ancestor and can develop a kind of 'potential qualities' through 'the pressure of such traumatic urgency'.[10] For Ferenczi, the fact that the shock can thus mature a part of the personality is not limited to the particular cases he works with in the psychoanalytic situation, although these, so to speak, open his eye to phenomena which he describes as for instance a 'precocious maturity' or traumatic progression through which 'the child can develop instantaneously all the emotions of a mature adult'.[11] Here, following Soreanu, we touch upon a thinking in 'register', which I find so very important for her analysis; it leads us to one of the perhaps most important aspects of her work, namely acknowledging the will and ability to survive. But if this will has the strength to create changes, how do we understand metapsychology – in other words: what is metapsychology?

Not leaving aside but thinking beyond a structural approach, we are ending up with trying to think again, rethinking our initial questions: what is psychic substrata? It becomes clear that it involves a further engaging in questions of how organisms begin to think; we ask ourselves what life is, what can create a sudden breakthrough of forces, of changes? 'Ferenczi', Soreanu writes, 'discusses this primal substrate in the first pages of his *Clinical Diary*, pointing to a process when different organs or body parts produce effects of thinking'.[12] All along there is this agonising concern: what is this *stuff* that constitutes psychic life? Leading us through this complex field, Soreanu again and again underlines the importance of discovering this psychic stuff as it appears in registers, in different and separate languages, in different modes of arranging things and objects, parts and connections. In my view, it not only brings us back to thinking fragments, but involves a creating of entanglements, links, assemblage. Finally, in my mind, it bring us to the processes of dreams.

'Psychic life', Soreanu writes in her critique of Klein, 'is from the onset based on *qualities*, and not on sheer polarities'.[13] In my view this is a most important point; quite simply, it makes all the difference. In the words of Soreanu: 'We can certainly be frustrated or satisfied, by the object or in the imagination, but the question of importance that should be formulated is: "in which particular way does frustration/satisfaction occur?"'[14] Asked in this way, the question leads to a key concept in Soreanu's work, that of an 'eventful' form of splitting that leaves more stable fragments as its traces.[15] The analysis takes her beyond Klein's detailed depiction of a first type of splitting, performed by the self in relation to the object and resulting in the polarity of the bad and the good object. Rather, and thinking with Ferenczi, what Soreanu explores are forms of change or transformation that take place through the body. Instead of thinking binary couples of good and bad, it invites an exploration of qualities. With Ferenczi, Soreanu conceives an investigation into a new kind of splitting within psychic life, which is at once stable and potentially irreversible. Suddenly, a new area of the unconscious can be uncovered, populated by terrifying fragments, beyond or untouched by the development of the self and with the capacity to overwhelm it. It is an integrated psychic life of fragments, split off from the self and the superego. To conclude, let me speculate further in my assumption of the strong resonance between this psychic life of fragments and dream processes.

Again, I would like to go back to the question Soreanu asked, as referred to in the beginning of my response: 'what is the "stuff" that the psyche is splitting?'[16] It might guide us to another way of understanding this *phenomenological gap*, now through poetry, a poetry guided by the notion Soreanu detects in Ferenczi of the very 'immediate materiality' of meaning.[17] It invites us to speculate, on amphibian life, on movement between water and land, and most importantly it brings forth the telling of new stories, whether they might be depicted, as in the following from our contemporary popular sciences, tales of original transition from sea to land, creating new forms of life – or from lived experience:

Green algae made their way out of fresh water and onto land, a broken and desolate environment, with wildly changing temperatures and nutrients locked in solid rock and minerals.[18] This movement constitutes a breakthrough, a sudden opening of biological possibilities, hitherto dormant in photosynthetic bacteria, extremophilic algae and fungi. The intermingling of these forms amounts to something unknown. Life on earth had hitherto taken place in the water. What made algae's perilous transition to dry land possible, with no roots, no means of transporting or storing water, was the ability to establish new relationships with sponges. This collective flourishing, with its co-operations, conflicts and competition, forms an intimate partnership, an alliance called 'mycorrhizal relations'. Fungi and algae thus form an association that gives rise to an evolutionary *refrain* where they merge into entirely new symbiotic relationships.

So the speculative answer to this question of what 'stuff' the psyche is made of would already have been given: when in a dream an image rises from the meshwork of its unfathomable network it does so like 'the mushroom out of its mycelium'.[19] But this makes sense only if we acknowledge that the dream world's signifying chains – with Ferenczi understood as involving 'different sensorial impressions and thing-presentations'[20] – constantly repeats this transition from sea to land. Thus the individual takes part in life, just as the symbiosis between fungi and algae can help them orient themselves in soils filled with structures and micropores, electrically charged cavities and labyrinthine root landscapes. And as the algae depended on fungi to make their way, so thought appears as a side effect of the intense work produced by mycelium. As Prospero in Shakespeare's *The Tempest*, restoring order after an imaginary shipwreck, sees his *revels* melt 'into thin air', and as the 'baseless fabric of this vision', with all it inherits, 'dissolves', he must conclude: 'We are such stuff/ As dreams are made on'.[21] So the dream-work, to conclude this Ferenczian speculation, is on the one hand concentrated in the overdetermined image, on the other – but not as a *baseless* fabric, rather comprised by 'matted and felted microbial and fungal tangles, probing creepers, swelling roots, reaching and climbing tendrilled ones' – it involves points of contact with the unknown, as it were, 'the navel of its female knot', perhaps linked to the perception of an archaic mother, a body; in Shoshana Felman's words: '*what the dreamer and the dream interpreter do not yet know*'.[22]

Notes

1. R. Soreanu, 'The Psychic Life of Fragments: Splitting from Ferenczi to Klein', *The American Journal of Psychoanalysis* 78(4), 2018, pp. 421–444, p. 425f.
2. Soreanu, Part 3, p. 148.
3. Soreanu, Part 3, p. 145.
4. D. J. Haraway, *Staying with the Trouble: Making Kin in the Chthulucene*. Durham: Duke UP, 2016, p. 32.
5. R. Soreanu, Part 3, p. 149.
6. E. Glissant, *Poetics of Relation*, transl. by B. Wing. Ann Arbor: University of Michigan Press, 1997, p. 5.
7. Ibid., pp. 6–7.
8. R. Soreanu, Part 3, p. 145.
9. S. Ferenczi, 'Confusion of Tongues between Adults and the Child' [1933], in: S. Ferenczi, *Final Contributions to the Problems and Methods of Psycho-Analysis*, ed. by M. Bálint, transl. by E. Mosbacher. London: Karnac, 1994, pp. 156–167, pp. 164–165.
10. Ibid., p. 165.
11. Idem.
12. R. Soreanu, 'The Time of Re-Living. For an Eventful Psychoanalysis', *Vestigia* 2(1), 2019, pp. 132–153, p. 138.
13. R. Soreanu, 'The Psychic Life of Fragments: Splitting from Ferenczi to Klein', p. 430.
14. Idem.
15. Idem.
16. Ibid., p. 422.
17. R. Soreanu, 'Something Was Lost in Freud's Beyond the Pleasure Principle: A Ferenczian Reading', *The American Journal of Psychoanalysis* 77(3), 2017, pp. 223–238, p. 234.
18. M. Sheldrake, *Entangled Life: How Fungi Make our Worlds, Change our Minds and Shape our Futures*. London: The Bodley Head, 2020.
19. S. Freud, 'The Interpretation of Dreams (II)' [1900], in: S. Freud, *The Interpretation of Dreams (Second Part) and On Dreams* (1900–1901), SE 5, pp. 339–627, p. 525.
20. R. Soreanu, 'Something Was Lost in Freud's Beyond the Pleasure Principle: A Ferenczian Reading', p. 234.
21. W. Shakespeare, *The Tempest*, ed. by V. M. Vaughan, A. T. Vaughan. London: Bloomsbury, 2011, 4.1.15–158.
22. S. Felman, 'Postal Survival, or the Question of the Navel', *Yale French Studies* 69, 1985, pp. 49–72, p. 66.

Bibliography

Abraham, N. & Torok, M., *The Wolf Man's Magic Word: A Cryptonymy*, transl. by N. Rand. Minneapolis: University of Minnesota Press, 1986.
Adorno, T. W., *Philosophische Terminologie. Zur Einleitung*. Frankfurt/M.: Suhrkamp, 1973.
Aron, L. & Harris, A. (eds.), *The Legacy of Sándor Ferenczi*. London: The Analytic Press, 1993.
Aron, L. & Starr, K., *A Psychotherapy for the People: Toward a Progressive Psychoanalysis*. London, New York: Routledge, 2013.
Aron, L. & Starr, K., 'Freud and Ferenczi: Wandering Jews in Palermo', in: A. Harris, S. Kuchuck (eds.), *The Legacy of Sándor Ferenczi: From Ghost to Ancestor*. London, New York: Routledge, 2015, pp. 150–167.
Aron, L. & Starr, K., 'Freud, Ferenczi, and the Case of Schreber: A Mutual Enactment of Homoerotic Longings, Homophobia, and Internalized Anti-Semitism', in: A. W. Rachmann (ed.), *The Origin of a Two-Person Psychology and Emphatic Perspective*. London, New York: Routledge, 2016, pp. 104–129.
Avelar, A., *Trauma e prática clínica: um percurso entre Freud e Ferenczi* [dissertation]. Universidade Federal do Rio de Janeiro, Instituto de Psicologia, 2013.
Avello, J. J., 'Metapsychology in Ferenczi: Death Instinct or Death Passion?', *International Forum of Psychoanalysis* 7, 1998, pp. 229–234.
Azzouni, S., 'Populärwissenschaft als fachwissenschaftliche Autorität: Wilhelm Bölsches "Das Liebesleben in der Natur" und die Anfänge der Sexualwissenschaft', *Jahrbuch Literatur und Medizin* 3, 2009, pp. 13–38.
Bacal, H., 'The Budapest School's Concept of Supervision: Michael Bálint's Legacy to the Development of Psychoanalytic Specificity Theory', in: A. Rachman (ed.), *The Budapest School of Psychoanalysis. The Origin of a Two-Person Psychology and Emphatic Perspective*. London, New York: Routledge, 2016, pp. 140–163.
Bálint, M., *The Basic Fault. Therapeutic Aspects of Regression*. London: Tavistock, 1968.
Bálint, M., 'The Disagreement Between Freud and Ferenczi and Its Repercussions', in: M. Bálint, *The Basic Fault. Therapeutic Aspects of Regression*. London: Tavistock, 1968, pp. 149–158.
Baraitser, L., *Enduring Time*. London: Bloomsbury, 2017.
Bar-Haim, S., *The Maternalists. Psychoanalysis, Motherhood, and the British Welfare State*. Philadelphia: University of Pennsylvania Press, 2021.
Bateson, G., *Mind and Nature: A Necessary Unity*. New York: Dutton, 1979.

Bayertz, K., 'Darwinismus als Politik. Zur Genese des Sozialdarwinismus in Deutschland 1860–1900', in: E. Aescht, G. Aubrecht, E. Krausse (eds.), *Welträtsel und Lebenswunder. Ernst Haeckel – Werk, Wirkung und Folgen*. Linz: Oberösterreichisches Landesmuseum, 1998, pp. 229–289.

Beer, G., 'Darwin and the Uses of Extinction', *Victorian Studies* [Special Issue: Darwin and the Evolution of Victorian Studies] 51(2), 2009, pp. 321–331.

Beer, G., *Darwin's Plots. Evolutionary Narrative in Darwin, George Eliot and Nineteenth Century Fiction*. Cambridge, New York: Cambridge UP, 2009.

Bell, D., *The Cultural Contradictions of Capitalism*. New York: Basic Books, 1976.

Benjamin, J., *Beyond Doer and Done to: Recognition Theory, Intersubjectivity and the Third*. London, New York: Routledge, 2018.

Benjamin, W., 'On the Concept of History', in: W. Benjamin, *Selected Writings, Vol. 4, 1938–1940*, ed. by H. Eiland, M. W. Jennings, transl. by E. Jephcott. Cambridge, Mass.: Belknap Press of Harvard UP, 2006, pp. 339–411.

Berentsen, A., *Vom Urnebel zum Zukunftsstaat – Zum Problem der Popularisierung der Naturwissenschaften in der deutschen Literatur (1880–1910)*. Berlin: Oberhofer, 1986.

Berz, P., 'Die Einzeller und die Lust. Bölsche, Freud, Ferenczi', in: C. Kirchhoff, G. Scharbert (eds.), *Freuds Referenzen*. Berlin: Kadmos, 2012, pp. 15–33.

Beyes, T. & Metelmann, J. (eds.), *The Creativity Complex. A Companion to Contemporary Culture*. Bielefeld: transcript, 2018.

Birksted-Breen, D., 'Time and the Après-Coup', *International Journal of Psychoanalysis* 84, 2003, pp. 1501–1515.

Biro, M., *The Dada Cyborg. Visions of the New Human in Weimar Berlin*. Minneapolis, London: University of Minnesota Press, 2009.

Bohleber, W., 'Remembrance, Trauma and Collective Memory: The Battle for Memory in Psychoanalysis', *International Journal of Psychoanalysis* 88(2), 2007, pp. 329–352.

Bohleber, W., *Destructiveness, Intersubjectivity, and Trauma: The Identity Crisis of Modern Psychoanalysis*. London: Karnac, 2010.

Bokanowski, T., 'Splitting, Fragmenting, and Mental Agony: The Clinical Thinking of Sándor Ferenczi', *International Forum of Psychoanalysis* 13(1–2), 2004, pp. 20–25.

Bókay, A., 'The Child as a Traumatic Self-Component in Ferenczi's Later Psychoanalysis', *American Journal of Psychoanalysis* 75(1), 2015, pp. 46–56.

Bölsche, W., *Das Liebesleben in der Natur. Eine Entwicklungsgeschichte der Liebe*, Vol. I. Florence, Leipzig: Diedrichs, 1889.

Bölsche, W., *Das Liebesleben in der Natur. Eine Entwicklungsgeschichte der Liebe*, Vol. II. Florence, Leipzig: Diedrichs, 1900.

Bölsche, W., *Das Liebesleben in der Natur. Eine Entwicklungsgeschichte der Liebe*, Vol. III. Leipzig: Diedrichs, 1903.

Bölsche, W., *Love-Life in Nature. The Story of the Evolution of Love*, Vol. I–II, transl. by C. Brown. New York: Albert & Charles Boni, 1926.

Bölsche, W., *Stirb und Werde! Naturwissenschaftliche und kulturelle Plaudereien*. Jena: Diederichs, 1913.
Bölsche, W., *Was muß der neue deutsche Mensch von Naturwissenschaft und Religion fordern?*. Berlin: Buchholz & Weißwange, 1934.
Boltanski, L. & Chiapello, È., *Der neue Geist des Kapitalismus*, transl. by M. Tillmann. Konstanz: UVK, 2003.
Bonomi, C., 'Between Symbol and Antisymbol: The Meaning of Trauma Reconsidered', *International Forum of Psychoanalysis* 12(1), 2003, pp. 17–21.
Bonomi, C., 'Trauma and the Symbolic Function of the Mind', *International Forum of Psychoanalysis* 13(1–2), 2004, pp. 45–50.
Bonomi, C., 'The Penis on the Trail: Re-reading the Origins of Psychoanalysis with Sándor Ferenczi', in: A. Harris, S. Kuchuck (eds.), *The Legacy of Sándor Ferenczi: From Ghost to Ancestor*. London, New York: Routledge, 2015, pp. 33–51.
Bonomi, C., *The Cut and the Building of Psychoanalysis, Vol. 2: Sigmund Freud and Sándor Ferenczi*. London, New York: Routledge, 2018.
Borgogno, F., 'Elasticity of Technique: The Psychoanalytic Project and the Trajectory of Ferenczi's Life', *The American Journal of Psychoanalysis* 61, 2001, pp. 391–407.
Borgogno, F., 'Ferenczi's Clinical and Theoretical Conception of Trauma: A Brief Introductory Map', *The American Journal of Psychoanalysis* 67, 2007, pp. 141–149.
Boyarin, D., *Unheroic Conduct. The Rise of Heterosexuality and the Invention of the Jewish Man*. Berkeley: University of California Press, 1997.
Brabant, É., 'Les voies de la passion. Les rapports entre Freud et Ferenczi', *Le Coq-Héron* 3, 2003, pp. 100–113.
Bragin, M., 'Knowing Terrible Things: Engaging Survivors of Extreme Violence in Treatment', *Clinical Social Work Journal* 35(4), 2007, pp. 229–236.
Bröckling, U., *The Entrepreneurial Self. Fabricating a New Type of Subject*, transl. by S. Black. Los Angeles, London: Sage, 2016.
Brook, P., *Reading for the Plot: Design and Intention in Narrative*. New York: A. A. Knopf, 1984.
Canetti, E., *Crowds and Power*, transl. by C. Stewart. New York: Continuum, 1984.
Caruth, C. (ed.), *Trauma. Explorations in Memory*. Baltimore, London: Johns Hopkins UP, 1995.
Caruth, C., *Unclaimed Experience: Trauma, Narrative, History*. Baltimore, London: Johns Hopkins UP, 1996.
Castoriadis, C., 'Done and to Be Done', in: D. A. Curtis (ed.), *The Castoriadis Reader*. Oxford: Blackwell, 1989, pp. 361–417.
Certeau, M. de, 'The Institution of Rot', in: D. Allison, P. de Oliveira, M. Roberts, A. Weiss (eds.), *Psychoanalysis and Identity. Toward a Post-Analytic View of the Schreber Case*. Albany: SUNY Press, 1988, pp. 88–100.
Culler, J., 'Story and Discourse in the Analysis of Narration', in: J. Culler, *The Pursuit of Signs: Semiotics, Literature, Deconstruction*. London: Routledge & Kegan Paul, 1981, pp. 169–187.

Dahl, G., 'The Two Time Vectors of *Nachträglichkeit* in the Development of Ego Organization: Significance of the Concept for the Symbolization of Nameless Traumas and Anxieties', *International Journal of Psychoanalysis* 91, 2010, pp. 727–744.

Darwin, C., *On the Origin of Species: A Facsimile of the First Edition* [1859]. Cambridge, Mass.: Harvard UP, 1964, p. 489.

Deleuze, G., *Nietzsche and Philosophy*, transl. by H. Tomlinson. London: Athlone Press, 1983.

Deleuze, G. & Guattari, F., *Anti-Oedipus. Capitalism and Schizophrenia*, transl. by R. Hurley, M. Seem, H. L. Lane. London: Penguin Books, 2009.

Deleuze, G. & Guattari, F., *Kafka: Toward a Minor Literature*, transl. by D. Polan. Minneapolis: University of Minnesota Press, 1986.

Deleuze, G. & Guattari, F., *A Thousand Plateaus: Capitalism and Schizophrenia*, transl. by B. Massumi. London: The Athlone Press, 1987.

Deleuze, G. & Guattari, F., *What is Philosophy?*, transl. by H. Tomlinson, G. Burchill. London: Verso, 1994.

Dimitrijević, A. & Cassullo, G. & Frankel, J. (eds.), *Ferenczi's Influence on Contemporary Psychoanalytic Traditions. Lines of Development. Evolution of Theory and Practice over Decades*. London, New York: Routledge, 2018.

Dinnage, R., 'Introduction', in: D. P. Schreber, *Memoirs of My Nervous Illness* [1903], ed. and transl. by I. Macalpine, R. A. Hunter. New York: New York Review of Books, 2000, pp. xi–xxiv.

Dinshaw, C. & Edelman, L. & Ferguson, R. A. & Freccero, C. & Freeman, E. & Halberstam, J. & Jagose, A. & Nealon, C. & Nguyen, T. H., 'Theorizing Queer Temporalities: A Roundtable Discussion', *GLQ: A Journal of Lesbian and Gay Studies* 13(2), 2007, pp. 177–195.

Doherty, B., '"We Are All Neurasthenics!" Or, the Trauma of Dada Montage', *Critical Inquiry* 24(1), 1997, pp. 82–132.

Dufresne, T., *The Late Sigmund Freud: Or, the Last Word on Psychoanalysis, Society, and all the Riddles of Life*. Cambridge, New York: Cambridge UP, 2017.

Dupont, J., 'Freud's Analysis of Ferenczi as Revealed by Their Correspondence', *The International Journal of Psycho-Analysis* 75(2), 1994, pp. 301–320.

Dupont, J., 'The Concept of Trauma According to Ferenczi and Its Effects on Subsequent Psychoanalytic Research', *International Forum of Psychoanalysis* 7(4), 2010, pp. 235–241.

Erős, F., 'Some Social and Political Issues Related to Ferenczi and the Hungarian School', in: T. Keve, J. Szekacs-Weisz (eds.), *Ferenczi and His World: Rekindling the Spirit of the Budapest School*. London: Karnac, 2012, pp. 39–54.

Erős, F., 'Freedom and Authority in the Clinical Diary', *American Journal of Psychoanalysis* 74(4), 2014, pp. 367–380.

Erős, F., 'Against Violence: Ferenczi and Liberal Socialism', in: A. Dimitrijević, G. Cassullo, J. Frankel (eds.), *Ferenczi's Influence on Contemporary Psychoanalytic Traditions. Lines of Development. Evolution of Theory and Practice over Decades*. London, New York: Routledge, 2018, pp. 248–254.

Erős, F., 'Violence, Trauma, and Hypocrisy', in: A. Borgos, J. Gyimesi, F. Erős (eds.), *Psychology and Politics: Intersections of Sciences and Ideology in the History of Psy-Sciences*. Budapest, New York: Central European UP, 2019, pp. 81–94.

Evzonas, N., 'Countertransference Madness: Supervision, Trans*, and the Sexual', *Psychoanalytic Review* 108(4), 2021, pp. 475–509.

Faimberg, H., *The Telescoping of Generations: Listening to the Narcissistic Links Between Generations*. London, New York: Routledge, 2005.

Faimberg, H., 'A Plea for a Broader Concept of *Nachträglichkeit*', *The Psychoanalytic Quarterly* 76, 2007, pp. 1221–1240.

Falzeder, E., 'The Significance of Ferenczi's Clinical Contributions for Working with Psychotic Patients', *International Forum of Psychoanalysis* 13(1–2), 2004, pp. 26–30.

Falzeder, E., 'Sándor Ferenczi Between Orthodoxy and Heterodoxy', *American Imago* 66(4), 2009, pp. 395–404.

Falzeder, E., 'Dreaming of Freud: Ferenczi, Freud, and Analysis without End', in: E. Falzeder, *Psychoanalytic Filiations. Mapping the Psychoanalytic Movement*. London, New York: Routledge, 2015, pp. 245–256.

Felman, S., 'Postal Survival, or the Question of the Navel', *Yale French Studies* 69, 1985, pp. 49–72.

Felman, S. & Laub, D., *Testimony. Crises of Witnessing in Literature, Psychoanalysis, and History*. London, New York: Routledge, 1992.

Felski, R., *The Limits of Critique*. Chicago: University of Chicago Press, 2015.

Felski, R., 'Postcritical Reading', *American Book Review* 38(5), 2017, pp. 4–5.

Ferenczi, S., 'États sexuels intermédiaires' [Intermediary Sexual States] [1905], in: S. Ferenczi, *Les écrits de Budapest* [The Budapest Writings]. Paris: EPEL, pp. 243–255.

Ferenczi, S., 'Psycho-Analysis and Education' [1908], in: S. Ferenczi, *Final Contributions to the Problems and Methods of Psycho-Analysis*, ed. by M. Bálint, transl. by E. Mosbacher. London: Karnac, 1994, pp. 280–290.

Ferenczi, S., 'The Analytic Conception of the Psycho-Neuroses' [1908], in: S. Ferenczi, *Further Contributions to the Theory and Technique of Psycho-Analysis*, comp. by J. Rickman, transl. by J. I. Suttie. London: Karnac, 1994, pp. 15–30.

Ferenczi, S., 'Introjection and Transference' [1909], in: S. Ferenczi, *First Contributions to Psycho-Analysis*, transl. by E. Jones. London: Karnac, 1994, pp. 35–93.

Ferenczi, S., 'On the Organization of the Psycho-Analytical Movement' [1911], in: S. Ferenczi, *Final Contributions to the Problems and Methods of Psycho-Analysis*, ed. by M. Bálint, transl. by E. Mosbacher. London: Karnac, 1994, pp. 299–307.

Ferenczi, S., 'Transitory Symptom-Constructions during the Analysis' [1912], in: S. Ferenczi, *First Contributions to Psycho-Analysis*, transl. by E. Jones. London: Karnac, 1994, pp. 193–194.

Ferenczi, S., 'A Lecture for Judges and Barristers' [1913], in: S. Ferenczi, *Further Contributions to the Theory and Technique of Psycho-Analysis*, comp. by J. Rickman, transl. by J. I. Suttie. London: Karnac, 1994, pp. 424–434.

Bibliography

Ferenczi, S., 'Stages in the Development of the Sense of Reality' [1913], in: S. Ferenczi, *First Contributions to Psycho-Analysis*, transl. by E. Jones. London: Karnac, 1994, pp. 213–239.

Ferenczi, S., 'The Dream of the Occlusive Pessary' [1915], in: S. Ferenczi, *Further Contributions to the Theory and Technique of Psycho-Analysis*, comp. by J. Rickman, transl. by J. I. Suttie. London: Karnac, 1994, pp. 304–311.

Ferenczi, S., 'Psycho-Analysis of the War-Neuroses' [1918], in: E. Jones (ed.), *Psychoanalysis and the War Neuroses*. London, Vienna, New York: International Psa. Press, 1921, pp. 5–21.

Ferenczi, S., 'The Phenomena of Hysterical Materialization' [1919], in: S. Ferenczi, *Further Contributions to the Theory and Technique of Psycho-Analysis*, comp. by J. Rickman, transl. by J. I. Suttie. London: Karnac, 1994, pp. 89–104.

Ferenczi, S., 'Psycho-Analytical Observations on Tic' [1920], in: S. Ferenczi, *Further Contributions to the Theory and Technique of Psycho-Analysis*, comp. by J. Rickman, transl. by J. I. Suttie. London: Karnac, 1994, pp. 142–174.

Ferenczi, S., 'The Symbolism of the Bridge' [1921], in: S. Ferenczi, *Further Contributions to the Theory and Technique of Psycho-Analysis*, comp. by J. Rickman, transl. by J. I. Suttie. London: Karnac, 1994, pp. 352–356.

Ferenczi, S., 'The Dream of the "Clever Baby"' [1923], in: S. Ferenczi, *Further Contributions to the Theory and Technique of Psycho-Analysis*, comp. by J. Rickman, transl. by J. I. Suttie. London: Karnac, 1994, pp. 349–350.

Ferenczi, S., 'Versuch einer Genitaltheorie' [1924], in: S. Ferenczi, *Schriften zur Psychoanalyse II*, ed. by M. Bálint. Gießen: Psychosozial-Verlag, 2004, pp. 317–400.

Ferenczi, S., *Thalassa. A Theory of Genitality* [1924], transl. by H. A. Bunker. London, New York: Karnac, 1989.

Ferenczi, S., 'The Problem of Acceptance of Unpleasant Ideas: Advances in Knowledge of the Sense of Reality' [1926], in: S. Ferenczi, *Further Contributions to the Theory and Technique of Psycho-Analysis*, comp. by J. Rickman, transl. by J. I. Suttie. London: Karnac, 1994, pp. 366–379.

Ferenczi, S., 'The Adaptation of the Family to the Child' [1928], in: S. Ferenczi, *Final Contributions to the Problems and Methods of Psycho-Analysis*, ed. by M. Bálint, transl. by E. Mosbacher. London: Karnac, 1994, pp. 61–76.

Ferenczi, S., 'The Elasticity of Psycho-Analytic Technique' [1928], in: S. Ferenczi, *Final Contributions to the Problems and Methods of Psycho-Analysis*, ed. by M. Bálint, transl. by E. Mosbacher. London: Karnac, 1994, pp. 87–101.

Ferenczi, S., 'The Principle of Relaxation and Neocatharsis' [1929], in: S. Ferenczi, *Final Contributions to the Problems and Methods of Psycho-Analysis*, ed. by M. Bálint, transl. by E. Mosbacher. London: Karnac, 1994, p. 123.

Ferenczi, S., 'The Unwelcome Child and His Death Instinct' [1929], in: S. Ferenczi, *Final Contributions to the Problems and Methods of Psycho-Analysis*, ed. by M. Bálint, transl. by E. Mosbacher. London: Karnac, 1994, pp. 102–107.

Ferenczi, S., 'Autoplastic and Alloplastic Adaptation' [1930], in: S. Ferenczi, *Final Contributions to the Problems and Methods of Psycho-Analysis*, ed. by M. Bálint, transl. by E. Mosbacher. London: Karnac, 1994, p. 221.

Ferenczi, S., 'Each Adaptation is Preceded by an Inhibited Attempt at Splitting' [1930], in: S. Ferenczi, *Final Contributions to the Problems and Methods of Psycho-Analysis*, ed. by M. Bálint, transl. by E. Mosbacher. London: Karnac, 1994, p. 220.

Ferenczi, S., 'On the Analytic Construction of Mental Mechanism' [1930], in: S. Ferenczi, *Final Contributions to the Problems and Methods of Psycho-Analysis*, ed. by M. Bálint, transl. by E. Mosbacher. London: Karnac, 1994, p. 222.

Ferenczi, S., 'Fantasies on a Biological Model of Super-Ego Formation' [1930], in: *Final contributions to the Problems and Methods of Psychoanalysis*, ed. by M. Bálint, transl. by E. Mosbacher. London: Karnac, 1994, pp. 227–230.

Ferenczi, S., 'Trauma and Striving for Health' [1930], in: S. Ferenczi, *Final Contributions to the Problems and Methods of Psycho-Analysis*, ed. by M. Bálint, transl. by E. Mosbacher. London: Karnac, 1994, pp. 230–231.

Ferenczi, S., 'Child-Analysis in the Analysis of Adults' [1931], in: S. Ferenczi, *Final Contributions to the Problems and Methods of Psycho-Analysis*, ed. by M. Bálint, transl. by E. Mosbacher. London: Karnac, 1994, pp. 126–142.

Ferenczi, S., 'On the Revision of the Interpretation of Dreams' [1931], in: S. Ferenczi, *Final Contributions to the Problems and Methods of Psycho-Analysis*, ed. by M. Bálint, transl. by E. Mosbacher. London: Karnac, 1994, pp. 238–243.

Ferenczi, S., 'The Birth of Intellect' [1931], in: S. Ferenczi, *Final Contributions to the Problems and Methods of Psycho-Analysis*, ed. by M. Bálint, transl. by E. Mosbacher. London: Karnac, 1994, pp. 244–246.

Ferenczi, S., 'Trauma and Anxiety' [1931], in: S. Ferenczi, *Final Contributions to the Problems and Methods of Psycho-Analysis*, ed. by M. Bálint, transl. by E. Mosbacher. London: Karnac, 1994, pp. 249–250.

Ferenczi, S., 'On Shock' [1932], in: S. Ferenczi, *Final Contributions to the Problems and Methods of Psycho-Analysis*, ed. by M. Bálint, transl. by E. Mosbacher. London: Karnac, 1994, pp. 253–254.

Ferenczi, S., *The Clinical Diary of Sándor Ferenczi* [1932], ed. by J. Dupont, transl. by M. Bálint, N. Z. Jackson. Cambridge, Mass.: Harvard UP, 1995.

Ferenczi, S., 'The Two Extremes: Credulity and Scepticism' [1932], in: S. Ferenczi, *Final Contributions to the Problems and Methods of Psycho-Analysis*, ed. by M. Bálint, transl. by E. Mosbacher. London: Karnac, 1994, p. 263.

Ferenczi, S., 'Confusion of Tongues between Adults and the Child' [1933], in: S. Ferenczi, *Final Contributions to the Problems and Methods of Psycho-Analysis*, ed. by M. Bálint, transl. by E. Mosbacher. London: Karnac, 1994, pp. 156–167.

Ferenczi, S., 'Freud's Influence on Medicine' [1933], in: S. Ferenczi, *Final Contributions to the Problems and Methods of Psycho-Analysis*, ed. by M. Bálint, transl. by E. Mosbacher. London: Karnac, 1994, pp. 143–155.

Bibliography

Ferenczi, S. & Groddeck, G., *Briefwechsel Sándor Ferenczi–Georg Groddeck*, ed. by M. Giefer. Frankfurt/M.: Stroemfeld, 2006.

Ferenczi, S. & Groddeck, G., *The Sándor Ferenczi–Georg Groddeck Correspondence*, ed. and transl. by C. Fortune. London: Open Gate Press, 2002.

Ferguson, S., 'The Face of Time between Haeckel and Bergson; Or, Toward an Ethics of Impure Vision', *Qui Parle* 19(1), 2010, pp. 107–151.

Fletcher, J., *Freud and the Scene of Trauma*. New York: Fordham UP, 2013.

Foucault, M., *Essential Works of Foucault, 1954–1984, Vol. 2: Aesthetics, Method and Epistemology*. New York: New Press, 1998.

Foucault, M., *Psychiatric Power: Lectures at the Collège de France, 1973–1974*, ed. by J. Lagrange, transl. by G. Burchell. Basingstoke: Palgrave, 2006.

Foucault, M., *Histoire de la sexualité I. La volonté de savoir*. Paris: Gallimard, 1976, pp. 197–198.

Frankel, J., 'Ferenczi's Trauma Theory', *American Journal of Psycho-Analysis* 58(1), 1998, pp. 41–61.

Frankel, J., 'Exploring Ferenczi's Concept of Identification with the Aggressor: Its Role in Trauma, Everyday Life, and the Therapeutic Relationship', *Psychoanalytic Dialogues* 12(1), 2002, pp. 101–139.

Frankel, J., 'The Persistent Sense of Being Bad: The Moral Dimension of the Identification with the Aggressor', in: A. Harris, S. Kuchuck (eds.), *The Legacy of Sándor Ferenczi: From Ghost to Ancestor*. London, New York: Routledge, 2015, pp. 204–222.

Frankel, J., 'The Narcissistic Dynamics of Submission: The Attraction of the Powerless to Authoritarian Leaders', *The American Journal of Psychoanalysis*, 30 August 2022, on-line ahead of print: https://link.springer.com/article/10.1057/s11231-022-09369-4.

Freud, A., *The Ego and the Mechanisms of Defence* [1936]. London: The Hogarth Press, 1936.

Freud, S., *The Standard Edition of the Complete Psychological Works of Sigmund Freud*, transl. under the general editorship of J. Strachey, in collaboration with A. Freud, assisted by A. Strachey, A. Tyson. London: The Hogarth Press, 1973. (*SE*)

Freud, S. & Breuer, J., 'On the Psychical Mechanism of Hysterical Phenomena: Preliminary Communication' [1893], in: S. Freud, J. Breuer, *Studies on Hysteria* (1893–1895), *SE* 2, pp. 1–18.

Freud, S., 'The Interpretation of Dreams (II)' [1900], in: S. Freud, *The Interpretation of Dreams (Second Part) and On Dreams* (1900–1901), *SE* 5, pp. 339–627.

Freud, S., 'Fragment of an Analysis of a Case of Hysteria' [1905], in: S. Freud, *A Case of Hysteria, Three Essays on Sexuality and Other Works* (1901–1905), *SE* 7, pp. 7–122.

Freud, S., 'Notes upon a Case of Obsessional Neurosis' [1909], in: S. Freud, *The Cases of 'Little Hans' and the 'Rat Man'* (1909), *SE* 10, pp. 151–249.

Freud, S., 'Psychoanalytic Notes on an Autobiographical Account of a Case of Paranoia' [1911], in: S. Freud, *Case History of Schreber, Papers on Technique and Other Works* (1911–1913), *SE* 12, pp. 1–79.

Freud, S., 'Recommendations to Physicians Practicing Psycho-Analysis' [1912], in: S. Freud, *The Case of Schreber, Papers on Technique and Other Works* (1911–1913), *SE* 12, pp. 111–120.

S. Freud, *A Phylogenetic Fantasy: Overview of the Transference Neuroses* [1915], ed. by Ilse Grubrich-Simitis, P. T. Hoffer, transl. by A. Hoffer, Cambridge, Mass.: Belknap Press of Harvard UP, 1987.

Freud, S., 'Some Thoughts on Development and Regression – Aetiology' [1917], in: S. Freud, *Introductory Lectures on Psycho-Analysis (Part III)* (1916–1917), *SE* 16, pp. 339–357.

Freud, S., 'A Difficulty in the Path of Psycho-Analysis' [1917], in: S. Freud, *An Infantile Neurosis and Other Works* (1917–1919), *SE* 17, pp. 137–144.

Freud, S., 'From the History of an Infantile Neurosis' [1918], in: S. Freud, *An Infantile Neurosis and Other Works* (1917–1919), *SE* 17, pp. 1–122.

Freud, S., 'Beyond the Pleasure Principle' [1920], in: S. Freud, *Beyond the Pleasure Principle, Group Psychology and Other Works* (1920–1922), *SE* 18, pp. 7–64.

Freud, S., 'Fetishism' [1927], in: S. Freud, *The Future of an Illusion, Civilization and its Discontents and Other Works* (1927–1931), *SE* 21, pp. 152–157.

Freud, S., 'Civilization and its Discontents' [1930], in: S. Freud, *The Future of an Illusion, Civilization and its Discontents and Other Works* (1927–1931), *SE* 21, pp. 21–145.

Freud, S., 'The Question of a *Weltanschauung*' [1933], in: S. Freud, *New Introductory Lectures on Psycho-Analysis and Other Works* (1932–1936), *SE* 22, pp. 158–182.

Freud, S., 'Sándor Ferenczi' [1933], in: S. Freud, *New Introductory Lectures on Psycho-Analysis and Other Works* (1932–1936), *SE* 22, pp. 227–229.

Freud, S., *The Complete Letters of Sigmund Freud to Wilhelm Fliess 1887–1904*. Cambridge, Mass.: Belknap Press of Harvard UP, 1985.

Freud, S. & Eitingon, M., *Briefwechsel 1906–1939. Sigmund Freud und Max Eitingon*, ed. by M. Schröter. Tübingen: edition diskord, 2004.

Freud, S. & Ferenczi, S., *The Correspondence of Sigmund Freud and Sándor Ferenczi, Vol. 1: 1908–1914*, ed. by É. Brabant, E. Falzeder, P. Giampieri-Deutsch, transl. by P. T. Hoffer. Cambridge, Mass.: Belknap Press of Harvard UP, 1993.

Freud, S. & Ferenczi, S., *The Correspondence of Sigmund Freud and Sándor Ferenczi, Vol. 2: 1914–1919*, ed. by É. Brabant, E. Falzeder, P. Giampieri-Deutsch, transl. by P. T. Hoffer. Cambridge, Mass.: Belknap Press of Harvard UP, 1996.

Freud, S. & Ferenczi, S., *The Correspondence of Sigmund Freud and Sándor Ferenczi, Vol. 3: 1920–1933*, ed. by É. Brabant, E. Falzeder, P. Giampieri-Deutsch, transl. by P. T. Hoffer. Cambridge, Mass.: Belknap Press of Harvard UP, 2000.

Freud, S. & Freud, A., *Briefwechsel 1904–1938*, ed. by I. Meyer-Palmedo. Frankfurt/M.: Fischer, 2006.

Freud, S. & Groddeck, G., *Briefe über das Es*, ed. by M. Honegger. Munich: Kindler, 1974.

Freud, S. & Jones, E., *The Complete Correspondence of Sigmund Freud and Ernest Jones 1908–1939*, ed. by R. A. Paskauskas. Cambridge, Mass.: Belknap Press of Harvard UP, 1993.

Freud, S. & Jung, C. G., *The Freud-Jung Letters: The Correspondence Between Sigmund Freud and C. G. Jung*. Princeton, NJ: Princeton UP, 1994.

Freudenberg, F., 'Liebesleben in der Natur', *Der Frauenarzt* 18(2), 1903, pp. 65–68.

Frosh, S., 'Psychoanalysis and Ghostly Transmission', *American Imago* 69(2), 2012, pp. 241–264.

Gandesha, S., 'Identifying with the Aggressor. From the Authoritarian to the Neoliberal Personality', *Constellations* 25(1), 2018, pp. 1–18.

Gandesha, S., 'Adorno, Ferenczi, and the New "Categorical Imperative" after Auschwitz', *International Forum of Psychoanalysis* 28(4), 2019, pp. 222–230.

Gasman, D., *Haeckel's Monism and the Birth of Fascist Ideology*. New York: Lang, 1998.

Gasman, D., 'The Monism of Georges Vacher de Lapouge and Gustave Le Bon', in: D. Gasman, *Haeckel's Monism and the Birth of Fascist Ideology*. New York: Lang, 1998.

Gay, P., *Freud: A Life for Our Time*. London: J. M. Dent, 1988.

Gherovici, P., 'Botched Bodies: Inventing Gender and Constructing Sex', in: V. Tsolas, C. Anzieu-Premmereur (eds.), *A Psychoanalytic Exploration of the Body in Today's World*. London, New York: Routledge, 2017, pp. 159–173.

Gilman, S. L., *Freud, Race, and Gender*. Princeton, NJ: Princeton UP, 1993.

Girard, R., *Le Bouc émissaire*. Paris: Grasset, 1983.

Glissant, E., *Poetics of Relation*, transl. by B. Wing. Ann Arbor: University of Michigan Press, 1997.

Goodfield, J., *An Imagined World: A Story of Scientific Discovery*. New York: Harper & Row, 1981.

Gould, S. J., *Ontogeny and Phylogeny*. Cambridge, Mass., London: Belknap Press, 1977.

Gradmann, C., 'Unsichtbare Feinde. Bakteriologie und politische Sprache im deutschen Kaiserreich', in: P. Sarasin, S. Berger, M. Hänseler, M. Spörri (eds.), *Bakteriologie und Moderne. Studien zur Biopolitik des Unsichtbaren 1879–1920*. Frankfurt/M.: Suhrkamp, 2007, pp. 327–353.

Graves, R., *The Greek Myths, Complete Edition*. New York: Penguin Books, 1992.

Green, A., *On Private Madness*. London: Karnac, 1996.

Groddeck, G., *The Book of the It*, transl. by V. M. E. Collins. New York: Funk & Wagnalls Company, 1923.

Grosz, E., *The Nick of Time. Politics, Evolution, and the Untimely*. Durham: Duke UP, 2004.

Grosz, E., 'Darwinian Matters: Life, Force, Change', in: E. Grosz, *The Nick of Time. Politics, Evolution, and the Untimely*. Durham: Duke UP, 2004, pp. 17–39.

Grubrich-Simitis, I., 'Metapsychologie und Metabiologie. Zu Sigmund Freuds Entwurf einer "Übersicht der Übertragungsneurosen"', in: S. Freud, Übersicht der Übertragungsneurosen. Ediert und mit einem Essay versehen von Ilse Grubrich-Simitis. Frankfurt/M.: Fischer, 1985, pp. 83–119.

Grubrich-Simitis, I., 'Trauma oder Trieb – Trieb und Trauma. Lektionen aus Sigmund Freuds phylogenetischer Phantasie von 1915', *Psyche. Zeitschrift für Psychoanalyse und ihre Anwendungen* 41, 1987, pp. 992–1023.

Grubrich-Simitis, I., 'Trauma oder Trieb – Trieb und Trauma: Wiederbetrachtet', *Psyche. Zeitschrift für Psychoanalyse und ihre Anwendungen* 61, 2007, pp. 637–656.

Guattari, F., *The Machinic Unconscious: Essays in Schizoanalysis*, transl. by T. Adkins. Los Angeles: Semiotext(e), 2011.

Gumbs, A. P., *Dub: Finding Ceremony*. Durham: Duke UP, 2020.

Gumbs, A. P., *Undrowned: Black Feminist Lessons from Marine Mammals*. Chico: AK Press, 2020.

Gurevich, H., 'Orpha, Orphic Functions, and the Orphic Analyst: Winnicott's "Regression to Dependence" in the Language of Ferenczi', *American Journal of Psychoanalysis* 76(4), 2016, pp. 322–340.

H. D. [Hilda Doolittle], *Tribute to Freud*. Boston: Godine, 1974.

Haeckel, E., 'Ueber die Entwicklungstheorie Darwins' [Jungfernrede, Stettiner Rede], in: C. A. Dohrn, Dr. Behm, *Amtlicher Bericht über die acht und dreißigste Versammlung deutscher Naturforscher und Ärzte in Stettin im September 1863*. Stettin: Hesselands Buchdruck, 1864, pp. 17–30.

Haeckel, E., *Generelle Morphologie der Organismen. Allgemeine Grundzüge der organischen Formen-Wissenschaft, mechanisch begründet durch die von C. Darwin reformirte Descendenz-Theorie*. Berlin: Georg Reimer, 1866.

Haeckel, E., *Natürliche Schöpfungsgeschichte*. Berlin: Reimer, 1872.

Haeckel, E., *Gott-Natur (Theophysis). Studien über die monistische Religion*. Leipzig: Alfred Kröner, 1914.

Haeckel, E., *Ewigkeit. Weltkriegsgedanken über Leben und Tod, Religion und Entwicklungslehre*. Berlin: Georg Reimer, 1915.

Hagner, M. & Sarasin, P., 'Wilhelm Bölsche und der "Geist". Populärer Darwinismus in Deutschland 1887–1934', *Nach Feierabend. Zürcher Jahrbuch für Wissensgeschichte* 4, 2008, pp. 47–68.

Haraway, D. J., *Crystals, Fabrics, and Fields: Metaphors of Organicism in Twentieth-Century Developmental Biology*. New Haven, London: Yale UP, 1976.

Haraway, D. J., *Staying with the Trouble: Making Kin in the Chthulucene*. Durham: Duke UP, 2016.

Harris, A. & Kuchuck, S. (eds.), *The Legacy of Sándor Ferenczi: From Ghost to Ancestor*. London, New York: Routledge, 2015.

Harris, A., '"Language is There to Bewilder Itself and Others": Theoretical and Clinical Contributions of Sabina Spielrein', *Journal of the American Psychoanalytic Association* 63(4), 2015, pp. 727–767.

Harris, A., 'Ferenczi's Work on War Neuroses', in: A. Harris, S. Kuchuck (eds.), *The Legacy of Sándor Ferenczi. From Ghost to Ancestor*. London, New York: Routledge, 2015, pp. 127–133.

Harris, A., 'Thalassa, Confusion of Tongues, The Unwelcome Child and his Death-Instinct: Sándor Ferenczi's Unfolding Model of Trauma', *Attachment* 14(1), 2020, pp. 1–22.

Hartmann, N. & Wedemeyer, A., 'Ankündigung eines Austauschs des RISS mit Catherine Malabou anlässlich ihres neuen Buches *Le plaisir effacé. Clitoris et pensée*', *RISS. Zeitschrift für Psychoanalyse: Bioanalysen II* 95, 2021, pp. 113–117.

Haute, P. v. & Westerink, H., 'Hysterie, Sexualität und Psychiatrie. Eine Relektüre der ersten Ausgabe der *Drei Abhandlungen zur Sexualtheorie*', in: P. v. Haute, C. Huber, H. Westerink (eds.), *Sigmund Freud: Drei Abhandlungen zur Sexualtheorie (1905)*. Göttingen: V&R unipress, 2015, pp. 9–56.

Haverkamp, A., 'Undone by Death. Umrisse einer Poetik nach Darwin', in: C. Blumenberg, A. Heimes, E. Weitzman, S. Witt (eds.), *Suspensionen. Über das Untote*. Paderborn: Wilhelm Fink, 2015, pp. 35–51.

Haynal, A. & King, J. E., *Controversies in Psychoanalytic Method. From Freud and Ferenczi to Michael Bálint*. New York, London: New York UP, 1990.

Haynal, A. E. & Haynal, V. D., 'Ferenczi's Attitude', transl. by S. K. Wang, in: A. Harris, S. Kuchuck (eds.), *The Legacy of Sándor Ferenczi. From Ghost to Ancestor*. London, New York: Routledge, 2015, pp. 52–74.

Haynal, A., 'Countertransference in the Work of Ferenczi', *The American Journal of Psychoanalysis* 59, 1999, pp. 315–331.

Haynal, A., 'Trauma – Revisited: Ferenczi and Modern Psychoanalysis', *Psychoanalytic Inquiry* 34(2), 2014, pp. 98–111.

Hayward, E., 'Fingeryeyes: Impressions of Cup Corals', *Cultural Anthropology* 25(4), 2010, pp. 577–599.

Hirsch, I., 'Countertransference and the Person of the Therapist', in: A. Dimitrijević, G. Cassullo, J. Frankel (eds.), *Ferenczi's Influence on Contemporary Psychoanalytic Traditions. Lines of Development. Evolution of Theory and Practice over Decades*. London, New York: Routledge, 2018, pp. 165–168.

Hobsbawm, E., *The Age of Empire 1875–1914*. New York: Vintage, 1987.

Höch, H., *Siebenmeilenstiefel* [1934], Photomontage, 23.1 x 23.8 cm. Hamburger Kunsthalle.

Hoffer, P. T., 'The Concept of Phylogenetic Inheritance in Freud and Jung', *Journal of the American Psychoanalytic Association* 40(2), 1992, pp. 517–530.

Hoffer, P. T., 'Freud's 'Phylogenetic Fantasy' and His Construction of the Historical Moses', in: L. J. Brown (ed.), *On Freud's 'Moses and Monotheism'*. London, New York: Routledge, 2022, pp. 35–51.

Howe, J. N., 'Kreativität', in: C. Benthien, E. M. de Mazza, U. Wirth (eds.), *Handbuch Literatur und Ökonomie*. Berlin, Boston: De Gruyter, 2019, p. 182–184.

Hristeva, G., '"Uterus Loquitur": Trauma and the Human Organism in Ferenczi's "Physiology of Pleasure"', *The American Journal of Psychoanalysis* 73(4), 2013, pp. 339–352.

Hristeva, G., '"Primordial Chant". Sandor Ferenczi as an Orphic Poet', *The American Journal of Psychoanalysis* 79(4), 2019, pp. 517–539.

Jahraus, O. & Kirchmeyer, C., 'Der Erste Weltkrieg als Katastrophe', in: N. Werber, S. Kaufmann, L. Koch (eds.), *Erster Weltkrieg. Kulturwissenschaftliches Handbuch*. Stuttgart, Weimar: Metzler, 2014.

Jones, E., *The Life and Work of Sigmund Freud. Vol. I: The Young Freud 1856–1900*. London: The Hogarth Press, 1954.

Jones, E., *The Life and Work of Sigmund Freud. Vol. II: Years of Maturity 1901–1919*. London: The Hogarth Press, 1954.

Jones, E., *Sigmund Freud. Life and Work. Vol. III: The Last Phase 1919–1939*. London: The Hogarth Press, 1957.

Jung, C. G., 'The State of Psychotherapy Today' [1934], in: C. G. Jung, *Collected Works of Carl Jung, Vol. 10: Civilization in Transition*, ed. by G. Adler, transl. by R. F. C. Hull. Princeton, NJ: Princeton UP, 1970, pp. 157–174.

Jung, C. G., *Erinnerungen, Träume, Gedanken*. Zurich: Racher, 1962.

Jung, C. G. & Jaffé, A., *Memories, Dreams, Reflections*. London: Fontana, 1993.

Kelly, A., *The Descent of Darwin: The Popularization of Darwin in Germany, 1860–1914*. Chapel Hill: UNC Press, 1981.

Kerényi, K., *The Heroes of the Greeks*. London: Thames and Hudson, 1959.

Keve, T. & Szekacs-Weisz, J. (eds.), *Ferenczi and His World: Rekindling the Spirit of the Budapest School*. London: Karnac, 2012.

Keve, T. & Szekacs-Weisz, J. (eds.), *Ferenczi for Our Time: Theory and Practice*. London: Karnac, 2012.

Kleeberg, B., *Theophysis. Ernst Haeckels Philosophie des Naturganzen*. Cologne, Weimar, Vienna: Böhlau, 2005.

Klein, M., 'The Early Development of Conscience in the Child' [1933], in: M. Klein, *The Writings of Melanie Klein*, Vol. 1. London: The Hogarth Press, 1975, pp. 248–257.

Klein, M., 'Notes on some Schizoid Mechanisms' [1946], in: M. Klein, *The Writings of Melanie Klein*, Vol. 3. London: The Hogarth Press, 1975, pp. 1–24.

Klein, M., 'On Identification' [1955], in: M. Klein, *The Writings of Melanie Klein*, Vol. 3. London: The Hogarth Press, 1975, pp. 141–175.

Koppenfels, M. v., *Schwarzer Peter, der Fall Littell, die Leser und die Täter*. Göttingen: Wallstein, 2012.

Koritar, E., 'Relaxation in Technique Leading to New Beginnings', *American Journal of Psychoanalysis* 76(4), 2016, pp. 341–353.

Koritar, E., 'Ferenczi's Researches in Technique', *The American Journal of Psychoanalysis* 82, 2022, pp. 210–221.

Kosofsky Sedgewick, E., *Between Men: English Literature and Male Homosocial Desire*. New York: Columbia UP, 1985.

Kupermann, D., 'Social Trauma and Testimony: A Reading of Maryan S. Maryan's Notebooks Inspired by Sándor Ferenczi', *American Journal of Psychoanalysis* 82(2), 2022, pp. 268–280.

Lacan, J., *The Four Fundamental Concepts of Psychoanalysis: The Seminar of Jacques Lacan Book XI*, transl. by A. Sheridan. New York: W.W. Norton, 1998.

Lacan, J., 'The Freudian Thing or the Meaning of the Return to Freud in Psychoanalysis', in: J. Lacan, *Écrits: The First Complete Edition in English*, transl. by B. Fink. New York: W.W. Norton, 2006, pp. 401–436.

LaCapra, D., *Writing History, Writing Trauma*. Baltimore, London: Johns Hopkins UP, 2014.

Laplanche, J. & Pontalis, J. B., 'Fantasy and the Origins of Sexuality', *The International Journal of Psychoanalysis* 49(1), 1968, pp. 1–18.

Laplanche, J. & Pontalis, J.-B., *The Language of Psychoanalysis*. London, New York: Routledge, 2018.

Laplanche, J., *Nouveaux fondements pour la psychanalyse*. Paris: PUF, 1987.

Laplanche, J., *Notes sur l'après-coup*, 1998 [Paper presented at the Conference on psychoanalytical intracultural and intercultural dialogue. International Psychoanalytical Association, Paris, 27–29 July].

Laplanche, J., *Essays on Otherness*. London, New York: Routledge, 1999.

Laub, D., Lee, S., 'Thanatos and Massive Psychic Trauma: The Impact of the Death Instinct on Knowing, Remembering, and Forgetting', *Journal of the American Psychoanalytic Association* 51(2), 2003, pp. 433–464.

Lavin, M., *Cut with the Kitchen Knife: The Weimar Photomontages of Hannah Höch*. New Haven, London: Yale UP, 1993.

Lénárd, K. & Tényi, T., 'Ferenczi's Concept on Trauma, connected with the Katonadolog – "Soldiers can take it" Concept', *International Forum of Psycho-Analysis* 12(1), 2003, pp. 22–29.

Luckhurst, R., *The Trauma Question*. London, New York: Routledge, 2008.

Makela, M., 'Grotesque Bodies. Weimar-Era Medicine and the Photomontages of Hannah Höch', in: F. S. Connelly (ed.), *Modern Art and the Grotesque*. Cambridge: Cambridge UP, 2003, pp. 193–219.

Marcaggi, G. & Guénolé, F., 'Freudarwin: Evolutionary Thinking as a Root of Psychoanalysis', *Frontiers in Psychology* 9, 2018, pp. 1–9.

Marks, L., *Touch: Sensuous Theory and Multisensory Media*. Minneapolis: University of Minnesota Press, 2002.

Martín-Cabré, L., 'Freud-Ferenczi: Controversy Terminable and Interminable', *International Journal of Psychoanalysis* 78(1), 1997, pp. 105–114.

Masson, J. M., *Assault on Truth. Freud's Suppression of the Seduction Theory*. New York: Farrar, Straus and Giroux, 1984.

May, U., 'Der dritte Schritt in der Trieblehre. Zur Entstehungsgeschichte von Jenseits des Lustprinzip', *Luzifer-Amor. Zeitschrift zur Geschichte der Psychoanalyse* 26(51), 2013, pp. 92–169.

Melville, H., *Bartleby, the Scrivener* [1856], in: H. Melville, *Billy Budd, Bartleby, and Other Stories*. New York: Penguin, 2016, pp. 17–54.
Mentz, S., *Shipwreck Modernity: Ecologies of Globalization, 1550–1719*. Minneapolis: University of Minnesota Press, 2015.
Mészáros, J., 'Sándor Ferenczi and the Budapest School of Psychoanalysis', *Psychoanalytic Perspectives* 7(1), 2010, pp. 69–89.
Mészáros, J., *Ferenczi and Beyond. Exile of the Budapest School and Solidarity in the Psychoanalytic Movement during the Nazi Years*. London: Karnac, 2014.
Michler, W., *Darwinismus und Literatur. Naturwissenschaftliche und literarische Intelligenz in Österreich 1859–1914*. Vienna, Cologne, Weimar: Böhlau, 1999.
Mitscherlich, A. & Mitscherlich, M., *The Inability to Mourn: Principles of Collective Behaviour*, transl. by B. R. Platzeck. New York: Grove Press, 1975.
Murray, J. & Bradley, H. & Craigie, W. & Onions, C. T. & Burchfield, R. & Weiner, E. & Simpson, J. (eds.), *Oxford English Dictionary* [Online ed.]. Oxford UP, 2022. https://www.oed.com.
Nagel, B. N., 'The Child in the Dark: On Child Abuse in Robert Walser', *New German Critique. An Interdisciplinary Journal of German Studies* 146(8), 2022, pp. 107–132.
Niederland, W., *Der Fall Schreber: Das psychoanalytische Profil einer paranoiden Persönlichkeit*. Frankfurt/M.: Suhrkamp, 1978.
Oliner, M., '"Non-Represented" Mental States', in: H. B. Levine, G. S. Reed, D. Scarfone (eds.), *Unrepresented States and the Construction of Meaning: Clinical and Theoretical Contributions*. London: Karnac, 2013, pp. 152–171.
Pick, D., *Faces of Degeneration: A European Disorder 1848–1918*. Cambridge: Cambridge UP, 1993.
Rachman, A. (ed.), *The Budapest School of Psychoanalysis. The Origin of a Two-Person Psychology and Emphatic Perspective*. London, New York: Routledge, 2016.
Ramponi, P. & Willner, J., 'Nachdarwinistische Obsessionen. Eine Vorgeschichte der Human-Animal-Studies', in: C. Ortlieb, P. Ramponi, J. Willner (eds.), *Das Tier als Medium und Obsession. Zur Politik des Wissens um Mensch und Tier um 1900*. Berlin: Neofelis, 2015, pp. 9–46.
Rand, N. T., 'Secrets and Posterity: The Theory of the Transgenerational Phantom. Editor's Note', in: N. Abraham, M. Torok, *The Shell and the Kernel. Renewals of Psychoanalysis*, Vol. 1, ed. and transl. by N. T. Rand. Chicago, London: The University of Chicago Press, 1994, pp. 165–169.
Reckwitz, A., *The Invention of Creativity. Modern Society and the Culture of the New*, transl. by S. Black. Malden, Mass.: Polity, 2017.
Reich, W., 'The Imposition of Sexual Morality', in: W. Reich, *Sex-Pol*, ed. by L. Baxandall. New York: Vintage Books, 1972.
Richards, R. J., *The Tragic Sense of Life: Ernst Haeckel and The Struggle over Evolutionary Thought*. Chicago: University of Chicago Press, 2008.
Ritvo, L., *Darwin's Influence on Freud: A Tale of Two Sciences*. New Haven: Yale UP, 1990.

Roith, E., 'Hysteria, Heredity and Anti-Semitism. Freud's Quiet Rebellion', *Psychoanalysis and History* 10(2), 2008, pp. 149–168.
Roudinesco, É., *Freud in His Time and Ours*, transl. by C. Porter. Cambridge, Mass.: Harvard UP, 2016.
Roussillon, R., 'Creativity: A New Paradigm for Freudian Psychoanalysis', in: G. Saragnano, C. Seulin (eds.), *Playing and Reality Revisited*. London: Karnac, 2015, pp. 89–110.
Roussillon, R., *Primitive Agony and Symbolization*. London: Karnac, 2011.
Rudnitzky, P. L. & Bókay, A. & Gampieri-Deutsch, P., *Ferenczi's Turn in Psychoanalysis*. New York, London: New York UP, 1996.
Sachs, H., *Freud: Master and Friend*. London: Imago, 1945.
Salgó, E., *Psychoanalytic Reflections on Politics: Fatherlands in Mothers' Hands*. London, New York: Routledge, 2014.
Santner, E. L., *My Own Private Germany: Daniel Paul Schreber and the Secret History of Modernity*. Princeton, NJ: Princeton UP, 1996.
Santner, E. L., *Untying Things Together. Philosophy, Literature, and a Life in Theory*. London, Chicago: University of Chicago Press, 2022.
Sarasin, P., 'Zäsuren biologischen Typs: Der Kampf ums Überleben bei Wilhelm Bölsche, H. G. Wells und Steven Spielberg', in: H. Schramm, L. Schwarte, J. Lazardzig (eds.), *Spuren der Avantgarde*. Berlin: De Gruyter, 2011, pp. 443–459.
Schatzmann, M., *Soul Murder: Persecution in the Family*. New York: Random House, 1973.
Schneider, M., *Le trauma et la filiation paradoxale: de Freud à Ferenczi*. Paris: Ramsay, 1988.
Schorske, C. E., *Fin-de-siècle Vienna*. New York: Vintage, 1980.
Schreber, D. P., *Memoirs of My Nervous Illness* [1903], ed. and transl. by I. Macalpine, R. A. Hunter. New York: New York Review of Books, 2000.
Schuller, K., *The Biopolitics of Feeling. Race, Sex, and Science in the Nineteenth Century*. Durham, London: Duke UP, 2018.
Shakespeare, W., *The Tempest*, ed. by V. M. Vaughan, A. T. Vaughan. London: Bloomsbury, 2011.
Sheldrake, M., *Entangled Life: How Fungi Make our Worlds, Change our Minds and Shape our Futures*. London: The Bodley Head, 2020.
Slavet, E., *Racial Fever. Freud and the Jewish Question*. New York: Fordham UP, 2009.
Smith, N. A., '"Orpha Reviving": Toward an Honorable Recognition of Elizabeth Severn', *International Forum of Psychoanalysis* 7(4), 1998, pp. 241–246.
Smith, N. A., 'From Oedipus to Orpha: Revisiting Ferenczi and Severn's Landmark Case', *American Journal of Psychoanalysis* 59(4), 1999, pp. 345–366.
Soreanu, R., 'Ferenczi's Times: The Tangent, the Segment, and the Meandering Line', *American Imago* 73(1), 2016, pp. 51–69.
Soreanu, R., 'Something Was Lost in Freud's Beyond the Pleasure Principle: A Ferenczian Reading', *The American Journal of Psychoanalysis* 77(3), 2017, pp. 223–238.

Soreanu, R., 'The Psychic Life of Fragments: Splitting from Ferenczi to Klein', *The American Journal of Psychoanalysis* 78(4), 2018, pp. 421–444.
Soreanu, R., *Working-Through Collective Wounds: Trauma, Denial, Recognition in the Brazilian Uprising*. London: Palgrave Macmillan, 2018.
Soreanu, R., 'Sándor Ferenczi's Epistemologies and their Politics: On Utraquism and the Analogical Method', in: F. Erős, A. Borgos, J. Gyimesi (eds.), *Psychology and Politics: Intersections of Science and Ideology in the History of Psy-Sciences*. Budapest, New York: Central European UP, 2019, pp. 95–106.
Soreanu, R., 'Supervision for Our Times: Countertransference and the Rich Legacy of the Budapest School', *The American Journal of Psychoanalysis* 79(3), 2019, pp. 329–351.
Soreanu, R., 'The Time of Re-Living. For an Eventful Psychoanalysis', *Vestigia* 2(1), 2019, pp. 132–153.
Spielrein, S., 'Destruction as the Cause of Coming into Being' [1912], *Journal of Analytical Psychology* 39(2), 1994, pp. 155–186.
Spillius, E., *Encounters with Melanie Klein: Selected Papers of Elizabeth Spillius*. London, New York: Routledge, 2007.
Staberg, J., 'Anstatt Sprache: Verwirrung. Eine verfehlte Begegnung zwischen Sigmund Freud und Sándor Ferenczi', *Psyche. Zeitschrift für Psychoanalyse und ihre Anwendungen* 74(5), 2020, pp. 321–343.
Stanton, M., *Sándor Ferenczi: Reconsidering Active Intervention*. London: Free Association Books, 1991.
Stewart, H., 'Regression Post-Ferenczi', in: T. Keve, J. Szekacs-Weisz (eds.), *Ferenczi and His World: Rekindling the Spirit of the Budapest School*. London: Karnac, 2012, pp. 129–137.
Sulloway, F. J., *Freud, Biologist of the Mind. Beyond the Psychoanalytic Legend*. Cambridge, Mass., London: Harvard UP, 1992.
Susen, G.-H. & Wack, E., 'Einleitung', in: G.-H. Susen, E. Wack (eds.), *'Was wir im Verstande ausjäten, kommt im Traume wieder'. Wilhelm Bölsche 1861–1939*. Würzburg: Königshausen & Neumann, 2012, pp. 7–16.
Thomé, H., 'Weltanschauungsliteratur. Vorüberlegungen zu Funktion und Texttyp', in: L. Danneberg, F. Vollhart (eds.), *Wissen in Literatur im 19. Jahrhundert*. Tübingen: Max Niemeyer, 2002, pp. 338–380.
Thurschwell, P., 'Ferenczi's Dangerous Proximities: Telepathy, Psychosis, and the Real Event', *differences: A Journal of Feminist Cultural Studies* 11, 1999, pp. 150–178.
Thurschwell, P., *Literature, Technology, and Magical Thinking*. Cambridge: Cambridge UP, 2001.
Voss, J., 'Das erste Bild der Evolution. Wie Charles Darwin die Unordnung der Naturgeschichte zeichnete und was daraus wurde', in: K. Bayertz, M. Gerhard, W. Jaeschke (eds.), *Weltanschauung, Philosophie und Naturwissenschaft im 19. Jahrhundert. Bd. 2: Der Darwinismus-Streit*. Hamburg: Felix Meiner, 2007, pp. 47–82.
Wallenstein, S. O., 'Hegels Shakespeare', *Agora* 37(1), 2019, pp. 25–44.

Webster, J. & Coelen, M., 'Two Analysts Ask, "What is Genitality?" Ferenczi's Thalassa and Lacan's Lamella', in: P. Gherovici, M. Steinkohler (eds.), *Psychoanalysis, Gender, and Sexualities. From Feminism to Trans**. London, New York: Routledge, 2023.

Wegener, M., 'Seinem großen Ozeanischen Freund das Landthier S. Fr.', *RISS. Zeitschrift für Psychoanalyse: Bioanalysen II* 95, 2021, pp. 27–41.

Weikart, R., *Socialist Darwinism: Evolution in German Socialist Thought from Marx to Bernstein*. San Francisco: International Scholars Publication, 1999, pp. 157–188.

Weiss, P., *The Aesthetics of Resistance* [1975], Vol. 1, transl. by J. Neugroschel. Durham, London: Duke UP, 2005.

Willey, A., 'A World of Materialisms: Postcolonial Feminist Science Studies and the New Natural', *Science, Technology, and Human Values* 41(6), 2016, pp. 991–1014.

Willner, J., 'Vom Fisch an aufwärts giebt es keinen Rückfall. Bedrohlicher Optimismus in Wilhelm Bölsches *Das Liebesleben in der Natur*', in: C. Ortlieb, P. Ramponi, J. Willner (eds.), *Das Tier als Medium und Obsession. Zur Politik des Wissens von Mensch und Tier um 1900*. Berlin: Neofelis, 2015, pp. 265–302.

Willner, J., 'Weltanschauung', in: T. Erthel, R. Stockhammer (eds.), *Welt-Komposita. Ein Lexikon*. Munich: Fink, 2019, pp. 15–25.

Willner, J., 'Neurotische Evolution. Bioanalyse als Kulturkritik in Jenseits des Lustprinzips', *Psyche. Zeitschrift für Psychoanalyse und ihre Anwendungen* 11(74), 2020, pp. 895–921.

Willner, J., 'Das Problem mit dem Erbe. Ferenczis Organologie und die Politik der Bioanalyse', *RISS. Zeitschrift für Psychoanalyse: Bioanalysen I* 94, 2021, pp. 81–97.

Willner, J., 'The Problem of Heredity: Ferenczi's Organology and the Politics of Bioanalysis', transl. by N. E. Levis, *Psychoanalysis and History* 24(2), 2022, pp. 205–219.

Wilson, E., *Gut Feminism*. Durham, London: Duke UP, 2015.

Young-Bruehl, E. & Schwartz, M., 'Why Psychoanalysis Has no History', *American Imago* 69(1), 2012, pp. 139–159.

Zaretsky, E., *Secrets of the Soul: A Social and Cultural History of Psychoanalysis*. New York: Vintage, 2005.

About the Authors

Adrienne Harris (PhD) is a member of faculty and supervisor at the New York University Postdoctoral Program in Psychotherapy and Psychoanalysis and at the Psychoanalytic Institute of Northern Carolina. She is an editor at *Psychoanalytic Dialogues*, and *Studies in Gender and Sexuality*. In 2012 she established the *Sándor Ferenczi Center* at the New School University together with Lewis Aron and and Jeremy Safran. In collaboration with Lewis Aron, Eyal Rozmarin and Steven Kuchuck, she co-edits the book series *Relational Perspectives in Psychoanalysis*, with over 100 published volumes. She is an editor of the IPA journal Psychoanalysistoday.com, which is developing cross cultural communications among the five language groups in the IPA. Her current work is on analytic subjectivity, on intersectional models of gender and sexuality, and on ghosts.

Jakob Staberg is a practising psychoanalyst and psychotherapist, and a member of the International Psychoanalytical Association. He is an assistant professor for Comparative Literature and lecturer in Aesthetics at Södertörn University, south of Stockholm. Staberg is working in the field of aesthetics, literature, and psychoanalytic theory. He received his PhD in 2002 at Stockholm University. In 2009, Staberg published the monograph *Sjukdomens estetik* [The Aesthetics of Illness]. Staberg is currently working on a project that seeks to rethink the genealogy of psychoanalysis. In particular, he has devoted himself to the relationship between Freud and Ferenczi from the perspective of the problem of transference and as it is expressed in dream interpretation. He has published on this topic in the journal *Psyche. Zeitschrift für Psychoanalyse und ihre Anwendungen* 5(74), 2020.

Jenny Willner is an assistant professor for Comparative Literature at the Ludwig Maximilians University in Munich. Her research is located at the intersection between literary theory, history of science, and psychoanalytic theory. She studied German Literature and Philosophy in Berlin and New York and earned her PhD at Freie Universität Berlin with the study *Wortgewalt. Peter Weiss und die deutsche Sprache* (Konstanz UP, 2014). In 2018, she organised the workshop *Sándor Ferenczi. Interdisciplinary Approaches* at the Center for Advanced Studies in Munich. Currently, she is completing her second monograph, which discusses the political dimension of phylogenetic speculation in Ferenczi and Freud. She has published on this topic in *Psyche. Zeitschrift für Psychoanalyse und ihre Anwendungen* 11(74), 2020, in *RISS. Zeitschrift für Psychoanalyse* 94, 2020, and in *Psychoanalysis and History* 24(2), 2022.

Raluca Soreanu is a psychoanalyst, member of the Círculo Psicanalítico do Rio de Janeiro, and Professor in Psychoanalytic Studies at the Department of Psychosocial and Psychoanalytic Studies, University of Essex. Her work sits at the intersection of psychosocial studies, psychoanalysis, social theory and medical humanities. She has a particular interest in the social, political and cultural applications of psychoanalysis. She is the author of *Working-through Collective Wounds: Trauma, Denial, Recognition in the Brazilian Uprising* (Palgrave, 2018) and of journal publications on Sándor Ferenczi and on Michael Bálint. Her most recent project is a monograph looking at psychic splitting and temporality, *The Psychic Life of Fragments: On Splitting and the Experience of Time in Psychoanalysis*. She is an Academic Associate of the Freud Museum London.

Index

A
Abraham, Nicholas 8, 117
adaptation 112, 167, 170, 174–175
  alloplastic vs. autoplastic 161–163, 174–175
  to renunciation 139
  to reality 182–183
  and development 111–112
Adorno, Theodor W. 12, 107
afterwardsness 153, *see also* deferred action, *Nachträglichkeit*
Alexander, Franz 111
algae 207
alienation 4, 105, 107, 113, 172
alien transmission 170
alien transplant 170
alien will 37, 162, 170
alloplastic, alloplasticity 161–163, 174–175
amphibian, amphibians 101–102, 105–106, 138, 148–149, 182, 184, 199, 204, 207
amphimixis XIV, 84–85, 116
  of eroticisms 85
anaesthesia 196
analogous, analogy, analogies 7, 43, 57, 111, 148, 154, 163, 166, 168, 174–175, 177, 182, 184, 197
ancestor, ancestors, ancestral XI, 8–9, 107, 114, 149, 166, 175
Anstoß 145
antisemitism, antisemitic 12, 28–30, 32, 38, 44, 73, 113, 117
anal, anus 78, 84–85, 99, 115
anxiety 23, 46, 50, 57, 77, 168–169, 175, 205
appeasement 139
Aron, Lewis XI–XII, 27, 29, 74

asymmetry, asymmetric encounter XV, 146–147, 164, 183
atomisation 51, 132, 145, 146, 166, 177, 197, 204
authoritarian, authoritarianism XIII, 4, 6, 12, 25–26, 32, 34, 37, 38, 43, 48, 77, 108, 119, 140, 198
authority 24–25, 26, 29, 34–37, 40, 42, 46–48, 50, 54, 58, 63, 64, 73–75, 168
autoplastic, autoplasticity 132, 161–162, 174–175, 205
autotomy 163, 174–175, 196
aquired capacities, characteristics, sensitivity 38, 62, 117

B
Bálint, Michael 8, 181
Bartleby 110
Bártok, Béla 3
Bateson, Gregory 163
Beer, Gillian 103
Benjamin, Walter 5, 78
beyond the phallus 62, 84, 86, 87
bioanalysis 7, 95–96, 98, 110, 112–113, 117, 118–119, 133, 149, 199
biogenetic law 94
biological fantasy 2, 112
biologism, biologistic 7, 94, 96, 97, 108, 110, 118, 133, 149, 199
biopolitical, biopolitics 113, 117, 119, 133
birth 32, 56, 58, 63, 79, 93–94
  of intellect 173
blue humanities 150
Bölsche, Wilhelm 7, 93, 95–97, 98–109, 113–114, 119, 133, 139, 199
Bonomi, Carlo 92

Index

breath, breathe, breathing 7, 99, 101, 140, 149, 165, 176, 178, 184, 196
Breuer, Josef 39
Brill, Abraham 23, 42, 53
Brooks, Peter 50
Budapest 3, 11–12, 27–28, 31, 86
Budapest School 11–12

C
Canetti, Elias 77
cartesian dualism 111
Castoriadis, Cornelius 145
castration 47, 105, 115
catastrophe, catastrophes 2–3, 5, 7, 73, 92–94, 116, 140, 145–146, 148, 150, 163, 172, 177, 181–182, 185, 195, 196, 198, 200, 203
cavalry 91
Charcot, Jean-Martin 28
cockroach 77
coitus 92, 101, 115–116
commodification 194
compromise 115, 139,
conciliation 59, 139–140
confusion of tongues XV, 10, 12, 62, 146–147, 166, 195
conversion 3, 115, 156–157
cooperation 13, 76, 95, 139, 140, 178
  of organs 139
cough
  coughing penis 115, 137–138, 140
  Dora's cough 115
counter-narrative 6, 98, 139
countertransference 10, 41
cow 105–106
creative, creativity 3, 7, 145, 148, 151, 176–177, 182, 184–185, 194–195, 197–198, 199
  creativity complex 198
  creativity dispositif 194–195, 198, 199
creature, creatures 91, 92, 100, 101, 103, 105–106, 110, 110, 184

crisis, crises 5, 8, 13, 29, 31, 37, 43, 45, 75, 103–105, 116, 148, 150, 194, 200
critical theory 5, 11, 12
critter, critters 7, 84, 109, 148–149, 177, 199
crocodile 99, 103
crowd 77, 108–109, 140
cyborg 198

D
Dada 1, 3–4
Dante Alighieri 196
Darwinian; Darwin, Charles 93, 94, 98, 102–105, 113, 132–133
Darwinism 7, 93, 94, 97, 102, 105, 119
de-libidinisation, de-libininised 160, 164, 176, 180, 195
de-Oedipalising 8, 11, 84
death 3, 37, 53, 62, 91, 104, 107, 118, 135, 147, 164, 171, 174, 175, 177, 178, 196, 203, 205
death drive 10, 58, 132–135, 138–140, 152, 154, 159, 163, 165, 168, 184, *see also* drive, drives
deep biology 95
defamiliarise, defamiliarisation 4, 93, 110, 113
deferred action 25, 50, 132, *see also* afterwardsness, *Nachträglichkeit*
defusion 10, 138, 175
degeneration, degenerate, degeneracy 33, 45, 46, 96, 98, 102, 107, 109, 110, 113
Deleuze, Gilles 6, 29–30, 34, 77–78, 131, 132, 134
dematerialisation 163, 166–167, 196
denial 140, 147, 156, 167, 178
desire, desires 23, 24, 34, 35, 41, 43, 50, 63, 76, 77, 79, 83, 87, 96, 97, 98, 115
destruction 4, 46, 73, 132, 161, 175–177, 178, 181, 182, 185, 198
Deutsch, Felix 111

Index

development 111, 112, 116, 139, 150
 biological 57, 94, 101
 embryonal 93, 94, 105
 evolutionary/of the species 103, 106, 114
 sexual 84, 92, 132
 of humanity 108
 of hyper-faculties 168
 of memory 150
 as a neurotic reaction 113, 118, 132
 of the (primacy of the) genital zone 93–94, 113
 of psychoanalysis 24, 30, 37, 41, 45, 53, 62
 of the superego 183
devil 196
dialogue, dialogues XII, 5, 6, 13, 54–55, 57, 62, 79, 83–84, 86, 111, 138, 148–149, 163, 194
Dinshaw, Caroline 83
disavow, disavowal 78, 102, 105, 113, 195
dog 168
Doherty, Brigid 3
Dora 33, 39, 40, 100, 114–115, 137, 196
dream, dreams 11, 25, 28, 32–33, 35, 41, 49, 50, 54–56, 61, 206–207
 of the clever/wise baby 173
 of the dissection of the pelvis 60–61
 of fragments 158–159, 181
 of Irma's injection 28, 53, 60
 of the occlusive pessary 54, 57–58, 61
dream-work 207
Dreyfus affair 28
drive, drives XIII, 10, 26, 58, 138, 165, 167
 death drive, death drives 10, 58, 132–135, 138–140, 152, 154, 159, 163, 165, 168, 184
 life drive, life drives 10, 58–59, 138–139, 154, 184

 of conciliation/conciliatory 140, 135
 of self-assertion 140
 sexual drives 4
dualism 111, 112, 138, 140, 199
Dupont, Judith 62

E
echinococci 57
economic liberalism 97
ego memories 151
Eibenschütz, Rosa 32
Eitingon, Max 23, 36, 38, 53
ejaculation 115
Elma affair 56, 63
embryo 78, 94, 100–102, 113, 184
endurance of suffering 139
entangled, entanglement 12–13, 42, 50, 74, 96, 97, 101, 111, 163, 184, 206
environment 6, 28, 32–33, 47, 145–146, 150, 151, 161, 174, 177, 179, 181, 203, 207
environmental factors, environmental conditions 114, 116–117
epistemology, epistemological 7, 103, 104, 111, 113, 148, 197, 199
 epistemological crisis 104
 epistemological optimism 103
erection 114–116, 118
Ernst, Max 4
erotic, erotics, eroticism 51, 84, 85–86, 116, 118, 182
erotic monism 95, 98, 119
eugenic, eugenic, eugenicist 7, 96–98, 109, 112–113, 117, 119, 199
Eurydice 179–180
event, events 2, 8, 10, 25, 42, 47–51, 56, 62, 116, 145, 147–148, 153, 155, 157, 158, 165, 197, 203, 205
eventful, eventfulness 148, 152, 160, 203, 206
 eventful psychoanalysis 7, 145, 176, 203–204

231

Index

evolutionary monism 103, 107, 112, 114
evolutionist enthusiasm 98, 100, 104
executive manager 115

F
Falzeder, Ernst 54–55
family 34–36, 45, 113, 118
  family doctor 31
  family organisation 34
fantasy 2, 10, 25, 26, 27, 36, 46, 47, 49, 50, 51, 74, 101, 107, 108, 113, 137, 140, 148, 157, 169, 179, 182, 183, *see also* biological fantasy
fascism 5, 73, 77, 97, 109
father figure 35, 44
Felman, Shoshana 207
Felski, Rita 137
female 44, 45, 58–59, 75, 99, 135, 207
  female body, female genital organ 78–79
  female homosexuality 31
  female Orpheus, *see also* Orpha
  female sexuality 44
feminine 44, 58–59, 62, 86, 109, 135
  feminine contraceptive 57
  feminine men 87
femininity 78–79
Ferenczi, Gizella 23, 56, 58, 63
Ferenczi, Sándor (works by)
  'États sexuels intermédiaires' [Intermediary Sexual States] [1905] 86
  'Psycho-Analysis and Education' [1908] 183
  'The Analytic Conception of the Psycho-Neuroses' [1908] 151 fn 17
  'Introjection and Transference' [1909] 25, 39–40, 41 fn 71, 110 fn 113, 111 fn 121
  'On the Organization of the Psycho-Analytical Movement' [1911] 26 fn 13, 34–35 fn 40 f.
  'Transitory Symptom-Constructions during the Analysis' [1912] 182 fn 129
  'A Lecture for Judges and Barristers' [1913] 118
  'Stages in the Development of the Sense of Reality' [1913] 168 fn 72
  'The Dream of the Occlusive Pessary' [1915] 32 fn 26, 54, 57–58 fn 148 f.
  'Psycho-Analysis of the War-Neuroses' [1918] 4–5 fn 19
  'The Phenomena of Hysterical Materialization' [1919] 3 fn 10, 138 fn 4, 157 fn 41–42
  'Psycho-Analytical Observations on Tic' [1920] 174
  'The Symbolism of the Bridge' [1921] 154 fn 31, 163 fn 57, 182 fn 128
  'The Dream of the "Clever Baby"' [1923] 173
  Thalassa. A Theory of Genitality [1924] XII–XIII, 2, 3, 6–7, 59, 84, 85, 91–119, 137–140, 148–150, 156, 163 fn 57, 184
  'The Problem of Acceptance of Unpleasant Ideas: Advances in Knowledge of the Sense of Reality' [1926] 151 fn 20, 175 fn 95 f.
  'The Problem of the Termination of Analysis' [1927] 55
  'The Adaptation of the Family to the Child' [1928] 53 fn 136, 54 fn 138
  'The Elasticity of Psycho-Analytic Technique' [1928] 54 fn 141
  'The Principle of Relaxation and Neocatharsis' [1929] 182
  'The Unwelcome Child and His Death Instinct' [1929] 138–139
  'Autoplastic and Alloplastic Adaptation' [1930] 161 fn 53, 174 fn 89, 178 fn 111

'Each Adaptation is Preceded by an Inhibited Attempt at Splitting' [1930] 167
'On the Analytic Construction of Mental Mechanism' [1930] 171, 176–177 fn 106
'Fantasies on a Biological Model of Super-Ego Formation' [1930] 183
'Trauma and Striving for Health' [1930] 175–176 fn 100
'Child-Analysis in the Analysis of Adults' [1931] 152, 164–165 fn 63, 177, 179 fn 119, 181 fn 126
'On the Revision of the Interpretation of Dreams' [1931] 165 fn 64
'The Birth of Intellect' [1931] 150 fn 16, 151 fn 19, 179 fn 118 f.
'Trauma and Anxiety' [1931] 175
'On Shock' [1932] 2 fn 3, 146, 164, 166–167, 197 fn 19
The Clinical Diary [1932] 2, 3, 12, 33, 37–42, 44, 48, 51–52, 54, 58, 63, 74, 80, 101 fn 66, 118, 133, 134, 139–140, 156–159, 161–162, 165, 168, 170, 172, 174, 176–179, 180–181, 193, 205
'The Two Extremes: Credulity and Scepticism' [1932] 185
'Freud's Influence on Medicine' [1933] 111–112, 199 fn 33 f.
Ferenczi revival 8–9, 11
fertilisation 59, 78, 93–94, 175
fetishistic disavowal 102, 105, 113, 195
fingers 84, 177
fingereyes 84, 86
fins 100
First World War XII, 5, 27–28, 45, 91, 93, 98–99, 119, 137
fish 92, 101, 105–108, 114, 115, 138, 149, 182, 184, 199, 204
 fish-orgy 98–101, 108–109, 139
 fish-tail 114
Fletcher, John 153–154
Fließ, Wilhelm XIV, 28, 33, 49, 74
flood 99, 109

fluid 61, 116, 139, 157, 183, 184
 amniotic fluid 184
 semifluid 157
 seminal fluid 99
Foucault, Michel 40, 42, 63–64, 98, 109
fragment, fragments 2–3, 5, 10, 12, 25, 30, 40, 51, 57, 74, 80, 85, 132, 134, 140, 145–185, 193, 196–199, *see also* psychic fragments
Franco-German War 97
Frankel, Jay 164, 169
Freud, Anna 23, 38, 166
Freud, Sigmund (works by)
 The Interpretation of Dreams [1900] 27, 28, 30, 39, 41, 54, 59, 297 fn 19
 'Fragment of an Analysis of a Case of Hysteria' [1905] 39–40, 100, 114–115, *see also* Dora
 Three Essays on the Theory of Sexuality [1905] 86, 91–93, 119, 132, 137
 'Notes upon a Case of Obsessional Neurosis' [1909] 156–157 fn 37, *see also* Rat Man
 'Psychoanalytic Notes on an Autobiographical Account of a Case of Paranoia' [1911] 75–76, *see also* Schreber, Daniel Paul
 'Recommendations to Physicians Practicing Psycho-Analysis' [1912] 38 fn 62
 Totem and Taboo [1913] 95
 'Some Thoughts on Development and Regression – Aetiology' [1917] 95 fn 28
 'A Difficulty in the Path of Psycho-Analysis' [1917] 102–103
 'From the History of an Infantile Neurosis' [1918] 30, *see also* Wolf Man
 'Beyond the Pleasure Principle' [1920] 3, 51, 58, 92, 95, 104, 110–111, 133, 135, 152
 'Fetishism' [1927] 105 fn 95
 'Civilization and its Discontents' [1930] 107

Index

'The Question of a Weltanschauung' [1933]   107 fn 100
'A Disturbance of Memory on the Acropolis' [1936]   48
'Analysis Terminable and Interminable' [1937]   39, 55
Moses and Monotheism [1939]   95, 117
Freud, Sigmund and Josef Breuer, *Studies on Hysteria*   39, 49 fn 109
fright, frighten, frightening   42, 51, 60–61, 135, 195
frog   103
Fromm, Erich   12
fungi, fungal   138, 149, 204, 207
fusion   10, 84–85, 116, 138–139, 168

G
gastropod   1
Gay, Peter   44
genealogy   8, 24, 30–31, 42–43, 63, 73, 92, 104, 131
genital, genitals   6, 58, 62, 77–78, 86–86, 92–93, 102, 113–114, 116, 118, 119, 131–132, 177
genitality   7–8, 84–85, 91–92, 98, 116, 118, 132, 139
genital reassignment surgery   4
getting beside oneself   163, 171–172, 196
Gherovici, Patricia   87
ghost, ghosts, ghostly   8–9, 59, 97, 101, 134, 175
gills, gill-slits   100–101, 184, 200
Gilman, Sander L.   113
Girard, René   45, 74
Glissant, Eduard   203–205
Greek tragedy   2
Groddeck, Georg   52, 56, 76, 127, 182
Grosz, George   4
Grubrich-Simitis, Ilse   92
guardian angel   10, 139, 171, 178
Guattari, Félix   6,9, 29–30, 34, 77–78, 163

guilt   48, 51, 118, 146, 161, 163, 168–171, 180, 196, 198
Gumbs, Alexis Pauline   7, 149, 165
gynaecology   100

H
H.D.; Hilda Dolittle   38, 44
Habsburg Monarchy   27, 45, 93
Haeckel, Ernst   7, 93–98, 101–109, 111–113, 116, 119, 133, 184, 199
hallucination, hallucinations   48, 101, 138, 157, 166–167, 169–170, 176, 178, 193, 196–197
    negative hallucination   166–167, 169
    positive hallucination   166–167, 169
Haraway, Donna   7–9, 84, 138, 148, 149, 163, 181, 199, 204
hard sciences   112
Harris, Adrienne   8–9, 13, 175
Hausmann, Raoul   4
Haverkamp, Anselm   104
Haynal, André   29
Haynal, Veronique   29
Hayward, Eva   84
Hegel, Georg Wilhelm Friedrich   43
herd   35, 108–109, 140
heredity   107, 116–117, 119
heritage   33, 95, 116
herring, herrings   98–99, 101, 106–107, 109
Hirschfeld, Magnus   4, 86
Hitler, Adolf   77, 108–109
horse   91
Höch, Hannah   1–5, 13
homosexuality, homosexual   31, 34–35, 44–45, 47, 76–78, 86, 115
homosocial desire   76
Huelsenbeck, Richard   4
horde   34–35
hyper-attunement   170
hyper-faculties   151, 161, 168, 178–179, 198
hypnosis   31, 37, 183

234

Index

hysteria   3, 5, 7, 37, 39–41, 44, 91–92, 97, 100, 110, 112–113, 115–116, 119, 131, 137–138, 157
hysterical   3, 11, 33, 46, 52, 56, 73–74, 111, 114–115, 134–135, 138, 153, 156–157
  hysterical acting out   24
  hysterical identification   39, 42
  hysterical materialisation   138, 157
  hysterical penis   116, 137–138
  hysterical woman   31, 43

I
ice age   93
id memory   156, 158, 165, 181
identification with the aggressor   6, 10, 12, 74, 146, 159, 161, 163, 166, 169, 183, 198
ideology, ideological   7, 11, 12, 110, 119, 199
imitation   14, 115, 140, 146, 161, 163, 166–169, 196
infection   11, 57
inheritance   97, 103, 117
integration   85, 158, 160–161, 175–176, 198
intensities   30, 61
inter-form, inter-forms   85–86, 184–185
intermediary sexual states   86
interspecies   149, 165–166
introjection, introjected   25, 51, 92, 159–161, 183–184
  introjection of guilt feelings   118, 161, 163, 169, 196, 198
  introjection of the aggressor   146, 163, 169, 196
ironic obedience   74

J
jellyfish   138, 149, 177, 182, 199, 204
Jewish   8, 12, 25, 27–29, 31–32, 44–45, 75, 117
Jones, Ernest   26, 33, 36, 38, 42, 44–45, 52–54, 74, 102
Judaism   113, 116
Jung, C. G.   25–26, 29, 31, 36, 42, 44, 46–47, 73, 76

K
Kafka, Franz   29–30, 77
Kautsky, Karl   97
Klein, Melanie   159–161, 171, 183, 204, 206
Kodály, Zoltán   3
Kränkung, Kränkungen   102
Kraus, Karl   27, 30
Kristeva, Julia   4

L
Lacan, Jacques   26, 40, 43, 53, 59, 63
Lamarck, Jean-Baptiste   7, 92–93, 95, 116–117, 119
Lamarckism   92–94, 102, 116–117
language of passion   51, 146–147, 153–154, 156, 169, 178
language of tenderness   146–147, 153, 156, 169, 178
Laplanche, Jean   8, 49–51, 147, 153–154
latency   93, 117
layering of organs   139–140
leap backwards   2, 200
legacy   5, 9–11, 37, 42, 95–96, 104, 134
Le Bon, Gustave   108
Lebensreform   98, 109
libido   29, 75, 95, 139, 160, 178, 181
life drive   10, 58–59, 138–139, 154, 184, *see also* drive, drives
linking   152, 154, 165, 175, 198
Lueger, Karl   28
Lukács, Georg   31
lung fish   101, 184
Lyell, Charles   2

M
male bonding   6, 76
Mann, Thomas   3
Mantegazza, Paolo   100, 114
Márai, Sándor   3

Index

marine beings 7, 149, 184
masculine protest 78
masculinity 6, 11, 44, 53, 75, 79, 118, 131, 135
mass, masses 99, 107, 204
 of affect 193
 of fish 99
 mass murder 38, 45
 mass psychology 108
 mass strike 4
materialisation 3, 138, 157, 167
materialist monism 111
maternal 32, 53, 56, 58, 79, 100, 135, 162, 173
Melusina (legend of) 114
memory 40, 48, 107, 140, 147, 149–156, 158, 162, 165, 168, 170, 181, 184, 197, 204
Mentz, Steve 150
Metabiology 95
metapsychology, metapsychological 2–3, 7–10, 12, 28, 40, 84, 91, 117, 133–134, 145, 148, 152–153, 159–160, 163, 174, 179–180, 183, 193, 195–196, 199–200, 203, 205
mimetic defence 74, 195
modernism 28
mollusc 1
monism 94, 95, 98, 103, 107–108, 111–112, 114, 119
montage 1, 3–4, 50
mother 32, 44, 55–56, 58–59, 61, 63, 79, 86, 100, 135, 173, 178, 184, 207
mourning 3, 44, 118, 150
mud-eel 101, 103, 184
mushroom 54, 207, *see also* fungi, fungal
mycelium, mycelial 54, 56, 207
mutuality 10, 168

N

Nachträglichkeit 25, 50, 102, 132, 153, 155, *see also* afterwardsness, deferred action

narcissism, narcissist 102–103, 107, 164, 173, 176, 178, 183, 195
 anthropological narcissism 103
 narcissistic reaction 104
 narcissistic splitting 178
National Socialism 5, 97
nationalism 4, 133
natural sciences 11, 96, 110, 133
natural selection 109, 116
negative hallucination 166–167, 169
neo-formation, neo-formations 80, 163, 175, 196
neoliberalism, neoliberal 194–195, 198–199
neurasthenia 113
neurosis 39, 49–50, 91, 110–112, 192
new beginning 181
Nietzsche, Friedrich 63, 133
non-phallic 73

O

ocean 93, 99, 107–108, 148–150, 203
oceanic 111, 150
oceanic feeling 107
octopus 138, 149, 182, 199, 204
Oedipal 47, 56–58, 61–62, 77, 180
Oedipus complex 11, 38, 46–48, 76
omnipotence 107, 170, 172, 180
ontogenesis, ontogenetic 92, 94, 100, 105–106, 156, 165
organ 3–4, 7, 11, 53, 60, 75, 77–78, 85, 92–93, 102, 111–117, 131–135, 137–140, 148, 156, 163, 165–166, 175–178, 181, 195–198, 200, 204–206
organ individuality 139
organ libido 139
organic matter 149, 156, 199
organology 93, 111, 116–117, 119, 137
Orpha 10, 58, 139, 159, 163, 168, 171, 178–180, 196, 203
Orpheus 10, 178–180, 203

Index

Other 2, 8, 85, 147, 164, 170–171, 185
overdetermination 11, 46–47, 57, 112, 115, 132

P

pain 52, 62, 174, 176–177, 197, 198
Pálos, Elma 56, 58, 63
Pálos, Gizella 23, 56, 58, 63, *see also* Ferenczi, Gizella
Pankejeff, Sergei 30, *see also* Wolf Man
paralysis 163–165, 171, 196
pathology 63, 76, 112, 114
pathologisation 42, 44–45, 74
penis 92, 99, 105, 114–116, 137–138, 140
perigenesis 94
perverse, perversion 91, 95, 97, 101, 157
phallus 4, 62, 84, 86–87
phantasmatic 24, 26, 35, 43
phenomenological gap 145, 159, 163, 204, 206
phenomenology 146
Phoenix 119
Photomontage 1, 3–4, 198
phylogenesis, phylogenetic 92, 94–97, 100, 106, 117–119, 156, 165, 199
phylogenetic fantasy 101
pig 105
pirouette 1, 4
plasticity 6, 11, 138–140, 148–149, 157, 165, 168, 172, 181, 184, 199
pollution 11, 57
Pontalis, Jean-Bertrand 49–51
positive hallucination 166–167, 169
post-critique, post-criticism, post-critical 11, 137, 199
post-humanist, post-humanism 148
post-traumatic 118–119, 185
  post-traumatic survival 119
  masculinity as post-traumatic phenomenon 118

potency 93, 107
power 12, 24, 26, 30–31, 33–35, 40, 44, 52, 63–64, 105, 108, 153, 156, 166–167
primal 151, 162
  primal catastrophe 93
  primal creature 93, 116
  primal fight 75
  primal scene 50–51, 74, 135
  primal substrate 165
  primal text 50
primitive 3, 32, 47, 58, 102, 110–111, 115, 118, 156, 160, 181
primordial memory 107, 156
productivity 4, 59, 134, 194
progress 5, 84, 86, 93, 94–95, 104, 107, 111–112, 133, 139–140, 163
progressive optimism 4, 98, 100–103
projection 25, 159, 160, 171, 182–183, 199
projective identification 150, 160,
protective bladder 139, 175, 176, 184
proto-ego 152, 162, 166
psychiatry, psychiatric science XIII, XIV, 26, 31, 34, 37, 49, 64, 80, 98, 113,
psychic fragments 2–3, 7, 12, 14, 51, 55, 70, 80, 85, 132, 134, 138, 145, 147, 149, 151, 153, 157, 158–163, 165, 167, 169, 171–173, 176, 178–185, 187, 193, 196–200, 203–204, 206, 208
psychoanalytic treatment, psychoanalytic situation XIV, 2, 24–25, 30, 37–42, 45–46, 52, 55, 63, 76, 148, 155, 177, 204–205
psychosis, psychotic 74, 75, 77, 101–102, 123, 126, 197
psychosoma 111–112, 115, 138–139
psychosomatic conversion 115
public health 117
pulverisation 145, 166–167, 204

237

Index

Q
queer spectrality 83, 85, 87
queer, queering 4, 79, 83–85, 87

R
R.N. (Elisabeth Severn) 158, 176, 179, 181, 193
rabbit 105
racial hygiene 96
raccoons 138
radical plasticity 6, 11, 138–140, 149, 157, 161, 165, 168, 172, 181, 184
Rank, Otto 36, 41, 53
Rat Man 156
re-libidinisation 161, 198
rebellion XIV, 74, 128, 195
recapitulation 94–96, 102, 106–107, 114
reconstruction 4, 73, 76, 112, 161, 163–164, 167–168, 174, 180, 196
regression, regress, regressive XII–XIII, 2, 11, 14–15, 42, 45–46, 61, 81, 91, 100–101, 111–113, 115, 148, 152, 156–157, 181, 200, 205
Reich, Wilhelm 109
reliving 152, 155, 156, 179
reparative repetition 152, 158
repetition XIV, 23, 24, 52, 59, 63, 74, 107, 138, 152, 158, 195
representation 3, 12, 39, 41, 48, 50, 61, 112, 115, 146, 151, 155, 158, 171, 172, 194, 197, 199, 200
repressive hypothesis 109, 194
reproduction 40, 57, 59, 60, 62–63, 79, 168
reptile 14, 101, 102, 105
resilience 7, 140, 149, 184
resistance, resistances 24, 30, 37, 42, 50, 58, 59, 94, 127, 146, 162, 165–166, 177, 179, 201
romanticist, romanticism 74, 105
Roudinesco, Elisabeth 29

S
Sachs, Hanns 36
salamander 101
Santner, Eric L. 75, 202 fn 29
scapegoat, scapegoating 24, 33, 35, 43, 45–46, 74–75, 83
scar 150–151, 160, 162, 168
scar-tissue 150–151
scene XI, XIII, XIV, XV, 1, 3, 5–7, 10, 16, 25, 42, 47, 50–51, 61, 73–74, 91–92, 100, 116, 119, 135, 138–140, 143, 145, 147–149, 152–159, 166, 168–173, 176–179, 181, 183–184, 186, 196, 203
Schnitzler, Arthur 27
Schönberg, Arnold 27
Schorske, Carl 28, 55
Schreber, Daniel Paul 75–79
Schreber, Fridoline 79
Schreber, Moritz 76
Schuller, Kyla 116, 199
Schwarz, Murray 8
screen memories 154
sea 7, 84, 86, 92, 99, 100, 116, 148–150, 177, 184, 200, 204, 207
secret 7, 24, 26, 31, 33, 34, 36, 38, 40, 49, 54, 73, 75, 86
Sedgewick, Eve Kosofsky 76
seduction theory 10, 49, 50–51, 77, 92, 119
self-analysis 30, 32–33, 47–48, 61, 63
self-caring 163, 178
self-castration 115
self-denial 139
self-destruction 161, 174–175
selflessness 139–140
semifluid 157
Seven-League Boots 1
Severn, Elisabeth (R.N.) 158, 176, 179, 181, 193, *see also* R.N.
sexology 4, 97
Shakespeare, William 207
shell 1, 4–5, 91
shell-shock, shell-shocked 5, 91

238

shock   2, 4–5, 104, 118, 133, 145–147, 150.151, 162–164, 166, 175, 179, 181, 196–197, 205
Siebenmeilenstiefel   1, 4, 5
snail   1
snake   114
Social Darwinism   9
social psychology   12, 100
soldier, soldiers   5, 7, 91, 93, 94, 97, 98, 102, 119
soma   XIII, 11, 92, 102, 111–112, 115–116, 138–139, 155–157, 165, 176, 181, 196, 199–200
spectrality   83, 87
Spielrein, Sabina   175
Spinoza   134
splitting   XII, 2, 7, 132, 140, 145, 149, 163, 166–167, 178–179, 181, 184, 195–198, 203, 206
  splitting by the ego   159–162, 176, 193–194
  splitting of the ego   155, 157, 173, 175, 177
squid   138, 149, 182, 199–200, 204
Starr, Karen   27, 29, 74
strapped on phallus   4
strategic dualism   112, 199
suffocation   176, 196
suggestion   37–38, 133
Sulloway, F.J.   95
superego   10, 54, 159, 162, 178, 183, 203, 206
survival   2–4, 10, 80, 92, 102, 113, 119, 131, 134, 140, 165, 176, 180, 184, 194, 197
swamp   60, 101, 103, 109
symbol, symbolic   30, 36, 39, 41, 46, 50, 87, 96, 115, 118, 154, 159, 168, 178
symbolisation   147, 151, 194
symbiosis, symbiotic   207
symptom   3, 11, 14, 24, 37, 41, 46–47, 49, 54, 58–59, 62, 64, 75–77, 80, 98, 114–116, 135, 138, 153, 157, 177, 196
synaesthesia   85

T
tact   10
tactile eye   XIV, 62, 83–85, 87, 148, 181, 184
tapeworms   57
teleplasty   176
tentacle, tentacles   84, 200
  tentacular knowledges   148
  tentacular psychoanalyst   84, 148
teratoma   159, 182–184
terrifying fragments   60, 206
thalassal, *see also* Ferenczi, Sándor: *Thalassa*
the basic fault   181
Theweleit, Klaus   109
Thurschwell, Pamela   97
tooth, teeth   115, 177
Torok, Mária   8, 117
tragedy   2, 102, 140
transference   XV, 6, 10, 24–26, 33, 37–48, 50, 52, 54–55, 58–59, 62–64, 77, 152, 205
transgenerational   117
trauma
  trauma history   8
  trauma model/trauma theory of hysteria   5, 92, 119, *see also* seduction theory
  trauma scene   139, 155, 166, 173, 177, *see also* traumatic scene
  trauma theory   9–10
  trauma theory, Ferenczi's   XI, 3–4, 9–10, 163, 177
  traumatic adaptation   170
  traumatic attack   2, 10, 139, 165, 167, 178
  traumatic bifurcation   173
  traumatic confusion   164, 168, 169, 170
  traumatic disturbances   3
  traumatic dissociation   173
  traumatic event   25, 50, 147, 155, 197
  traumatic guilt   168
  traumatic ground   25
  traumatic hyper-faculties   168

Index

traumatic imitation 163, 166, 167–168, 169, 196
traumatic lack 105
traumatic mimicry 162, 167–168
traumatic omnipotence 169–170, 172
traumatic paralysis 163–165, 171, 196
traumatic progression 117, 163, 173, 196, 205
traumatic re-enactment 177
traumatic repetition 74
traumatic scene 155, 166, 169, 196, *see also* trauma scene
traumatic shock 2
traumatic splitting 179, 195
traumatolytic function 158
triumph 102, 104, 114, 140, 172, 176, 195

U
unwelcome child 139
urethra, urethral 57, 85, 115
uterus 92, 101
utraquism 111, 188

V
Verfremdung 4
Verleugnung 105, 147
Vienna 6, 12, 15, 23, 25–28, 31–32

vitalism 114, 139, 199
vulnerability 44, 107

W
war machine 26, 30, 34–36, 38, 77
Weismann, August 94, 116, 119
Weltanschauung 94, 102, 105, 107–108
Wilson, Elizabeth 156
wise baby 173
wise organs 7, 78
wish, wishes XIV, 10, 13, 32, 41, 47, 48, 57–58, 61, 63, 83, 84, 86, 92, 110, 115, 119, 157, 166, 178, 183, 193
Wolf Man 30, 50, *see also* Pankejeff, Sergei
work through, working through 3, 8, 36, 95, 152, 156, 163
wound 49, 103, 107, 147, 150–151, 162, 174

Y
Young-Bruehl, Elisabeth 8

Z
Zaretsky, Eli 44
Zoology 93
Zweig, Stefan 27